DNS and BIND in a Nutshell

DNS and BIND
in a Nutshell

Paul Albitz and Cricket Liu

O'Reilly & Associates, Inc.
103 Morris Street, Suite A
Sebastopol, CA 95472

DNS and BIND in a Nutshell
by Paul Albitz and Cricket Liu

Editor: Mike Loukides

Printing History:

October 1992:	First Edition.
March 1993:	Minor corrections.
July 1994:	Minor corrections.

This book is printed on acid-free paper with 85% recycled content, 15% post-consumer waste. O'Reilly & Associates is committed to using paper with the highest recycled content available consistent with high quality.

ISBN: 1-56592-010-4   [2/96]

Table of Contents

7: *Maintaining BIND*   *125*

Figures

Preface

You may not know much about the Domain Name System—yet—but if you have an account on an Internet host, you probably use DNS all the time. Every time you send electronic mail or use *telnet* or *rlogin* to reach another host, you rely on the Domain Name System.

You see, while you, as a human being, prefer to remember *names* of computers, computers like to address each other by number. On an internet, that number is 32 bits long, or between one and four billion or so. That's easy for a computer to remember, because computers have lots of memory dedicated to storing numbers, but it isn't nearly as easy for us humans. Try picking ten phone numbers out of the phone book at random and try to remember them. Not easy? Now flip to the front of the book and attach random area codes to the phone numbers. That's about how difficult it would be to remember ten arbitrary internet addresses.

This is part of the reason we need the Domain Name System. DNS handles mapping between host names, which we humans find convenient, and internet addresses, which computers deal with. In fact, DNS is the standard mechanism on the Internet for advertising and accessing all kinds of information about hosts, not just addresses. And DNS is used by virtually all internetworking software, including electronic mail, remote terminal programs like *telnet*, and file transfer programs like *ftp*.

Another important feature of DNS is that it makes host information available *all over* the Internet. Keeping information about hosts in a formatted file on a single computer only helps users on that computer. DNS provides a means of retrieving information remotely, from anywhere on the network.

More than that, DNS lets you distribute the management of host information between many sites and organizations. You don't need to submit your data to some central site or periodically retrieve copies of the "master" database. You simply make sure your section, called a *domain*, is up-to-date on your *name servers*. Your name servers make your domain's data available to all the other name servers on the network.

Because the database is distributed, the system also needs the ability to locate the data you're looking for from among a number of possible locations. The Domain Name System gives name servers the intelligence to navigate through the database and find data in any domain.

Of course, DNS does have a few problems. For example, the system allows more than one name server to store the same data, for redundancy's sake. But inconsistencies can crop up between copies of the data.

But the *worst* problem with DNS is that, despite its widespread use on the Internet, there's really very little documentation about managing and maintaining it. Most administrators on the Internet make do with the documentation their vendors see fit to provide and what they can glean from following the two Internet mailing lists on the subject.

This lack of documentation means that the understanding of an enormously important internet service—one of the linchpins of today's Internet—is either handed down from administrator to administrator like a closely-guarded family recipe, or relearned repeatedly by isolated programmers and engineers. New administrators of domains suffer through the same mistakes made by countless others.

Our aim with this book is to help remedy this situation. We realize that not all of you have the time or the desire to become DNS experts. Most of you, after all, have plenty to do besides managing a domain or a name server: system administration, network engineering, or software development. It takes an awfully big institution to devote a whole person to DNS. We'll try to give you enough information to do what you need to do, whether that's running a small domain or managing a multinational monstrosity, tending a single name server or shepherding a hundred of them. Read as much as you need to know now, and come back later if you need to know more.

DNS is a big topic—big enough to require two authors, anyway—but we've tried to present it as sensibly and understandably as possible. The first two chapters give you a good theoretical overview and enough practical information to get by, and later chapters fill in the nitty-gritty details. We provide a roadmap up-front to suggest a path through the book appropriate for your job or interest.

When we talk about actual DNS software, we'll concentrate almost exclusively on BIND, the Berkeley Internet Name Domain software, as the most popular implementation of the DNS specs (and the one we know best). We've tried to distill our experience in managing and maintaining a domain with BIND into this book—a domain, incidentally, which is one of the largest on the Internet (we don't mean to brag, but we can use the credibility). Where possible, we've included the real programs that we use in administration, many of them rewritten into *perl* recently for speed and efficiency.

We hope that this book will help you get acquainted with DNS and BIND if you're just starting out, let you refine your understanding if you're already familiar with them, and provide valuable insight and experience even if you know 'em like the back of your hand.

Versions

This book deals primarily with the 4.8.3 version of BIND, the most recent version as of this writing. We do occasionally mention two earlier versions, 4.8 and 4.8.1, because many vendors continue to ship code based on this older software as part of their UNIX products. Where we feel it's significant, we point out differences in the behavior of these versions.

We use *nslookup*, a name server utility program, a great deal in our examples. The version of *nslookup* we use is the one shipped with the 4.8.3 BIND code. Older versions of *nslookup* provide much, but not quite all, of the functionality in the 4.8.3 *nslookup*. We have tried to use commands available in older *nslookup*s in our examples; when this was not possible, we tried to note it.

Organization

This book is organized, more or less, to follow the evolution of a domain and a domain administrator. Chapters 1 and 2 discuss Domain Name System theory. Chapters 3 through 6 help you to decide whether or not to set up your own domain, then describe how to go about it, should you choose to. The middle chapters, 7, 8 and 9, describe how to maintain your domain, to configure hosts to use your name server, to plan for the growth of your domain, and how to create subdomains. The last chapters, 10 through 14, deal with troubleshooting tools and problems, and the lost art of programming with the resolver library routines.

Here's a more detailed, chapter-by-chapter breakdown:

- Chapter 1, *Background*, provides a little historical perspective and discusses the problems that motivated the development of DNS, then presents an overview of DNS theory.

- Chapter 2, *How Does DNS Work?* goes over DNS theory in more detail, including how the DNS name space is organized, domains, and name servers. We also introduce important concepts like name resolution and caching.

- Chapter 3, *Where Do I Start?* covers how to get the BIND software, if you don't already have it, and what to do with it once you've got it: how to figure out what your domain name should be, and how to contact the organization that can delegate your domain to you.

- Chapter 4, *Setting Up BIND*, details how to set up your first two BIND name servers, including creating your name server database, starting up your name servers, and checking their operation.

- Chapter 5, *DNS and Electronic Mail*, deals with DNS's MX record, which allows administrators to specify alternate hosts to handle a given destination's mail. The chapter covers mail routing strategies for a wide variety of networks and hosts, including networks with security firewalls and hosts without direct Internet connectivity.

- Chapter 6, *Configuring Hosts*, explains how to configure a BIND resolver. We also include notes on the idiosyncrasies of many major UNIX vendors' resolver implementations.

- Chapter 7, *Maintaining BIND*, describes the periodic maintenance administrators need to perform to keep their domains running smoothly, like checking name server health and authority. This chapter also explains more advanced name server configuration.

- Chapter 8, *Growing Your Domain*, covers how to plan for the growth and evolution of your domain, including how to get big, and how to plan for moves and outages.

- Chapter 9, *Parenting*, explores the joys of becoming a parent domain. We explain when to become a parent (create subdomains), what to call your children, how to create them (!), and how to watch over them.

- Chapter 10, *nslookup*, shows the ins and outs of the most popular tool for doing DNS debugging, including techniques for digging obscure information out of remote name servers.

- Chapter 11, *Reading BIND Debugging Output*, is the Rosetta Stone of BIND's debugging information. This chapter should help you make sense of the cryptic debugging information that BIND emits, which in turn will help you understand your name server better.

- Chapter 12, *Troubleshooting DNS and BIND*, covers a dozen common DNS and BIND problems and their solutions, then describes a number of less common, harder-to-diagnose scenarios.

- Chapter 13, *Programming with the Resolver Library Routines*, demonstrates how to use BIND's resolver routines to query name servers and retrieve data from within a C program. We include a useful (we hope!) program to check the health and authority of your name servers.

- Chapter 14, *Miscellaneous*, ties up all the loose ends. We cover DNS wildcarding, special configurations for networks with Internet connectivity through firewall hosts, network name encoding, and new, experimental record types.

- Appendix A, *DNS Message Format and Resource Records*, contains a byte-by-byte breakdown of the formats used in DNS queries and responses, as well as a comprehensive list of the currently defined resource record types.

- Appendix B, *Compiling and Installing BIND on a Sun*, contains step-by-step instructions on how to port the 4.8.3 version of BIND to SunOS.

- Appendix C, *Existing Top-Level Domains*, lists the current top-level domains in the Internet's domain name space.

- Appendix D, *DOMAIN-TEMPLATE.TXT*, is the Network Information Center's current form for requesting the establishment of a subdomain of a NIC-run domain.

- Appendix E, *IN-ADDR-TEMPLATE.TXT*, is the Network Information Center's current form for requesting the establishment of a subdomain of the **in-addr.arpa** domain.

Audience

This book is primarily intended for system administrators who manage a domain and one or more name servers, but also includes material for programmers, network engineers, and others. Not all of the book's chapters will be equally interesting to a diverse audience, though, and you don't want to wade through fourteen chapters to find the information pertinent to your job. We hope this roadmap will help you plot your way through the book.

System administrators setting up their first domain should read Chapters 1 and 2 for DNS theory, Chapter 3 for information on getting started and selecting a good domain name, then Chapters 4 and 5 to learn how to set up a domain for the first time. Chapter 6 explains how to configure hosts to use the new name servers. Soon after, they should read Chapter 7 to "flesh out" their domain implementation, by setting up additional name servers and adding additional data. Then, Chapters 10, 11 and 12 describe troubleshooting tools and techniques.

Experienced administrators could benefit from reading Chapter 6 to learn how to configure DNS resolvers on different hosts and Chapter 7 for information on maintaining their domains. Chapter 8 contains instructions on how to plan for your domain's growth and evolution, which should be especially valuable to administrators of large domains. Chapter 9 explains parenting—creating subdomains—which is *de rigeur* reading for those considering the big move. Chapters 10 through 12 describe tools and techniques for troubleshooting, which even advanced administrators may find worthwhile.

System administrators on networks without full Internet connectivity should read Chapter 5 to learn how to configure mail on such networks, and Chapter 14 to set up an independent DNS infrastructure.

Programmers can read Chapters 1 and 2 for DNS theory, then Chapter 13 for detailed coverage of how to program with the BIND resolver library routines.

Network administrators not directly responsible for a domain should still read Chapters 1 and 2 for DNS theory, then Chapter 10 to learn how to use *nslookup*, plus Chapter 12 for troubleshooting tactics.

Postmasters should read Chapters 1 and 2 for DNS theory, then Chapter 5 to find out how DNS and electronic mail coexist. Chapter 10, which describes *nslookup*, will also help postmasters grub mail routing information out of the domain name space.

Interested users can read Chapters 1 and 2 for DNS theory, and then whatever else they like!

Note that we assume you're familiar with basic UNIX system administration, TCP/IP networking, and programming using simple shell scripts and *perl*. We don't assume you have any other specialized knowledge, though. When we introduce a new term or concept, we'll do our best to define or explain it. Whenever possible, we'll use analogies from UNIX (and from the real world) to help you understand.

Obtaining the Example Programs

The example programs in this book are available electronically in a number of ways: by *ftp*, *ftpmail*, *bitftp*, and *uucp*. The cheapest, fastest, and easiest ways are listed first. If you read from the top down, the first one that works for you is probably the best. Use *ftp* if you are directly on the Internet. Use *ftpmail* if you are not on the Internet but can send and receive electronic mail to Internet sites (this includes CompuServe users). Use BITFTP if you send electronic mail via BITNET. Use UUCP if none of the above works.

FTP

To use FTP, you need a machine with direct access to the Internet. A sample session is shown, with what you should type in boldface.

```
% ftp ftp.uu.net.
Connected to ftp.uu.net.
220 FTP server (Version 6.21 Tue Mar 10 22:09:55 EST 1992) ready.
Name (ftp.uu.net:kismet): anonymous
331 Guest login ok, send domain style e-mail address as password.
Password: kismet@ora.com (use your user name and host here)
230 Guest login ok, access restrictions apply.
ftp> cd /published/oreilly/nutshell/dnsbind
250 CWD command successful.
ftp> binary (Very important! You must specify binary transfer for compressed files.)
200 Type set to I.
ftp> get dns.tar.Z
200 PORT command successful.
150 Opening BINARY mode data connection for dns.tar.Z.
226 Transfer complete.
ftp> quit
221 Goodbye.
%
```

If the file is a compressed *tar* archive, extract the files from the archive by typing:

```
% zcat dns.tar.Z | tar xf -
```

System V systems require the following *tar* command instead:

```
% zcat dns.tar.Z | tar xof -
```

If *zcat* is not available on your system, use separate uncompress and *tar* commands.

FTPMAIL

FTPMAIL is a mail server available to anyone who can send electronic mail to and receive it from Internet sites. This includes any company or service provider that allows email connections to the Internet. Here's how you do it.

You send mail to *ftpmail@online.ora.com*. In the message body, give the FTP commands you want to run. The server will run anonymous FTP for you and mail the files back to you. To get a complete help file, send a message with no subject and the single word "help" in the body. The following is an example mail session that should get you the examples. This command sends you a listing of the files in the selected directory, and the requested example files. The listing is useful if there's a later version of the examples you're interested in.

```
% mail ftpmail@online.ora.com
Subject:
reply-to alan@ora.com          (where you want files mailed)
open
cd /published/oreilly/nutshell/dnsbind
dir
mode binary
uuencode                       (or btoa if you have it)
get dns.tar.Z
quit
```

A signature at the end of the message is acceptable as long as it appears after "quit."

All retrieved files will be split into 60KB chunks and mailed to you. You then remove the mail headers and concatenate them into one file, and then *uudecode* or *atob* it. Once you've got the desired file, follow the directions under FTP to extract the files from the archive.

BITFTP

BITFTP is a mail server for BITNET users. You send it electronic mail messages requesting files, and it sends you back the files by electronic mail. BITFTP currently serves only users who send it mail from nodes that are directly on BITNET, EARN, or NetNorth. BITFTP is a public service of Princeton University. Here's how it works.

To use BITFTP, send mail containing your *ftp* commands to **BITFTP@PUCC**. For a complete help file, send HELP as the message body.

The following is the message body you should send to BITFTP:

```
FTP   ftp.uu.net   NETDATA
USER   anonymous
PASS   your Internet email address (not your bitnet address)
CD    /published/oreilly/nutshell/dnsbind
DIR
BINARY
GET   dns.tar.Z
QUIT
```

Once you've got the desired file, follow the directions under FTP to extract the files from the archive. Since you are probably not on a UNIX system, you may need to get versions of *uudecode, uncompress, atob*, and *tar* for your system. VMS, DOS, and Mac versions are available. The VMS versions are on **gatekeeper.dec.com** in */archive/pub/VMS.*

Questions about BITFTP can be directed to Melinda Varian, **MAINT@PUCC** on BITNET.

Conventions Used in This Book

We use the following font and format conventions for UNIX commands, utilities, and system calls:

- Excerpts from scripts or configuration files are shown in a constant width font:

```
if test -x /etc/named -a -f /etc/named.boot
then
    /etc/named
fi
```

- Sample interactive sessions, showing command line input and corresponding output, will be shown in a constant width font, with user-supplied input in bold:

```
% cat /etc/named.pid
78
```

If the command can be typed by any user, we use the percent sign (%) as the prompt. If the command must be executed by the superuser, we use the pound sign (#) as the prompt:

```
# /etc/named
```

- Command lines, when they appear exactly as a user would type them, are printed in bold text when they appear in the body of a paragraph. For example, run **ls** to list the files in a directory.

- Domain names are also printed in bold text when they appear within a paragraph. We use a special period, six points larger than the standard period, as the separator between labels in the domain name. This distinguishes the separator from regular punctuation. For example, there's a standard period (period-as-punctuation) at the end of the domain name **ns.nic.ddn.mil**.

- UNIX commands (when mentioned in passing, and not as part of a command line) and UNIX manual pages mentioned in the body of a paragraph appear italicized. For example, to find more information on *named*, a user could consult the *named*(1m) manual page.

- Filenames are printed in italics; for example, the BIND name server's boot file is usually */etc/named.boot*.

Quotations

The Lewis Carroll quotations which begin each chapter are from the Millennium Fulcrum Edition 2.9 of the Project Gutenberg electronic text of *Alice in Wonderland* and *Through the Looking-Glass*. Quotations in Chapters 1, 2, 5, 6, 8, and 12 come from *Alice in Wonderland*, and those in Chapters 3, 4, 7, 9, 10, 11, and 14 come from *Through the Looking-Glass*.

Acknowledgements

The authors would like to thank Ken Stone, Jerry McCollom, Peter Jeffe, Christopher Durham, Hal Stern, Bill Wisner, Dave Curry and Jeff Okamoto for their (in?)valuable contributions to this book. We'd also like to thank our reviewers, Eric Pearce, Jack Repenning, Andrew Cherenson, Dan Trinkle, Bill LeFebvre and John Sechrest for their criticism and suggestions. Without their help, this book would not be what it is (it'd be much shorter!).

Cricket would particularly like to thank his manager, Rick Nordensten, who is the very model of a modern HP manager, his neighbors, who have borne his occasional crabbiness for lo these many months, and of course his wife, Paige, for her (mostly) unflagging support and for putting up with his tap-tap-tapping during her nap-nap-napping.

Paul would like to thank his wife Katherine for her patience, many review sessions, and for proving that she could make a quilt in her spare time quicker than her spouse could write his half of a book.

We would also like to thank the folks at O'Reilly and Associates for their hard work and patience. Credit is especially due our editor, Mike Loukides; our indexer, Ellie Cutler; our production copyeditor, Kismet McDonough; and our illustrator, Chris Reilley. Thanks besides to Jerry Peek, for all sorts of miscellaneous help, and to Tim O'Reilly, for inspiring us to put it all in print.

And thanks, Edie, for the cricket on the cover!

We'd Like to Hear From You

We have tested and verified all of the information in this book to the best of our ability, but you may find that features have changed (or even that we have made mistakes!). Please let us know about any errors you find, as well as your suggestions for future editions, by writing:

```
O'Reilly & Associates, Inc.
103 Morris Street, Suite A
Sebastopol, CA 95472
1-800-998-9938 (in the US or Canada)
1-707-829-0515 (international/local)
1-707-829-0104 (FAX)
```

You can also send us messages electronically. To be put on the mailing list or request a catalog, send email to:

info@ora.com   (via the Internet)
uunet!ora!info   (via UUCP)

To ask technical questions or comment on the book, send email to:

bookquestions@ora.com   (via the Internet)

1

Background

> *The White Rabbit put on his spectacles. "Where shall I begin, please your Majesty?" he asked.*
>
> *"Begin at the beginning," the King said, very gravely, "and go on till you come to the end: then stop."*

It's important to know a little ARPANET history to understand the Domain Name System. DNS was developed to address particular problems on the ARPANET, and the Internet—a descendant of the ARPANET—remains its main user.

If you've been living on the Internet for years, you can probably skip this chapter. If you haven't, we hope it'll give you enough background to understand what motivated the development of DNS.

A (Very) Brief History of the Internet

In the late 1960's, the U.S. Department of Defense's Advanced Research Projects Agency, ARPA (later DARPA), began funding an experimental wide-area computer network that spanned the United States, called the *ARPANET.* The original goal of the ARPANET was to allow government contractors to share expensive or scarce computing resources. From the beginning, however, users of the ARPANET also used the network for collaboration. This collaboration ranged from sharing files and software and exchanging electronic mail—now commonplace— to joint development and research using shared remote computers.

The *TCP/IP* protocol suite was developed in the early 1980's, and quickly became the standard host networking protocol on the ARPANET. The inclusion of the protocol suite in the University of California at Berkeley's popular *BSD UNIX* operating system was instrumental in democratizing internetworking. BSD UNIX was virtually free to universities. This meant that internetworking—and ARPANET connectivity—were suddenly available cheaply to many more organizations than were previously attached to the ARPANET. Many of the computers being connected to the ARPANET were being connected to local networks, too, and very shortly the other computers on the local networks were communicating via the ARPANET, as well.

The network grew from a handful of hosts to a network of tens of thousands of hosts. The original ARPANET became the backbone of a confederation of local and regional networks based on TCP/IP, called the *Internet*.

In 1988, however, DARPA decided the experiment was over. The Department of Defense began dismantling the ARPANET. Another network, funded by the National Science Foundation and called the *NSFNET*, replaced the ARPANET as the backbone of the Internet.

Today, the Internet connects hundreds of thousands of hosts across the world. In fact, a significant proportion of the non-PC computers in the world are connected to the Internet. The current backbone can carry a volume of 45 megabits per second, almost one thousand times the bandwidth of the original ARPANET. Hundreds of thousands of people use the network for communication and collaboration daily.

On the Internet and internets

A word on "the Internet," and on "internets" in general, is in order. In print, the difference between the two seems slight: one is always capitalized, one isn't. The distinction between their meanings, however, *is* significant. The Internet, with a capital "I", refers to the network that began its life as the ARPANET and continues today as, roughly, the confederation of all TCP/IP networks directly or indirectly connected to the NSFNET. Seen close up, it's actually quite a few different networks—regional TCP/IP networks, corporate and U.S. government TCP/IP networks, even TCP/IP networks in other countries—interconnected by high-speed digital circuits.

A lowercase internet, on the other hand, is simply any network made up of multiple smaller networks using the same internetworking protocols. An internet (little "i") isn't necessarily connected to the Internet (big "I"), nor does it necessarily use TCP/IP as its internetworking protocol. There are isolated corporate internets, and there are Xerox XNS-based internets and DECnet-based internets.

The History of the Domain Name System

Through the 1970's, the ARPANET was a small, friendly community of a few hundred hosts. A single file, *HOSTS.TXT*, contained all the information you needed to know about those hosts: it held a name-to-address mapping for every host connected to the ARPANET. The familiar UNIX host table, */etc/hosts*, was compiled from *HOSTS.TXT* (mostly by deleting fields UNIX didn't use).

The file was maintained by SRI's* *Network Information Center* (dubbed "the NIC") and distributed from a single host, **SRI-NIC**. ARPANET administrators typically e-mailed their changes to the NIC, and periodically *ftp*'d to **SRI-NIC** and grabbed the current *HOSTS.TXT*. Their changes were compiled into a new *HOSTS.TXT* once or twice a week. As the ARPANET grew, however, this scheme became unworkable. The size of *HOSTS.TXT* grew proportionally to the growth in the number of ARPANET hosts. Moreover, the traffic generated by the update process increased even faster: every additional host meant not only another line in *HOSTS.TXT*, but potentially another host updating from **SRI-NIC**.

And when the ARPANET moved to the TCP/IP protocols, the population of the network exploded. Now there were a host of problems with *HOSTS.TXT*:

Traffic and load
> The toll on **SRI-NIC**, in terms of network traffic and processor load, was becoming unbearable.

Name collisions
> No two hosts in *HOSTS.TXT* could have the same name. However, while the NIC could assign addresses in a way that guaranteed uniqueness, it had no authority over host names. There was nothing to prevent someone from adding a host with a conflicting name and breaking

---

*SRI is the Stanford Research Institute in Menlo Park, California. SRI conducts research into many different areas, including computer networking.

the whole scheme. Someone adding a host with the same name as a major mail hub, for example, could disrupt mail service to much of the ARPANET.

Consistency

Maintaining consistency of the file across an expanding network became harder and harder. By the time a new *HOSTS.TXT* could reach the farthest shores of the enlarged ARPANET, a host across the network had changed addresses, or a new host had sprung up that you wanted to reach.

The essential problem was that the *HOSTS.TXT* mechanism didn't scale well. Ironically, the success of the ARPANET as an experiment led to the failure and obsolescence of *HOSTS.TXT*.

The ARPANET's governing bodies chartered an investigation into a successor for *HOSTS.TXT*. Their goal was to create a system that solved the problems inherent in a unified host table system. The new system should allow local administration of data yet make that data globally available. The decentralization of administration would eliminate the single-host bottleneck and relieve the traffic problem. And local management would make the task of keeping data up-to-date much easier. It should use a hierarchical name space to name hosts. This would ensure the uniqueness of names.

Paul Mockapetris, of USC's Information Sciences Institute, was responsible for designing the architecture of the new system. In 1984, he released RFCs* 882 and 883, which describe the Domain Name System, or DNS. These RFCs were superceded by RFCs 1034 and 1035, the current specifications of the Domain Name System.

The Domain Name System, in a Nutshell

The Domain Name System is a distributed database. This allows local control of the segments of the overall database, yet data in each segment are available across the entire network through a client-server scheme. Robustness and adequate performance are achieved through replication and caching.

---

*RFCs are *Request for Comments* documents, part of the relatively informal procedure for introducing new technology on the Internet. RFCs are usually freely distributed and contain fairly technical descriptions of the technology, often intended for implementors.

Programs called *name servers* comprise the server half of DNS's client-server mechanism. Name servers contain information about some segment of the database and make it available to clients, called *resolvers*. Resolvers are often just library routines that create queries and send them across a network to a name server.

The structure of the DNS database, shown in Figure 1.1, is very similar to the structure of the UNIX filesystem (or the MSDOS filesystem, for that matter). The whole database (or filesystem) is pictured as an inverted tree, with the root at the top. In UNIX, the root is written as a slash "/". In DNS, the root's name is the null label (""), but is written as a single dot "." in text.

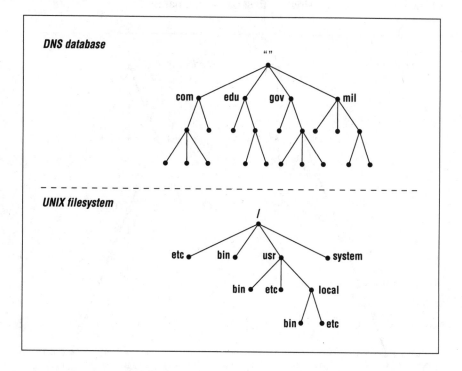

Figure 1.1: The DNS database versus a UNIX filesystem

Each node in the tree represents a partition of the overall database—a "directory" in the UNIX filesystem, or a *domain* in the Domain Name System. Each domain or directory can be further divided into partitions, called *subdomains* in DNS, like a filesystem's "subdirectories." Subdomains, like subdirectories, are drawn as children of their parent nodes.

Every domain is named, like every directory. A domain has a label, which identifies it relative to its parent domain. This is analogous to a directory's "relative name." A domain also has a *domain name*, which identifies its position in the database, much like a directory's "absolute pathname" specifies its place in the filesystem. In DNS, the full domain name is the sequence of labels from the domain to the root, with "." separating the labels. In the UNIX filesystem, a directory's absolute pathname is the list of relative names read from root to leaf (the opposite direction to DNS, as shown in Figure 1.2), using "/" to separate the names.

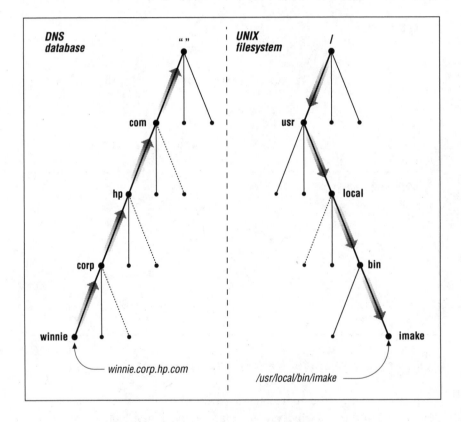

Figure 1.2: Reading names in DNS and in a UNIX filesystem

In DNS, each domain can be administered by a different organization. Each organization can then break its domain into a number of subdomains and dole out responsibility for those subdomains to other organizations. For example, the Internet's Network Information Center runs the **edu** (educational) domain, but assigns U.C. Berkeley authority over the **berkeley.edu** subdomain (Figure 1.3). This is something like NFS-mounting a filesystem: certain directories in a filesystem may actually be filesystems on other hosts, mounted remotely via NFS. The administrator on host **winken**, for example (again, Figure 1.3), is responsible for the filesystem that appears on the local host as the directory */usr/nfs/winken.*

In a filesystem, directories contain files and are sometimes said to "contain" subdirectories, too. Likewise, domains can contain both hosts and other domains: their subdomains. Domain names are used as indexes into the DNS database. You might think of data in DNS as "attached" to a domain name.

Each host on a network has a domain name, which points to information about the host (see Figure 1.4). This information may include IP addresses, information about mail routing, etc. Hosts may also have one or more *domain name aliases*, which are simply pointers from one domain name (the alias) to another (the official or *canonical* domain name).

Why all the complicated structure? To solve the problems that *HOSTS.TXT* had. For example, making names hierarchical eliminates the pitfall of name collisions. Domains are given unique domain names, so organizations are free to choose names within their domains. Whatever name they choose, it won't conflict with other domain names, since it'll have their unique domain name tacked onto the end. You can have two hosts named **puella** (as shown in Figure 1.5), provided that they have different parent domains.

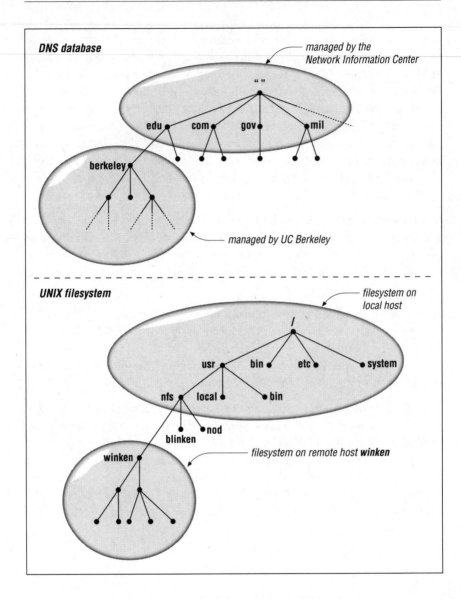

Figure 1.3: Remote management of subdomains and of filesystems

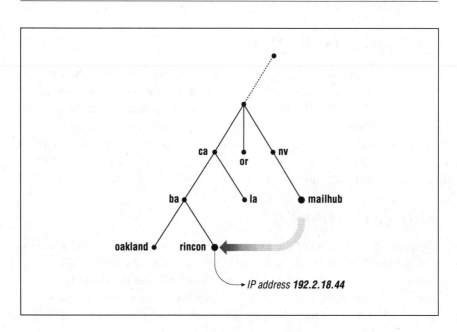

Figure 1.4: An alias in DNS pointing to a canonical name

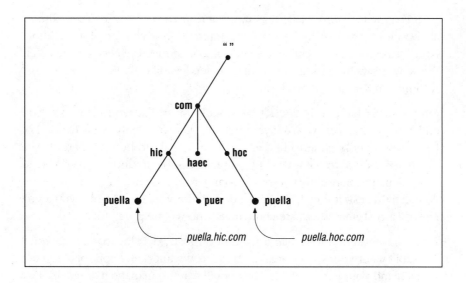

Figure 1.5: Solving the name collision problem

The History of BIND

The first implementation of the Domain Name System was called JEEVES, written by Paul Mockapetris himself. A later implementation was *BIND*, written for Berkeley's 4.3BSD UNIX operating system by Kevin Dunlap. BIND, which stands for *Berkeley Internet Name Domain*, is the implementation we'll concentrate on in this book. BIND is by far the most popular implementation of DNS today. It has been ported to most flavors of UNIX, and is shipped as a standard part of most vendors' UNIX offerings.

But Do I Need It?

Despite the usefulness of the Domain Name System, there are still some situations in which it doesn't pay to use it. Sometimes the overhead involved in managing a domain and its name servers outweighs the benefits. On the other hand, there are circumstances in which you have no other choice but to set up and manage a domain. Here are some guidelines to help you make that decision:

If you're connected to the Internet . . .

DNS is a must. Think of DNS as the *lingua franca* of the Internet: almost all business that gets done over the Internet wouldn't get done without DNS. That includes electronic mail, remote terminal access, file transfer, the X Window System, and information services like WAIS (the Wide Area Information Server) and *archie*.

On the other hand, this doesn't necessarily mean that you have to set up and run a domain *by* yourself *for* yourself. If you've only got a handful of hosts, you may be able to find an existing domain to become part of (see the *Where Do I Start?* chapter). Or you may be able to find someone else to run a domain for you. If you pay a commercial IP vendor for your Internet connectivity, ask if they'll manage a domain for you, too. Even if you aren't already a customer, there are companies who will help out, for a price.

If you have a little more than a handful of hosts, or a lot more, then you'll probably want your own domain. And if you want direct control over your domain and your name servers, then you'll want to manage it yourself. Buy the book and read on!

If you have a UUCP connection to a host on the Internet...

it's a good idea to set up a domain. *user@domain*-style addressing has become standard on the Internet. Once you've set up a domain, your correspondents on the Internet will be able to send you mail using these simpler addresses. You'll also be prepared if you decide later to get a connection to the Internet.

It's a common misconception that you actually need to be connected to the Internet to set up a domain and use *user@domain* addresses. You'll need hosts on the Internet to act as name servers for your domain, but they don't have to be *your* hosts. You'd be surprised how many people are willing to "host" your domain gratis: the Internet is still a pretty neighborly place. (And even if you can't find anyone willing, there are companies who'll do it for you for cheap.)

If you have your own TCP/IP-based internet...

you probably want DNS. By an internet, we don't mean just a single Ethernet of workstations using TCP/IP (see below if you thought that was what we meant); we mean a fairly complex "network of networks." Maybe you have a forest of Appletalk nets and a handful of Apollo token rings.

If your internet is basically homogeneous and your hosts don't need DNS (say you have a big DECnet or OSI internet), then you may be able to do without it. But if you've got a variety of hosts, especially if some of those run some variety of UNIX, you'll want DNS. It'll simplify the distribution of host information and rid you of any kludgy host table distribution schemes you may have cooked up.

If you have your own local area network or site network...

and that network isn't connected to a larger network, you can probably get away without using DNS. You might consider using host tables, or Sun's Network Information Service (NIS) product.

But if you need distributed administration or have trouble maintaining the consistency of data on your network, DNS may be for you. And if your network is likely to be connected to another network soon, like your corporate internet or the Internet, it'd be wise to start up a domain now.

2

How Does DNS Work?

"...and what is the use of a book," thought Alice, "without pictures or conversations?"

The Domain Name System is basically a database of host information. Admittedly, you get a lot with that: funny dotted names, networked name servers, a shadowy "name space." But you should keep in mind that, in the end, the service DNS provides is information about internet hosts.

We've already covered some important aspects of DNS, including its client-server architecture and the structure of the DNS database. However, we haven't gone into much detail, and we haven't explained the nuts and bolts of DNS's operation.

In this chapter, we'll explain and illustrate the mechanisms that make DNS work. We'll also introduce the terms you'll need to know to read the rest of the book (and to converse intelligently with your fellow domain administrators).

First, though, let's take a more detailed look at concepts introduced in the previous chapter. We'll try to add enough detail to spice it up a little.

The Domain Name Space

Each unit of data in DNS's distributed database is indexed by a name. These names are essentially just paths in a large inverted tree, called the *domain name space*. The tree's hierarchical structure, shown in Figure 2.1, is very similar to the structure of the UNIX filesystem. The tree has a single root at the top.* In UNIX, this is called the root directory, represented by a "/". DNS simply calls it "the root," or occasionally "the root domain." Like a filesystem, DNS's tree can branch any number of ways at each intersection point, called a *node*. BIND's implementation limits the tree's depth to 127 levels (a limit you're not likely to run into).

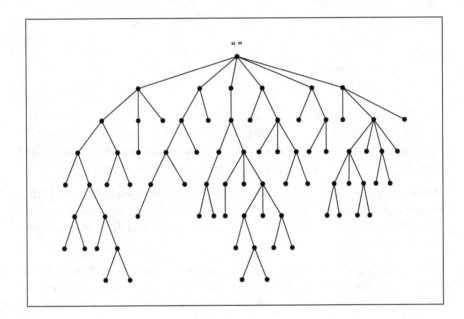

Figure 2.1: The structure of the DNS name space

---

*Clearly this is a computer scientist's tree, not a botanist's.

Domain Names

Each node in the tree is labeled with a simple name (without dots). The label can be up to 63 characters in length. The root domain has a null (zero-length) label, which is reserved. The full *domain name* of any node in the tree is the sequence of labels on the path from that node to the root. Domain names are always read from the node toward the root ("up" the tree), and with dots separating the names in the path.

If the root domain actually appears in a node's domain name, the name *looks* as though it ends in a dot. (It actually ends with a dot—the separator—and a null label.) When the root domain appears by itself, it is written as a single dot, ".", for convenience. Consequently, some software interprets a trailing dot in a domain name to indicate that the domain name is *absolute*. An absolute domain name is written relative to the root and unambiguously specifies a node's location in the hierarchy. An absolute domain name is also referred to as a *fully-qualified domain name*, often abbreviated *FQDN*. Names without trailing dots are sometimes interpreted as relative to some domain other than the root.

DNS requires that sibling nodes—nodes that are children of the same parent—be named uniquely. This restriction guarantees that a domain name uniquely identifies a single node in the tree. The restriction really isn't a limitation, since the names only need to be unique among the children, not among all the nodes in the tree. The same restriction applies to the UNIX filesystem: you can't name two sibling directories the same name. Just as you can't have two **hobbes.pa.ca.us** nodes in the name space, you can't have two */usr/bin* directories (Figure 2.2). You can, however, have both a */bin* directory and a */usr/bin* directory.

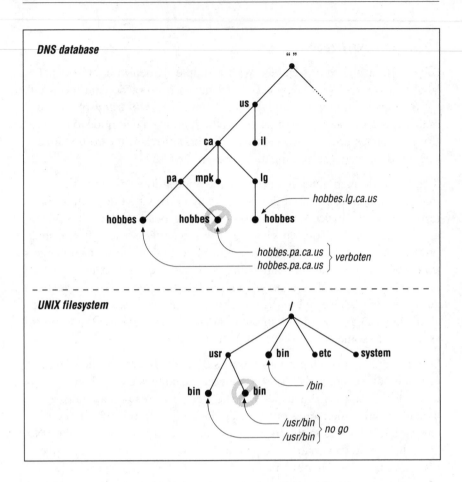

Figure 2.2: Ensuring uniqueness in domain names and in UNIX pathnames

Domains

A *domain* is simply a subtree of the domain name space. A domain's domain name is the same as the domain name of the root node of the subtree. That just means that the name of a domain is the name of the node at the very top of the domain. So, for example, the top of the **purdue.edu** domain is a node named **purdue.edu**, as shown in Figure 2.3.

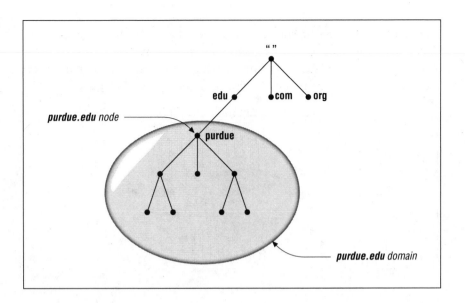

Figure 2.3: The purdue.edu domain

Likewise, in a filesystem, at the top of the */usr* directory, you'd expect to find a node called */usr*, as shown in Figure 2.4.

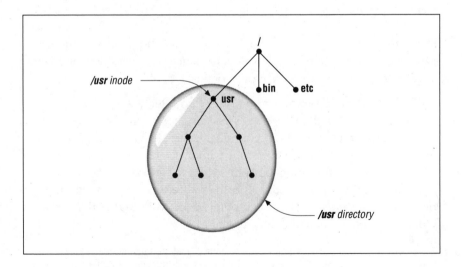

Figure 2.4: The /usr directory

Any domain name in the subtree is considered a part of the domain. Since a domain name can be in many subtrees, a domain name can also be in many domains. For example, the domain name **pa.ca.us** is part of the **ca.us** domain, and also part of the **us** domain, as shown in Figure 2.5.

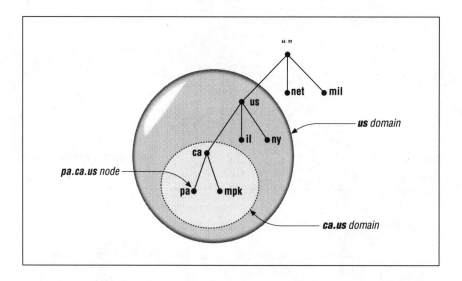

Figure 2.5: A node in multiple domains

So in the abstract, a domain is just a subtree of the domain name space. But if a domain is just made up of domain names and other domains, where are all the hosts? Domains are groups of hosts, right?

The hosts are there, but they're domains, too. Remember, domain names are just indexes into the DNS database. The "hosts" are the domain names that point to information about individual hosts. And a domain contains all the hosts whose domain names are within the domain.* The hosts are related *logically*, often by geography or organizational affiliation, and not necessarily by network or address or hardware type. You might have ten different hosts, each of them on a different network and perhaps even in different countries, all in the same domain.

---

*One note of caution: don't confuse domains in the Domain Name System with domains in Sun's Network Information Service (NIS). Though an NIS domain also refers to a group of hosts, and both types of domains have similarly structured names, the concepts are quite different. NIS uses hierarchical names, but the hierarchy ends there: hosts in the same NIS domain share certain data about hosts and users, but can't navigate the NIS name space to find data in other NIS domains.

Domains at the leaves of the tree generally represent individual hosts. Their domain names may point to network addresses, hardware information, and mail routing information. Domain names in the interior of the tree can name a host *and* can point to structural information about the domain's children, or *subdomains.** Interior domain names aren't restricted to one or the other. They can represent both the domain they correspond to and a particular host on the network. For example, **hp.com** is both the name of the Hewlett-Packard Company's domain and the domain name of a host that forwards mail between HP and the Internet.

Which type of information—host or structural—a search retrieves depends on the context the domain name is used in. A search for the children of the node would return the structural data, while *telnet*'ing to the domain name would look up the host information (in Figure 2.6, for example, **hp.com**'s IP address).

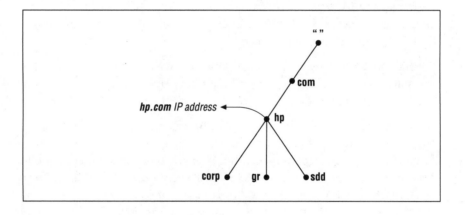

Figure 2.6: An interior node with both host and structural data

A simple way of deciding whether a domain is a subdomain of another domain is to compare their domain names. A subdomain's name ends with the name of its parent domain. For example, the domain **la.tyrell.com** must be a subdomain of **tyrell.com** since **la.tyrell.com** ends with **tyrell.com**. Similarly, it's a subdomain of **com**, as is **tyrell.com**.

---

*Note: The terms *domain* and *subdomain* are often used interchangeably, or nearly so, in DNS and BIND documentation. In this book, we use *subdomain* only as a relative term: a domain is a subdomain of another domain if the root of the subdomain is within the domain.

Besides being referred to in relative terms, as subdomains of other domains, domains are often referred to by *level*. On mailing lists and in USENET newsgroups, you may see the terms *top-level* or *second-level* bandied about. This just refers to a domain's position in the domain name space:

- a top-level domain is a child of the root,
- a first-level domain is a child of the root (a top-level domain),
- a second-level domain is a child of a first-level domain,

. . . and so on.

Resource Records

The data associated with domain names are contained in *resource records*, or *RRs* for short. Records are divided into classes. Each class of records pertains to a type of network or software. Currently, there are classes for internets (any TCP/IP-based internet), networks based on the Chaosnet protocols, and networks that use Hesiod software. (Chaosnet is an old network of largely historic significance.)

The internet class is by far the most popular. (We're not really sure if anyone still uses the Chaosnet class, and use of the Hesiod class is mostly confined to MIT.) In this book, we'll concentrate on the internet class.

Records come in several types, which correspond to the different varieties of data that may be stored in the domain name space. Different classes may define different record types, though some types may be common to more than one class. For example, almost every class defines an *address* type. Each record type defines a particular record syntax, which all resource records of that type must adhere to. (For details on all internet resource record types and their syntaxes, see Appendix A, *DNS Message Format and Resource Records.*)

If this information seems sketchy, don't worry: we'll cover each record in more detail later. The common records are described in Chapter 4, *Setting Up BIND*, and a comprehensive list is included as part of Appendix A.

The Internet Domain Name Space

We've talked so far about the theoretical structure of the domain name space, and what sorts of data are stored in it, and we've even hinted at the types of names you might find in it with our (sometimes fictional) examples. But this won't help you decode the domain names you see on a daily basis on the Internet.

The Domain Name System doesn't impose many rules on the labels in domain names, and it doesn't attach any *particular* meaning to the labels at a particular level. When you manage a part of the domain name space, you can decide on your own semantics for your domain names. Heck, you could name your subdomains A through Z and no one would stop you (though they might strongly suggest against it).

The existing Internet domain name space, however, has some self-imposed structure to it. Especially in the upper-level domains, the domain names follow certain traditions. (Not rules, really, since they can and have been broken.) This helps domain names from appearing totally chaotic. Understanding these traditions is an enormous asset if you're trying to decipher a domain name.

Top-Level Domains

The original top-level domains divided the Internet domain name space organizationally. There were seven main top-level domains:

com Commercial organizations, like Hewlett-Packard (**hp.com**), Sun Microsystems (**sun.com**) and IBM (**ibm.com**)

edu Educational organizations, like U.C. Berkeley (**berkeley.edu**) and Purdue University (**purdue.edu**)

gov Government organizations, like NASA (**nasa.gov**) and the National Science Foundation (**nsf.gov**)

mil Military organizations, like the U.S. Army (**army.mil**) and Navy (**navy.mil**)

net Networking organizations, like NSFNET (**nsf.net**)

org Non-commercial organizations, like the Electronic Frontier Foundation (**eff.org**)

int International organizations, like NATO (**nato.int**)

There's also a top-level domain called **arpa**, which was originally used during the ARPANET's transition from host tables to DNS. All ARPANET hosts originally had host names under **arpa**, so they were easy to find. Later, they moved into various subdomains of the organizational top-level domains.

You may notice a certain nationalistic prejudice in the examples: all of them are primarily U.S. organizations. That's easier to understand—and forgive—when you remember that the Internet began as the ARPANET, a U.S.-funded research project. No one anticipated the success of the ARPANET, or that it would eventually become as international as the Internet is today.

To accommodate the internationalization of the Internet, the implementors of DNS compromised. Instead of insisting that all top-level domains describe organizational affiliation, they decided to allow geographical designations, too. New top-level domains were reserved (but not necessarily created) to correspond to individual countries. Their domain names followed an existing international standard called ISO 3166.* ISO 3166 establishes official, two-letter abbreviations for every country in the world. We've included the current list of top-level domains as Appendix C of this book.

Further Down

Within these top-level domains, the traditions and the extent to which they are followed vary. Some of the ISO 3166 top-level domains follow the U.S.'s original organizational scheme closely. For example, Australia's top-level domain, **au**, has subdomains like **edu.au** and **com.au**. Some other ISO 3166 top-level domains follow the **uk** domain's lead, and have subdomains like **co.uk** for corporations, and **ac.uk** for the "academic community." In most cases, however, even these geographically-oriented top-level domains are divided up organizationally.

That's not true of the **us** top-level domain, though. The **us** domain has fifty subdomains that correspond to—guess what?—the fifty U.S. states.† Each is named according to the standard two-letter abbreviation for the state—the same abbreviation the U.S. Postal Service standardized on. Within each state's domain, the organization is still geographical: there are subdomains that correspond to individual cities. Beneath the cities, the subdomains usually correspond to individual hosts.

---

*Except for Great Britain. According to ISO 3166 and Internet tradition, Great Britain's top-level domain should be **gb**. Instead, Great Britain and Northern Ireland (the United Kingdom) use the top-level domain **uk**. They drive on the wrong side of the road, too.

†Actually, there are a few more domains under **us**: one for Washington, D.C., one for Guam, and so on.

Reading Domain Names

Now that you know what most top-level domains represent and how their name spaces are structured, you'll probably find it much easier to make sense of most domain names. Let's dissect a few for practice:

```
lithium.cchem.berkeley.edu
```

You've got a headstart on this one, since we've already told you that **berkeley.edu** is U.C. Berkeley's domain. (Even if you didn't already know that, though, you could have inferred that the name belonged to a U.S. university, because it's in the top-level **edu** domain.) **cchem** is the College of Chemistry's subdomain of **berkeley.edu**. **lithium**, finally, is the name of a particular host in the domain—and probably one of about a hundred or so, if they've got one for every element.

```
winnie.corp.hp.com
```

This is a bit harder, but not much. The **hp.com** domain in all likelihood belongs to the Hewlett-Packard Company (in fact, we gave you this earlier, too). Their **corp** subdomain is undoubtedly their corporate headquarters. And **winnie** is probably just some silly name someone thought up for a host.

```
fernwood.mpk.ca.us
```

Here you'll need to use your understanding of the **us** domain. **ca.us** is obviously California's domain, but **mpk** is anybody's guess. In this case, it'd be awfully hard to know that it's Menlo Park's domain unless you knew your San Francisco Bay Area geography. (And no, it's not the same Menlo Park that Edison lived in.)

```
daphne.ch.apollo.hp.com
```

We've included this one just so you don't start thinking that all domain names have only four labels. **apollo.hp.com** is the former Apollo Computer's subdomain of the **hp.com** domain. (When HP acquired Apollo, they also acquired Apollo's Internet domain, **apollo.com**, which became **apollo.hp.com**.) **ch.apollo.hp.com** is Apollo's Chelmsford, Massachusetts, site. And **daphne** is a host at Chelmsford.

Delegation

Remember that one of the main goals of the design of the Domain Name System was decentralizing administration? This is achieved through *delegation*. Delegating domains works a lot like delegating tasks at work. A manager may break a large project up into smaller tasks and delegate responsibility for each of these tasks to different employees.

Likewise, an organization administering a domain can divide it into subdomains. Each of those subdomains can be *delegated* to other organizations. This means that the organization delegated to becomes responsible for maintaining all the data in that subdomain. They can freely change the data, and can even divide their subdomain up into more subdomains and delegate those. The parent domain contains only pointers to sources of the subdomain's data, so that it can refer queriers there. The domain **stanford.edu**, for example, is delegated to the folks at Stanford who run the university's networks (Figure 2.7).

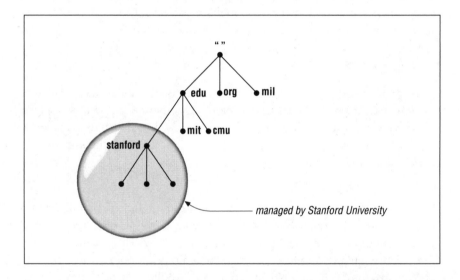

Figure 2.7: stanford.edu is delegated to Stanford University

Not all organizations delegate their whole domain away, just as not all managers delegate all their work. A domain may have several subdomains and also contain hosts that don't belong in the subdomains. For example, the Acme Corporation (they supply a certain coyote with most of his gadgets), which has a division in Rockaway and its headquarters in Kalamazoo, might have a **rockaway.acme.com** subdomain and a **kalamazoo.acme.com** subdomain. However, the few hosts in the Acme sales offices scattered throughout the U.S. would fit better under **acme.com** than under either subdomain.

We'll explain how to create and delegate subdomains later. For now, it's only important that you understand that the term *delegation* refers to assigning responsibility for a subdomain to another organization.

Name Servers

The programs that store information about the domain name space are called *name servers*. Name servers generally have complete information about some part of the domain name space, called a *zone*. The name server is then said to have *authority* for that zone. Name servers can be authoritative for multiple zones, too.

The difference between a zone and a domain is subtle. A zone contains the domain names and data that a domain contains, except for domain names and data that are delegated elsewhere. For example, the top-level domain **ca** (for Canada) may have the subdomains **ab.ca**, **on.ca** and **qb.ca**, for the provinces Alberta, Ontario and Quebec. Authority for the **ab.ca**, **on.ca** and **qb.ca** domains may be delegated to organizations in each of the provinces. The *domain* **ca** contains all the data in **ca** plus all the data in **ab.ca**, **on.ca** and **qb.ca**. But the *zone* **ca** contains only the data in **ca** (see Figure 2.8).

However, if a subdomain of the domain isn't delegated away, the zone contains the domain names and data in the subdomain. So the **bc.ca** and **sk.ca** (British Columbia and Saskatchewan) subdomains of the **ca** domain may exist, but not be delegated. (Perhaps the provincial authorities aren't yet ready to manage the domain, but the authorities running the top-level **ca** domain want to preserve the consistency of the name space and implement domains for all the Canadian provinces right away.) In this case, the zone **ca** has a ragged bottom edge, containing **bc.ca** and **sk.ca**, but not the other **ca** subdomains as shown in Figure 2.9.

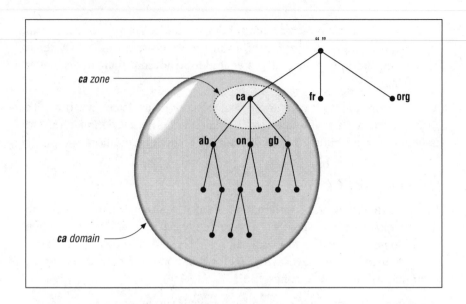

Figure 2.8: The domain ca versus the zone ca

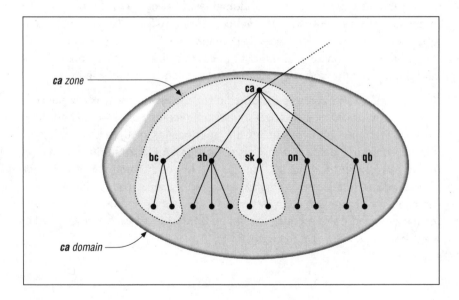

Figure 2.9: The domain ca vs. the zone ca

So why do name servers load zones instead of domains? Because a domain might contain more information than the name server would need: it could contain data delegated to other name servers.

If you're just starting out, though, your domain probably won't have any subdomains. In this case, since there's no delegation going on, your domain and your zone contain the same data.

Delegating Domains

Even though you may not need to delegate parts of your domain just yet, it's helpful to understand a little more about how it works. Delegation, in the abstract, involves assigning responsibility for some part of your domain to another organization. What really happens, though, is the assignment of authority for your subdomains to different name servers. (Note that we said "name servers," not just "name server.")

Your data, instead of containing information about the subdomain you've delegated, includes pointers to the name servers authoritative for that subdomain. Now if your name server is asked for data in the subdomain, it can reply with a list of the right name servers to talk to.

Types of Name Servers

The DNS specs define two types of name servers, *primary masters* and *secondary masters*. A *primary master* name server gets the data for the zones it's authoritative for from files on the host it runs on. A *secondary master* name server gets its zone data from another name server authoritative for the zone. When a secondary starts up, it contacts the name server it updates from and pulls the zone data over. This is referred to as a *zone transfer*.

DNS provides these two types of name servers to make administration easier. Once you've created the data for your zone and set up a primary master name server, you don't need to fool with copying that data from host to host to create new name servers for the zone. You simply set up secondary master name servers that load their data from the primary. Once they're set up, the secondaries will periodically query the primary to keep the zone data up-to-date.

This is important because it's a very good idea to set up more than one name server for any given zone. You'll want more than one for redundancy, to spread the load around, and to make sure that all the hosts in the zone have a name server close-by. Using secondary master name servers makes this administratively workable.

Calling a *given* name server a primary master name server or a secondary master name server is a little silly, though. We mentioned earlier that a name server can be authoritative for more than one zone. Similarly, a name server can be a primary master for one zone, and a secondary master for another. Most name servers, however, are either primary for most of the zones they load or secondary for most of the zones they load. So if we call a particular name server a primary or a secondary, we mean that it's the primary or a secondary master, respectively, for *most* of the zones it loads.

Data Files

The files that primary master name servers load their zone data from are called, simply enough, data files. We often refer to them as *db files*, short for *database files*. Secondary master name servers sometimes load their zone data from data files, too. Secondaries can be configured to back up the zone data they transfer to data files. If the secondary is later killed and restarted, it will read the backup data files first, then check to see whether the data are current.

The data files contain resource records that describe the zone. The resource records describe all the hosts in the zone, and mark any delegation of subdomains. BIND also allows special *directives* to include the contents of other data files in a data file, much like the #include statement in C programming.

Resolvers

Resolvers are the clients that access name servers. Programs running on a host that need information from the domain name space use the resolver. The resolver handles:

- Querying a name server
- Interpreting responses (which may be resource records or an error)
- Returning the information to the programs that requested it

In BIND, the resolver is just a set of library routines that are compiled into programs like *telnet* and *ftp*. They're not even separate processes. They have the smarts to put together a query, send it and wait for an answer, and to resend the query if it isn't answered, but that's about all. Most of the burden of finding an answer to the query is placed on the name server. The DNS specs call this kind of resolver a *stub resolver.*

Other implementations of DNS have smarter resolvers, which can do more sophisticated things like build up a cache of information already retrieved from name servers. But these aren't nearly as common as the stub resolver implemented in BIND.

Resolution

Name servers are adept at retrieving data from the domain name space. They have to be, given the limited intelligence of some resolvers. Not only can they give you data about zones they're authoritative for, they can also search through the domain name space to find data they're not authoritative for. This process is called *name resolution* or simply *resolution.*

Because the name space is structured as an inverted tree, a name server only needs one piece of information to find its way to any point in the tree: the names and addresses of the root name servers (is that more than one piece?). A name server can issue a query to a root name server for any name in the domain name space, and the root name server will start the name server on its way.

Root Name Servers

The root name servers know where name servers authoritative for all the top-level domains are. (In fact, the root name servers *are* authoritative for the top-level, U.S. organizational domains.) Given a query about any domain name, the root name servers can at least provide the names and addresses of the name servers authoritative for the top-level domain the domain name is in. And those top-level name servers can provide the list of name servers authoritative for the second-level domain the domain name is in. Each name server queried gives the querier information about how to get "closer" to the answer it's seeking, or provides the answer itself.

The root name servers are clearly very important to resolution. Since they're so important, DNS provides mechanisms—like caching, which we'll discuss a little later—to help offload the root name servers. But in the absence of other information, resolution has to start at the root name servers. This makes the root name servers crucial to the operation of DNS: if all the Internet root name servers were unreachable for an extended period, all resolution on the Internet would fail. To protect against this, the

Internet has seven root name servers (as of this writing), spread across different parts of the network. Some are on the MILNET, the U.S. military's portion of the Internet, one is on SPAN, NASA's internet, one is in Europe, and others are close to the NSFNET backbone.

Being the focal point for so many queries keeps the roots busy: even with seven, the traffic to each root name server is very high. A recent study by U.S.C. reported that their root received as many as 20,000 query packets in an hour, or almost six queries per second.

Despite the load placed on root name servers, resolution on the Internet works quite well. Figure 2.10 shows the resolution process for the address of a real host in a real domain, including how the process corresponds to traversing the domain name space tree.

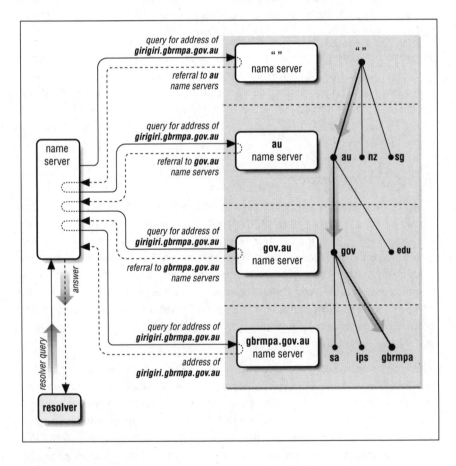

Figure 2.10: Resolution of girigiri.gbrmpa.gov.au on the Internet

The local name server queries a root name server for the address of **giri-giri.gbrmpa.gov.au**, and is referred to the **au** name servers. It asks an **au** name server the same question, and is referred to the **gov.au** name servers. The **gov.au** name server refers the local name server to the **gbrmpa.gov.au** name servers. Finally, the local name server asks a **gbrmpa.gov.au** name server for the address, and gets the answer.

Recursion

You may have noticed a big difference in the amount of work done by the name servers in the previous example. Four of the name servers simply returned the best answer they already had—mostly referrals to other name servers—to the queries they received. They didn't have to send their own queries to find the data requested. But one name server—the one queried by the resolver—had to follow successive referrals until it received an answer.

Why couldn't it simply have referred the resolver to another name server? Because a stub resolver wouldn't have had the intelligence to follow a referral. And how did the name server know not to answer with a referral? Because the resolver issued a *recursive* query.

Queries come in two flavors, *recursive* and *iterative*, or simply *non-recursive*. Recursive queries place most of the burden of resolution on a single name server. *Recursion*, or *recursive resolution*, is just a name for the resolution process used by a name server when it receives recursive queries.

Iteration or *iterative resolution*, on the other hand, refers to the resolution process used by a name server when it receives iterative queries.

In recursion, a resolver sends a recursive query to a name server for information about a particular domain name. The queried name server is then obliged to respond with the requested data, or with an error stating that data of the requested type doesn't exist or that the domain name specified doesn't exist. The name server can't just refer the querier to a different name server, because the query was recursive.

If the queried name server isn't authoritative for the data requested, it will have to query other name servers to find the answer. It could send recursive queries to those name servers, thereby obliging them to find the answer and return it (and passing the buck). Or it could send iterative queries, and possibly be referred to other name servers "closer" to the domain name it's looking for. Current implementations are polite and do the latter, following the referrals until an answer is found.

You can probably already see the analogy between recursive resolution and recursion in programming. In recursive programming, the same process originally used to ask the question is used at each level to ask a refined version of the question. Similarly, in recursive resolution, a name server uses the basic querying process over and over to find the answer to the initial query, refining the process along the way by asking name servers further down the domain tree.

Iteration

Iterative resolution, on the other hand, doesn't require nearly as much work on the part of the queried name server. In iterative resolution, a name server simply gives the best answer *it already knows* back to the querier. There's no additional querying required. The queried name server consults its local data (including its cache, which we're about to talk about), looking for the data requested. If it doesn't find the data there, it makes its best attempt to give the querier data that will help it continue the resolution process. Usually these are the names and addresses of name servers "closer" to the data its seeking.

What this amounts to is a resolution process which, taken as a whole, looks like Figure 2.11.

A resolver queries a local name server, which then queries a number of other name servers in pursuit of an answer for the resolver. Each name server it queries refers it to another name server further down the name space and closer to the data sought. Finally the local name server queries the authoritative name server, which returns an answer.

Mapping Addresses to Names

One major piece of functionality missing from the resolution process as explained so far is how addresses get mapped back to names. Address-to-name mapping is used to produce output that is easier for humans to read and interpret (in log files, for instance). It's also used in some authorization checks. UNIX hosts map addresses to host names to compare against entries in *.rhosts* and *hosts.equiv* files, for example.

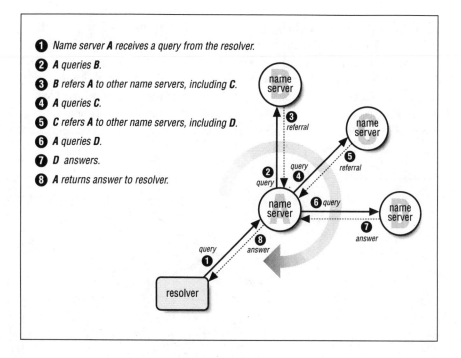

① *Name server* **A** *receives a query from the resolver.*

② *A queries* **B**.

③ *B refers* **A** *to other name servers, including* **C**.

④ *A queries* **C**.

⑤ *C refers* **A** *to other name servers, including* **D**.

⑥ *A queries* **D**.

⑦ *D answers.*

⑧ *A returns answer to resolver.*

Figure 2.11: The resolution process

When using host tables, address-to-name mapping is trivial. It requires a straightforward sequential search through the host table for an address. The search returns the official host name listed. In DNS, though, address-to-name mapping isn't so simple. Data, including addresses, in the domain name space are indexed by name. Finding an address given a domain name is relatively easy. But finding the domain name that maps to a given address would seem to require an exhaustive search of every domain name in the tree.

Actually, there's a better solution that's both clever and very effective. Since it's easy to find data once you're given the name that indexes that data, why not create a part of the domain name space that uses addresses as names? In the Internet's domain name space, this portion of the name space is the **in-addr.arpa** domain.

Nodes in the **in-addr.arpa** domain are named after the numbers in the dotted-octet representation of IP addresses. (Dotted-octet representation refers to the common method of expressing 32-bit IP addresses as four numbers in the range 0 to 255, separated by dots.) The **in-addr.arpa** domain, for example, could have up to 256 subdomains, one corresponding to each possible value in the first octet of an IP address. Each of these subdomains could have up to 256 subdomains of its own, corresponding to the possible values of the second octet. Finally, at the fourth level down, there are resource records attached to the final octet giving the full domain name of the host or network at that IP address. That makes for an awfully big domain: **in-addr.arpa**, shown in Figure 2.12, is roomy enough for every IP address on the Internet.

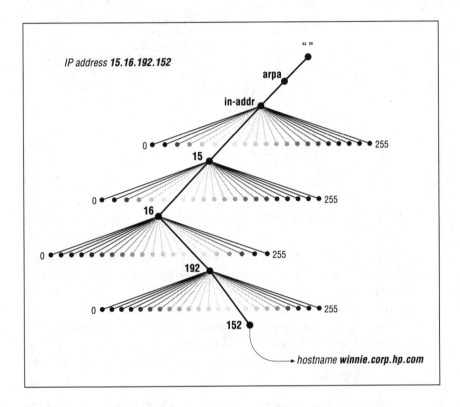

Figure 2.12: The in-addr.arpa Domain

Note that when read as a domain name, the IP address appears backwards, since the name is read leaf-to-root. For example, if **winnie.corp.hp.com** has the IP address 15.16.192.152, the corresponding **in-addr.arpa** subdomain is **152.192.16.15.in-addr.arpa**, which maps back to the domain name **winnie.corp.hp.com**.

IP addresses could have been represented the opposite way in the name space, with the first octet of the IP address at the bottom of the **in-addr.arpa** domain. That way, the IP address would have read correctly (forward) in the domain name.

However, IP addresses are hierarchical, just like domain names. Network numbers are doled out much like domain names are, and administrators can then subnet their address space and further delegate numbering. The difference is that IP addresses get more specific from left to right, while domain names get less specific from left to right. Figure 2.13 shows what we mean.

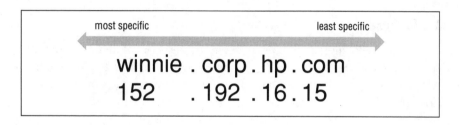

Figure 2.13: Hierarchical names and addresses

Making the first octets in the IP address appear highest in the tree gives administrators the ability to delegate authority for **in-addr.arpa** domains along network lines. For example, the **15.in-addr.arpa** domain can be delegated to the administrators of network 15. This would be impossible if the octets appeared in the opposite order. If the IP addresses were represented the other way around, **15.in-addr.arpa** would consist of every host whose IP address ended with 15—not a practical domain to try to delegate.

Inverse Queries

The **in-addr.arpa** name space is clearly only useful for IP address-to-domain name mapping, though. Searching for a domain name that indexes an *arbitrary* piece of data—something besides an address—in the domain name space would require another specialized name space like **in-addr.arpa**, or an exhaustive search.

That exhaustive search is to some extent possible, and it's called an inverse query. An inverse query is a search for the domain name that indexes a given datum. It's processed solely by the name server receiving the query. That name server searches all of its local data for the item sought and returns the domain name that indexes it, if possible. If it can't find the data, it gives up. No attempt is made to forward the query to another name server.

Since any one name server only knows about part of the overall domain name space, an inverse query is never guaranteed to return an answer. For example, if a name server receives an inverse query for an IP address it knows nothing about, it can't return an answer, but it also doesn't know that the IP address doesn't exist, since it only holds part of the DNS database. What's more, the implementation of inverse queries is optional according to the DNS specification; future versions of BIND may drop it.

Caching

The whole resolution process may seem awfully convoluted and cumbersome to someone accustomed to simple seeks through the host table. Actually, though, it's usually quite fast. One of the features that speeds it up considerably is *caching*.

A name server processing a recursive query may have to send out quite a few queries to find an answer. However, it discovers a lot of information about the domain name space as it does so. Each time it's referred to another list of name servers, it learns that those name servers are authoritative for some zone, and it learns the addresses of those servers. And, at the end of the resolution process, when it finally finds the data the original querier sought, it can store that data for future reference, too.

Name servers cache all of this data to help speed up successive queries. The next time a resolver queries the name server for data about a domain name the name server knows something about, the process is shortened quite a bit. The name server may have cached the answer, in which case it simply returns the answer to the resolver. Even if it doesn't have the answer cached, it may have learned the identities of the name servers authoritative for the zone the domain name is in, and be able to query them directly.

For example, say our name server has already looked up the address of **eecs.berkeley.edu**. In the process, it cached the names and addresses of the **eecs.berkeley.edu** and **berkeley.edu** name servers (plus **eecs.berkeley.edu**'s IP address). Now if a resolver were to query our name server for the address of **baobab.cs.berkeley.edu**, our name server could skip querying the root name servers. Recognizing that **berkeley.edu** is the closest ancestor of **baobab.cs.berkeley.edu** that it knows about, our name server would start by querying a **berkeley.edu** name server, as shown in Figure 2-14.

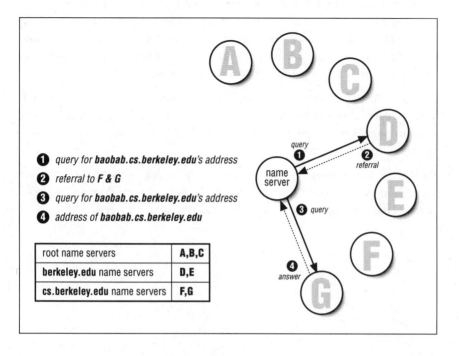

1 query for *baobab.cs.berkeley.edu's* address

2 referral to *F & G*

3 query for *baobab.cs.berkeley.edu's* address

4 address of *baobab.cs.berkeley.edu*

root name servers	A,B,C
berkeley.edu name servers	D,E
cs.berkeley.edu name servers	F,G

Figure 2.14: Resolving baobab.cs.berkeley.edu

In addition to speeding up resolution, caching prevented us from having to query the root name servers again. This means that we're not as dependent on the roots and they won't suffer as much from all our queries.

Time to Live

Name servers can't cache data forever, of course. If they did, changes to that data on the authoritative name servers would never reach the rest of the network. Remote name servers would just continue to use cached data. Consequently, the administrator of the zone that contains the data decides on a *time to live*, or *TTL*, for the data. The time to live is the amount of time that any name server is allowed to cache the data. After the time to live expires, the name server must discard the cached data and get new data from the authoritative name servers.

Deciding on a time to live for your data is essentially deciding on a tradeoff between performance and consistency. A small TTL will help ensure that data about your domain is consistent across the network, because remote name servers will time it out more quickly and be forced to query your authoritative name servers more often for new data. On the other hand, this will increase the load on your name servers and lengthen resolution time for information in your domain, on the average.

A large TTL will shorten the average time it takes to resolve information in your domain, since the data can be cached longer. The drawback is that your information will be inconsistent longer if you make changes to your data on your name servers.

Enough of this theory—I'll bet you're antsy to get on with this. There's some homework necessary before you can set up your domain and your name servers, though, and we'll assign it in the next chapter.

3

Where Do I Start?

*"What do you call yourself?" the Fawn said at last. Such a soft
sweet voice it had!*

*"I wish I knew!" thought poor Alice. She answered, rather sadly,
"Nothing, just now."*

"Think again," it said: "that won't do."

*Alice thought, but nothing came of it. "Please, would you tell me
what you call yourself?" she said timidly. "I think that might help
a little."*

*"I'll tell you, if you come a little further on," the Fawn said. "I
can't remember here."*

Now that you understand the theory behind the Domain Name System, we
can attend to more practical matters. Before you set up a domain, you may
need to get the BIND software. Usually, it's included as a standard part of
most UNIX-based operating systems. Occasionally, however, you'll need to
seek out a version for a more obscure operating system, or you'll want the
current version with all the latest functionality.

Once you've got BIND, you need to decide on a domain name—which may
not be quite as easy as it sounds, as it entails finding an appropriate parent
domain in the Internet name space. That decided, you need to contact the
administrators of the parent domain of the domain name you've chosen.

One thing at a time, though. Let's talk about where to get BIND.

Getting BIND

If you plan to set up your own domain and run name servers for that
domain, you'll need the BIND software first. Even if you're planning on
having someone else run your domain, it's helpful to have the software
around. For example, you can use your local copy of BIND to test your data
files before giving them to your remote domain administrator.

Most commercial UNIX vendors ship BIND with the rest of their standard TCP/IP networking software. And, quite often, the networking software is included with the operating system, so you get BIND free. Even if the networking software is priced separately, you've probably already bought it, since you clearly do enough networking to need DNS, right?

If you don't have a version of BIND for your flavor of UNIX, though, or if you want the latest, greatest version, you can always get the source code. As luck would have it, it's freely distributed. The most up-to-date BIND source as of this writing (BIND 4.8.3) is available via anonymous *ftp* from **ftp.uu.net** in */networking/ip/dns/bind/bind.4.8.3.tar.Z.** Compiling it may be relatively straightforward, and on the other hand it may be fairly difficult, depending on how closely your vendor's version of UNIX resembles Berkeley's BSD UNIX (the closer the better). SunOS is based on BSD UNIX, and is therefore a relatively easy port. We include instructions on porting BIND to SunOS as Appendix B.

Handy Mailing Lists

Instructions on how to port BIND to every other version of UNIX could consume another book this size, so we'll have to refer you to the BIND mailing list, **bind@vangogh.cs.berkeley.edu**,† for further help. The folks who read and contribute to the BIND list can be enormously helpful in your porting efforts. Be sure to ask whether the port you're after has already been done—you may be pleasantly surprised. For example, DEC currently makes an unsupported version of BIND 4.8.3 already ported to Ultrix available via anonymous *ftp* on two of its hosts, **gatekeeper.dec.com** and **crl.dec.com**. All you need to do is compile it.

Another mailing list you might be interested in is the *namedroppers* list. Folks on the *namedroppers* mailing list usually discuss DNS issues, rather than BIND-specific problems. For example, a discussion of extensions to the DNS protocol or proposed DNS record types would probably take place

---

*Unfortunately, **ftp.uu.net** doesn't allow *ftp* access to hosts that aren't registered in the DNS, so you may have to use an account on a registered host to *ftp* the source.

†To ask a question on an Internet mailing list, all you need to do is send a message to the mailing list's address. If you'd like to join the list, however, you have to send a message to the list's maintainer first, requesting him or her to add your electronic mail address to the list. Don't send a request to be added to the list itself—it's considered rude. The Internet convention is that you can reach the maintainer of a mailing list by sending mail to *list*-request@*domain*, where *list*@*domain* is the address of the mailing list. So, for example, you can reach the BIND mailing list's administrator by sending mail to **bind-request@vangogh.cs.berkeley.edu**.

on *namedroppers* instead of the *bind* mailing list. Avoid sending the same message to both mailing lists: many people are on both.

The *namedroppers* mailing list is **namedroppers@nic.ddn.mil**, and is gatewayed into the Internet newsgroup **comp.protocols.tcp-ip.domains**. To join the *namedroppers* mailing list, send mail to **namedroppers-request@nic.ddn.mil**.

Finding IP Addresses

You'll notice we gave you a number of domain names of hosts that have *ftp*'able software, and the mailing lists we mentioned include domain names. That should underscore the importance of DNS to you: see what valuable software and advice you can get with the help of DNS? Unfortunately, it's also something of a chicken-and-egg problem. You can't *ftp* to **gatekeeper.dec.com** unless your host is configured to use DNS, so how can you get the BIND source for Ultrix?

Well, we could give you the IP addresses for all the hosts we mentioned, but since IP addresses change often (in publishing timescales, anyway), we'll show you how you can use someone else's name server to find the information instead. As long as your host has Internet connectivity and the *nslookup* program, you can retrieve information from the Internet name space. To look up the IP address for **gatekeeper.dec.com**, for example, you could use

```
% nslookup gatekeeper.dec.com. 128.32.130.2
```

This instructs *nslookup* to query the name server running on the host at IP address 128.32.130.2 to find the IP address for **gatekeeper.dec.com**, and should produce output like:

```
Server:   vangogh.CS.Berkeley.EDU
Address:  128.32.130.2

Name:     gatekeeper.dec.com
Address:  16.1.0.2
```

Now you can *ftp* to **gatekeeper.dec.com**'s IP address, 16.1.0.2.

How did we know the host at IP address 128.32.130.2 runs a name server? Truthfully, we cheated: we knew **vangogh.cs.berkeley.edu** was a **berkeley.edu** name server and we looked up its IP address with *nslookup* and found 128.32.130.2. How should you choose an IP address to query? Well, if you don't already have a name server in mind, you could use one we list in this book. As long as you only use it to look up a few IP addresses or other data, the administrators probably won't mind.

Of course, if you've already got access to a host with Internet connectivity *and* DNS configured, you can use it to *ftp* the stuff you need.

Once you've got a working version of BIND, you're ready to start thinking about your domain name.

Choosing a Domain Name

Choosing a domain name is more involved than it may sound, because it entails both choosing a name *and* finding a parent. In other words, you need to find out where you fit in the Internet domain name space, and decide what you'd like to call your particular corner of that name space.

The first step in picking a domain name is finding where in the existing domain name space you belong. It's easiest to start at the top and work your way down: decide which top-level domain you belong in, then which of that top-level domain's subdomains you fit into.

Note that in order to find out what the Internet domain name space looks like (beyond what we've already told you), you'll need access to the Internet. You don't need access to a host that already has Domain Name Service configured, but it would help a little. If you don't have access to a host with DNS configured, you'll have to "borrow" name service from other name servers (as in our previous **ftp.uu.net** example) to get you going.

Where in the World Do I Fit?

If your organization is attached to the Internet outside of the United States, you should check whether your country's top-level domain is registered, and if it is, what kind of structure it has. Consult our list of the current top-level domains (Appendix C) if you're not sure what your country's top-level domain is.

Some countries' top-level domains, like New Zealand's **nz**, Australia's **au**, and the United Kingdom's **uk**, are divided organizationally into second-level domains. The names of their second-level domains, like **co** or **com** for commercial entities, reflect organizational affiliation. Others, like France's **fr** domain, and Canada's **ca** domain, are divided into a multitude of domains managed by individual universities and companies, like the University of St. Etienne's domain, **univ-st-etienne.fr** and Bell Northern

Research's **bnr.ca**. You'll have to use a tool like *nslookup* to grope around and discover your top-level domain's structure if it isn't well-known. (If you're uncomfortable with our rushing headlong into *nslookup* without giving it a proper introduction, you might skim Chapter 10, *nslookup*.) For example, here's how you could list the **au** domain's subdomains using *nslookup*:

```
% nslookup - 128.32.130.2   --Use the name server at 128.32.130.2
Default Server:  vangogh.CS.Berkeley.EDU
Address:  128.32.130.2

> set type=ns             --Find the name servers (ns)
> au.                     --for the au domain
Server:  vangogh.CS.Berkeley.EDU
Address: 128.32.130.2

au        nameserver = munnari.OZ.AU
au        nameserver = mulga.cs.mu.OZ.AU
au        nameserver = jatz.aarnet.EDU.AU
au        nameserver = ucbvax.Berkeley.EDU
au        nameserver = ns.UU.NET
au        nameserver = mcsun.eu.NET
munnari.OZ.AU   internet address = 128.250.1.21
munnari.OZ.AU   internet address = 192.43.207.1
mulga.cs.mu.OZ.AU      internet address = 192.43.207.2
mulga.cs.mu.OZ.AU      internet address = 128.250.35.21
jatz.aarnet.EDU.AU     internet address = 139.130.204.4
ucbvax.Berkeley.EDU    internet address = 128.32.137.3
ucbvax.Berkeley.EDU    internet address = 128.32.133.1
ucbvax.Berkeley.EDU    internet address = 128.32.130.12
ucbvax.Berkeley.EDU    internet address = 128.32.149.36
ns.UU.NET       internet address = 137.39.1.3
ns.eu.NET       internet address = 192.16.202.11

> server ucbvax.berkeley.edu.   --Now query one of these name servers--
                                --preferably a close one!
Default Server:  ucbvax.berkeley.edu
Addresses:  128.32.137.3, 128.32.133.1, 128.32.130.12, 128.32.149.36

> ls -t ns au.  --List all name server records in the domain au
                --(which mark delegation to subdomains and will give
                --you the names of the subdomains)

                --Note that not all name servers will allow you to
                --list domains for security reasons. Also, some
                --versions of nslookup don't understand ls -t.
                --If your nslookup doesn't, use ls instead.
                --ls will produce this output and much more.

[ucbvax.berkeley.edu]
AU.                          server = munnari.OZ.AU
AU.                          server = mulga.cs.mu.OZ.AU
```

```
AU.                        server = jatz.aarnet.EDU.AU
AU.                        server = ucbvax.Berkeley.EDU
AU.                        server = ns.UU.NET
AU.                        server = ns.eu.NET
ORG                        server = munnari.OZ.AU
ORG                        server = mulga.cs.mu.OZ.AU
GW                         server = mulga.cs.mu.OZ.AU
GW                         server = munnari.OZ.AU
GW                         server = muwaya.ucs.unimelb.EDU.AU
GW                         server = jatz.aarnet.EDU.AU
CSIRO                      server = munnari.OZ.AU
CSIRO                      server = wanda.mel.dit.CSIRO.AU
CSIRO                      server = manta.mel.dit.CSIRO.AU
CSIRO                      server = dmssyd.syd.dms.CSIRO.AU
OZ                         server = mulga.cs.mu.OZ.AU
OZ                         server = munnari.OZ.AU
OZ                         server = dmssyd.syd.dms.CSIRO.AU
OZ                         server = ns.UU.NET
COM                        server = mulga.cs.mu.OZ.AU
COM                        server = munnari.OZ.AU
COM                        server = mundoe.maths.mu.OZ.AU
GOV                        server = nameserver.arc.NASA.GOV
GOV                        server = mulga.cs.mu.OZ.AU
GOV                        server = munnari.OZ.AU
GOV                        server = jatz.aarnet.EDU.AU
EDU                        server = mundoe.maths.mu.OZ.AU
EDU                        server = mulga.cs.mu.OZ.AU
EDU                        server = munnari.OZ.AU
EDU                        server = jatz.aarnet.EDU.AU
EDU                        server = ucbvax.Berkeley.EDU
> ^D
```

The basic technique we use is straightforward: look up the list of authoritative name servers for the top-level domain—because they're the only ones with complete information about the domain—then connect to one of those name servers, and list the name servers for the second-level domains.

If the purpose of a particular domain isn't intuitively obvious to you (what's **CSIRO**, or **OZ**, for that matter?), you can always ask the folks who administer it what it's for. In each domain's start of authority (SOA) record, there's a field that contains the electronic mail address of the domain's technical contact. (The other fields in the start of authority record provide general information about a domain—we'll discuss them in more detail later.) You can look up the domain's SOA record with *nslookup*, too:

```
% nslookup - 128.32.130.2
Default Server: vangogh.CS.Berkeley.EDU
Address: 128.32.130.2

> set type=soa    --Look for start of authority data
> csiro.au.       --for csiro.au
```

```
Server:   vangogh.CS.Berkeley.EDU
Address:  128.32.130.2

csiro.au
          origin = manta.mel.dit.csiro.AU
          mail addr = smart.manta.mel.dit.csiro.AU
          serial = 1992021800
          refresh = 10800 (3 hours)
          retry   = 3600 (1 hour)
          expire  = 3600000 (41 days 16 hours)
          minimum ttl = 86400 (1 day)
```

The mail addr field is the Internet address of **csiro.au**'s contact. To use the address with most UNIX mailers, you'll need to change the first "**.**" in the address into a "**@**".* So **smart.manta.mel.dit.csiro.AU** becomes **smart@manta.mel.dit.csiro.AU**.

domain-contacts.txt

Another possibility is to *ftp* the current *domain-contacts.txt* file from **nic.ddn.mil** (it's in the *netinfo* subdirectory). The *domain-contacts.txt* file lists the current administrative, zone, and technical contact for all first- and second-level domains. For example, under **movie.edu**, you might find:

```
MOVIE.EDU

  Admin: LeDomaine, Al      al@MOVIE.EDU      (213) 555-4242
  Tech : LeDomaine, Al      al@MOVIE.EDU      (213) 555-4242
  Zone : LeDomaine, Al      al@MOVIE.EDU      (213) 555-4242
```

An alternate way to get this file is to e-mail a letter to **service@nic.ddn.mil** with the subject field **netinfo domain-contacts.txt**. The file will be mailed back to you.

whois

The NIC's *whois* service can also help you figure out what a given domain is for. Many vendors ship a simple *whois* client that queries a database at the NIC for information about domains, networks, or people registered in the database. For example:

---

*This form of Internet mail address is a vestige of two former DNS records, MB and MG. MB (mail box) and MG (mail group) were to be DNS records specifying Internet mailboxes and mail groups (mailing lists) as subdomains of the appropriate domain. MB and MG never took off, but the address format they would have dictated is used in the SOA record, maybe for sentimental reasons.

```
% whois bob
```

will turn up every match for *bob* in the database, including people, networks and domains. To restrict the search to domains or networks, you can use the keywords *dom* or *net*, respectively:

```
% whois dom foo   # print information on all domains that match foo
% whois net 17    # print information on network number 17
```

If you don't have a *whois* client, you can *telnet* to **nic.ddn.mil** and use the *whois* service. At the "@" prompt, you can use the same *whois* commands we've shown above, for example:

```
% telnet nic.ddn.mil.
```

nic.ddn.mil *displays a long, informative banner...*

```
@ whois dom foo
```

Unfortunately, the *whois* database only lists contacts for top-level country domains and second-level U.S. organizational domains, so you won't find **csiro.au**. Still, you can use it to find the contact for **au**:

```
% whois dom au
```

will connect to a host at the NIC and search their database for information on the domain **au**:

```
Australian Research Network (AU-DOM)
    Computer Science
    University of Melbourne
    Parkville, Victoria 3052
    AUSTRALIA

    Domain Name: AU

    Administrative Contact, Technical Contact, Zone Contact:
        Elz, Robert  (RE18)  kre@MUNNARI.OZ.AU
        +61 3 344 5225

    Record last updated on 18-Jun-91.

    Domain servers in listed order:

    MUNNARI.OZ.AU              128.250.1.21
    MULGA.CS.MU.OZ.AU          192.43.207.2
    JATZ.AARNET.EDU.AU         139.130.204.4
    UCBVAX.Berkeley.EDU        128.32.133.1, 128.32.130.12,
                               128.32.149.36
    NS.UU.NET                  137.39.1.3
    NS.EU.NET                  192.16.202.11

    Top Level domain for Australia
```

You could send a message to the administrative contact for the **au** domain and ask what the **CSIRO** subdomain is all about, or even describe your organization and ask for suggestions on where you might fit.

If your copy of *whois* is outdated, it'll probably try to query the NIC's database using an old domain name, **sri-nic.arpa**. That'll produce either a pleasant message from the NIC staff or a gruff error message like:

```
sri-nic.arpa: Unknown host
```

If this happens and you have access to the source code, just recompile *whois* to query **nic.ddn.mil**. If you don't have the source, you can still direct *whois* to use **nic.ddn.mil** from the command line with the –*h* option, as in:

```
% whois -h nic.ddn.mil dom au
```

Elsewhere in the World

In true cosmopolitan spirit, we covered international domains first. But what if you're from the good ol' U.S. of A.?

If you're in the U.S., where you belong depends mainly upon how many hosts you have. If you only have one or two, or maybe a handful of hosts you'd like registered in the Internet's domain name space, you can join the **us** domain. The **us** domain registers individual hosts under third-level domains named after cities; the second-level domains correspond to the appropriate U.S. Postal Service's two-letter state acronym (recall our discussion in *The Internet Domain Name Space*). So, for example, if all you need is to register the two internetworked hosts in your basement in Colorado Springs, Colorado, you can just have them added to the **colospgs.co.us** domain.

You won't, however, get your own domain to manage. That's partly because of the structure of the **us** domain, and partly a policy decision by the administrators of the **us** domain. Your hosts will become part of an existing Internet domain, managed by others. The **us** administrators will add address and mail handling information for your host (more on this in the next two chapters—be patient), but not name server information—in other words, they won't delegate a portion of their domain to you. They'll free you from the burden of managing name servers for your hosts, but also keep you from creating subdomains.

If you want your own domain and you're in the U.S., you'll have to ask for a subdomain of one of the original, organizational top-level domains, like **edu** and **com**. As long as you don't ask for an overly-long domain name (the NIC recommends 12 letters or fewer), or one that's already taken, you should get the one you ask for. We'll cover membership under the organizational top-levels later in this chapter.

The US Domain

Let's go through an example to give you an idea of how to comb the **us** domain name space for the perfect domain name. Say you live in Rockville, Maryland, and you want to register the UNIX workstation you just bought out of the back of a truck. You're not directly connected to the Internet, but you do have a UUCP connection to UMD in College Park.

Since you only need to have a single host registered, you really don't need your own domain to manage. You just need to have your host registered in the Internet domain name space somewhere. The **us** top-level domain is the one for you. Letting someone else take care of the name server and domain administration will save you a lot of administrative effort.

Using an account you still have on a host at UMD (from your undergrad days), you can check to see whether a domain for Maryland exists. (If you didn't have an account there, but you did have Internet connectivity, you could still use *nslookup* to query a well-known name server.)

```
% nslookup
Default Server:  noc.umd.edu
Address: 128.8.5.2

> set type=ns          --Look up the name servers
> md.us.               --for md.us
Server:  noc.umd.edu
Address:  128.8.5.2

md.us    nameserver = VENERA.ISI.EDU
md.us    nameserver = VAXA.ISI.EDU
md.us    nameserver = NNSC.NSF.NET
md.us    nameserver = HERCULES.CSL.SRI.COM
```

Sure enough, there's a domain for Maryland. Now change servers to a **md.us** name server and check to see if there are any subdomains (you haven't exited out of *nslookup* yet):

```
> server venera.isi.edu.  --Change server to venera.isi.edu
Default Server:  venera.isi.edu
Address:  128.9.0.32
```

```
> ls -t ns md.us.    --List all name server records in the domain md.us
[venera.isi.edu]
MD.US.                                server = VENERA.ISI.EDU
MD.US.                                server = VAXA.ISI.EDU
MD.US.                                server = NNSC.NSF.NET
MD.US.                                server = HERCULES.CSL.SRI.COM
```

Hmm. Well, you know there aren't any delegated subdomains under
md.us. But what if **md.us** were just one zone? It could have subdomains
that weren't delegated to other name servers. You should check for other
types of data, too:

```
> ls -t any md.us.    --List any data under md.us
[venera.isi.edu]
md.us.                     SOA   VENERA.ISI.EDU Westine.ISI.EDU.
   (920215 4 3200 1800 604800 604800)
MD.US.                     NS    VENERA.ISI.EDU
VENERA.ISI.EDU.            A     128.9.0.32
MD.US.                     NS    VAXA.ISI.EDU
VAXA.ISI.EDU.              A     128.9.0.33
MD.US.                     NS    NNSC.NSF.NET
NNSC.NSF.NET.              A     128.89.1.178
MD.US.                     NS    HERCULES.CSL.SRI.COM
HERCULES.CSL.SRI.COM.      A     192.12.33.51
paladin.aberdeen           MX    10   ctj.paladin.aberdeen.md.us
ctj.paladin.aberdeen       A     128.63.30.24
ctj.paladin.aberdeen       A     128.63.17.254
ctj.paladin.aberdeen       HINFO MacII        A/UX
ctj.paladin.aberdeen       WKS   tcp  ftp telnet smtp
ctj.paladin.aberdeen       WKS   tcp  smtp
jetson.UPMA                HINFO compaq-386/20   SCO-Xenix/386
jetson.UPMA                MX    10   RELAY1.UU.NET
jetson.UPMA                MX    10   RELAY2.UU.NET
n3dmc.svr                  HINFO INTEL-386    UNIX
n3dmc.svr                  MX    10   RELAY1.UU.NET
n3dmc.svr                  MX    10   RELAY2.UU.NET
fe2o3.LAUREL               MX    10   MIMSY.CS.UMD.EDU
fe2o3.LAUREL               HINFO NSC/ICM-3216   UNIX-4.2bsd
DUMMY-HOST.CITY            A     10.0.0.0
TEST-HOST.CITY             CNAME VENERA.ISI.EDU
md.us.                     SOA   VENERA.ISI.EDU Westine.ISI.EDU.
   (920215 43 200 1800 604800 604800)
>
```

Aha! So there *is* life in Maryland! There are subdomains called **aberdeen**,
UPMA, **svr**, and **LAUREL**. But there doesn't seem to be a domain for Rockville. No matter—you may be the first host in Rockville to want to register
under the **md.us** domain. The administrators of **md.us** would probably be
willing to create a subdomain of **md.us** for Rockville. Since it'll just be part
of the **md.us** zone, it won't require very much work for them: there's no
need to set up separate servers.

What to call the domain? **rockville.md.us**? **rock.md.us**? Turns out there's a convention in the **us** domain that city-level domains be named after the appropriate Western Union's "City Mnemonic." (Don't worry: the **us** administrators have a copy.) The alternative is to use the full name of the city.

Actually, with any parent domain, it's possible the administrators of the domain will have some strong feelings about the names of their child domains. They may want to preserve the consistency of their name space. We think it's polite to defer to your parent if they feel strongly about naming—after all, they could simply refuse to let you join the domain. You still get to choose the name of your host, after all.

How do you find out how to contact your parent domain's administrator? You can try *whois*, but since **md.us** isn't a top-level country domain or an organizational U.S. domain, you probably won't find much. Your best bet is probably to use *nslookup* to find the SOA record for **md.us**, just like you did to find out who to ask about **csiro.au**. Though the person or persons who read mail sent to the address in the SOA record may not handle registration themselves—technical and administrative functions for the domain may be divided—it's a good bet they know the folks who do and can direct you to them.

Here's how you'd use *nslookup* to dig up the SOA record for **md.us**:

```
% nslookup
Default Server:  noc.umd.edu
Address:  128.8.5.2

> set type=soa      --Look up SOA record
> md.us.            --for md.us
Server:  noc.umd.edu
Address:  128.8.5.2

md.us
        origin = VENERA.ISI.EDU
        mail addr = Westine.ISI.EDU
        serial = 920215
        refresh = 43200 (12 hours)
        retry   = 1800 (30 mins)
        expire  = 604800 (7 days)
        minimum ttl = 604800 (7 days)
```

As in the **csiro.au** example, you need to swap the first "." in the mail addr field for a "@" before you use it. Thus **Westine.ISI.EDU** becomes **Westine@ISI.EDU**.

The Organizational U.S. Domains

As we said, if you'd wanted your own domain to manage, you'd have to ask for a subdomain of one of the U.S. top-level organizational domains, like **com**, **edu**, and **org**. Let's go through a short example of choosing a domain name under an organizational top-level domain.

Imagine you're the student administrator of a small university network in Hopkins, Minnesota. You've just gotten a grant for Internet connectivity, and are about to be connected to your regional network, MRNet. Your university has never had so much as a UUCP link, so you're not currently registered in the Internet name space.

Since you're in the U.S., you have the choice of joining either **us** or **edu**. You've already got over a dozen computers on your local network, though, and you expect more, so **us** wouldn't be a good choice. A subdomain of **edu** would be best.

Your university is known as The Gizmonics Institute, so you decide **gizmo.edu** might be an appropriate domain name. Now you've got to check if the name **gizmo.edu** has been taken by anyone, so you use an account you have at UMN:

```
% nslookup
Default Server:  ns.unet.umn.edu
Address:  128.101.101.101

> set type=any     --Look for any records
> gizmo.edu.       --for gizmo.edu
Server:  ns.unet.umn.edu
Address:  128.101.101.101

*** ns.unet.umn.edu can't find gizmo.edu.: Non-existent domain
```

Looks like there's no **gizmo.edu** yet (hardly surprising), so you can go on to the next step: finding out who runs your intended parent domain. You use *whois*:

```
% whois dom edu
Educational Domain (EDU-DOM)

   Domain Name: EDU

   Administrative Contact, Technical Contact, Zone Contact:
      Government Systems, Inc.  (HOSTMASTER)  HOSTMASTER@NIC.DDN.MIL
      (800) 365-3642 (703) 802-4535

   Record last updated on 25-Sep-91.

   Domain servers in listed order:
```

```
NS.NIC.DDN.MIL              192.112.36.4
KAVA.NISC.SRI.COM           192.33.33.24
C.NYSER.NET                 192.33.4.12
TERP.UMD.EDU                128.8.10.90
NS.NASA.GOV                 128.102.16.10, 192.52.195.10
AOS.BRL.MIL                 128.63.4.82, 26.3.0.29, 192.5.25.82
NIC.NORDU.NET               192.36.148.17
```

Checking that Your Network Number is Registered

If your network isn't connected to the Internet yet, but will be soon, and you've been using an Internet-connected host to grope the Internet's domain name space for information, there's one thing you should check before you go any further: whether or not your network number is registered with the NIC. A network number defines a range of IP addresses. For example, the network number *15* is composed of all IP addresses in the range 15.0.0.0 to 15.255.255.255. The network number *199.10.25* starts at 199.10.25.0 and ends at 199.10.25.255.

The NIC is the official source of all network numbers: they assign network numbers to Internet-connected networks and make sure no two ranges overlap. If your network number isn't registered, the NIC won't let you register any of your network's hosts in their domains.

If you're not sure your network number is official, there are a number of ways you can check. You can retrieve the file */netinfo/networks.txt* from **nic.ddn.mil** via anonymous *ftp*. *networks.txt* lists all official network numbers. Or you can use the NIC's *whois* service and look for your network number:

```
% whois net 15
Hewlett-Packard Company (NET-HP-INTERNET)
   1501 Page Mill Road
   Palo Alto, CA 94303

   Netname: HP-INTERNET
   Netnumber: 15.0.0.0

   Coordinator:
      Liu, Cricket  (CL142)  cricket@WINNIE.CORP.HP.COM
      (415) 424-3723
```

```
Domain System inverse mapping provided by:

RELAY.HP.COM                     15.255.152.2
HPLABS.HPL.HP.COM                15.255.176.47
NNSC.NSF.NET                     128.89.1.178
HPFCLA.FC.HP.COM                 15.254.48.2
HPLB.HPL.HP.COM                  15.255.59.2
HPCUOC.CUP.HP.COM                15.255.208.5

Record last updated on 27-Feb-91.
```

Or you can even send mail to **hostmaster@internic.net** (hostmaster@nic.ddn.mil if you're on the MILNET) and ask. Hostmasters are awfully busy people, though, so your other alternatives may well be quicker.

If you find out your network number isn't registered, you'll need to request an official one. The file */netinfo/network-template.txt*, which you can *ftp* from **nic.ddn.mil**, explains how to apply for an official network number. If you were lucky enough to choose an unused network number, the NIC may assign it to you. If not, you'll have to reassign your hosts' IP addresses to addresses in a NIC-blessed range.

Once all your Internet-connected hosts are on NIC-registered networks, you can give your parent domain a call.

Registering with Your Parent

Different domains have different registration policies. We've included the NIC's current registration form for second-level domains as Appendix D. The form is only valid for registration under the NIC-run, organizational top-level domains like **com** and **edu**. (In other words, don't submit it to the administrators of the **au** or **fr** domain and expect them to honor it.) It should, however, give you an idea of what to expect in a registration form (especially if you're registering under one of the NIC's domains). Other domains often have more informal registration processes. Sometimes simply sending the "registrar" the necessary information in a mail message will do.

The basic information that your parent needs is the names and addresses of your domain name servers. If you're not connected to the Internet, give them the addresses of the Internet hosts that will act as your name servers. Some parent domains also require that you already have operational name servers for your domain. (The NIC doesn't, but they ask for an estimate of when the domain will be fully operational.) If that's the case with your parent, skip ahead to *Setting Up BIND* and set up your name servers. Then contact your parent with the requisite information.

If the NIC runs your parent domain, they'll also ask for some information about your organization, and for an administrative contact and a technical contact for the domain (which can be the same person). If your contacts aren't already registered in the NIC's *whois* database, you'll also need to provide information to register them in *whois*. This includes their names, surface mail addresses, phone numbers, and electronic mail addresses. If they are already registered in *whois*, just specify their NIC *whois* "handle" (a unique alphanumeric ID) in the registration.

If you're directly connected to the Internet, you should also have the **in-addr.arpa** domains corresponding to your network numbers delegated to you. For example, if your company was allocated the class C network 192.201.44, you should manage the **44.201.192.in-addr.arpa** domain. This will let you control the IP address-to-name mappings for hosts on your network. *Setting Up BIND* also explains how to set up your **in-addr.arpa** domains.

The NIC manages all **in-addr.arpa** delegation, and uses a special form, *in-addr-template.txt*, for **in-addr.arpa** domain registration (included as Appendix E).

Now that you've sent your prospective parent word that you'd like to be adopted, you'd better take some time to get your things in order. You've got a domain to set up, and in the next chapter, we'll show you how.

4

Setting Up BIND

"It seems very pretty," she said when she had finished it, *"but it's* **rather** *hard to understand!" (You see she didn't like to confess, even to herself, that she couldn't make it out at all.) "Somehow it seems to fill my head with ideas—only I don't exactly know what they are!"*

If you have been diligently reading each chapter of this book, you're probably anxious to get a name server running. This chapter is for you. Let's set up a couple of name servers. Others of you may have read the table of contents and skipped directly to this chapter. (Shame on you!) If you are one of those people who cut corners, be aware that we may use concepts from earlier chapters and expect you to understand them already.

There are several factors that influence how you should set up your name servers. The biggest factor is what sort of access you have to the Internet: complete access (e.g., you can *ftp* to **nic.ddn.mil**), limited access (limited by a security "firewall"), or no access at all. This chapter assumes you have complete access. We'll discuss the other cases in Chapter 14, *Miscellaneous*.

In this chapter, we'll set up two name servers for a fictitious domain as an example for you to follow in setting up your own domain. We'll cover the topics in this chapter in enough detail to get your first two name servers running. Subsequent chapters will fill in the holes and go into greater depth. If you already have your name servers running, skim through this chapter to familiarize yourself with the terms we use or just to verify that you didn't miss something when you set up your servers.

Our Domain

Our fictitious domain is for a college. Movie University studies all aspects of the film industry and researches novel ways to distribute films. One of the most promising projects is research into using Ethernet as the distribution media. After talking with the folks at the NIC, they have decided on the domain name **movie.edu**. A recent grant has enabled them to connect to the Internet.

Movie U. currently has two Ethernets and they have plans for another network or two. The Ethernets have network numbers 192.249.249 and 192.253.253. A portion of their host table shows the following entries:

```
127.0.0.1       localhost

# These are our killer machines

192.249.249.2  robocop.movie.edu robocop
192.249.249.3  terminator.movie.edu terminator bigt
192.249.249.4  diehard.movie.edu diehard dh

# These machines are in horror(ible) shape and will be replaced
# soon.

192.253.253.2  misery.movie.edu misery
192.253.253.3  shining.movie.edu shining
192.253.253.4  carrie.movie.edu carrie

# A wormhole is a fictitious phenomenon that instantly transports
# space travelers over long distances and is not known to be
# stable.  The only difference between wormholes and routers is
# that routers don't transport packets as instantly--especially
# ours.

192.249.249.1  wormhole.movie.edu wormhole wh wh249
192.253.253.1  wormhole.movie.edu wormhole wh wh253
```

And the network is pictured in Figure 4.1.

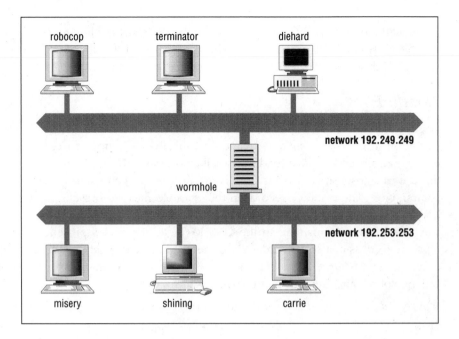

Figure 4.1: The Movie University network

Setting Up DNS Data

Our first step in setting up the Movie U. name servers is to translate the host table into equivalent DNS data. The DNS version has multiple files. One file maps all the host names to addresses. Other files map the addresses back to host names. The address-to-name lookup is sometimes called *reverse mapping*. Each network has its own file for the reverse mapping.

As a convention in this book, a file mapping host names to addresses is called *db.DOMAIN*. In **movie.edu**, this file is *db.movie*. The files mapping addresses to host names are called *db.ADDR* where *ADDR* is the network number without the trailing zeroes. In our example, the files are *db.192.249.249* and *db.192.253.253*; there's one for each network. The *db* is short for database. We'll call the collection of *db.DOMAIN* and *db.ADDR* files *db files* or DNS *database files*. There are a couple other data files: *db.cache* and *db.127.0.0*. These files are overhead. Each name server must have them and they are, more or less, the same for each server.

To tie all the db files together, a name server needs a startup file—for BIND this file is usually */etc/named.boot*. The db files are DNS specific. The startup file is specific to the name server implementation; in this case BIND.

The db Files

Most entries in db files are called *DNS resource records*. DNS lookups are case-insensitive so you can enter names in your db files in uppercase, lowercase, or mixed case. We tend to use all lower case. Even though lookups are case-insensitive, case is preserved. Resource records must start in column one. The resource records in the example files we present in this book do start in column one, but they may look indented because of the way this book is formatted. In the DNS RFCs, the examples present the resource records in a certain order. Most people have chosen to follow that ordering, as we have here, but this ordering is not a requirement. The ordering of resource records in the db files is as follows:

SOA record	Indicates *authority* for this domain data
NS record	Lists a *name server* for this domain
Other records	Data about hosts in this domain

Of the other records, this chapter covers:

A	Name-to-address mapping
PTR	Address-to-name mapping
CNAME	Canonical name (for aliases)
TXT	Textual information
WKS	Well-known services
HINFO	Host information

Those of you who have some experience with the DNS file format will look, no doubt, at our data and say to yourself, "It would have been shorter to specify it this other way . . ." We are not using abbreviations or shortcuts in our data, at least not initially. Once you understand the long version, we'll go back and "tighten up" the files.

Comments

The db files are easier to read if they contain comments and blank lines. Comments start with a semicolon and finish at the end of the line. As you might guess, the name server ignores comments and blank lines.

SOA Records

The first entry in each of these files is the SOA (start of authority) resource record. The SOA record indicates that this name server is the best source of information for the data within this domain. Our name server is *authoritative* for the domain **movie.edu** because of the SOA record. An SOA record is required in each *db.DOMAIN* and *db.ADDR* file. There can be one and only one SOA record in a db file.

We added the following SOA record to the *db.movie* file:

```
movie.edu. IN SOA terminator.movie.edu. al.robocop.movie.edu. (
                      1        ; Serial
                      10800    ; Refresh after 3 hours
                      3600     ; Retry after 1 hour
                      604800   ; Expire after 1 week
                      86400 )  ; Minimum TTL of 1 day
```

The name **movie.edu.** must start in column one of the file. Make sure the names end with a trailing dot, as we have done here, or you will be surprised at the result! (We'll explain later in this chapter.)

The *IN* stands for Internet. This is one *class* of data. Other classes exist, but none of them are currently in widespread use. Our examples only use the IN class.

The first name after *SOA* (**terminator.movie.edu.**) is the host this data was created on. The second name (**al.robocop.movie.edu.**) is the mail address of the person in charge of the data (if you replace the first "." with an "@"). Often you'll see root or postmaster as the e-mail address. Name servers won't use these names—they are meant for human consumption. If you have a problem with someone's domain, you can send an e-mail message to the mail address.

The parentheses allow the SOA record to span more than one line. Parentheses are supposed to allow *any* resource record data to span lines, but BIND 4.8.3 and earlier versions only allow parentheses for the SOA and WKS records. Most of the fields within the parentheses of the SOA record are for use by secondary name servers and are discussed when we introduce secondary name servers later in this chapter. For now, assume these are reasonable values.

We added similar SOA records to the beginning of *db.192.249.249* and *db.192.253.253* files. In these files, we changed the first name in the SOA record from **movie.edu.** to the name of the appropriate **in-addr.arpa**

domain: 249.249.192.in-addr.arpa.   and   253.253.192.in-addr.arpa.,
respectively.

NS Records

The next entries we added to each file are NS (name server) resource
records. We added one NS record for each name server for our domain.
Here are the NS records from the *db.movie* file:

```
movie.edu.   IN NS   terminator.movie.edu.
movie.edu.   IN NS   wormhole.movie.edu.
```

These records indicate that there are two name servers for the domain
movie.edu. The name servers are on the hosts **terminator** and **wormhole**.
Multi-homed hosts, like **wormhole**, are excellent choices for name servers
since they are "well-connected." They are directly accessible by hosts on
more than one network and, if they also serve as routers, are not often
down because they are closely monitored. We'll cover more on where to
place your name servers in Chapter 8, *Growing Your Domain*.

Like the SOA record, we added NS records to the *db.192.249.249* and
db.192.253.253 files.

Address and Alias Records

Next, we created the name-to-address mappings. We added the following
resource records to the *db.movie* file:

```
;
; Host addresses
;
localhost.movie.edu.   IN A    127.0.0.1
robocop.movie.edu.     IN A    192.249.249.2
terminator.movie.edu.  IN A    192.249.249.3
diehard.movie.edu.     IN A    192.249.249.4
misery.movie.edu.      IN A    192.253.253.2
shining.movie.edu.     IN A    192.253.253.3
carrie.movie.edu.      IN A    192.253.253.4
;
; Multi-homed hosts
;
wormhole.movie.edu.    IN A    192.249.249.1
wormhole.movie.edu.    IN A    192.253.253.1
;
; Aliases
;
bigt.movie.edu.        IN CNAME terminator.movie.edu.
dh.movie.edu.          IN CNAME diehard.movie.edu.
wh.movie.edu.          IN CNAME wormhole.movie.edu.
```

```
wh249.movie.edu.      IN A    192.249.249.1
wh253.movie.edu.      IN A    192.253.253.1
```

The first two blocks are probably not a surprise. The A stands for address and each resource record maps a name to an address. **wormhole** acts as a router. It has two addresses associated with its name and therefore two address records. Unlike host table lookups, a DNS lookup can return more than one address for a name. A lookup of **wormhole** will return two. If the requestor and name server are on the same network, the name server will place the "closest" address first in the response for better performance. This feature is called *address sorting* and is covered in Chapter 7, *Maintaining BIND*.

The third block has the host table aliases. For the first three aliases, we created CNAME (canonical name) resource records. However, we created address records for the other two aliases—more on this in a moment. The name server handles CNAME records in a different manner than aliases are handled in the host table. When a name server looks up a name and finds a CNAME record, it replaces the name with the canonical name and looks up the new name. For example, when the name server looks up **wh**, it finds a CNAME record pointing to **wormhole**. **wormhole** is then looked up and both addresses are returned.

The final two entries solve a special problem. Suppose you have a router, like **wormhole**, and you want to check one of the interfaces. One common troubleshooting technique is to *ping* the interface to verify that it is responding. If you *ping* the name **wormhole**, the name server returns both addresses when the name is looked up. *ping* uses the first address in the list. But which address is first?

With the host table, we chose the address we wanted by using either **wh249** or **wh253**—each name referred to *one* of the host's addresses. To provide equivalent capability with DNS, we didn't make **wh249** and **wh253** into aliases (CNAME records). That would result in both addresses for **wormhole** being returned when the alias was looked up. Instead, we used address records. Now, to check the operation of the 192.253.253.1 interface on **wormhole**, we *ping* **wh253** since it refers to only one address. The same applies to **wh249**.

To state this as a general rule: if a host is multi-homed (has more than one network interface), create an address (A) record for each alias unique to one address. Create a CNAME record for each alias common to all the addresses.

Since we used A (address) records for the **wh249** and **wh253** aliases, you might ask: "Is it okay to use address records instead of CNAME records in *all* cases?" Well, using address records instead of CNAME records doesn't cause problems with most applications since the application only cares that it finds the IP address. There is one application—*sendmail*—whose behavior changes, though. *sendmail* usually replaces aliases in mail headers with their canonical name; this *canonicalization* only happens if the name in the mail header has CNAME data associated with it. Without CNAME records for aliases, your *sendmail* will have to understand all of the possible aliases your host might be known by, which will require extra *sendmail* configuration work on your part.

In addition to the problem with *sendmail*, users might be confused when they try to figure out the canonical name to enter in their *.rhosts* file. Looking up a name that has CNAME data leads them to the canonical name, whereas address data won't. In this case, users *should* instead be looking up the *IP address* to get the canonical name, as *rlogind* does, but users like these never seem to be on systems we administer.

PTR Records

Next we created the address-to-name mappings. The file *db.192.249.249* maps addresses to host names for the 192.249.249 network. The DNS resource records used for this mapping are PTR (pointer) records. There is one record for each host interface on this network. (Recall that addresses are looked up as names in DNS. The address is reversed and **in-addr.arpa** is appended.)

Here are the PTR records we added for network 192.249.249:

```
1.249.249.192.in-addr.arpa.   IN PTR wormhole.movie.edu.
2.249.249.192.in-addr.arpa.   IN PTR robocop.movie.edu.
3.249.249.192.in-addr.arpa.   IN PTR terminator.movie.edu.
4.249.249.192.in-addr.arpa.   IN PTR diehard.movie.edu.
```

There are a couple things to notice about this data. First, addresses can only point to a single name: the canonical name. Thus, 192.249.249.1 maps to **wormhole** and not **wh249**. Second, even though **wormhole** has two addresses, you only see one of them here. That's because this file shows only the direct connections to network 192.249.249 and **wormhole** has only one connection there.

We created similar data for the 192.253.253 network.

The Completed Data Files

Now that the various resource records of the db files have been explained, we'll show you what they look like when all the data are in one place. . Again, the actual order of these resource records does not matter.

Contents of file *db.movie*:

```
movie.edu. IN SOA terminator.movie.edu. al.robocop.movie.edu. (
                        1        ; Serial
                        10800    ; Refresh after 3 hours
                        3600     ; Retry after 1 hour
                        604800   ; Expire after 1 week
                        86400 )  ; Minimum TTL of 1 day

;
; Name servers
;
movie.edu.   IN NS  terminator.movie.edu.
movie.edu.   IN NS  wormhole.movie.edu.

;
; Addresses for the canonical names
;
localhost.movie.edu.    IN A    127.0.0.1
robocop.movie.edu.      IN A    192.249.249.2
terminator.movie.edu.   IN A    192.249.249.3
diehard.movie.edu.      IN A    192.249.249.4
misery.movie.edu.       IN A    192.253.253.2
shining.movie.edu.      IN A    192.253.253.3
carrie.movie.edu.       IN A    192.253.253.4

wormhole.movie.edu.     IN A    192.249.249.1
wormhole.movie.edu.     IN A    192.253.253.1

;
; Aliases
;
bigt.movie.edu.         IN CNAME terminator.movie.edu.
dh.movie.edu.           IN CNAME diehard.movie.edu.
wh.movie.edu.           IN CNAME wormhole.movie.edu.

;
; Interface specific names
;
wh249.movie.edu.        IN A    192.249.249.1
wh253.movie.edu.        IN A    192.253.253.1
```

Contents of file *db.192.249.249*:

```
249.249.192.in-addr.arpa. IN SOA terminator.movie.edu. al.robocop.movie.edu. (
                        1        ; Serial
                        10800    ; Refresh after 3 hours
```

```
                         3600      ; Retry after 1 hour
                         604800    ; Expire after 1 week
                         86400 )   ; Minimum TTL of 1 day


;
; Name servers
;
249.249.192.in-addr.arpa.  IN NS  terminator.movie.edu.
249.249.192.in-addr.arpa.  IN NS  wormhole.movie.edu.


;
; Addresses point to canonical name
;
1.249.249.192.in-addr.arpa.  IN PTR wormhole.movie.edu.
2.249.249.192.in-addr.arpa.  IN PTR robocop.movie.edu.
3.249.249.192.in-addr.arpa.  IN PTR terminator.movie.edu.
4.249.249.192.in-addr.arpa.  IN PTR diehard.movie.edu.
```

Contents of file *db.192.253.253*:

```
253.253.192.in-addr.arpa. IN SOA terminator.movie.edu. al.robocop.movie.edu. (
                         1         ; Serial
                         10800     ; Refresh after 3 hours
                         3600      ; Retry after 1 hour
                         604800    ; Expire after 1 week
                         86400 )   ; Minimum TTL of 1 day


;
; Name servers
;
253.253.192.in-addr.arpa.  IN NS  terminator.movie.edu.
253.253.192.in-addr.arpa.  IN NS  wormhole.movie.edu.


;
; Addresses point to canonical name
;
1.253.253.192.in-addr.arpa.  IN PTR wormhole.movie.edu.
2.253.253.192.in-addr.arpa.  IN PTR misery.movie.edu.
3.253.253.192.in-addr.arpa.  IN PTR shining.movie.edu.
4.253.253.192.in-addr.arpa.  IN PTR carrie.movie.edu.
```

The Loopback Address

A name server needs one additional *db.ADDR* file to cover the *loopback* network: the special address that hosts use to direct traffic to themselves. This network is (almost) always 127.0.0, and the host number is (almost) always 127.0.0.1. Therefore, the name of this file is *db.127.0.0*. No surprise here; it looks like the other *db.ADDR* files.

Contents of file *db.127.0.0*:

```
0.0.127.in-addr.arpa. IN SOA terminator.movie.edu. al.robocop.movie.edu. (
                            1          ; Serial
                            10800      ; Refresh after 3 hours
                            3600       ; Retry after 1 hour
                            604800     ; Expire after 1 week
                            86400 )    ; Minimum TTL of 1 day

0.0.127.in-addr.arpa.  IN NS  terminator.movie.edu.
0.0.127.in-addr.arpa.  IN NS  wormhole.movie.edu.

1.0.0.127.in-addr.arpa.  IN PTR localhost.
```

Why do name servers need this silly little file? Think about it for a second. No one was given responsibility for network 127 yet systems use it for a loopback address. Since no one has direct responsibility, everyone who uses it is responsible for it individually. You could omit this file and your name server would operate. However, a lookup of 127.0.0.1 would either fail because the root name server contacted wasn't configured itself to map 127.0.0.1 to a name, or the root name server contacted might provide an answer like **localhost**. You ought to provide the mapping yourself so there are no surprises.

The Cache Data

Besides your local information, the name server also needs to know where the name servers for the root domain are. This information must be retrieved from the Internet host **nic.ddn.mil**. Use anonymous *ftp* to retrieve the file *root-servers.txt* from the *netinfo* subdirectory. An alternate way to get this file is to e-mail a letter to **service@nic.ddn.mil** with the subject field **netinfo root-servers.txt**. The file will be mailed back. For example, sending the following letter:

```
To: service@nic.ddn.mil
Subject: netinfo root-servers.txt
--------
```

resulted in the following file being sent back:

```
HOSTNAME            NET ADDRESSES       SERVER PROGRAM


NS.NIC.DDN.MIL      192.112.36.4        BIND (UNIX)

KAVA.NISC.SRI.COM   192.33.33.24        BIND (UNIX)

AOS.BRL.MIL         128.63.4.82         BIND (UNIX)
                    26.3.0.29
                    192.5.25.82
```

```
       C.NYSER.NET            192.33.4.12         BIND (UNIX)

       TERP.UMD.EDU           128.8.10.90         BIND (UNIX)

       NS.NASA.GOV            192.52.195.10       BIND (UNIX)
                              128.102.16.10

       NIC.NORDU.NET          192.36.148.17       BIND (UNIX)
```

This information must be translated to DNS format for the cache file. In the *db.cache* file, the lines look like the following:

```
  .                   99999999   IN NS   ns.nic.ddn.mil.
  .                   99999999   IN NS   kava.nisc.sri.com.
  .                   99999999   IN NS   aos.brl.mil.
  .                   99999999   IN NS   c.nyser.net.
  .                   99999999   IN NS   terp.umd.edu.
  .                   99999999   IN NS   ns.nasa.gov.
  .                   99999999   IN NS   nic.nordu.net.
  ns.nic.ddn.mil.     99999999   IN A    192.112.36.4
  kava.nisc.sri.com.  99999999   IN A    192.33.33.24
  aos.brl.mil.        99999999   IN A    128.63.4.82
  aos.brl.mil.        99999999   IN A    26.3.0.29
  aos.brl.mil.        99999999   IN A    192.5.25.82
  c.nyser.net.        99999999   IN A    192.33.4.12
  terp.umd.edu.       99999999   IN A    128.8.10.90
  ns.nasa.gov.        99999999   IN A    192.52.195.10
  ns.nasa.gov.        99999999   IN A    128.102.16.10
  nic.nordu.net.      99999999   IN A    192.36.148.17
```

The domain name "." refers to the root domain. Since the root domain's name servers change over time, don't assume *this* list is current. Pull a new version of *root-servers.txt*.

How is this file kept up-to-date? As the network administrator, you must keep it up-to-date. Some versions of BIND did update this file periodically. That feature was disabled; apparently, it didn't work as well as the authors had hoped. Sometimes the changed *db.cache* file is mailed to the *bind* or *namedroppers* mailing list. If you are on one of these lists, you are likely to hear about changes.

Can you put data other than root name server data in this file? You can, but it won't be used. Originally, the name server installed this data in its cache. However, the cache file has changed (subtly) to be root name server *hints* (but the name "cache file" stuck). The name server stores the hints data in a special place and does not discard the hints if their TTLs drop to zero as it would with cache data. The name server uses the hint data to query the root name servers for the current list of root name servers, which it caches.

When the cached list of root name servers times out, the name server again uses the hints to get a new list.

What are the 99999999s for? Since this was originally cache data, the name server needed to know how long to keep these records active. The 99999999 meant *a very long time*. The root name server data was to be kept active for as long as the server ran. Since the name server now stores this data in a special place and doesn't discard it if it times out, the TTL is unnecesary. But it's not harmful to have the 99999999s and it makes for interesting BIND folklore when you pass responsibility to the next name server administrator.

Setting Up a BIND Boot File

Now that the db files have been created, a name server must be instructed to read each of the files. For BIND, the mechanism for pointing the server to its db files is the boot file. Up to this point, we've been discussing files whose data and format are described in the DNS specification. The boot file, though, is specific to BIND and is not defined in the DNS RFCs.

Usually, boot files contain a line indicating the directory where the files are located. The name server changes directory to this location before reading the files. This allows the filenames to be relative to the current directory instead of being complete path names. Here is how a directory line looks:

```
directory /usr/local/named
```

On a primary server, the boot file contains one line for each file to be read. This line is comprised of three fields: the word *primary*, starting in the first column, the domain the server is authoritative for, and the filename:

```
primary   movie.edu                   db.movie
primary   249.249.192.in-addr.arpa    db.192.249.249
primary   253.253.192.in-addr.arpa    db.192.253.253
primary   0.0.127.in-addr.arpa        db.127.0.0
```

Here is the boot file line to read the cache file:

```
cache   .   db.cache
```

As mentioned earlier, this file is not for general cache data. It only contains the root name server *hints*.

By default, BIND expects the boot file to be named */etc/named.boot*, but it can be changed with a command line option. The db files for our example are in the directory */usr/local/named*. Which directory you use does not matter. Avoid putting the directory in the root filesystem if the root filesystem is short on space. Here is the complete */etc/named.boot* file:

```
directory /usr/local/named

primary  movie.edu                 db.movie
primary  249.249.192.in-addr.arpa  db.192.249.249
primary  253.253.192.in-addr.arpa  db.192.253.253
primary  0.0.127.in-addr.arpa      db.127.0.0
cache    .                         db.cache
```

Abbreviations

At this point, we have created all the files necessary for a primary name server. Let's go back and revisit the DNS database files; there are shortcuts we didn't use. Without seeing and understanding the long form first, though, the short form can look very cryptic. Now that you know the long form and have seen the BIND boot file, we'll show you the shortcuts.

Appending Domains

The second field of a *primary* boot file line specifies a domain. This domain is the key to the most useful shortcut. This domain is the *origin* of all the data in the db file. The origin is appended to all names in the db file not ending in a dot. The origin will be different for each db file.

Since the origin is appended to names, instead of entering **robocop**'s address in *db.movie* as this:

```
robocop.movie.edu.    IN A    192.249.249.2
```

We could have entered it like this:

```
robocop    IN A    192.249.249.2
```

In the *db.192.24.249* file we entered this:

```
2.249.249.192.in-addr.arpa.  IN PTR robocop.movie.edu.
```

Since **249.249.192.in-addr.arpa** is the origin, we could have entered:

```
2  IN PTR robocop.movie.edu.
```

Remember we warned you earlier not to omit the trailing dot when using the long names? Suppose you forgot the trailing dot. An entry like:

```
robocop.movie.edu    IN A    192.249.249.2
```

turns into an entry for **robocop.movie.edu.movie.edu** and you didn't intend that at all.

@ *Notation*

If the domain name is the *same* as the origin, the name can be specified as
"@". This is most often seen in the SOA record of the db files. The SOA
records could have been entered this way:

```
@ IN SOA terminator.movie.edu. al.robocop.movie.edu. (
                        1         ; Serial
                        10800     ; Refresh after 3 hours
                        3600      ; Retry after 1 hour
                        604800    ; Expire after 1 week
                        86400 )   ; Minimum TTL of 1 day
```

Repeat Last Name

If a resource record name (that starts in column one) is a space or tab, then
the name from the last resource record is used. You would use this if there
were multiple resource records for a name. Here is an example where
there are two address records for one name:

```
wormhole    IN A    192.249.249.1
            IN A    192.253.253.1
```

In the second address record, the name **wormhole** is implied. You can use
this shortcut even if the resource records are of different types.

The Shortened db Files

Now that we have shown you the abbreviations, we'll repeat the db files
making use of these shortcuts.

Contents of file *db.movie*:

```
;
; Origin added to names not ending
; in a dot: movie.edu
;

@ IN SOA terminator.movie.edu. al.robocop.movie.edu. (
                        1         ; Serial
                        10800     ; Refresh after 3 hours
                        3600      ; Retry after 1 hour
                        604800    ; Expire after 1 week
                        86400 )   ; Minimum TTL of 1 day


;
; Name servers (The name '@' is implied)
;
            IN NS   terminator.movie.edu.
            IN NS   wormhole.movie.edu.
```

```
;
; Addresses for the canonical names
;
localhost  IN A      127.0.0.1
robocop    IN A      192.249.249.2
terminator IN A      192.249.249.3
diehard    IN A      192.249.249.4
misery     IN A      192.253.253.2
shining    IN A      192.253.253.3
carrie     IN A      192.253.253.4

wormhole   IN A      192.249.249.1
           IN A      192.253.253.1


;
; Aliases
;
bigt       IN CNAME terminator
dh         IN CNAME diehard
wh         IN CNAME wormhole
;
; Interface specific names
;
wh249      IN A      192.249.249.1
wh253      IN A      192.253.253.1
```

Contents of file *db.192.249.249*:

```
;
; Origin added to names not ending
; in a dot: 249.249.192.in-addr.arpa
;

@ IN SOA terminator.movie.edu. al.robocop.movie.edu. (
                           1        ; Serial
                           10800    ; Refresh after 3 hours
                           3600     ; Retry after 1 hour
                           604800   ; Expire after 1 week
                           86400 )  ; Minimum TTL of 1 day


;
; Name servers (The name '@' is implied)
;
   IN NS  terminator.movie.edu.
   IN NS  wormhole.movie.edu.


;
; Addresses point to canonical name
;
1  IN PTR wormhole.movie.edu.
2  IN PTR robocop.movie.edu.
3  IN PTR terminator.movie.edu.
4  IN PTR diehard.movie.edu.
```

Contents of file *db.192.253.253*:

```
;
; Origin added to names not ending
; in a dot: 253.253.192.in-addr.arpa
;

@ IN SOA terminator.movie.edu. al.robocop.movie.edu. (
                        1         ; Serial
                        10800     ; Refresh after 3 hours
                        3600      ; Retry after 1 hour
                        604800    ; Expire after 1 week
                        86400 )   ; Minimum TTL of 1 day


;
; Name servers (The name '@' is implied)
;
    IN NS  terminator.movie.edu.
    IN NS  wormhole.movie.edu.


;
; Addresses point to canonical name
;
1   IN PTR wormhole.movie.edu.
2   IN PTR misery.movie.edu.
3   IN PTR shining.movie.edu.
4   IN PTR carrie.movie.edu.
```

Contents of file *db.127.0.0*:

```
@ IN SOA terminator.movie.edu. al.robocop.movie.edu. (
                        1         ; Serial
                        10800     ; Refresh after 3 hours
                        3600      ; Retry after 1 hour
                        604800    ; Expire after 1 week
                        86400 )   ; Minimum TTL of 1 day

    IN NS  terminator.movie.edu.
    IN NS  wormhole.movie.edu.

1   IN PTR localhost.
```

While looking at the new *db.movie* file, you may notice that we could have removed **movie.edu** from the host names of the the SOA and NS records like this:

```
@ IN SOA terminator al.robocop (
                        1         ; Serial
                        10800     ; Refresh after 3 hours
                        3600      ; Retry after 1 hour
                        604800    ; Expire after 1 week
                        86400 )   ; Minimum TTL of 1 day
```

```
IN NS   terminator
IN NS   wormhole
```

You *can't* do this in the other db files because their origins are different. In *db.movie*, we left these names as fully qualified domain names so that the NS and SOA records are exactly the same for *all* the db files.

Tools

Wouldn't it be handy to have a tool to translate your host table into name server file format? There is such a beast, written in *perl*: *h2n*—a host table to name server file converter. You can use *h2n* to create your data the first time and then maintain your DNS data manually. Or, you can use *h2n* over and over again. As you have seen, the format of the host table is much simpler to understand and to modify correctly. So, you could maintain */etc/hosts* and re-run *h2n* to update your DNS data after each modification.

If you plan to use *h2n*, you might as well start with it, since it uses */etc/hosts*—not your hand-crafted DNS data—to generate the new DNS files. We could have saved ourselves lots of work by generating the sample data in this chapter with the following:

```
% h2n -d movie.edu -s terminator -s robocop \
  -n 192.249.249 -n 192.253.253 \
  -u al.robocop.movie.edu
```

The **-d** and **-n** options specify the domain name and network numbers. You'll notice the db filenames are derived from these options. The **-s** options list the name servers for the NS records. The **-u** (user) is the e-mail address in the SOA record. We'll cover *h2n* in more detail in Chapter 7, *Maintaining BIND*, after we've covered how DNS affects e-mail.

Running a Primary Name Server

Now that you've created your DNS database files, you are ready to start a couple of name servers. You'll need to set up two name servers: a primary name server and a secondary name server. Before you start a name server, though, make sure the syslog daemon is running. If the name server sees an error, it logs a message to the syslog daemon. If the error is bad enough, the name server will exit.

Starting Up the Name Server

At this point, we assume the machine you are running on has the BIND name server and the support tool *nslookup*. Check the *named** manual page to find the directory the server is in and verify that the executable is on your system. On BSD systems, the name server started out its life in */etc*, but may have migrated elsewhere. On SunOS, the name server is */usr/etc/in.named*. The descriptions below assume that the name server is still in */etc*.

To start up the name server, you must become root. The name server operates on a reserved port requiring root privileges. The name server doesn't require root access for anything else. Start the name server from the command line the first time you run it, to test that it is operating correctly. Later, we'll show you how to start up the name server automatically when your system boots.

The following command starts the name server. In the **movie.edu** domain, we ran this command on the host **terminator**.

```
# /etc/named
```

This command assumes your boot file is */etc/named.boot*. You can have your boot file elsewhere, but you have to tell the name server where it is by using the **-b** command line option:

```
# /etc/named -b bootfile
```

Check for Syslog Errors

The first thing to do after starting your name server is to check the *syslog* file for error messages. If you are not familiar with syslog, look at the *syslog.conf* manual page for a description of the syslog configuration file, or the *syslogd* manual page for a description of the syslog daemon. The name server logs messages as *daemon* under the name *named*. You might be

---

**/etc/named* is pronounced name-dee and stands for name server daemon. BIND is pronounced like "kind." Some creative people have noticed the similarities in the names and choose to mispronounce them bin-dee and named (like "tamed").

able to find out where syslog messages are logged by looking for *daemon* in */etc/syslog.conf*:

```
% grep daemon /etc/syslog.conf
*.err;kern.debug;daemon,auth.notice /var/adm/messages
```

On this host, the name server syslog messages are logged to */var/adm/messages*.

When the name server starts, it logs a *restarted* message:

```
% grep named /var/adm/messages
Jan 10 20:48:32 terminator named[3221]: restarted
```

The *restarted* message is not an error message, but there might be other messages with it that are error messages. The most common errors are syntax errors in the db files or boot file. For example, if you forgot the resource record type in an address record:

```
robocop  IN  192.249.249.2
```

you'll see the following syslog error messages:

```
Jan 10 20:48:32 terminator named[3221]]: Line 13: Unknown type:
                192.249.249.2
Jan 10 20:48:32 terminator named[3221]]: db.movie Line 13:
                database format error (192.249.249.2)
```

Or, if you misspelled the word `primary` in */etc/named.boot*:

```
prmary  movie.edu  db.movie
```

you'll see the following syslog error message:

```
Jan 10 20:50:12 terminator named[3227]: /etc/named.boot:
                line 9: unknown field 'prmary'
```

If you have a syntax error, check the line mentioned in the syslog error message to see if you can figure out the problem. You've seen what the db files are supposed to look like; that should be enough to figure out most simple syntax errors. Otherwise, you'll have to go through Appendix A, *DNS Message Format and Resource Records*, to see the gory syntax details of all the resource records. If you can fix the syntax error, do so and then send the name server a HUP signal:

```
# kill -HUP <pid>
```

so that it re-reads the data files. You'll see more information in Chapter 7, *Maintaining BIND*, on sending signals to the name server.

Testing Your Setup with nslookup

If you have correctly set up your local domain and your connection to the Internet is up, you should be able to look up a local and a remote name. We'll step you through the lookups below with *nslookup*. There is a whole chapter in this book on *nslookup*, but we will cover *nslookup* in enough detail here to do basic name server testing.

Initialize the Default Domain

Before running *nslookup*, set *hostname*(1) to be a domain name. On the host **terminator**, we set *hostname*(1) to **terminator.movie.edu**. Don't add a trailing dot to the name. With this in place, you can look up a name like **carrie** instead of spelling out **carrie.movie.edu**—the system adds the domain for you.

NOTE

> SunOS doesn't use *hostname*(1) for the default DNS domain. To test your name server operation, create a file called */etc/resolv.conf* with the following line starting in column one. (Substitute your domain for **movie.edu**.)
>
> ```
> domain movie.edu
> ```
>
> In addition to the difference in using *hostname*(1) on SunOS, you have to run NIS to query */usr/etc/in.named* from any service besides *nslookup* (e.g., *ftp* or *telnet*). See Chapter 6, *Configuring Hosts*, for more information on Sun systems and NIS after you have tested your name servers with *nslookup*.

Look Up a Local Name

nslookup can be used to look up any type of resource record, and it can be directed to query any name server. By default, it looks up A (address) records using the name server on the local system. To look up a host's address with *nslookup*, run *nslookup* with the host's name as the only argument. A lookup of a local name should return almost instantly.

We ran *nslookup* to look up **carrie**:

```
% nslookup carrie
Server: terminator.movie.edu
Address: 192.249.249.3

Name:    carrie.movie.edu
Address: 192.253.253.4
```

If looking up a local name works, your local name server has been configured properly for your domain. If the lookup fails, you'll see something like this:

```
*** terminator.movie.edu can't find carrie: Non-existent domain
```

This means that either *carrie* is not in your data—check your db file—or you didn't set your default domain in *hostname*(1), or some name server error occurred (but you should have caught the error when you checked the syslog messages). If you see a message like this:

```
*** Can't find initialize address for server : Non-existent domain
```

your host's name is not in your name server database (i.e., *nslookup* looked up **terminator.movie.edu**—the name of the host *nslookup* was run on—as part of its initialization, but the name server didn't have the name in its database).

Look Up a Remote Name

The next step is to try using the local name server to look up a remote name, like **uunet.uu.net**, or another system you know on the Internet. This command may not return as quickly as the last one. If *nslookup* fails to get a response from your name server, it will wait a little longer than a minute before giving up:

```
% nslookup uunet.uu.net.
Server: terminator.movie.edu
Address: 192.249.249.3

Name:     uunet.uu.net
Addresses: 137.39.1.2, 192.48.96.2
```

If this works, your name server knows where the root name servers are and knows how to contact them to find out information about domains other than your own. If it fails, either you forgot to initialize the cache file (and a syslog message will show up) or the network is broken somewhere and you can't reach the name servers for the remote domain. Try a different remote domain name.

If these first two lookups succeeded, congratulations! You have a primary name server up and running. At this point, you are ready to start configuring your secondary name server.

One More Test

While you are testing, though, run one more test. Try having a remote name server look up a name in your domain. This is only going to work if your parent name servers have already delegated your domain to the name server you just set up. If your parent required you to have your two name servers running before delegating your domain, skip down to the "Editing the Startup Files" section.

To make *nslookup* use a remote name server to look up a local name, give the local host's name as the first argument and the remote server's name as the second argument. Again, if this doesn't work it may take a little longer than a minute before *nslookup* gives you an error message. For instance, to have **vangogh.cs.berkeley.edu** look up **carrie**:

```
% nslookup carrie vangogh.cs.berkeley.edu.
Server: vangogh.cs.berkeley.edu
Address: 128.32.130.11

Name:    carrie.movie.edu
Address: 192.253.253.4
```

If the first two lookups worked, but using a remote name server to look up a local name failed, you may not be registered with your parent name server. That is not a problem, at first, because systems within your domain can look up the names of other systems within your domain and outside of your domain. You'll be able to send e-mail and to *ftp* to local and remote systems. But this situation will shortly become a problem. Hosts outside of your domain cannot look up names within your domain. You will be able to send e-mail to friends in remote domains, but you won't get their responses. To fix this problem, contact someone responsible for your parent domain and have them check the delegation of your domain.

Editing the Startup Files

Once you have confirmed that your name server is running properly and can be used from here on, you'll need to start it automatically and set *hostname*(1) to a domain name in your systems startup files. Check to see if your vendor has already set up the name server to start on boot up. You may have to remove comment characters from the startup lines or the startup file may test to see if */etc/named.boot* exists. To look for automatic startup lines:

```
% grep named /etc/*rc*
```

or if you have System V style *rc* files:

```
% grep named /etc/rc*/S*
```

If you don't find anything, add lines like the following to the appropriate startup file somewhere after your interfaces are initialized by *ifconfig*:

```
if test -x /etc/named -a -f /etc/named.boot
then
        echo "Starting named"
        /etc/named
fi
```

You may want to wait to start the name server until after the default route is installed or your routing daemon (*routed* or *gated*) is started, depending upon whether these services need the name server or they can get by with */etc/hosts*.

Find out which startup file initializes the host name. Change *hostname*(1) to a domain name. For example, we changed:

```
hostname terminator
```

to:

```
hostname terminator.movie.edu
```

Running a Secondary Name Server

You need to set up another name server for robustness. You can (and probably will) set up more than two name servers. Two servers are the minimum. If you have only one name server and it goes down, no one can look up names. A second name server splits the load with the first server or handles the whole load if the first server is down. You *could* set up another primary name server, but we don't recommend it. Set up a secondary name server. You can always change a secondary name server into a primary name server later if you decide that you want to expend the extra work it takes to run multiple primary name servers.

How does a server know if it is a primary or a secondary for a zone? The *named.boot* file tells the server it is a primary or a secondary on a per zone basis. The NS records don't tell us which servers are primary for a zone and which servers are secondary for a zone—they only say who the servers are.

(Globally, DNS doesn't care; as far as the actual name resolution goes, secondary servers are as good as primary servers.)

What is different between a primary name server and a secondary name server? The crucial difference is where the server gets its data. A primary name server reads its data from files. A secondary name server loads its data over the network from another name server. This process is called a *zone transfer*.

A secondary name server is not limited to loading zones from a *primary* name server; a secondary server can load from another *secondary* server. We'll call the server from which a secondary loads a *master* server, as in primary master server or secondary master server.

The big advantage of secondary name servers is that you only maintain one set of the DNS database files, the ones on the primary name server. You don't have to worry about synchronizing the files among name servers: the secondaries do that for you. The caveat is that a secondary does not re-synchronize instantly. It polls to see if it is current. The polling interval is one of those numbers in the SOA record that we haven't explained yet.

A secondary name server doesn't need to retrieve *all* of its db files over the network; the overhead files, *db.cache* and *db.127.0.0*, are the same as on a primary, so keep a local copy on the secondary. That means that a secondary name server is a *primary* for **0.0.127.in-addr.arpa**. Well, you *could* make it a secondary for **0.0.127.in-addr.arpa**, but that data never changes—it might as well be a primary.

Setup

To set up your secondary name server, create a directory for the db files on the secondary name server host (e.g., */usr/local/named*) and copy over the following files: */etc/named.boot*, *db.cache*, and *db.127.0.0*.

```
# rcp /etc/named.boot host:/etc
# rcp db.cache db.127.0.0 host:db-file-directory
```

You must modify */etc/named.boot* on the secondary name server host. Change every occurrence of `primary` to `secondary` except for **0.0.127.in-addr.arpa**. Before the filename on each of these lines, add the

IP address of the primary server you just set up. For example, if the original boot file line was this:

```
primary movie.edu      db.movie
```

then the modified line looks like:

```
secondary movie.edu       192.249.249.3 db.movie
```

This tells the name server that it is a secondary for the zone **movie.edu** and that it should track the version of this zone that is being kept on the host 192.249.249.3. The secondary name server will keep a backup copy of this zone in the local file *db.movie.*

For Movie U., we set up our secondary name server on **wormhole**. Recall that the boot file on **terminator** (the primary) looked like this:

```
directory /usr/local/named

primary movie.edu                 db.movie
primary 249.249.192.in-addr.arpa db.192.249.249
primary 253.253.192.in-addr.arpa db.192.253.253
primary 0.0.127.in-addr.arpa      db.127.0.0
cache  .                          db.cache
```

We copied */etc/named.boot, db.cache,* and *db.127.0.0* to **wormhole** and edited the boot file as described above. The boot file on **wormhole** now looks like this:

```
directory /usr/local/named

secondary  movie.edu                 192.249.249.3 db.movie
secondary  249.249.192.in-addr.arpa 192.249.249.3 db.192.249.249
secondary  253.253.192.in-addr.arpa 192.249.249.3 db.192.253.253
primary    0.0.127.in-addr.arpa      db.127.0.0
cache      .                          db.cache
```

This causes the name server on **wormhole** to load **movie.edu**, **249.249.192.in-addr.arpa**, and **253.253.192.in-addr.arpa** over the network from 192.249.249.3 (**terminator**). It also saves a backup copy of these files in */usr/local/named* because we left a filename at the end of the secondary lines. You may find it handy to isolate the backup files in a subdirectory or to name them with a unique suffix like *.bak*; on rare occasions, you may have to delete all of the backup files manually. We'll cover more on backup files later.

Start up the name server on your secondary. Check for error messages in the *syslog* file as you did for the primary server. As on the primary, the command to start up a name server is:

```
# /etc/named
```

One extra check to make on the secondary that you didn't have to make on the primary is to see that the name server created the backup files. Shortly after we started our secondary name server on **wormhole**, we saw *db.movie*, *db.192.249.249*, and *db.192.253.253* show up in the */usr/local/named* directory. This means the secondary has successfully loaded these domains from the primary and has saved a backup copy.

To complete setting up your secondary name server, try looking up the same names you looked up when the primary server was started. This time *nslookup* must be run on the secondary name server host so that the secondary server is queried. If your secondary is working fine, add the proper lines to your system startup files so that the secondary name server is started when your system boots up and *hostname*(1) is set to a domain name.

Backup Files

Secondaries are not *required* to save a backup copy of the zone data. If there is a backup copy, the secondary server reads it on startup and later checks with the master server to see if the master server has a newer copy instead of loading a new copy of the zone immediately. If the master server has a newer copy, the secondary pulls it over and saves it in the backup file.

Why save a backup copy? Suppose the master server is down when the secondary starts up. The secondary will be unable to transfer the zone and therefore won't function as a server for that zone until the master server is up. With a backup copy, the secondary has some data, although it might be slightly out of date. Since the secondary does not rely on the master server always being up, it is a more robust system.

To run without a backup copy, omit the filename at the end of the secondary lines in the boot file. We recommend having all your secondary servers save backup copies, though. There is very little extra cost to having a backup file, but there is a very high cost if you get caught without a backup file when you need it most.

Multiple Master Servers

Are there other ways to make your secondary server configuration more robust? Yes, you can specify up to ten IP addresses of master servers. Just add them after the first IP address, before the backup filename. The secondary will try the master server at each IP address, in the order listed, until it successfully transfers the zone.

SOA Values

Remember this SOA record?

```
movie.edu. IN SOA terminator.movie.edu. al.robocop.movie.edu. (
                    1        ; Serial
                    10800    ; Refresh after 3 hours
                    3600     ; Retry after 1 hour
                    604800   ; Expire after 1 week
                    86400 )  ; Minimum TTL of 1 day
```

We never explained what the values in between the parentheses were for.

The serial number applies to all the data within the zone. When a secondary name server contacts a master server for zone data, it first asks for the serial number on the data. If the secondary's serial number is lower than the master server's, the secondary's zone data are out of date. In this case, the secondary pulls a new copy of the zone. When a secondary starts up and there is no backup file to read, it always loads the zone. As you might guess, when you modify the db files on the primary, you must increment the serial number. Updating your db files is covered in Chapter 7, *Maintaining BIND*.

The next four fields specify various time intervals in seconds.

refresh   The refresh interval tells the secondary how often to check the accuracy of its data. (10800 seconds is three hours.)

retry   If the secondary fails to reach the master name server(s) after the refresh period (the host(s) could be down), then it starts trying to connect every **retry** seconds. In this case the retry interval is one hour. Normally, the retry interval is shorter than the refresh interval, but it doesn't have to be.

expire   If the secondary fails to contact the master server(s) for **expire** seconds, the secondary expires its data. (604800 seconds is one week.) Expiring the data means the secondary stops giving out

answers about the data because the data are too old to be useful. Essentially, this field says: at some point, the data are so
old that having *no* data is better than having stale data.

TTL   TTL stands for *time to live*. This value applies to all the resource
records in the db file. The name server supplies this TTL in
query responses, allowing other servers to cache the data for
the TTL interval. (86400 seconds is one day.)

We discuss changing these values in Chapter 8, *Growing Your Domain.*

Additional db File Entries

After you've been running a name server for a while, you may want to add
data to your name server to help you manage your domain. Have you ever
been stumped when someone asked you *where* one of your hosts is?
Maybe you don't even remember what kind of host it is. Administrators
have to manage larger and larger populations of hosts these days, making it
easy to lose track of this information. The name server can help you out.

So far in the book, we've covered SOA, NS, A, CNAME, and PTR records.
These records are critical to everyday operation—name servers need them
to operate and applications look up data of these types. DNS defines more
data types. The most useful of the types we have not already described is
MX. MX records are for e-mail; they get their own chapter—Chapter 5, *DNS
and Electronic Mail.* The next most useful resource record types are HINFO
and TXT; these can be used to tell you the machine's type and location.
The WKS type can also be useful. It indicates which well-known Internet
services a host provides. For a complete list of the resource records, see
Appendix A, DNS Message Format and Resource Records.

Host Information

HINFO stands for *Host INFOrmation.* The data are a pair of strings identify-
ing the host's hardware type and the operating system. The strings should
come from the MACHINE NAMES and SYSTEM NAMES listed in the "Assigned
Numbers" RFC (currently RFC 1340), but this requirement is not enforced;
you can use your own abbreviations. The RFC isn't at all comprehensive,
so it is quite possible you won't find your system in the list anyway. Originally, host information records were designed to let services like FTP determine how to interact with the remote system. This would have made it
possible to negotiate data type transformations automatically. Unfortunately, this didn't happen—few sites supply accurate HINFO values for all

their systems. Some network administrators use HINFO records to help them keep track of the machine types, instead of recording the machine types in a notebook. Here are two examples of HINFO records; note that the hardware type or operating system must be surrounded with quotes if it includes any white space:

```
;
; These machine names and system names did not come from RFC 1340
;
wormhole   IN   HINFO   ACME-HW  ACME-GW
cujo       IN   HINFO   "Watch Dog·Hardware"   "Rabid OS"
```

General Text Information

TXT stands for *TeXT.* These records are simply a list of strings, each less than 256 characters in length. Versions of BIND prior to 4.8.3 do not support TXT records. In version 4.8.3, BIND limits the db file TXT record to a single string of almost 2K of data. Later BIND implementations may handle TXT records better, allowing multiple strings instead of a single string. TXT records can be used for anything you want; a common use is to list a host's location:

```
cujo   IN   TXT   "Location: machine room dog house"
```

The folks at MIT originally requested the creation of both the TXT record type and the HS (Hesiod) class. They use TXT records to store information that, at another site, would be handled by NIS: */etc/passwd* entries, */etc/group* entries, etc. While the */etc/passwd* information, less the password itself, is available on the network from name servers, the passwords are handled separately by Kerberos. (Kerberos is a secure network authentication service.) Kerberos is a critical ingredient to this scheme—since *any* Internet site could look up the *passwd* file entries from a name server, including the password in the entry would be unsafe. For more information on the Hesiod work, mail to **hesiod@athena.mit.edu**.

Well-Known Services

WKS stands for *Well-Known Services.* This record describes the services provided by a particular protocol on a particular interface. The protocol is usually UDP or TCP, although it can be any of the entries in */etc/protocols.* The services are the services below port number 256 from the file */etc/services.* The data is tied to a particular interface although, in practice, the same protocol/service list is usually used for each interface. Below is an example for a multi-homed host that provides SMTP and DNS (referred to as "domain") over TCP, but only DNS over UDP:

```
wormhole  IN  WKS  192.249.249.1  UDP  domain
          IN  WKS  192.249.249.1  TCP  smtp domain
          IN  WKS  192.253.253.1  UDP  domain
          IN  WKS  192.253.253.1  TCP  smtp domain
```

If the list of services is long, you can encapsulate it in parentheses so that it can span several lines. For example:

```
terminator  IN  WKS 192.249.249.3  TCP ( telnet smtp ftp
                                         shell domain )
```

These records were intended to be used by various services. SMTP mailers would use WKS to verify that the destination host provided the SMTP service. This would allow mailers to return mail quickly when a destination host did not support SMTP, rather than waiting three days before giving up on the letter. This restriction (requiring WKS records for mail) proved unworkable and was dropped—too many sites failed to provide WKS records.

What Next?

In this chapter, we showed you how to create name server data files by translating */etc/hosts* to equivalent name server data and how to set up a primary and a secondary name server. There is more work to do to complete setting up your local domain: you need to modify your DNS data for e-mail, configure the other hosts in your domain to use name servers, and possibly to start up more name servers. These topics are covered in the next few chapters.

In this chapter:
- *MX Records*
- *Structuring MX Lists*
- *Internal Domain Addresses*

5

DNS and Electronic Mail

And here Alice began to get rather sleepy, and went on saying to herself, in a dreamy sort of way, "Do cats eat bats? Do cats eat bats?" and sometimes "Do bats eat cats?" for, you see, as she couldn't answer either question, it didn't much matter which way she put it.

I'll bet you're drowsy too, after that looong chapter. Thankfully, this next chapter discusses a topic that'll probably be very interesting to you system administrators and postmasters: how DNS impacts electronic mail. And even if it isn't interesting to you, at least it's shorter than the last chapter.

One of the advantages of the Domain Name System over host tables is its support of advanced mail routing. When mailers only had *HOSTS.TXT* (and its derivative, */etc/hosts*) to work with, the best they could do was to attempt delivery to a host's IP address. If that failed, they could either defer delivery of the message and try again later, or bounce the message back to the sender.

DNS offers a mechanism for specifying backup hosts for mail delivery. The mechanism also allows hosts to assume mail handling responsibilities for other hosts. This lets diskless hosts that don't run mailers, for example, have mail addressed to them processed by their server. Together, these features give administrators much more flexibility in configuring electronic mail on their network.

MX Records

DNS uses a single type of resource record to implement enhanced mail routing, the **MX** record. Originally, this functionality was split between two records, the **MD** (mail destination) and **MF** (mail forwarder) records. MD specified the final destination to which a message addressed to a given domain name should be delivered. MF specified a host that would forward mail on to the eventual destination should that destination be unreachable.

Early experience with DNS on the Internet showed that separating the functionality didn't work very well. A mailer needed both the MD and MF records attached to a domain name (if both existed) to decide where to send the mail—one or the other alone wouldn't do. But an explicit lookup of one type or another (either MD or MF) would cause a name server to cache just that record type. So mailers either had to do two queries, one for MD and one for MF data, or could no longer accept cached answers. This meant that the overhead of running mail was higher than that of running other services, and was eventually deemed unacceptable.

The two records were integrated into a single record type, MX, to solve this problem. Now a mailer just needed all the MX records for a particular domain name destination to make a mail routing decision. Using cached MX records was fine, as long as the TTLs matched.

MX records specify a *mail exchanger* for a domain name: a host that will *either* process or forward mail for the domain name. "Processing" the mail means either delivering it to the individual it's addressed to, or gatewaying it to another mail transport, like UUCP. "Forwarding" means sending it to its final destination or to another mail exchanger "closer" to the destination via SMTP, the Internet's Simple Mail Transfer Protocol. Sometimes forwarding the mail involves queuing it for some amount of time, too.

In order to prevent mail routing loops, the MX record has an extra parameter, besides the domain name of the mail exchanger: a preference value. The preference value is an unsigned 16 bit number (between 0 and 65535) that indicates the mail exchanger's priority. For example, the MX record:

```
peets.mpk.ca.us.    IN    MX    10 relay.hp.com.
```

specifies that **relay.hp.com** is a mail exchanger for **peets.mpk.ca.us** at preference value 10.

Taken together, the preference values of a host's mail exchangers determine the order in which a mailer should use them. The preference value itself isn't important, only its relationship to the values of other mail exchangers: Is it higher or lower than the values of this host's other mail exchangers? Unless there are other records involved, the following:

```
plange.puntacana.dr.    IN    MX    1 listo.puntacana.dr.
plange.puntacana.dr.    IN    MX    2 hep.puntacana.dr.
```

does exactly the same thing as:

```
plange.puntacana.dr.   IN   MX   50  listo.puntacana.dr.
plange.puntacana.dr.   IN   MX   100 hep.puntacana.dr.
```

Mailers should attempt delivery to the mail exchangers with the *lowest* preference values first. This seems a little counterintuitive at first: the *most* preferred mail exchanger has the *lowest* preference value. But since the preference value is an unsigned quantity, this lets you specify a "best" mail exchanger at preference value 0.

If delivery to the most preferred mail exchanger(s) fails, mailers should attempt delivery to less preferred mail exchangers (those with *higher* preference values) in order of increasing preference value. That is, mailers should try more preferred mail exchangers before they try less preferred mail exchangers. More than one mail exchanger may share the same preference value, too. This gives the mailer its choice of which to send to first. The mailer should try all the mail exchangers at a given preference value before proceeding to the next higher value, though.

For example, the MX records for **ora.com** might be:

```
ora.com.    IN    MX    0 ora.ora.com.
ora.com.    IN    MX    10 ruby.ora.com.
ora.com.    IN    MX    10 opal.ora.com.
```

Interpreted together, these MX records instruct mailers to attempt delivery to **ora.com** by sending to:

1. **ora.ora.com** first,
2. either **ruby.ora.com** or **opal.ora.com** next, and finally
3. the remaining preference 10 mail exchanger (the one not used in 2).

Of course, once the mailer successfully delivers the mail to one of **ora.com**'s mail exchangers, it can stop. A mailer successfully delivering **ora.com** mail to **ora.ora.com** doesn't need to try **ruby** or **opal**.

What if a host doesn't have any MX records? Will a mailer simply not deliver mail to that host? Actually, some purist versions of *sendmail* do just that. Many vendors, however, have modified their *sendmails* to be more forgiving: if no MX records exist, they'll at least attempt delivery to the host's address. Check your vendor's documentation if you're not sure which variety your *sendmail* is.

What's a Mail Exchanger, Again?

The idea of a mail exchanger is probably new to many of you, so let's go over it in a little more detail. A simple analogy should help here: imagine a mail exchanger is an airport, and instead of setting up MX records to instruct mailers where to send messages, you're advising your inlaws on which airport to fly into when they come visit you.

Say you live in Los Gatos, California. The closest airport for your inlaws to fly into is San Jose, the second closest is San Francisco, and the third Oakland. (We'll ignore other factors like price of the ticket, Bay Area traffic, etc.) Don't see the parallel? Then picture it like this:

```
los-gatos.ca.us.     IN    MX    1 san-jose.ca.us.
los-gatos.ca.us.     IN    MX    2 san-francisco.ca.us.
los-gatos.ca.us.     IN    MX    3 oakland.ca.us.
```

The MX list is just an ordered list of destinations that tells mailers (your inlaws) where to send messages (fly) if they want to reach a given domain (your house). The preference value tells them how desirable it is to use that destination—you can think of it as a logical "distance" from the eventual destination (in any units you choose), or simply a "top-ten"-style ranking of the proximity of those mail exchangers to the final destination.

With this list, you're saying, "Try to fly into San Jose, and if you can't get there, try San Francisco and Oakland, in that order." It *also* says that if you reach San Francisco, you should take a commuter flight to San Jose. If you wind up in Oakland, you should try to get a commuter to San Jose, or at least San Francisco.

What makes a good mail exchanger, then? The same qualities that make a good airport:

Size   You wouldn't want to fly into tiny Reid-Hillview Airport to get to Los Gatos, because the airport's not equipped to handle large planes or many people. (You'd probably be better off landing a big jet on Highway 280 than at Reid-Hillview.) Likewise, you don't want to use an emaciated, underpowered host as a mail exchanger: it won't be able to handle the load.

Uptime   You know better than to fly through Denver International Airport in the winter, right? Then you should know better than to use a host that's rarely up or available as a mail exchanger.

Connectivity If your relatives are flying in from far away, you've got to make sure they can get a direct flight to at least one of the airports in the list you give them. You can't tell them their only choices are San Jose and Oakland if they're flying in from Helsinki. Similarly, you've got to make sure that at least one of your hosts' mail exchangers is reachable to anyone who might conceivably send you mail.

Keep this example in mind, because we'll use it again later.

The MX Algorithm

That's the basic idea behind MX records and mail exchangers, but there are a few more wrinkles you should know about. Mailers need to use a slightly more complicated algorithm than what we've described when they determine where to send mail, to avoid routing loops.

Imagine what would happen if mailers didn't check for routing loops. Let's say you send mail from your workstation to **nuts@ora.com**, raving (or raging) about the quality of this book. Unfortunately, **ora.ora.com** is down at the moment. No problem! Recall **ora.com**'s MX records:

```
ora.com.    IN    MX    0  ora.ora.com.
ora.com.    IN    MX    10 ruby.ora.com.
ora.com.    IN    MX    10 opal.ora.com.
```

Your mailer falls back and sends your message to **ruby.ora.com**, which is up. **ruby**'s mailer then tries to forward the mail on to **ora.ora.com**, but can't, because **ora.ora.com** is down. Now what? Unless **ruby** checks the sanity of what she is doing, she'll try to forward the message to **opal.ora.com**, or maybe even to herself. That's certainly not going to help get the mail delivered. If **ruby** sends the message to herself, we have a mail routing loop. If **ruby** sends the message to **opal**, **opal** will either send it back to **ruby** or send it to herself, and we again have a mail routing loop.

To prevent this from happening, mailers discard certain MX records before they decide where to send a message. A mailer sorts the list of MX records by preference value and looks for the domain name of the host it's running on in the list. If the local host appears as a mail exchanger, the mailer discards that MX record and all MX records at equal or lower preferences (*higher* preference values). That prevents the mailer from sending messages to itself or to mailers "further" from the eventual destination.

Let's think about this in the context of our airport analogy. This time, imagine you're an airline passenger (a message), and you're trying to get to Greeley, Colorado. You can't get a direct flight to Greeley, but you can fly to either Fort Collins or Denver (the two next highest mail exchangers). Since Fort Collins is closer to Greeley, you opt to fly to Fort Collins.

Now, once you've arrived in Fort Collins, there's no sense in flying to Denver, away from your destination (a lower preference mail exchanger). (And flying from Fort Collins to Fort Collins would be silly, too.) So the only acceptable flight to get you to your destination is now a Fort Collins-Greeley flight. You eliminate flights to less-preferred destinations to prevent frequent flyer looping and wasteful travel time.

One caveat: most mailers only look for their local host's *canonical* (official) domain name in the list of MX records. They don't check for aliases. Unless you always use canonical names in your MX records, there's no guarantee a mailer will be able to find itself in the MX list and you'll run the risk of having your mail loop. The moral: in an MX record, always use the mail exchanger's canonical name.

In case you're interested, two of the most common symptoms of this problem—mail looping—are the *sendmail* errors:

```
553 Local configuration error, host name not recognized as local
```

and the perennial favorite:

```
553 foo.bar.baz  I refuse to talk to myself
```

You'd see these errors in a message once it was returned from the mailer.

To go back to our **ora.com** example, when **ruby** received the message from your workstation, her mailer would have checked the list of MX records:

```
ora.com.    IN    MX    0  ora.ora.com.
ora.com.    IN    MX    10 ruby.ora.com.
ora.com.    IN    MX    10 opal.ora.com.
```

Finding the local host's domain name in the list at preference value 10, **ruby**'s mailer would discard all the records at preference value 10 or higher (the records in bold below):

```
ora.com.    IN    MX    0  ora.ora.com.
ora.com.    IN    MX    10 ruby.ora.com.
ora.com.    IN    MX    10 opal.ora.com.
```

leaving only:

```
ora.com.   IN   MX   0 ora.ora.com.
```

Since **ora.ora.com** is down, **ruby** would defer delivery until later, and queue the message.

What happens if a mailer finds *itself* at the highest preference (lowest preference value), and has to discard the whole MX list? Some vendors have enhanced *sendmail* slightly to attempt delivery directly to the destination host's IP address, as a last-ditch effort. In the stock BSD *sendmail*, however, it's an error. It may indicate that DNS thinks the mailer should be processing (not just forwarding) mail for the destination, but the mailer hasn't been configured to know that. Or it may indicate that the administrator has ordered the MX records incorrectly by using the wrong preference values. In either situation, you'll probably see an error like:

```
550 ora.com (tcp)... Host unknown
550 <nuts@ora.com>... Host unknown
```

Adding diskless nodes sometimes causes this problem. The administrator of the domain name server may remember to update the name server so that the highest preference (again, *lowest* preference value) mail exchanger is the node's server:

```
diskless.acme.com.   IN   MX   10 server.acme.com.
```

but the server's system administrator may forget to reconfigure the server's mailer after the change.

Many mailers, *sendmail* included, need to be configured to identify their aliases and the names of other hosts they process mail for. Many versions of *sendmail* use class *w* or fileclass *w* as the list of "local" destinations. Depending on your *sendmail.cf* file, adding an alias can be as easy as adding the line

```
Cwdiskless.acme.com
```

to *sendmail.cf.*

You may have noticed that we tend to use multiples of ten for our preference values. Ten is convenient because it allows you to insert other MX records temporarily at intermediate values without changing the other weights.

One last caveat: the hosts you list as mail exchangers *must* have address records. A mailer needs to find an address for each mail exchanger you name, or else it can't attempt delivery there.

Structuring MX Lists

Now that you know what *not* do with MX records, let's talk about the right ways to use them. The structure of your MX lists—how many mail exchangers to have, which ones and at what preference—should depend on your hosts, your network, and your goals. Diskless clusters on your network may require one set of MX records, standalone hosts another. Hosts connected to the Internet via UUCP and hosts behind security "firewalls" also require special MX records.

This implies that the administrator of a domain needs to keep careful track of the state of the hosts in the domain, and needs a thorough understanding of his network (or networks). If a system administrator swipes the disks off of a workstation and sets it up as diskless, she needs to let the domain administrator know, so the MX records can be updated.

By keeping close tabs on hosts in the local domain and understanding how to set up MX lists for common configurations, a domain administrator can go a long way toward keeping mail flowing smoothly.

MX Lists for UUCP-connected Hosts

If you're not directly connected to the Internet, but have a UUCP connection to an Internet host, your MX records need to show that this Internet host handles your mail. Your own host won't appear as one of its own mail exchangers—the UUCP software on your mail exchanger gets the information it needs from a different source, out of a *Systems* or *L.sys* file.

If you have any backup UUCP connections to the Internet, you should create MX records for them, too. Be sure to add them at higher preference values (*lower* preference) than that of your primary UUCP connection.

For example, **movie.edu** is helping out a little movie consulting company, The Plot Thickeners, by providing them with a UUCP connection to a **movie.edu** host on the Internet. (The Plot Thickeners specialize in reworking the plots of thrillers to introduce startling twists and unexpected developments.) The Plot Thickeners only have one host, registered under the **ca.us** domain as **plotthickens.la.ca.us**, which is connected via UUCP to **sleuth.movie.edu**.

The Plot Thickeners should ask the administrators of the **ca.us** domain to add an MX record for **plotthickens.la.ca.us**. Since **plotthickens** has UUCP connectivity, they could mail this request to the **ca.us** admins, or simply call them on the phone, if they have the phone number (and spell the domain names *very carefully*). The record might look like this:

```
plotthickens.la.ca.us.    IN    MX    10 sleuth.movie.edu.
```

(Any preference value will do, but a preference value above 0 will allow you to insert a lower value later should you get a better UUCP connection.)

Note that this record needs to be added to the **ca.us** domain, not the **movie.edu** domain. The MX record points to a host in **movie.edu**, but the record itself is in **ca.us**.

MX Lists for Diskless Clusters

Diskless hosts typically have their mail directed to their servers. This eliminates the CPU overhead of running a mailer on each node in the cluster and the extra administration involved in configuring mail on the diskless nodes.

Basic MX lists to direct diskless hosts' mail to their server look a lot like the UUCP example above, with the server playing the part of the Internet-connected host.

For example, one of our labs has just been set up with a new cluster of graphics workstations to do colorization. To maximize the CPU power available for graphics applications, they want to run as few processes on the diskless hosts as possible. The server is configured to run *sendmail* and handle mail addressed to the diskless hosts (with class *w*), so we add these MX records:

```
gwtw.movie.edu.            IN    MX    10 tturner.movie.edu.
wonderfulife.movie.edu.    IN    MX    10 tturner.movie.edu.
tturner.movie.edu.         IN    MX    10 tturner.movie.edu.
```

Mail for **gwtw** and **wonderfulife** (the diskless hosts) will now be forwarded to **tturner** (the server).

Incidentally, the MX record for **tturner** could point to an entirely different host. For example, it could forward **tturner**'s mail to **diehard**:

```
tturner.movie.edu.    IN    MX    10 diehard.movie.edu.
```

This wouldn't affect mail addressed to **gwtw** or **wonderfulife**—MX records aren't applied recursively, so their mail would be sent to **tturner**'s IP address. Mail addressed to **tturner**, though, would be sent to **diehard**.

You might think of this as listing a group of neighboring cities and the airport—or airports—that serve them. Not all cities have their own airport, so you fly into the one that's closest to them.

MX Lists to Deal with Security

movie.edu, as a university, doesn't worry much about security. Corporations, on the other hand, often protect their internets by using some sort of a security scheme. One of the most common security schemes is the "firewall." Most of the hosts on the network are prevented from accessing the Internet directly. This is usually implemented using access control lists on the routers that connect the network to the Internet, or by attaching one or more multi-homed hosts to both the internal corporate network and the Internet, while disabling packet routing on that host. In either implementation, only a small number of hosts have direct Internet access—sometimes just a single host. These hosts act as a firewall between the Internet and the internal network. Users accessing the internal network from the Internet must go through a firewall host, as must internal users accessing the Internet. This isolates the risk to the network overall, since any access must occur through a firewall host, and allows administrators to focus their attention on securing those hosts.* Unfortunately, security firewalls present problems for mail connectivity. How do you handle mail addressed to a host that doesn't have direct access to the Internet? Well, through a little cleverness with MX records, you can work it out.

Let's say your company, preferring to err on the side of conservatism, has only one host with Internet connectivity, **relay.pink.com**. On the other side of your security firewall, however, are a flock of hosts that you'd like to receive mail. In particular, you'd like your correspondents to be able to address mail to your workstation, **deadend.pink.com**.

If you could visualize the **pink.com** firewall, it might look like Figure 5-1.

---

*For a much more comprehensive discussion of security firewalls, see Chapter 14 in O'Reilly & Associates' Nutshell handbook, *Practical UNIX Security*, by Simson Garfinkel and Gene Spafford.

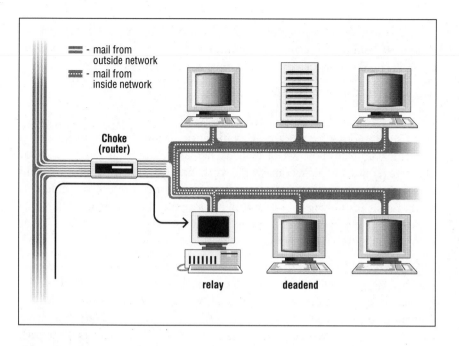

Figure 5.1: pink.com's firewall

Using MX records like this:

```
deadend.pink.com.    IN    MX    10 deadend.pink.com.
deadend.pink.com.    IN    MX    20 relay.pink.com.
```

your mail will get through to you. Mailers on the Internet will try sending mail addressed to **deadend** directly, but will fail because **deadend** is on the other side of the firewall. Then the mailers will attempt delivery to **relay**, which should succeed because **relay** is a firewall host. **relay** will then send the mail on to **deadend**—a firewall host can talk directly to a host on the internal network. And hosts on the protected side of the firewall can still send to **deadend** directly.

This setup is like international air travel (well, at least a little). If you want to fly to Shizuoka, Japan, you probably have to fly through Tokyo or Nagoya first, because you need to pass through customs before you enter the country. Japan only allows international flights into a few major Japanese cities, so they can better monitor who comes in and who leaves.

You'll need to create MX records like this for *each* host in your domain on the "wrong" side of the firewall (i.e., that isn't directly reachable from the Internet). That may seem like a lot of work, but *h2n*, which we introduced in *Setting Up BIND*, will make it a lot easier. You can use *h2n*'s **-m** option to create MX records *en masse*. For example, to create MX records at weight 10 pointing to **relay.pink.com** for all hosts in **pink.com**, the administrators could simply use the option **-m 10:relay.pink.com**.

Can you take a shortcut and use:

```
pink.com.    IN    MX    10 relay.pink.com.
```

to get the job done for all of **pink.com**, since all **pink.com** hosts will need **relay.pink.com** in their list of mail exchangers? Unfortunately, you can't. The MX record for **pink.com** won't work because it only applies to mail that's addressed to *user*@**pink.com** (though you may want to promote that kind of mail addressing—more on that before the chapter's out). There *is* a "wildcard" name you can use to apply to all names under a domain. Will it help? You'll find out in Chapter 14, *Miscellaneous*.

Wildcard records may be useful to you in another way. What we've shown you here is only half the solution for coping with security firewalls—the incoming half. Getting outgoing mail working—mail from inside the firewall to the Internet—often requires wildcard MX records *and* "internal root name servers" (yikes!). Since this is just part of the larger issue of providing name service inside a network without direct Internet connectivity, we'll put it off until Chapter 14.

MX Lists for Mail Hubs

Quite often, firewall hosts are major mail hubs: hosts which act as a mailing address for a large number of users. Those users may actually read their mail on the mail hub, or may have it forwarded automatically to their own workstation.

Even on networks without security firewalls, there are usually a number of mail hubs. Since these hosts are shared resources, administrators usually go to a lot of trouble to ensure that they're up and available. This makes them good candidates for mail exchangers.

On a network without a security firewall, the mail hub belongs at a higher preference value than the destination host:

```
fisherking.movie.edu.    IN    MX    10 fisherking.movie.edu.
fisherking.movie.edu.    IN    MX    20 postmanrings2x.movie.edu.
```

Here, if **fisherking** is down for some reason, mailers will fall back and attempt delivery to **postmanrings2x**. **postmanrings2x**, as a mail hub, should be available. If our mail administrator knows that **fisherking** will be down for an extended amount of time, she may reconfigure the mailer on

postmanrings2x to deliver the mail elsewhere, or to send it to her users' local accounts.

If your network employs a security firewall, your mail hubs may be on the inside. You can still use your mail hubs as mail exchangers, though. Set up your MX records like this:

```
deadend.pink.com.    IN    MX    10 deadend.pink.com.
deadend.pink.com.    IN    MX    20 mailhub.pink.com.
deadend.pink.com.    IN    MX    30 relay.pink.com.
```

This will give you the best of both worlds for two reasons:

1. Mail sent from the Internet to **deadend** will go through **relay** (after trying **deadend** and **mailhub**). **relay** will then send the mail on to **deadend**, or to **mailhub** if **deadend** is unreachable.

2. Mail sent from elsewhere on your own network (inside the firewall) to **deadend** will go directly to its destination. If **deadend** is down, the message will be delivered to **mailhub**.

Internal Domain Addresses

There's one more feature of MX records you may be interested in—one we alluded to earlier when we discussed firewalls. In order to make e-mail addresses easier to remember, many sites allow you to mail directly to their domain's name, instead of a host's name. After all, MX records aren't restricted to domain names that correspond to hosts. MX records can apply to any domain name in the name space (except an alias—remember, that's a violation of the DNS spec). For example, **movie.edu** is a small enough university to give almost all their students accounts on the mail hub, **postmanrings2x.movie.edu**. Students who don't have accounts on **postmanrings2x** have system aliases pointing to their home systems (via */usr/lib/aliases*, for example). So as not to force users' correspondents to type (and remember) long, unwieldy addresses like **abercrombie@postmanrings2x.movie.edu**, we added these records to *db.movie*:

```
movie.edu.    IN    MX    10 postmanrings2x.movie.edu.
movie.edu.    IN    A     192.249.249.66
```

With a minor configuration change to the mailer on **postmanrings2x** (adding **movie.edu** to the class defining names local to the mailer), Internet users can now send to **abercrombie@movie.edu**, thereby saving fourteen characters of typing, no small amount to a poor typist. This also simplifies mail addressing quite a bit: correspondents no longer need to keep track of which host a student at **movie.edu** is on. If a user moves from one host in **movie.edu** to another, our mail administrator only needs to change an alias in */usr/lib/aliases* on **postmanrings2x**.

Why did we include an address record for **movie.edu**? Unfortunately, some mailers on the Internet don't use MX records; they only use address records. Although that violates some Internet standards (the Host Requirements RFC, RFC 1123, for one), it's a fact of life on the Internet.

When you use a host's domain name in a mail address, the host usually has an address, so you don't have to worry about these boneheaded mailers. Most parent domains, however, don't have addresses associated with them. Consequently, it's prudent to add an address record to a parent domain name to placate those less-than-compliant mailers. In this case, the address record points to the IP address of **postmanrings2x**, which for mail purposes is the same as **movie.edu**.

These mailers do cause problems with diskless clients that don't run mailers, though, since the hosts *do* have addresses but *don't* accept mail. Boneheaded mailers effectively ignore DNS and send mail directly to the host. We haven't figured out the best way to deal with this yet. One clever solution a friend uses is to run the mailer on his diskless clients out of the UNIX super-server, *inetd*. (*inetd* starts other servers on an as-needed basis, when requests for their services are received.) The *inetd.conf* entry to do this usually looks like:

```
smtp    tcp    nowait    root    /usr/lib/sendmail    sendmail -bs
```

This way, mailers that ignore MX records can still deliver their mail, but the diskless client doesn't need to run a mailer all the time.

Well, since we've already started talking about configuring hosts to run mail, let's go on to talk about configuring hosts to use DNS.

6

Configuring Hosts

They were indeed a queer-looking party that assembled on the bank—the birds with draggled feathers, the animals with their fur clinging close to them, and all dripping wet, cross, and uncomfortable.

Now that you or someone else in your organization has set up name servers for your domain, you'll want to configure the other hosts on your network to use them. That involves configuring those hosts' resolvers. You should also check files like *hosts.equiv* and *.rhosts* and make any changes dictated by using DNS: you may need to convert some of the host names in these files to domain names. And you may also want to add aliases, both for your users' convenience and to minimize the shock of the conversion to DNS.

This chapter covers these topics, and also describes the major differences in resolver configuration between many common versions of UNIX.

The Resolver

We introduced resolvers way back in Chapter 2, *How Does DNS Work?* but didn't say much more about them. The resolver, you'll remember, is the client half of the Domain Name System. It's responsible for translating a program's request for host information into a query to a name server, and for translating the response into an answer for the program.

We haven't done any resolver configuration yet, because the occasion for it hasn't arisen. When we set up our name servers in Chapter 4, *Setting Up BIND*, the default resolver behavior worked just fine for our purposes. But if we'd needed the resolver to do more than what it does by default, or to behave differently from the default, we would have had to configure the resolver.

There's one thing we should mention up front: what we'll describe in the next few sections is the behavior of the vanilla BIND resolver, in the absence of other naming services. Not all resolvers behave quite this way: some vendors have implemented special resolver functionality that lets you modify the resolver algorithm. We'll cover various vendors' extensions later in this chapter.

So what exactly does the resolver allow you to configure? Most resolvers let you configure at least three aspects of the resolver's behavior: the default domain, the search list, and the name server(s) that the resolver queries. Many UNIX vendors allow you to configure other resolver behavior, too, through non-standard extensions to BIND. Sometimes these extensions are necessary to cope with other software, like Sun's Network Information Service (NIS);* sometimes they're simply value added by the vendor.

Almost all resolver configuration is done in the file */etc/resolv.conf* (this may be */usr/etc/resolv.conf* or similar on your host—check the *resolver* manual page, usually in section 4 or 5, to make sure). There are three main *directives* you can use in *resolv.conf*: the *domain* directive, the *search* directive and the *nameserver* directive. These directives control the behavior of the resolver. There are other, vendor-specific directives available on some versions of UNIX—we'll discuss them at the end of this chapter.

The Default Domain

The default domain is the domain considered "local" to the host. For example, when you add an entry like

```
relay mark
```

into your *.rhosts* file, the name **relay** is assumed to be in your default domain. This makes a lot more sense than allowing access to every host on the Internet whose domain name starts with **relay**. Other authorization files like *hosts.equiv* and *lpd.allow* work the same way.

Normally, the default domain is determined from the host's *hostname*: the default domain is everything after the first "**.**" in the name. If the name doesn't contain a "**.**", the default domain is assumed to be the root domain. So the *hostname* **asylum.sf.ca.us** implies a default domain of **sf.ca.us**, while the *hostname* **dogbert** implies a root default domain.

---

*NIS used to be called "Yellow Pages," or "YP," but was changed to NIS because the British phone company had a copyright on the name Yellow Pages.

You can also set the default domain with the *domain* directive in *resolv.conf.* If the *domain* directive is specified, it overrides the domain in the *hostname.*

The domain directive has a very simple syntax, but you've got to get it right, since the resolver doesn't report errors. The keyword *domain* starts the line in column one, followed by white space (one or more blanks or tabs), then the name of the default domain. The default domain should be written without a trailing dot, like:

```
domain colospgs.co.us
```

Trailing spaces *are not allowed* on the line, and will cause your default domain to be set to a name ending with one or more spaces, which is certainly not what you want.

And there's yet another way to set the default domain—via the LOCAL-DOMAIN environment variable. LOCALDOMAIN is handy because you can set it on a per-user basis. For example, you might have a big, massively-parallel box in your corporate computing center that employees from all over the world log in to. Each may do most of his work in a different company subdomain. With LOCALDOMAIN, each employee can set his default domain to the appropriate domain in his shell startup file.

Which method should you use—*hostname,* the *domain* directive, or LOCALDOMAIN? We prefer using *hostname,* but primarily because that's the way Berkeley does it and it seems "cleaner." Also, some Berkeley software, particularly software that uses the *ruserok()* library call to authenticate users, allows short host names in files like *hosts.equiv* only if *hostname* is set to the full domain name.

If you run software that can't tolerate long *hostnames,* though, you can use the *domain* directive. The *hostname* command will continue to return a short name, and the resolver will fill in the domain from *resolv.conf.* You may even find occasion to use LOCALDOMAIN on a host with lots of users.

The Search List

The default domain, whether derived from *hostname* or *resolv.conf,* also determines the default *search list.* The search list was designed to make users' lives a little easier by saving them some typing. The idea is to search the default domain and the default domain's parent domains for names typed at the command line. The default domain and its parent domains form the list of domains to search, hence the term *search list.*

The default search list includes the default domain and each of its parent domains with two or more labels. Therefore, if a host's *hostname* is set to dizzy.cv.hp.com, the default domain is inferred to be cv.hp.com, the first domain in the default search list. If a query in cv.hp.com doesn't return an answer, the resolver checks the next domain in the search list: the default domain's parent, hp.com. If that query doesn't turn up an answer, the resolver doesn't check com (which has only one label). One reason the BIND resolver doesn't append just the top-level domain is that there are very few hosts at the second level of the Internet's name space, so tacking on just com or edu to foo is unlikely to result in a valid domain name. Also, looking up the address of a foo.com or foo.edu would require sending a query to a root name server, which taxes the roots' resources and can be time consuming.

If the local domain is ch.apollo.hp.com, the default search list includes the domains ch.apollo.hp.com, apollo.hp.com and hp.com—the local domain and each parent domain with at least two parts.

Programs that take domain names as arguments, like *telnet*, *ftp*, *rlogin*, and *rsh*, apply the search list to those domain names unless the domain name ends in a dot. A domain name with a trailing dot is considered an *absolute* domain name—like an absolute pathname in a UNIX or MSDOS filesystem. In an absolute domain name, everything to the left of the final dot is the full domain name, written relative to the root domain. There's no need to search multiple domains for the name, since you know exactly which domain it's in.

There's one more wrinkle in the way the resolver applies the search list, and some of you may have already anticipated it. What happens if you type:

```
% telnet listo.hp.com
```

specifying the full domain name but forgetting the trailing dot? According to our explanation, the resolver would never look up just listo.hp.com, unless the default domain were the root! Actually, the resolver does check the name you type, *verbatim et literatim*, as long as the name has at least one dot in it. But the name only gets checked as you typed it in after the search list has been applied. If your search list is long, that can take some time.

The search Directive

What if you don't like the default search list you get when you set your default domain? In BIND 4.8.3, you can set the search list explicitly, domain by domain, in the order you want the domains searched. You do this with the *search* directive.

The syntax of the *search* directive is very similar to that of the *domain* directive, except that it can take multiple domains as arguments. The keyword *search* starts the line in column one, followed by from one to six domain names, in the order you want them searched. The first domain in the list is interpreted as the default domain, so the *search* and *domain* directives are mutually exclusive. If you use both in *resolv.conf,* the one that appears last will override the other.

The directive:

```
search corp.hp.com paloalto.hp.com hp.com
```

for example, would instruct the resolver to search the **corp.hp.com** domain first, then **paloalto.hp.com**, and then both domains' parent, **hp.com**. If the name typed had a dot in it, the resolver would check the root domain, too.

This directive might be useful on a host whose users access hosts in both **corp.hp.com** and **paloalto.hp.com** frequently. On the other hand, the directive:

```
search corp.hp.com
```

would have the resolver skip searching the default domain's parent domain when the search list is applied. This might be useful if the host's users only access hosts in the local domain, or if connectivity to the parent name servers isn't good (because it minimizes unnecessary queries to the parent name servers).

The nameserver Directive

Back in Chapter 4, *Setting Up BIND*, we talked about two types of name servers: primary master name servers and secondary master name servers. But what if you don't want to run a name server on a host, yet still want to use DNS? Or, for that matter, what if you *can't* run a name server on a host (because the operating system doesn't support it, for example)? Surely you don't have to run a name server on *every* host, right?

No, of course you don't. By default, the resolver looks for a name server running on the local host—which is why we could use *nslookup* on **terminator** and **wormhole** right after we configured their name servers. You can, however, instruct the resolver to look elsewhere.

The *nameserver* directive (yep, all one word) tells the resolver the IP address of a name server to query. For example, the line:

```
nameserver 15.32.17.2
```

instructs the resolver to send queries to the name server running at IP address 15.32.17.2, instead of to the local host. This means that on hosts that don't run name servers, you can use the *nameserver* directive to point them at a remote name server. In fact, since most name servers don't have any notion of access control, you can configure your resolver to query almost *anyone's* name server. Of course, configuring your host to use someone else's name server without first asking permission is somewhat presumptuous, and using one of your own will usually give you better performance, so we'll consider this only an emergency option.

You can also configure the resolver to query the host's local name server, by using either the local host's IP address or the zero address. The zero address, 0.0.0.0, is interpreted by most TCP/IP implementations to mean "this host." The host's real IP address, of course, also means "this host." On hosts that don't understand the zero address, you can use the loopback address, 127.0.0.1.

Now what if the name server your resolver queries is down? Isn't there any way to specify a backup? Do you just fall back to using the host table?

The resolver will also allow you to specify up to three (count 'em, three) name servers using multiple *nameserver* directives. The resolver will query those name servers, in the order listed, until it receives an answer or times out. The number of name servers you configure dictates other aspects of the resolver's behavior, too.

NOTE

If you use multiple *nameserver* directives, *don't* use the loopback address! There's a bug in BIND 4.8.3 that will cause problems if the local name server is down. The resolver will send query packets to the remote name servers with a source address of 127.0.0.1. When the remote name server tries to reply, it'll end up sending the reply packet to itself.

One Name Server Configured

If there's only one name server configured,* the resolver queries that name server (obviously) with a timeout of five seconds. The timeout is the length of time the resolver will wait for a response from the name server before sending another query. If the resolver encounters an error that indicates the name server is really down or unreachable, or times out, it will double the timeout and query the name server again. The errors that would cause this include:

- Receipt of an ICMP *port unreachable* message, which means that no name server is listening on the name server port
- Receipt of an ICMP *host unreachable* or *network unreachable* message, which means that queries can't be sent to the destination IP address

Note that the list of errors doesn't include the non-existence of the domain name or data looked up. Theoretically, at least, each name server should have an equivalent "view" of the name space; there's no reason to believe one and not another.† So if one name server tells you a given domain name doesn't exist, or that the type of data you're looking for doesn't exist for the domain name you specified, any other name server should give you the same answer. If the resolver receives an error *each* time it sends a query (for a total of four errors), it falls back to using the host table. Note that these are *errors*, not timeouts. If it times out on even one query, the resolver returns a null answer and does not fall back to */etc/hosts*.

More Than One Name Server Configured

With more than one name server configured, the behavior is a little different. Here's what happens: the resolver starts by querying the first name server in the list, with a timeout of five seconds, just like in the single name server case. If the resolver times out or receives an error, it will fall back to the next name server, using the same timeout. Unfortunately, the resolver won't receive many of the possible errors: the socket the resolver uses is "unconnected," since it must be able to receive responses from any of the

---

*When we say "one name server configured," that means either one *nameserver* directive in *resolv.conf* or no *nameserver* directive with a name server running locally.

†The built-in latency of DNS makes this a small fib: a primary can have authority for a zone and have different data from a secondary that also has authority for the zone. The primary may have just loaded new zone data from disk, while the secondary may not have had time to transfer the new zone data from the primary. Both name servers return authoritative answers for the zone, but the primary may know about a brand-new host that the secondary doesn't know about.

name servers it queries, and unconnected sockets don't receive ICMP error messages. If the resolver queries all the configured name servers, to no avail, it updates the timeouts and cycles through them again.

The new resolver timeout is based on the number of name servers configured in *resolv.conf.* The timeout for the second round of queries is ten seconds divided by the number of name servers configured, rounded down. Each successive round's timeout is double the previous timeout. After three sets of retransmissions (a total of four timeouts for every name server configured), the resolver gives up trying to query name servers.

For you mathophobes, Table 6-1 shows what the timeouts look like when you have one, two, or three name servers configured.

Table 6.1: Resolver Timeouts

Retry	Name Servers Configured		
	1	**2**	**3**
0	5s	(2x) 5s	(3x) 5s
1	10s	(2x) 5s	(3x) 3s
2	20s	(2x) 10s	(3x) 6s
3	40s	(2x) 20s	(3x) 13s
Total	75s	80s	81s

(Note that this is 4.8.3 BIND's behavior. The behavior of older versions of BIND is similar, but not identical.)

So if you configure three servers, the resolver queries the first server, with a timeout period of five seconds. If that query times out, the resolver queries the second server with the same timeout, and similarly for the third. If the resolver cycles through all three servers, it doubles the timeout period and divides by three (to three seconds, 10/3 rounded down) and queries the first server again.

Do these times seem awfully long? Remember, this describes a worst-case scenario. With properly functioning name servers running on tolerably fast hosts, your resolvers should get their answers back in well under a second. Only if all the configured servers are really busy or down will the resolver ever make it all the way through the retransmission cycle and give up.

What does the resolver do after it gives up? It times out and returns an error. Typically this results in an error like:

```
% telnet tootsie
tootsie: Host name lookup failure
```

Of course, it'll take about 75 seconds of waiting to see this message, so be patient.

Sample Resolver Configurations

So much for the theory—let's go over what *resolv.conf* files look like on real hosts. Resolver configuration needs vary depending on whether or not a host runs a local name server, so we'll cover both cases: hosts with local name servers, and hosts with remote name servers.

Resolver-Only

We, as the administrators of **movie.edu,** have just been asked to configure a professor's new standalone workstation, which doesn't run a name server. Deciding which domain the workstation belongs in is easy: there's only **movie.edu** to choose from. However, she *is* working with researchers at Pixar on new shading algorithms, so perhaps it'd be wise to put **pixar.com** in her workstation's search list. The *search* directive:

```
search movie.edu pixar.com
```

will put her workstation in the **movie.edu** domain, and will search **pixar.com** for names not found in **movie.edu.**

The new workstation is on the 192.249.249 network, so the closest name servers are **wormhole.movie.edu** (192.249.249.1) and **terminator.movie.edu** (192.249.249.3). As a rule, you should configure hosts to use the closest name server available first. (The closest possible name server is a name server on the local host, the next closest is a name server on the same network or subnet.) In this case, both name servers are equally close, but we know that **wormhole** is bigger (it's a faster host, with more capacity). So the first *nameserver* directive in *resolv.conf* should be:

```
nameserver 192.249.249.1
```

Since this particular professor is known to get awfully vocal when she has problems with her computer, we'll also add **terminator.movie.edu** (192.249.249.3) as a backup name server. That way, if **wormhole** is down for any reason, the professor's workstation can still get name service (assuming **terminator** and the rest of the network are up).

The *resolv.conf* file ends up looking like this:

```
search movie.edu pixar.com
nameserver 192.249.249.1
nameserver 192.249.249.3
```

Local Name Server

Next, we have to configure the university mail hub, **postmanrings2x**, to use domain name service. **postmanrings2x** is shared by all groups in the **movie.edu** domain. We've recently configured a caching-only name server on the host to help cut down the load on the other name servers, so we should make sure the resolver queries the name server on the local host first.

The simplest resolver configuration for this case is no configuration at all: don't create a *resolv.conf* file, and let the resolver default to using the local name server. The *hostname* should be set to the full domain name of the host, so the resolver can determine the local domain.

If we decide we need a backup name server, we can use *resolv.conf.* Whether or not we configure a backup name server depends largely on the reliability of the local name server. A good implementation of the BIND 4.8.3 *named* will keep running for longer than some operating systems, so there may be no need for a backup. If the local name server has a history of problems, though—say it hangs occasionally and stops responding to queries—it might be prudent to add a backup name server.

To add a backup name server, just list the local name server first in *resolv.conf* (at the host's IP address or the zero address, 0.0.0.0—either will do), then one or two backup name servers. Remember not to use the loopback address unless you've patched the bug in BIND we mentioned earlier.

Minimizing Pain and Suffering

Now that you've configured your host to use DNS, what's going to change? Will your users be forced to type long domain names? Will they have to change their mail addresses and mailing lists?

Thanks to the search list, much of this will continue working as before. There are some exceptions, though, and there are notable differences in the way that some programs behave when they use DNS. We'll try to cover all of the common ones.

Differences in Service Behavior

As you've seen earlier in this chapter, programs like *telnet, ftp, rlogin* and *rsh* apply the search list to domain name arguments that aren't dot-terminated. That means that if you're in **movie.edu** (i.e., your default domain is **movie.edu** and your search list includes **movie.edu**), you can type either:

```
% telnet misery
```

or:

```
% telnet misery.movie.edu
```

or even:

```
% telnet misery.movie.edu.
```

and get to the same place. The same holds true for the other services, too. There's one other behavioral difference you may benefit from: because a name server may return more than one IP address when you look up an address, *telnet* and *ftp* will try to connect to the first address returned, and if the connection is refused or times out, for example, try the next, and so on:

```
% ftp tootsie
ftp: connect to address 192.249.249.244: Connection timed out
Trying 192.253.253.244...
Connected to tootsie.movie.edu.
220 tootsie.movie.edu FTP server (Version 16.2 Fri Apr 26
    18:20:43 GMT 1991) ready.
Name (tootsie: guest):
```

One oddball service is NFS. The *mount* command can handle domain names just fine, and you can put domain names into */etc/fstab* (your vendor may call it */etc/checklist*), too. But watch out for */etc/exports* and */etc/netgroup*. */etc/exports* controls which filesystems you allow various clients to NFS-mount. You can also assign a name to a group of hosts in *netgroup* and then allow them access via *exports* by using the name of the group.

Unfortunately, older versions of NFS don't *really* use DNS to check *exports* or *netgroup*—the client tells the NFS server its identity in an RPC (Remote Procedure Call) packet. Consequently, the client's identity is whatever the client claims it is. And the identity a host uses in Sun RPC is the local host's *hostname*. So the name you use in either file needs to match the client's *hostname*, which isn't necessarily its domain name.

Electronic Mail

Some electronic mail programs, including *sendmail*, also don't work as expected: *sendmail* doesn't use the search list quite the same way other programs do. Instead, when configured to use a name server, it uses a process called *canonicalization* to convert names in electronic mail addresses to full, canonical domain names.

In canonicalization, *sendmail* applies the search list to a name and looks for data of type CNAME.* If the name server queried finds a CNAME record (an alias), it replaces the name looked up with the canonical name the alias points to. *sendmail* uses canonicalization several times when processing an SMTP message: it canonicalizes the destination address and several fields in the SMTP headers.

sendmail also sets macro *w* (not to be confused with class *w*) to the canonicalized *hostname* when you freeze the *sendmail.cf* file, or, if you don't freeze your configuration file, when the *sendmail* daemon starts up. So even if you set your *hostname* to a short, single-part name, *sendmail* will canonicalize the *hostname* using the search list defined in *resolv.conf.*

This is important because the local host's canonical name is the only name *sendmail* recognizes, by default, as the local host's name. *sendmail* will attempt to forward mail that's addressed to a domain name it thinks isn't local. So, for example, unless you configure *sendmail* to recognize the host's aliases (using class *w* or fileclass *w*, as we showed in Chapter 5, *DNS and Electronic Mail*), the host would try to forward messages that arrived addressed for anything other than the canonical domain name.

There's another important implication of the way *sendmail* canonicalizes the local *hostname*: *sendmail* only recognizes the local host's canonical name in MX lists. Consequently, if you use anything other than a host's canonical name in an MX record, you run the risk that the host will not recognize it. This can cause mail to loop and then be returned to the sender.

---

*Some versions of *sendmail* use a different technique for doing canonicalization: they apply the search list and query the name server for type ANY records for the name in question. ANY matches most types of resource record (not quite "any," though). If a record is found, the name is replaced with the name that turned up the data. These queries can cause problems, however, when they encounter wildcard records, because names in mail addresses may canonicalize to bogus domain names. Consequently, many vendors go the CNAME route (it's a compile-time option).

One last note on *sendmail*: when you start running a name server, you should also set the *I* option in your *sendmail.cf* file. Option I determines what *sendmail* does if a lookup for a destination host fails. When using */etc/hosts*, a failed lookup is fatal: if you search the host table once for a name and don't find it, it's doubtful it'll miraculously appear later, so the mailer may as well return the message. When using DNS, however, a lookup failure may be temporary, because of intermittent networking problems, for example. Setting option *I* instructs *sendmail* to queue mail if a lookup fails, instead of returning it to the sender. Just add:

```
OI
```

to your *sendmail.cf* file, and refreeze it, if you use a frozen configuration file.

Updating .rhosts, hosts.equiv, etc.

Once you start using DNS, you may also need to disambiguate host names in your host's authorization files. Entries which use simple, one-part host names will now be assumed to be in the local domain. For example, the *lpd.allow* file on **wormhole** might include:

```
wormhole
terminator
diehard
robocop
mash
twins
```

If we move **mash** and **twins** into the **comedy.movie.edu** domain, though, they won't be allowed to access *lpd*: the entries in **lpd.allow** only allow **mash.movie.edu** and **twins.movie.edu**. So we'd have to add the proper domains to host names outside of the local host's default domain:

```
wormhole
terminator
diehard
robocop
mash.comedy.movie.edu
twins.comedy.movie.edu
```

Some other files you should check for host names in need of domain-ification are:

```
hosts.equiv
.rhosts
X0.hosts
sendmail.cf
```

Sometimes, simply running these files through a canonicalization filter—a program that translates host names to domain names using the search list—is enough to disambiguate them. Here's a short canonicalization filter in perl to help you out:

```perl
#!/usr/bin/perl

# Perl canonicalization filter
#
# Expects one hostname per line, in the first field (a la .rhosts,
# X0.hosts)

require 'sys/socket.ph';

while(<>){
    if(($hostname, $null) = split){
      ($domainname, $aliases, $addrtype, $length, @addrs) =
          gethostbyname($hostname);
      if($domainname) {s/$hostname/$domainname/;}
    }
    print;
}
```

Providing Aliases

Even if you cover all your bases and convert all your *.rhosts, hosts.equiv,* and *sendmail.cf* files after you configure your host to use DNS, your users will still have to adjust to using domain names. Hopefully, the confusion they feel will be minimal, and will be more than offset by the benefits of DNS.

One way to make your users' lives less confusing after configuring DNS is to provide aliases for well-known hosts that are no longer reachable using their familiar names. For example, our users are accustomed to typing **telnet doofy** or **rlogin doofy** to get to the bulletin board system run by the movie studio on the other side of town. Now they'll have to start using doofy's full domain name, **doofy.maroon.com**. But most of our users don't know the full domain name, and it'll be some time before we can tell all of them and they get used to it.

Luckily, BIND will let you define aliases for your users. All we need to do is set the environment variable *HOSTALIASES* to the pathname of a file that contains mappings between aliases and domain names. For example, to

set up a system-wide alias for **doofy**, we could set HOSTALIASES to
/etc/host.aliases in the system's shell startup files, and add:

```
doofy     doofy.maroon.com
```

to */etc/host.aliases*. The format of the alias file is simple: the alias starts the
line in column one, followed by white space, and then the domain name
that corresponds to the alias. The domain name is written without a trailing
dot. The alias can't contain dots.

Now, when our users type **telnet doofy** or **rlogin doofy**, the resolver will
transparently substitute **doofy.maroon.com** for **doofy** in the name server
query. The message the users see will look something like:

```
Trying...
Connected to doofy.maroon.com.
Escape character is '^]'.


IRIX System V.3 (sgi)

login:
```

If the resolver falls back to using */etc/hosts*, though, our HOSTALIASES won't
have any effect. So we should also keep a similar alias in */etc/hosts*.

With time, and perhaps a little instruction, the users will start to associate
the full domain name they see in the *telnet* banner with the bulletin board
they use.

With HOSTALIASES, as long as you know the domain names your users are
likely to have trouble with, you can save them a little frustration. If you
don't know which hosts they're trying to get to, you can let your users create their own alias files, and have each point the HOSTALIASES variable in
his shell startup file to his personal alias file.

Vendor-specific options

UNIX is ostensibly a standard operating system, but there are almost as
many UNIX standards as flavors of UNIX. Likewise, there are almost as
many different styles of resolver configuration as there are UNIXes. Almost
all support the original Berkeley syntax, but most add non-standard
enhancements or variations, too. We'll cover as many of the major styles of
resolver configuration as we can.

Sun's SunOS

Configuring a host running SunOS can be a challenge. The behavior of the Sun resolver is arguably as different from standard BIND as major vendors get—primarily because Sun's resolver is integrated with Sun's Network Information Service, or NIS (nee Yellow Pages).

NIS, briefly, provides a mechanism for keeping important files synchronized between hosts on a network. This includes not just */etc/hosts*, but also */etc/services*, */etc/passwd*, and others. Sun positions DNS as a backup option to NIS: if the NIS resolver can't find a host name (or IP address) in the NIS hosts map, you can configure it to query a name server.

Note that the resolver functionality is implemented as part of the *ypserv* program, which also handles other types of NIS queries. So if *ypserv* isn't running, neither is your resolver! One benefit of using *ypserv* to resolve all queries is that you don't need to configure the resolvers on NIS clients, only on NIS servers. The NIS clients will query an NIS server for host data, and the NIS server will query DNS, if necessary.

You can follow the party line and configure your resolver to use DNS as a backup to NIS, or you can choose to run NIS without host maps, or you can buck convention and recompile your resolver to use DNS exclusively—or you can pick up free copies of modified resolvers on the Internet. However, we must warn you that, according to our sources, Sun *will not support* the modified resolver option.

Modified Resolvers

We won't go into much detail about this option here, primarily because the instructions on how to do this are fairly long, because they change with each new release of SunOS, and because the instructions are widely available on the Internet. The process itself usually involves creating a new *libc.so*, the standard, shared C library, by pulling out routines that call NIS and replacing them with pure DNS versions. Sun generously provides the necessary replacement routines, even though they don't support them. Unfortunately, the routines supplied with SunOS 4.1 are based on BIND 4.8.1.

The detailed instructions on this process are often posted to USENET newsgroups like *comp.sys.sun.admin*. Browse there if you're looking for up-to-date instructions. If you don't find them, you can post there and someone will probably send them to you.

If you're interested in the latest BIND, Dave Curry has packaged up patches to the 4.8.3 BIND source to make the 4.8.3 resolver compile and run under SunOS 4.1 along with instructions on how to build *libc.so* with those resolver routines. His package, called *bindon41*, is currently available via anonymous *ftp* from **germany.eu.net** as */pub/comp/sun/bindon41*.

If you'd rather skip the potentially edifying experience of creating your own shared C library and leverage someone else's efforts, there are a couple of options available to you:

- UUNet makes a DNS-only version of the shared C library available from **ftp.uu.net** under the */systems/sun/sun-fixes* directory. The library is available for both Sun 3's and Sun 4's, as *libc_resolv.so.sun3* and *libc_resolv.so.sun4*, respectively. These libraries may be a little old for your release of SunOS, though: they only work with the 4.0, 4.0.1 and 4.0.3 versions of SunOS.

- Bill Wisner has written an enhanced version of the resolver routines for SunOS, which allows administrators to choose the order in which NIS and DNS are queried (much like the extensions DEC added to Ultrix, which we'll discuss later). The new routines are available, with instructions on how to build them into *libc.so*, from **ftp.uu.net** as the *file /networking/ip/dns/resolv+2.1.tar.Z*.

Using DNS with NIS

If you go the socially-acceptable route, though, you'll need to make NIS and DNS coexist peacefully. That's a little tricky, so we'll go over it in some detail. We won't cover how to set up NIS—that's already been covered in gory detail in Hal Stern's *Managing NFS and NIS* (O'Reilly & Associates, 1991). Note that these instructions only apply to versions of SunOS after 4.1. If you run an older version of SunOS, consider the replacement libraries on **ftp.uu.net**.

First, you'll need to modify the *Makefile* NIS uses to build its maps—the files that it distributes to other hosts on the network. You should make this modification on the master NIS server, not on the slaves.

The NIS *Makefile* lives in */var/yp/Makefile* on a SunOS host. The change you need to make is simple: you need to uncomment one line and comment another. Find the lines that read:

```
#B=-b
B=
```

and change them to read:

```
B=-b
#B=
```

Then rebuild your NIS hosts map:

```
# cd /var/yp
# make hosts.time
updated hosts

pushed hosts
```

This will insert a "magic cookie" into the hosts map that instructs NIS to query DNS if it can't find a host name in the hosts map. Now, when the *ypserv* program looks up a name, it will check the appropriate hosts map for the local NIS *domainname*, and if it can't find the name there, will query a name server. The search list *ypserv* uses when it queries the name server is derived from either the local NIS *domainname*, or from the *domain* directive in *resolv.conf.*

Next, you should create a *resolv.conf* file, if you need one. The rules for configuring the resolver change slightly with SunOS:

- You *can't* set the *hostname* to a domain name and have the resolver infer the local domain.

- You also can't use the *search* directive in *resolv.conf* (yet) since the SunOS 4.1.1 resolver is based on BIND 4.8.1. The resolver will silently ignore it.

- You *can* set the NIS *domainname* to a domain name (you have to set it to the name of your NIS domain if you're using NIS) and the resolver will derive the name of the local DNS domain from it. However, this doesn't work quite the same it does with BIND: if you set *domainname* to **fx.movie.edu**, for example, the search list will only include **movie.edu**. Why doesn't the search list include **fx.movie.edu**? Because NIS assumes it's already checked an authoritative source of **fx.movie.edu** host data—the **fx.movie.edu** hosts map.

- If you want to set the default domain to the same name as your NIS *domainname*, you can prepend a dot or a plus ("+") to the *domainname*. To set your default domain to **fx.movie.edu**, you could set *domainname* to either **+fx.movie.edu** or **.fx.movie.edu**.

- You can also override NIS's normal behavior by setting the local domain with the *domain* directive in *resolv.conf.* So if you wanted to force the resolver to include **fx.movie.edu** in the search list, you could add `domain fx.movie.edu` to *resolv.conf.*

- You can even set the *domain* directive in *resolv.conf* to a DNS domain name totally unrelated to your NIS *domainname*. In some unfortunate situations, the local NIS *domainname* isn't the same or even similar to the DNS domain name. Say the Information Technology department at Movie U. originally set up the NIS domain **it.dept.movieu**, and still uses it. To prevent spurious DNS queries in the non-existent **dept.movieu** domain, hosts in this NIS domain should be configured with domain movie.edu (or something similar) in *resolv.conf.*

Finally, Sun's *resolv.conf* treats the *nameserver* directive just like vanilla BIND does. So once you're done inserting magic cookies, configuring your NIS *domainname* and possibly your DNS domain, you can add any name servers to *resolv.conf* and be done.

Ignoring NIS

If you want to retain Sun's support but would rather not use icky NIS, you still have an option: you can run NIS with an empty hosts map. First, set up your *resolv.conf* file, then insert the magic cookie into the NIS *Makefile* as we described in *Using DNS with NIS* and create an empty hosts map. Creating an empty hosts map just requires moving the NIS master server's */etc/hosts* file aside temporarily, generating your hosts NIS map, then replacing the */etc/hosts* file:

```
% mv /etc/hosts /etc/hosts.tmp
% touch /etc/hosts   # to keep make from complaining
% cd /var/yp
% make hosts.time
updated hosts

pushed hosts
% mv /etc/hosts.tmp /etc/hosts
```

Now, when the resolver checks NIS, it won't find anything, and will go directly to querying a domain name server.

If you periodically rebuild your NIS maps, you should make sure the hosts map doesn't accidentally get rebuilt from */etc/hosts*. The best way to do this is to remove the hosts target from the NIS *Makefile*. You can just comment out everything in the *Makefile* from the line that begins with:

```
hosts.time: $(DIR)/hosts
```

to the next blank line.

HP's HP-UX

HP's resolver implementation is basically straight BIND: the HP-UX 8.0 resolver is based on BIND 4.8.3, and supports the standard *domain*, *nameserver*, and *search* directives. The order in which a host consults DNS, NIS and the host table is hard-wired: the host will use DNS, if DNS is configured. If DNS isn't configured, and NIS is running, the host will use NIS. If neither DNS nor NIS is running, the host will use the host table. The host only falls back to using the other services under the circumstances described earlier in the chapter (i.e., the resolver only uses one name server—either listed in *resolv.conf* or on the local host by default—and four errors received while contacting that name server).

The hard-wired algorithm is less flexible than what other vendors provide, but it's easy to troubleshoot. When you can consult DNS, NIS, and the host table in any order, diagnosing user problems can be awfully difficult.

IBM's AIX

The resolver shipped with the current version of AIX, 3.2, is also relatively standard. The code is based on BIND 4.8.1, so it only understands the *domain* and *nameserver* directives; AIX supports up to three *nameserver* directives.

One difference between AIX's behavior and the stock BSD behavior is that AIX uses the existence of the *resolv.conf* file to determine whether or not to query a name server. If *resolv.conf* doesn't exist on the local host, the resolver reads */etc/hosts*. This means that, on a host running a name server, you should create a zero length */etc/resolv.conf* file, even if you don't intend to put any directives in it.

IBM has also modified the resolver so that it checks NIS and then */etc/hosts* even if DNS claims there's no such domain name or no such data. This gives you the ability to add hosts to */etc/hosts* temporarily before they make it into the name server, and will let you maintain your own, host-specific name-to-address mappings.

We should also note that you can configure the resolver using AIX's System Management Interface Tool (SMIT).

DEC's Ultrix

Ultrix allows you to configure the order in which the resolver checks NIS, DNS, and the host table via a file called *svc.conf* (see *svc.conf(5)*). *svc.conf* also allows you to configure which services are consulted for other "databases," including mail aliases, authentication checks (mapping from IP address to host or domain names), password and group information, and a slew of other things. Older versions of Ultrix (up to 3.1) provide just the resolver configuration functionality in a file called */etc/svcorder.*

To configure the resolver with *svc.conf*, use the database name *hosts*, followed by an "=" and the keywords for the services you want checked, separated by commas, in the order you want them checked. The legal keywords for *hosts* are *local* (the local host table), *yp* (for "Yellow Pages," the old name for NIS) and *bind* (for DNS). *local* must be the first service listed for *hosts*. Don't use any white space on the line, except (optionally) after commas and at the end of the line.

The line:

```
hosts=local,bind
```

instructs the resolver to check */etc/hosts* for host names first, and if no match is found, to use domain name service. This is very useful when the host has a small local host table that includes the local host's domain name and IP address, the host's default router, and any other hosts referenced during startup. Checking the local host table first avoids any problems using domain name service during startup, when networking and *named* may not have started.

Ultrix also includes a utility called *svcsetup* (see the *svcsetup(8)* manual page), which allows you to set up the *svc.conf* file interactively, without the aid of an editor. Typing *svcsetup* will throw you into a mode where you can choose the database you'd like to configure, and prompt you for the order of the services you want checked.

Silicon Graphics' Irix

As of Irix 4.0, Irix has a BIND 4.8.3 resolver and name server. The Irix *resolv.conf* file, which lives in */usr/etc/resolv.conf*, adds a *hostresorder* directive. The *hostresorder* directive allows the administrator to determine the order in which NIS, DNS and the local host table are searched. Individual users can set the environment variable *HOSTRESORDER* to determine the order in which the services are used for their commands.

hostresorder takes one or more of the keywords *nis*, *bind*, and *local* as arguments. (The keywords correspond to the obvious services.) The keywords may be separated by either white space or a "/" (slash). White space indicates that the next service should be tried if the previous service doesn't return an answer (e.g., the name isn't found in the host table, or the name server returns "no such domain") or isn't available (e.g., the name server isn't running). A slash indicates that the preceding service is authoritative, and if no answer is returned, resolution should stop. The next service is only tried if the previous isn't available.

SCO's SCO UNIX

SCO UNIX is basically straight pre-4.8.3 BIND, with a twist. The resolver configuration file lives in */etc/resolv.conf*, just where you'd expect it to be. The *domain* and *nameserver* directives are valid and follow standard syntax. The *search* directive, a 4.8.3-ism, isn't understood. SCO's resolver falls back to the host table only if there's one name server configured and the resolver receives an error each time it tries to query that name server.

The twist is the resolver's integration with NIS. SCO hosts don't really *use* NIS, per se. To satisfy SCO UNIX's C2 security subsystem (which affects operation even if the lowest level of security is configured), SCO's NIS never acts as a true NIS client. A host running NIS on SCO UNIX copies NIS maps from a master server, then runs scripts to translate the NIS maps back into their original ASCII form, essentially recreating */etc/hosts* and other system files. Consequently, the resolver never needs to query NIS at all.

FTP's PC/TCP

So far, we've only covered resolver configuration for various UNIXes. Since there's a good chance you have a PC or two on your network, too, we'll go over how to configure the resolver in one of the most popular PC-based TCP/IP packages, FTP Software's PC/TCP. Not only is FTP's product popular, some major computer manufacturers remarket PC/TCP, so there's hope this section covers your PCs' networking software.

Configuring the resolver in PC/TCP is markedly different—but no more difficult—than configuring a BIND resolver. The *ipconfig* command controls all resolver configuration settings. There's no *resolv.conf* file at all. There *is* the *ipcust.sys* file, which contains all permanent networking configuration information (i.e., configuration saved after a reboot), but the file isn't human-readable.

Another difference between configuring PC/TCP and a standard BIND resolver is that PC/TCP's resolver separates configuring permanent configuration and configuring the in-memory (running) configuration. This is handy if you want to test a configuration change before making it permanent. However, it means that to change the resolver's current behavior *and* have that change saved, you must use *ipconfig* to change the in-memory configuration, then run *ipconfig* again to save that configuration to the *ipcust.sys* file.

ipconfig's first argument indicates whether you're changing the running configuration or the permanent configuration. To specify the running configuration, use the keyword *$ipcust*. To indicate the permanent configuration, use the keyword *ipcust.sys*, the name of the configuration file.

This argument is usually followed by one or more option-value pairs. The options pertinent to resolver configuration are:

show   Displays the current network configuration information in summary format. *show* doesn't take a value, and can't be used with other options.

hostname Sets the host name of the PC. The *hostname* option should be followed by a legal host name—without dots—as a value. This is analogous to *hostname(1)* on a UNIX host, except that FTP's *hostname* option doesn't understand domain names.

domain   Sets the name of the PC's default domain, which is appended to the host name to form the fully-qualified domain name. This is analogous to the *domain* directive in *resolv.conf*, except that PC/TCP doesn't infer a search list from *domain*: it just appends the default domain to host names typed at the command line, and doesn't try parent domains.

fqdn   Sets the PC's fully-qualified domain name (its domain name, relative to the root), and therefore *both* the hostname and default domain. The *fqdn* option takes a domain name as a value. The PC's *hostname* is then set to the first label of the domain name, and the default domain is set to everything following the first label (minus the dot separator). Since *fqdn* sets both the host name and the default domain, you can use it instead of the *hostname* and *domain* options. Older versions of PC/TCP (before release 2.05 or so) don't understand the *fqdn* option, though.

ds   Specifies the domain name servers the PC's resolver will query. The *ds* option takes up to three name servers' IP addresses as a value, which the resolver queries in the order specified. This is exactly analogous to the *nameserver* directive in *resolv.conf.* Note that since *ds* may have more than one value, it *must* be the last option specified in an *ipconfig* command.

ns   Specifies the **IEN-116 n**ame servers the PC's resolver will query. We mention this because people often confuse this configuration option with *ds*. IEN-116 name servers *are not* domain name servers, and you likely don't have any on your network and don't need them, so you won't use this option.

So, for example, to set your PC's domain name and the domain name servers it queries in one fell swoop, you could execute

```
C> ipconfig $ipcust fqdn peechee.movie.edu
   ds 192.249.249.3 192.249.249.1
```

This sets the PC's host name to **peechee**, the default domain to **movie.edu**, and the list of domain name servers to query to 192.249.249.3, then 192.249.249.1.

Note that this command affects the in-memory configuration, not the permanent configuration. To save the running configuration to the permanent configuration file, *ipcust.sys*, you'd run

```
C> ipconfig ipcust.sys copy $ipcust
```

which copies *$ipcust* to *ipcust.sys* (and yes, we know it doesn't read that way, but that's the order they want the values specified).

In case you need to clear any of these settings, you can use the null value "", except for the *ds* option, which requires the value *clear*:

```
C> ifconfig ipcust.sys fqdn "" ds clear
```

7

Maintaining BIND

> *"Well, in our country," said Alice, still panting a little, "you'd generally get to somewhere else—if you ran very fast for a long time as we've been doing."*
>
> *"A slow sort of country!" said the Queen. "Now, here, you see, it takes all the running you can do, to keep in the same place. If you want to get somewhere else, you must run at least twice as fast as that!"*

This chapter discusses a number of related topics pertaining to name server maintenance. We'll talk about sending signals to name servers, modifying the db files, and keeping *db.cache* up-to-date. We'll list common syslog error messages and explain the statistics BIND keeps. This chapter also includes a couple of topics that could have been included in Chapter 4, *Setting Up BIND*: additional DNS database file and BIND boot file entries. These aren't necessary for getting your first servers running and will only be used at some sites, so we include them in this chapter instead.

This chapter doesn't cover troubleshooting problems. Maintenance involves keeping your data current and watching over your name servers as they operate. Troubleshooting involves putting out fires—those little DNS emergencies that flare up periodically. Firefighting is covered in Chapter 12, *Troubleshooting DNS and BIND*.

BIND Name Server Signals

In day-to-day operation, the BIND name server, */etc/named*, is manipulated with signals. We'll use them in this chapter and in other chapters. Here's a list of the signals you can send to a name server and a short description of the action each signal causes. Each of these signals will be discussed in more detail elsewhere in this book.

HUP Restart the name server. Send this signal to a primary name server after modifying its boot file or one of its database files.

INT Dump a copy of the name server's internal database to */usr/tmp/named_dump.db*.

ABRT Append the name server's statistics to */usr/tmp/named.stats*. This signal may be called IOT on your system.

USR1 Append debugging information to */usr/tmp/named.run*. Each subsequent USR1 signal increases the amount of detail in the debugging information.

USR2 Turn off debugging.

To send a name server a signal, you must first find the name server's process ID. The BIND name server leaves its process ID in a disk file, making it easier to chase the critter down: you don't have to use *ps*. The most common place for the process ID to be left is */etc/named.pid*. On some systems, the process ID is in */var/run/named.pid*. Check the *named* manual page to see which directory *named.pid* is in on your system. Since the name server process ID is in a file, sending a HUP signal can be as simple as:

```
# kill -HUP `cat /etc/named.pid`
```

Instead of looking for the process ID in a file, you can find the process ID with *ps*. On a BSD-based system use:

```
% ps -ax | grep named
```

On a SYS V-based system use:

```
% ps -ef | grep named
```

However, you may find more than one name server running if you use *ps*, since name servers spawn children to perform zone transfers. During a zone transfer, the name server pulling the zone data starts a child process and the name server providing the zone data starts a child process. We'll digress a little here and explain why child processes are used.

A secondary name server starts a child process to perform a zone transfer. This allows the secondary name server to keep answering queries while the zone data is being transferred from the master server to the local disk by the child process. Once the zone is on the local disk, the secondary name server reads in the new data. Using a child process to do the zone transfer fixed a problem with older versions of BIND in which secondary name servers wouldn't answer queries during a zone transfer. This could be a real nuisance on name servers which loaded lots of zones: they'd go silent for long periods of time.

A master (primary or secondary) name server also creates a child process to provide a zone to a secondary name server. There are two reasons to create a separate process to handle the zone transfer: The child process reduces the load on the master server by taking over what could be a long transfer. And, since the child process inherits a complete copy of the database (the master server process' data area) from its parent, it is free to traverse the database without watching out for database changes during the traversal. If the update were done from "live" data instead of a copy, some of the zone information might change during the transfer, and the secondaries could end up with inconsistent data.

If the *ps* output shows multiple name servers, you should be able to tell easily which name server process is the parent and which processes are children. A child name server started by a secondary server to pull a copy of a zone is called *named-xfer* instead of *named*:

```
root  548 547  0 22:03:17 ?    0:00 named-xfer -z movie.edu
      -f /usr/tmp/NsTmp0 -s 0 -P 53 192.249.249.3
```

A child name server started by a master name server changes its command line options to indicate which secondary server it is providing the zone to:

```
root 1137 1122 6 22:03:18 ?    0:00 /etc/named -zone XFR
      to [192.249.249.1]
```

You may encounter a version of *named* that doesn't change its command line, but you can still figure out the relationship between multiple *named* processes by examining their process IDs and parent process IDs. All the child processes will have the parent name server's process ID as their parent process ID. This may seem like stating the obvious, but only send signals to the *parent* name server process. The child processes will go away after the zone transfers complete.

Updating db Files

There is always something changing on your network: the new workstations arrive, you finally retire or sell the relic, or you move a host to a different network. Each change means the db files must be modified. Should
you make the changes manually? Should you wimp out and use a tool to
help you?

First, we'll discuss how to make the changes manually. Then we'll talk
about a tool to help out: *h2n*. Actually, we recommend that you use a tool
to create the db files—we were kidding about that wimp stuff, okay?—or,
at least, use a tool to increment the serial number for you. The syntax of
the DNS files lends itself to making mistakes. It doesn't help that the
address and pointer records are in different files which must agree with
each other. Nonetheless, it is critical to know what goes on when the files
are updated, so we'll start with the manual method.

Adding and Deleting Hosts

After creating your db files initially, it should be fairly apparent what needs
to be changed when you add a new host. We'll go through the steps here
in case you weren't the one to set up those files, or if you'd just like a
checklist to follow. Make these changes to your *primary* name server's
DNS database files. If you make the change to your *secondary* name
server's backup files, the secondary's data will change, but the next zone
transfer will overwrite it.

1. First, add any A (address), CNAME (alias), and MX (mail exchanger)
   records for the host to the *db.DOMAIN* file. We added the following
   resource records to the *db.movie* file when a new host (**cujo**) was added
   to our network:

   ```
   cujo  IN A  192.253.253.5   ; cujo's internet address
         IN MX 10 cujo         ; if possible, mail directly to cujo
         IN MX 20 terminator   ; otherwise, deliver to our mail hub
   ```

2. Add PTR records to *each db.ADDR* file for which the host has an
   address. **cujo** only has one address, on network **192.253.253**; therefore,
   we added the following PTR record to the *db.192.253.253* file:

   ```
   5  IN PTR cujo.movie.edu.
   ```

3. Update the serial numbers. We incremented the serial number in *both*
   the *db.movie* and *db.192.253.253* files, since **cujo** was added to both.

4. Restart the primary name server by sending it a HUP signal; this forces it to load the new information:

```
# kill -HUP `cat /etc/named.pid`
```

After it has been restarted, the primary name server will load the new data. Secondary name servers will load this new data sometime within the time interval defined in the SOA record for refreshing their data.

Sometimes your users won't want to wait for the secondaries to pick up the new data—they'll want it available right away. (Are you wincing or nodding knowingly as you read this?) Can you force a secondary to load the new information right away? You can, but the system wasn't designed for it. If you really want all the name servers to be updated instantaneously, consider making all your servers primary name servers, transfering the db files to all the name server hosts with *rcp* or *rdist*, and signaling each primary to re-read the new data files. If you really, really want to force the secondary to load new data *just this one time*, remove all of the secondary's backup files (or just the ones you want to force), kill the secondary server and start up a new one. Since the backup files are gone, the secondary must immediately pull new copies of the zones.

To delete a host, remove the resource records from the *db.DOMAIN* and from each *db.ADDR* file pertaining to that host. Increment the serial number in each file you changed and restart your primary name server.

SOA Serial Numbers

Each of the DNS database files has a serial number. Every time the data in the db file is changed the serial number must be incremented. If the serial number is not incremented, secondary name servers for the zone will not pick up the updated data. The change is simple. If the original db file had the following SOA record:

```
movie.edu. IN SOA terminator.movie.edu. al.robocop.movie.edu. (
                    100      ; Serial
                    10800    ; Refresh
                    3600     ; Retry
                    604800   ; Expire
                    86400 )  ; Minimum TTL
```

the updated db file would have the following SOA record:

```
movie.edu. IN SOA terminator.movie.edu. al.robocop.movie.edu. (
                        101      ; Serial
                        10800    ; Refresh
                        3600     ; Retry
                        604800   ; Expire
                        86400 )  ; Minimum TTL
```

This simple change is the key to distributing the data to all of your secondaries. Failing to increment the serial number is the most common mistake made when updating a name server. The first few times you make a change to a DNS database file, you'll remember to update the serial number because this process is new and you are paying close attention. After the db file modifications become second nature, you'll make some "quickie" little change, forget to update the serial number... and none of the secondaries will pick up the new data. That's why you should use a tool that updates the serial number for you! Your tool could be *h2n*, SCCS, or something written locally, but use a tool.

Suppose you use SCCS. Here's an example of an SOA record that uses the SCCS branch for the serial number:

```
movie.edu. IN SOA terminator.movie.edu. al.robocop.movie.edu. (
                        %B%      ; Serial
                        10800    ; Refresh
                        3600     ; Retry
                        604800   ; Expire
                        86400 )  ; Minimum TTL
```

Each modification requires you to check out the file, make the modification, check in the file, and check out a new copy. SCCS updates the serial number for you using a dotted revision number. That's okay; BIND can accept the serial number with a single dot in it.

Here's how BIND version 4.8.3 and earlier handles decimal serial numbers. If there is a decimal point in the serial number, BIND multiplies the digits to the left of the decimal by 1000. The digits to the right of the decimal point are then concatenated to the digits on the left. Therefore, a number like 1.1 is converted to 10001 internally. 1.10 is converted to 100010. This creates certain anomalies; for example, 1.1 is "greater" than 2, and 1.10 is "greater" than 2.1. Because this is so counterintuitive, it's best to stick with integer serial numbers, unless you're using a tool like SCCS to handle the numbers for you. Don't be surprised if the handling of serial numbers with decimal points changes in later versions of BIND.

There are several good ways to manage integer serial numbers. The obvious way is just to use a counter: increment the serial number by one each time the file is modified. Another method is to derive the serial number from the date. For example, you could use the eight-digit number formed by *<year><month><day>*. Suppose today is January 15, 1992. In this form, your serial number would be 19920115. This scheme only allows one update per day, though, and that may not be enough. Add another digit to this number to indicate how many times the file has been updated that day. The first number for January 15, 1992, would then be 199201150. The next modification that day would change the serial number to 199201151. This scheme allows 10 updates per day. If you update your files more than 10 times a day, you are probably spending too much of your time on name server operation and need to streamline your update process. Whatever scheme you choose, the serial number must fit in a 32-bit integer.

What should you do if you started out using floating point numbers and now want to switch to integers? It isn't obvious, but it can be done. There are two ways to convert: an easy way and a hard way. The easier way is to change to the integer equivalent of your floating point number and continue from there. Look at the backup DNS database file on your secondary name server. The SOA record has the integer serial number. Replace the floating point number in your primary's db file with the integer version. The disadvantage to this method of conversion is that you'll be dealing with large integers from here on.

The harder way is to purge your secondaries of any knowledge of the old serial numbers. Then you can start numbering from one (or any convenient point). First, change the serial number on your primary server and restart it; now the primary server has the new integer serial numbers. Log onto one of your secondary name server hosts and kill the server process with the command **kill `cat /etc/named.pid`**. Remove its backup copies of the db files (i.e., **rm db.movie db.192.249.249 db.192.253.253**). Start up your secondary name server. Since the backup copies were removed, the secondary must load a new version of the DNS database files—picking up the new serial numbers. This process must be repeated for each secondary server. If there are any servers not under your control backing up your domains, you'll have to contact their administrators to get them to do the same.

Generating the BIND Database from the Host Tables

As you saw in Chapter 4, *Setting Up BIND*, we defined a well-structured process for converting host table information to name server information. We've written a tool in *perl* to automate this process, called *h2n*. Using a tool to generate your data has one big advantage: there will be no syntax errors or inconsistencies in your database files—assuming we wrote *h2n* correctly! One common inconsistency is having an A (address) record for a host, but no corresponding PTR (pointer) record or the other way around. Because these data are in separate files, it is easy to err.

What does *h2n* do? Given the */etc/hosts* file and some command line options, *h2n* creates the db files for your domain. As a system administrator, you keep the host table current. Each time you modify the host table, you run *h2n* again. *h2n* rebuilds each db file from scratch, assigning each new file the next higher serial number. It can be run manually, or from a *cron* script each night. If you use *h2n*, you'll never need to worry about forgetting to update the serial number.

First, *h2n* needs to know the name of your domain and your network numbers. These map conveniently into the db filenames; **movie.edu** data goes in *db.movie*; network 192.249.249 data goes into *db.192.249.249*. The domain name and network number are specified with the –d and –n flags, as follows:

–d *domain*   The name of your domain.

–n *network*   The network number of your network. If you are generating files for several networks, use several –n options on the command line. Omit trailing zeros from the network numbers.

The *h2n* command requires the –d flag, and at least one –n flag; they have no default values. For example, to create the BIND database for the domain **movie.edu**, which consists of two networks, give the command:

```
% h2n -d movie.edu -n 192.249.249 -n 192.253.253
```

For greater control over the data, you can use other options:

–s *server*   The servers for the NS records. As with –n, use several –s options if you have multiple primary or secondary master servers. This defaults to the host on which you run *h2n*.

–h *host*   The host for the SOA record. This defaults to the host on which you run *h2n*.

–u *user*   The mail address of the person in charge of the domain's data. This defaults to *root* on the host on which you run *h2n*.

-o *other*   Other SOA values, not including the serial number, as a colon-separated list. These default to 10800:3600:604800:86400.

-f *file*   Read the *h2n* options from the named *file*, rather from the command line. If you have lots of options, keep them in a file.

Here is an example that uses all the options mentioned so far:

```
% h2n -f opts
```

Contents of file *opts*:

```
-d movie.edu
-n 192.249.249
-n 192.253.253
-s terminator.movie.edu
-s wormhole
-u al
-h terminator
-o 10800:3600:604800:86400
```

If an option requires a host name, you can provide either a full domain name (e.g., **terminator.movie.edu**), or just the host's name (e.g., **terminator**). If you give the host name only, *h2n* will form a complete domain name by adding the domain name given with the **-d** option. (If a trailing dot is necessary on the name, *h2n* will add it also.)

There are more options to *h2n* than we've shown here. You'll see them used in the chapters discussing mail and parenting. For the complete list of options, you'll have to look at the manual page.

Of course, a few kinds of resource records aren't easy to generate from */etc/hosts*—the necessary data simply isn't there. You may need to add these records in manually. But since *h2n* always rewrites db files, won't your changes be overwritten?

h2n provides a "back door" for inserting this kind of data. Put these special records in a file named *spcl.DOMAIN*, where *DOMAIN* is the name of your domain. When *h2n* finds this file, it will "include" it within the database files by adding the line:

```
$INCLUDE spcl.DOMAIN
```

to the end of the db.DOMAIN file. (The $INCLUDE directive is described later in this chapter.) For example, the administrator of **movie.edu** may add extra MX records into the file *spcl.movie* so that users can mail to **movie.edu** directly instead of sending mail to hosts within **movie.edu**.

Upon finding this file, *h2n* would put the line:

```
$INCLUDE spcl.movie
```

at the end of the database file *db.movie.*

Keeping db.cache Current

As explained in Chapter 4, *Setting Up BIND*, the *db.cache* file tells your server where the servers for the "root" domain are. It must be updated periodically. The root name servers do not change very often, but they do change. A good practice is to check your *db.cache* file every month or two. In Chapter 4, we told you to get the servers by sending mail to **service@nic.ddn.mil** (with the subject line **netinfo root-servers.txt**). However, in that chapter, we were assuming that you didn't have a name server running. If you already have a working name server, you can use *nslookup*, which makes the job much easier. To look up the name servers for the root domain, give the following **nslookup** command:

```
% nslookup -type=ns . terp.umd.edu.
```

You can use any valid root name server instead of **terp.umd.edu**. You can also make this request interactively by using the following sequence of commands:

```
% nslookup
Default Server:  terminator.movie.edu
Address: 192.249.249.3

> server terp.umd.edu.
Server:  terp.umd.edu
Address:  128.8.10.90

> set type=ns
> .
Server:  terp.umd.edu
Address:  128.8.10.90

(root)   nameserver = NS.NIC.DDN.MIL
(root)   nameserver = AOS.BRL.MIL
(root)   nameserver = KAVA.NISC.SRI.COM
(root)   nameserver = C.NYSER.NET
(root)   nameserver = TERP.UMD.EDU
(root)   nameserver = NS.NASA.GOV
(root)   nameserver = NIC.NORDU.NET
NS.NIC.DDN.MIL  internet address = 192.112.36.4
AOS.BRL.MIL     internet address = 128.63.4.82
AOS.BRL.MIL     internet address = 26.3.0.29
AOS.BRL.MIL     internet address = 192.5.25.82
KAVA.NISC.SRI.COM      internet address = 192.33.33.24
```

```
C.NYSER.NET        internet address = 192.33.4.12
TERP.UMD.EDU       internet address = 128.8.10.90
NS.NASA.GOV        internet address = 128.102.16.10
NS.NASA.GOV        internet address = 192.52.195.10
NIC.NORDU.NET      internet address = 192.36.148.17
> ^D
```

Compare your *nslookup* output to the contents of your *db.cache* file, and update *db.cache* appropriately. (The nameserver lines in *nslookup* output map into NS records in *db.cache*; the internet address lines map into the address records.) If you want to automate this process, here's a shell script that looks up the root name servers and generates a *db.cache* file:

```
#!/bin/sh

ROOT=terp.umd.edu.
TMPFILE=/tmp/ns.$$
CACHETMP=/tmp/db.cache.tmp

#
# Look up root server information and store it in a temporary file.
#
nslookup >$TMPFILE <<-EOF
server $ROOT
set type=ns
.
EOF

#
# Generate the the db.cache file from the nslookup output.  Store
# it in a temporary file.
#
cat $TMPFILE | awk '
  /(root)/ {printf "%-20s 99999999 IN  NS %s.\n", ".", $NF}
  /address/ {printf "%-20s 99999999 IN  A  %s\n", $1 ".", $NF}
  ' > $CACHETMP

#
# Move the new db.cache in place if it is not empty.
#
if test -s $CACHETMP
then
  mv $CACHETMP db.cache
else
  rm $CACHETMP
fi

#
# Clean up.
#
rm $TMPFILE
```

db File Control Entries

Two *control* entries are allowed in the DNS database files: *$ORIGIN* and *$INCLUDE.* $ORIGIN changes the origin, and $INCLUDE inserts a new file into the current file. The control entries are not resource records; they facilitate the maintenance of DNS data. In particular, these directives make it easier for you to divide your domain into subdomains: they allow you to store the data for each subdomain in a separate database file.

Changing the Origin

With BIND, the default origin for the DNS database files is the second field of the `primary` or `secondary` line in the *named.boot* file. The origin is a domain name that is appended automatically to all names not ending in a dot. This origin can be changed in the db file with $ORIGIN. In the db file, $ORIGIN is followed by a domain name. (Don't forget the trailing dot if you give the full domain name!) From this point on, all names not ending in a dot have the new origin appended. If your name server (e.g., **movie.edu**) is responsible for a number of subdomains, you can use the $ORIGIN entry to reset the origin and simplify the files. For example:

```
$ORIGIN classics.movie.edu.
maltese      IN  A  192.253.253.100
casablanca   IN  A  192.253.253.101

$ORIGIN comedy.movie.edu.
mash         IN  A  192.253.253.200
twins        IN  A  192.253.253.201
```

We'll cover more on creating subdomains in Chapter 9, *Parenting.*

Including Other Database Files

Once you've subdivided your domain like this, you might find it more convenient to keep the subdomain records in separate files. The $INCLUDE statement lets you do this:

```
$ORIGIN classics.movie.edu.
$INCLUDE db.classics

$ORIGIN comedy.movie.edu.
$INCLUDE db.comedy
```

To simplify the file even further, the new origin can be specified on the $INCLUDE line:

```
$INCLUDE db.classics classics.movie.edu.
$INCLUDE db.comedy  comedy.movie.edu.
```

When you specify the origin on the $INCLUDE line, it only applies to the particular file that you're including. For example, the **comedy.movie.edu** origin only applies to the names in *db.comedy*. After *db.comedy* has been included, the origin returns to what it was before $INCLUDE, even if there was an $ORIGIN entry within *db.comedy*.

There is a bug in the 4.8.3 version of BIND that you might trip across if you use $INCLUDE: the SOA record was not allowed in the included file. No doubt this will be fixed in later releases.

Additional Boot File Directives

We've already talked about the *directory, primary, secondary,* and *cache* boot file directives. There are a couple other dials and buttons we haven't told you about that help you solve specific problems: when you need your name server to return addresses in a certain order for multi-homed hosts or you need to limit the traffic that goes off your network because of delays or costs. Both of these problems can be solved with additional boot file directives.

Address Sorting

When you are contacting a host that has multiple network interfaces, using one of the interfaces may give you better performance. If the multi-homed host is local and shares a network with your host, one of the multi-homed host's addresses is "closer." If the multi-homed host is remote, there *may* be a performance gain by using one of the interfaces instead of another, but often it doesn't matter much which address is used. In days past, net 10 (the former ARPANET "backbone") was always closer than any other remote address. The Internet has improved drastically since those days, so you won't often see a marked improvement by preferring one network over another for remote multi-homed hosts, but we'll cover that case anyway.

Local Multi-homed Hosts

Let's deal with the local multi-homed host first. Suppose you have a source host (i.e., a host that keeps your master sources) on two networks, cleverly called network A and network B, and this host uses NFS to export filesystems to hosts on both networks. Hosts on network A will experience better performance if they use the source host's interface to network A. Likewise, hosts on network B would benefit from using the source host's interface to network B for the address of the NFS mount.

In Chapter 4, *Setting Up BIND*, we mentioned that BIND returns all the addresses for a multi-homed host. There was no guarantee of the order in which a DNS server would return the addresses, so we assigned aliases (**wh249** and **wh253** for **wormhole**) to the individual interfaces. If one interface was preferable, you (or more realistically, a DNS client) could use an appropriate alias to get the correct address. Aliases *can* be used to choose the "closer" interface (e.g., for setting up NFS mounts), but because of address sorting, they are not always necessary.

BIND, by default, sorts addresses if one condition holds: if the host that sent the query to the name server *shares* a network with the name server host (e.g., both are on network A), then BIND sorts the addresses in the response. How does BIND know when it shares a network with the querier? It knows because when BIND starts up, it finds out all the interface addresses of the host it is running on. BIND extracts the network numbers from these addresses to create the default sort list. When a query is received, BIND checks if the sender's address is on a network in the default sort list. If it is, then the query is local and BIND sorts the addresses in the response.

In Figure 7.1, assume the name server is on **notorious**. The name server's default sort list would contain network A and network B. When **spellbound** sends a query to **notorious** looking up the addresses of **notorious**, it will get an answer back with **notorious'** network A address first. That's because **notorious** and **spellbound** share network A. When **charade** looks up the addresses of **notorious**, it will get an answer back with **notorious'** network B address first. Both hosts are on network B. In both of these

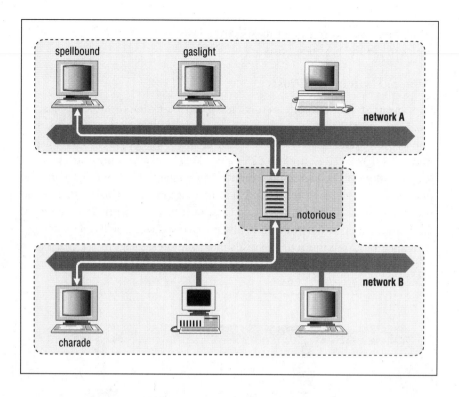

Figure 7.1: Communicating with a local multi-homed host

cases, the name server sorts the addresses in the response because the hosts share a network with the name server host. The sorted address list has the "closer" interface first.

Let's change the situation slightly. Suppose the name server is running on **gaslight**. When **spellbound** queries **gaslight** for **notorious**' address, **spellbound** will see the same response as in the last case because **spellbound** and **gaslight** share network A, which means the name server will sort the response. However, **charade** may see a different response since it does not share a network with **gaslight**. The closer address for **notorious** may still be first in the response to **charade**, but only because of luck, not name server address sorting. In this case, you'd have to run an additional name server on network B for **charade** to benefit from address sorting.

As you can see, you benefit by running a name server on each network: not only is your name server available if your router goes down, it also sorts addresses of multi-homed hosts. Because the name server sorts addresses, you do not need to specify aliases for NFS mounts or network logins to get the best response.

Remote Multi-homed Hosts

Suppose that your site often contacts a particular remote site or a "distant" local site, and that you get better performance by favoring addresses on one of the remote site's networks. For instance, the **movie.edu** domain has networks 192.249.249 and 192.253.253. Let's add a connection to net 10 (the old ARPANET). The remote host being contacted has two network connections, one to network 10 and one to network 26. This host does not route to network 26, but for special reasons it has a network 26 connection. Since the router to network 26 is always overloaded, you'll get better performance by using the remote host's net 10 address. Figure 7.2 is a picture of the situation.

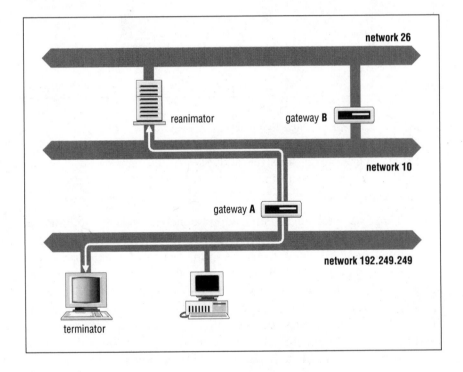

Figure 7.2: Communicating with a remote multi-homed host

If a user on **terminator** is contacting **reanimator**, it's preferable to use the network 10 address because access through **gateway B** to the network 26 address will be slower. Unfortunately, the name server running on **termina-tor** will not *intentionally* place network address 10 first in the list when it looks up the addresses for **reanimator**; the only network that **terminator** is attached to is 192.249.249 and so it doesn't know that network 10 is "closer" than network 26. This is where the *sortlist* boot file entry comes into play. To indicate a preference for network 10 addresses, add the following line to */etc/named.boot*:

```
sortlist 10.0.0.0
```

The *sortlist* entries are *appended* to the default sort list. With this *sortlist* entry, the sort list on **terminator** now contains networks 192.249.249 and 10. Now, when a user on **terminator** queries the name server on **termina-tor**, and the name server sorts the response because the query is local, the name server will check for addresses on the 192.249.249 network and place them first in the response. If there are no addresses on network 192.249.249, it will check for network 10 addresses and place them first in the response. This solves the problem we described earlier—when **reani-mator** is looked up, its network 10 address will be placed first in the response.

Address Sorting on Subnetted Networks

Subnetted networks change address sorting only slightly. When the name server creates its default sort list, it adds both the subnet number and the network number to the list. Like before, when the query is local and the name server sorts the response, the common subnet address will be placed first. Unfortunately, not everything is perfect—you can't add *sortlist* entries for other subnets of your network. Here's why: the name server assumes all the *sortlist* entries are network numbers (not subnet numbers) and your network number is already on the sort list. Since your network number is already on the list, the subnet *sortlist* entry is discarded.

Multiple Sortlist Entries

One last thing—if you want to add more than one *sortlist* entry, you must specify them all on the same line like this:

```
sortlist 10.0.0.0 26.0.0.0
```

Building up a Large Site-wide Cache with Forwarders

Certain network connections discourage sending large volumes of traffic off-site, either because the network connection is pay-by-packet or the network connection is a slow link with a high delay, like a remote office's satellite connection to their company's network. In these situations, you'll want to limit the off-site DNS traffic to the bare minimum. BIND provides a mechanism to do this: *forwarders.*

If you designate one or more servers at your site as forwarders, all the off-site queries are sent to the forwarders first. The idea is that the forwarders handle all the off-site queries generated at the site, building up a rich cache of information. For any given query in a remote domain, there is a high probability that the forwarder can answer the query from its cache, avoiding the need for the other servers to send packets off-site. Nothing special is done to these servers to make them forwarders; you modify all the *other servers* at your site to direct their queries through the forwarders.

A primary or secondary name server's mode of operation changes slightly when it is directed to use a forwarder. If the requested information is already in its database of authoritative data and cache data, it answers with this information; this part of the operation hasn't changed. However, if the information is not in its database, the name server will send the query to a forwarder and wait a short period for an answer before resuming normal operation and contacting the remote servers itself. What the name server is doing different is that it is sending a *recursive* query to the forwarder, expecting it to find the answer. At all other times, the name server sends out *non-recursive* queries to other name servers and deals with responses that only refer to other name servers.

Here is an example *forwarders* boot file directive for name servers in the **movie.edu** domain. Both **wormhole** and **terminator** are the site forwarders. This *forwarders* directive is added to every name server boot file *except* the boot files for the forwarders, **wormhole** and **terminator**.

```
forwarders 192.249.249.1 192.249.249.3
```

When you use forwarders, though, try to keep your site configuration simple. You *can* end up with configurations that are really twisted.

- Avoid having "mid-level" servers forward packets (i.e., avoid having a *forwarders* line in your mid-level name server's boot file). Mid-level servers mostly refer name servers to subdomain name servers. If they were configured to forward packets, do they refer to subdomain name servers or do they contact the subdomain name server to find out the answer? Whichever way it works, you're probably making your site configuration too hard for mere mortals (and subdomain administrators) to understand.

- Avoid chaining your forwarders. Don't configure server A to forward to server B and configure server B to forward to server C (or worse yet, back to server A).

A More Restricted Name Server

You may want to restrict your name servers even further—stopping them from even *trying* to contact an off-site server. You can do this by making the server a *slave* server. (A slave server is still a primary, secondary, or caching-only server; don't get confused here. We call it a slave server because calling it a primary, secondary, or caching-only slave server is just too long of a name.) A *slave* server is a variation on a server that uses *forwarders*. It still answers queries from its authoritative data and cache data. However, it relies *completely* on the forwarders; it *doesn't* try to contact other servers to find out information if the forwarders don't give it an answer. Here is an example of what a slave server's boot file would contain:

```
forwarders 192.249.249.1 192.249.249.3
slave
```

You must have the *forwarders* line in the boot file. It does not make sense to have only the *slave* line. If you do create a slave name server, you might want to consider including the forwarders more than once:

```
forwarders 192.249.249.1 192.249.249.3 192.249.249.1 192.249.249.3
slave
```

The slave server contacts each forwarder only once and it waits a short time for the forwarder to respond. Listing the forwarders multiple times directs the slave to *retransmit* queries to the forwarders, and increases the overall length of time that the slave name server will wait for an answer from a forwarder.

However, you must ask yourself if it *ever* makes sense to use a slave server. A slave server is completely dependent on the forwarders. You can achieve much the same configuration (and dependence) by not running a slave server at all; instead, create a *resolv.conf* file that contains *nameserver* lines that point to the forwarders you were using. Thus, you are still relying on the forwarders, but now your applications are querying the forwarders directly instead of having a slave name server query them for the applications. You lose the local caching that the slave server would have done and the address sorting, but you reduce the overall complexity of your site configuration by running fewer "restricted" name servers.

Keeping Everything Running Smoothly

A significant part of maintenance is being aware when something has gone wrong before it becomes a real problem. If you catch a problem early, chances are it'll be that much easier to fix. As the old adage says, an ounce of prevention is worth a pound of cure.

This isn't quite troubleshooting—we'll devote an entire chapter to troubleshooting later—think of it as "pre-troubleshooting." Troubleshooting (the pound of cure) is what you have to do if you ignore maintenance, after your problem has developed complications, and you need to identify the problem by its symptoms.

The next two sections deal with preventative maintenance: looking periodically at the *syslog* file and at the BIND name server statistics to see whether or not any problems are developing. Consider this a name server's medical checkup.

Common Syslog Error Messages

There are a large number of syslog messages *named* can emit. In practice, you'll only see a few of them. We'll cover the most common syslog messages here, excluding reports of syntax errors in DNS database files.

Every time you start *named*, it sends out this message at level LOG_NOTICE:

```
Jan 10 20:48:32 terminator named[3221]: restarted
```

This message just logs the fact that *named* started at this time. This is, of course, nothing to be concerned about.

Every time you send the name server a HUP signal, it sends out this message at level LOG_NOTICE:

```
Jan 10 20:50:16 terminator named[3221]: reloading nameserver
```

The "reloading" message just tells you that *named* reloaded its database (as a result of a HUP signal) at this time. Again, this is nothing to be concerned about. This message will most likely be of interest when you are tracking down how long a bad resource record has been in your name server data or how long a whole zone has been missing because of a mistake during an update.

Another syslog message, sent at LOG_ERR, is a warning message about the zone data:

```
Jan 10 20:48:38 terminator named[3221]: terminator2 has CNAME
                  and other data (illegal)
```

This message means that there's a problem with your zone data. For example, you may have entries like these:

```
terminator2  IN  CNAME t2
terminator2  IN  MX    10 t2
t2           IN  A     192.249.249.10
t2           IN  MX    10 t2
```

The MX record for **terminator2** is incorrect, and would cause the message given above. **terminator2** is an alias for **t2**, which is the canonical name. As described earlier, when DNS looks up a name and finds a CNAME, it replaces the original name with the canonical name, and then tries looking up the canonical name. Thus, when the server looks up the MX data for **terminator2**, it finds a CNAME record, and then looks up the MX record for **t2**. Since the server follows the CNAME record for **terminator2**, it will never use the MX record for **terminator2**; in fact, this record is illegal. In other words, all resource records for a host have to use the *canonical name*; it's an error to use an alias in place of the canonical name.

The following message indicates that a secondary was unable to reach any master server when it tried to do a zone load:

```
Jan 10 20:52:42 wormhole named[2813]: zoneref: Masters for
                  secondary zone movie.edu unreachable
```

This message is sent at level LOG_WARNING, and is only sent the first time the zone load fails. When the zone load finally succeeds, there is no syslog message to indicate success. No more syslog messages are sent until the zone expires, even if the load continues to fail. When this message first appears, you don't need to take any immediate action. The name server will continue to attempt to load the zone, according to the retry period in the SOA record. After a few days (or half the expire time), you might check that the server was able to load the zone. You can do this by checking the timestamp on the backup file. When a zone load succeeds, a new backup file is created. When a zone is found to be up-to-date, the backup file is *touched* (a la the UNIX *touch* command). In both cases, the timestamp on the backup file is updated, so go to the secondary and give the command **ls -l /usr/local/named/db.***. This will tell you when the secondary last synchronized each zone with the master server. We'll cover how to troubleshoot secondaries failing to load zones in Chapter 12, *Troubleshooting DNS and BIND*.

The last of the common syslog messages is only seen if you capture LOG_INFO syslog messages:

```
Jan 10 20:52:42 wormhole named[2813]: Malformed response
               from 192.1.1.1
```

Most often, this message means that some bug in a name server caused it to send an erroneous response packet. The error probably occurred on the remote name server (192.1.1.1) rather than the local server (**wormhole**). Diagnosing this kind of error involves capturing the response packet in a network trace and decoding it. Decoding DNS packets manually is beyond the scope of this book. But without going into much detail, you would see this type of error when the response packet says it has several answers in the answer section (like four address resource records) and yet the answer section only contains a single answer. The only course of action is to notify the postmaster (or root) of the offending host via e-mail (assuming you can get the name of the host by looking up the address). You would also see this message if the underlying network altered (damaged) the UDP response packets in some way. Checksumming of UDP packets is optional, so this error might not be caught at a lower level.

Understanding the BIND Statistics

Periodically, you should look over the statistics on some of your name servers, if only to see how busy they are. The statistics can sometimes uncover problems that need further attention. We will show you an example of the name server statistics and discuss what each line means. Name servers handle many queries and responses during normal operation, so first we need to show you what a typical exchange might look like.

Reading the explanations for the statistics is hard without a mental picture of what goes on during a lookup. To help you understand the name server's statistics, Figure 7.3 shows what might go on when an application tries to look up a name. The application, *ftp*, queries a local name server. The local name server had previously looked up data from this domain and knows where the remote name servers are. It queries each of the remote name servers—one of them twice—trying to find the answer. In the meantime, the application times out and sends yet another query, asking for the same information.

Keep in mind that even though a name server sends a query to a remote name server, the remote name server may not receive the query right away. The query might be delayed by the underlying network or, perhaps, the remote name server host might not pass the query immediately to the name server process because it is inactive and swapped out to disk.

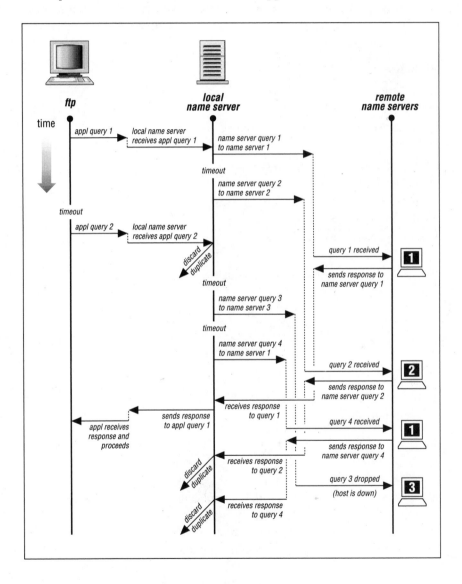

Figure 7.3: Example query/response exchange

Notice that a BIND name server is only able to detect duplicate queries while it is still trying to answer the original query. The local name server detects the duplicate query from the application because the local name server is still working on it. But, remote name server 1 does not detect the duplicate query from the local name server because it answered the previous query. After the local name server receives the first response from remote name server 1, all other responses are discarded as duplicates. This dialog required the following exchanges:

Exchange	Number
Application to local name server	2 queries
Local name server to application	1 response
Local name server to remote name server 1	2 queries
Remote name server 1 to local name server	2 responses
Local name server to remote name server 2	1 query
Remote name server 2 to local name server	1 response
Local name server to remote name server 3	1 query
Remote name server 3 to local name server	0 responses

These exchanges would make the following contributions to the local name server's statistics:

Statistic	Cause
5 input packets	2 queries + 3 query responses
5 output packets	4 queries + 1 query response
2 queries	From the application
1 duplicate query	From the application
3 responses	From remote name servers
2 duplicate responses	From remote name servers
1 OK answers	Sent to the application
1 A queries	Queries for address information

In our example, the local name server only received queries from an application, yet it sent queries to remote name servers. Normally, the local name server would also receive queries from remote name servers (that is, in addition to asking remote servers for information it needs to know, remote servers would be asking the local server for information they need to know), but we didn't show any remote queries, for the sake of simplicity.

Now that you've seen a typical exchange between applications and name servers and the statistics it generated, let's go over a more extensive example of the statistics. To get the statistics from your name server, send the name server an ABRT signal (on many systems, called IOT):

```
% kill -ABRT `cat /etc/named.pid`
```

Wait a few seconds and look at the file */usr/tmp/named.stats*. If the statistics are not dumped to this file, your server may not have been compiled with STATS defined and, thus, may not be collecting statistics. Here are the statistics from one of our name servers:

```
###  Mon Dec  9 10:11:50 1991
1443325  time since boot (secs)
1443325  time since reset (secs)
325802   input packets
326871   output packets
277054   queries
0        iqueries
56       duplicate queries
48819    responses
162      duplicate responses
273807   OK answers
3191     FAIL answers
0        FORMERR answers
66       system queries
7        prime cache calls
6        check_ns calls
94       bad responses dropped
107      martian responses
0        Unknown query types
113088   A queries
15       NS queries
2        CNAME queries
6        SOA queries
5        WKS queries
159077   PTR queries
451      MX queries
4410     ANY queries
```

Let's look at these statistics one line at a time. At the end of this section, we'll discuss some "red flags" to look for and what you can do about them.

```
1443325   time since boot (secs)
```

This is how long the local name server has been running. To convert to days, divide by 86400 (60*60*24, the number of seconds in a day). This server has been running for a bit more than 16 days.

```
1443325   time since reset (secs)
```

This is how long the local name server has run since the last HUP signal—i.e., the last time it loaded its database. You'll probably only see this number differ from the `time since boot` if the server is a primary name server. Secondary name servers automatically pick up new data with zone transfers and are not usually sent HUP signals. Since *this* server hasn't been restarted for 16 days, it is probably a secondary name server.

```
325802    input packets
```

The local name server has received 325802 UDP datagrams. These datagrams include:

- Queries from applications and remote name servers
- Query responses from remote name servers

```
326871    output packets
```

The local name server has sent 326871 UDP datagrams. This number *can be* larger than the number of input packets (as it is here). Some queries made to remote name servers may not be answered; the local name server may have to send out several queries to get a single response. The local name server may also initiate queries of its own (e.g., queries to find out who the name servers are for the root domain, and what their addresses are). Thus, the local name server may send out more UDP datagrams than it receives. If the number of output packets is considerably larger than the number of input packets, you may have a problem to look into like a break in network connectivity.

```
277054    queries
```

These are the queries received by the local name server. Queries may come from applications or from remote name servers. The number of queries *may be* larger than the number of input packets because some of the queries are made over TCP connections instead of in UDP packets; the DNS protocol allows both.

```
0         iqueries
```

Inverse queries were originally intended to map addresses to names. The local name server would get a packet saying "the answer is address X, what was the question?" (sort of like playing Jeopardy, huh?) The server would then look up the name for address X. Mapping addresses to names is now handled by PTR records, so not many inverse queries are issued these days. Older versions of *nslookup* use an inverse query on startup, so you may see a few iqueries.

```
56      duplicate queries
```

It may take the local name server a while to look up an answer from a remote name server. During this period, the *application* that generated the original query may retransmit the same query to the local name server, as we saw in the sample exchange. Since the local name server is still working on the original query, the retransmitted query is counted as a duplicate and dropped.

```
48819   responses
```

This statistic reports the number of responses that the local name server received from remote name servers.

```
162     duplicate responses
```

Since the local name server may retransmit the same query several times to a remote name server (as we saw in the sample exchange), it may receive a response to each one of its retransmitted queries. After the first response is received from the remote name server, each subsequent response to the same query is counted as a duplicate.

```
273807  OK answers
```

The local name server issued 273807 "OK" responses to the queries it received. A response is not OK when there is a format error (FORMERR), server failure (SERVFAIL), no such domain (NXDOMAIN), not implemented (NOTIMP), or refused (REFUSED) return code in the response. An OK response means the name exists. It does not necessarily mean that there is data of the requested type (e.g., MX).

```
3191    FAIL answers
```

FAIL answers mean the name does not exist, or that there was some sort of server failure. Therefore, this figure includes all kinds of errors (server failure, no such domain, not implemented, refused) except for format errors. In many cases, the name that doesn't exist (NXDOMAIN response) is a name like **foo.sub.company.com.company.com** generated by the resolver search algorithm. In other cases, the fail answer results from a user mistyping a name.

```
0        FORMERR answers
```

FORMERR answers occur when:

- The DNS query packet from an application violated the DNS protocol resulting in the local name server sending a FORMERR response.
- The DNS query packet from a remote name server violated the DNS protocol resulting in the local name server sending a FORMERR response.
- The DNS response packet from a remote name server violated the DNS protocol; as a result, the response was dropped. Since the format error was in a *response* packet and not a *query* packet, there is no point in sending back a FORMERR response.

If the packet is a DNS *query* packet, the only way to track down the error and the offender is to turn on debugging (at level one). If the packet is a *query response*, a syslog message is issued as well as a debug level one message. As you might guess (since it generates a syslog message), most of the FORMERRs are in response packets from remote name servers. The likely reason for the erroneous DNS packet is a defect in the remote name server implementation or a defect in the resolver code compiled into the application. The less likely (but still possible) reason for the FORMERR is that the UDP packet was altered in transit.

```
66       system queries
```

System queries are queries *initiated* by the local name server. For example, on startup the local name server sends out an NS query (a query for NS records) to discover which name servers are currently authoritative for the root domain. No application process requested this information about the root domain; therefore it is a "system query."

System queries also occur when the local name server sends out an address query for a remote name server, in order to satisfy an application's query for data within a domain served by the remote name server. A domain has several NS records listing remote name servers. The address records for those name servers are in separate resource records. These address records may have timed out (their TTLs decremented to zero) even though the NS records are still valid. Thus, to query the remote name server, the local name server has to look up the remote name server's address.

The local server's request for the remote server's address is a "system query" because it was initiated locally. The local server's subsequent request for information about the remote domain is not a system query, because a client requested the data. If you understand this, you understand the distinction between system queries and other queries.

```
7        prime cache calls
```

Priming the cache means using the hints provided in *db.cache* to find out the current root name server list (i.e., making an NS query for the domain "."). Every now and then, the root server's NS records time out. When this happens, the cache has to be primed again; this results in a system query.

```
6        check_ns calls
```

This statistic reports the number of times the name server made sure that it had an address for every root name server. If an address is missing (because the address timed out before the NS record did), then the name server issues a system query to find out the address.

```
94       bad responses dropped
```

This is the number of responses that the server received from other (remote) servers that it discarded for one reason or another. There are several reasons for a DNS response from a remote name server to be labelled "bad." The only way to track down the cause of the error is to turn on debugging at level two or above. Here's a list of reasons for the bad responses counter to be incremented. In each case, the packet being referred to is a response from a remote name server.

- The return code in the packet is SERVFAIL. This indicates some sort of server failure. Server failure responses often occur because the remote server read a db file and found a syntax error. Any queries for data in that domain (the one from the erroneous db file) will result in a server failure answer from the remote name server. This is probably the most common bad response. Server failure responses also occur when the remote name server tries to allocate more memory and can't, or the remote name server's domain data expires.

- The return code in the packet is FORMERR. The remote name server said the local name server's query was bad; in turn, this indicates a defect in the local name server's implementation. Note that this isn't related to the FORMERR statistic; that is incremented when the local name server declares the application's or remote name server's query in error. Here, we're talking about bad queries that the local server generated, which (in turn) led to a FORMERR response.

- The remote name server sent a response saying that the name doesn't exist (return code is NXDOMAIN), but the remote server doesn't indicate that it is authoritative for the domain (by setting the authority bit in the response). A name server is authoritative when it reads the SOA record from the db file. This bad response indicates a defect in the remote server's implementation.

- The response packet's opcode wasn't "query." For standard DNS, the only valid opcode choices are "query" and "inverse query." The local name server doesn't send inverse queries to remote name servers, and thus it should never get an inverse query response. (There are a few other non-standard opcodes for experimental dynamic update capability, but very few sites use the dynamic update code.) This bad response indicates a defect in the remote server's implementation or, perhaps, someone experimenting with new name server functionality.

```
107     martian responses
```

Didn't know your server sent queries to Mars, did you? A martian response is a response that came from an address your local name server didn't send to. It's like ordering a book from a bookstore in Atlanta and receiving the book in the mail from a bookstore in Denver. If the local name server sent a query to a remote name server at address X, the local name server received a response from address Y, and the local name server didn't know the remote host *had* an address Y, then the local name server considers the response "martian." Instead of trusting the response, the local server drops it. There shouldn't be many martian responses. BIND makes every attempt to send back the response with the same return address as the query was sent to. As you can see from the non-zero count, though, the Internet world isn't perfect.

```
0       Unknown query types
```

There is a well-known set of query types. If this number is non-zero, someone must be experimenting with new types, or there is a defective implementation somewhere.

```
113088  A queries
```

There have been 113088 address lookups. Address queries are normally the most common type of query.

```
15      NS queries
```

There have been 15 name server queries. Name servers only generate NS queries when they are trying to look up servers for the root domain. Since the local name server is not a name server for the root domain, this probably means that someone is looking up NS records interactively, with a tool like *dig* or *nslookup*.

```
2       CNAME queries
```

Some versions of *sendmail* make CNAME queries in order to canonicalize a mail address (replace an alias with the canonical name). Other versions of *sendmail* use ANY queries instead (see below). Otherwise, the CNAME lookups are most likely from *dig* or *nslookup*.

```
6       SOA queries
```

SOA queries are made by secondary name servers to check if their zone data are current. If the data are not current, an AXFR query follows to cause the zone transfer. Since this set of statistics does not show any AXFR queries, we can conclude that this server is not a master for any secondary name servers; i.e., no secondary name servers load zone data from this server. The SOA queries counted here are either from someone interactively looking up SOA records, or a support tool looking up SOA records. Support tools can help keep the DNS system running smoothly by checking that each name server *is* authoritative for the domains it is supposed to be authoritative for.

```
5       WKS queries
```

The well-known services queries are most likely from someone interactively looking up WKS records.

```
159077  PTR queries
```

The pointer queries map addresses to names. Many kinds of software look up IP addresses: *inetd, rlogind, rshd*, network management software, network tracing software. In this set of statistics, there have been more PTR queries than address queries. Most name servers will see more address (A) queries than PTR queries. A greater number of PTR queries may mean that this host is a network management station, a network traffic monitor, or a mail hub that receives more mail than it sends out.

```
451     MX queries
```

Mail exchanger queries are made by mailers like *sendmail* as part of the normal electronic mail delivery process.

```
4410    ANY queries
```

ANY queries request data of any type for a name. This query type is used most often by *sendmail*. Since *sendmail* looks up CNAME, MX, and address records for a mail destination, it will make a query for ANY data type so that all the resource records are cached right away at the local name server.

Overall, the statistics generated by this name server indicate the server is healthy. How do you know what "healthy" operation is? You have to watch the statistics generated by your server over a period of time to get a feel for what sorts of numbers are normal for your configuration. These numbers will vary markedly depending on the mix of applications generating lookups, the type of server (primary, secondary, caching-only), and the level in the domain tree it is serving.

There are several things you can watch for in the statistics. Keep track of how many queries per second your name server typically answers. This name server is handling one query every five seconds on average. This seems quite reasonable for a secondary server handling a few hosts and serving only "bottom-level" domains (i.e., it's not a "mid-level" server). The number of FAIL answers looks reasonable; there will always be names mistyped or other data that can't be looked up because there is no name server answering for it. A "mid-level" name server (like **hp.com**) receives lots of queries for names like **foo.sub.hp.com.hp.com** because of the resolver search algorithm, driving up the number of FAIL answers. There were no FORMERR answers, so we don't have to track down protocol violations. We would be a little concerned about the number of "bad responses dropped" and "martian responses." To check out the bad responses dropped, we would turn on name server debugging to level two for half hour periods and look for the packets that are dropped because of an error. The martian responses will also require name server debugging, but only at level one. See Chapter 11, *Reading BIND Debugging Output*, for details on reading the debugging output.

You might wonder why we didn't flag the duplicate queries and responses—there were some counted in the statistics. The duplicates are not something to be alarmed about unless they seem excessive and, again, you won't know what excessive is until you get a feel for what normal statistics are for your server. As our example exchange showed earlier, duplicates are part of normal operation. DNS primarily uses UDP, which is an unreliable protocol, so resolvers and name servers re-send queries anticipating that some datagrams will be lost. You could see a high number of duplicate queries if your network was cut off from the rest of the Internet for a long period of time, but you won't need to check the name server statistics to figure that problem out.

8

Growing Your Domain

"What size do you want to be?" it asked.

"Oh, I'm not particular as to size," Alice hastily replied; "only one doesn't like changing so often, you know . . . "

"Are you content now?" said the Caterpillar.

*"Well, I should like to be a **little** larger, sir, if you wouldn't mind . . . . "*

How Many Name Servers?

We set up two name servers in Chapter 4, *Setting Up BIND*. Two servers are as few as you'll ever want to run. Depending on the size of your network, you may need to run many more than just two servers. It is not uncommon to run from five to seven servers with one of them off-site. How many name servers are enough? You'll have to decide that based on your network. Here are some guidelines to help out:

1. Have at least one name server available directly on each network or subnet you have. This removes routers as a failure point. Make the most of any multi-homed hosts you may have, since they're (by definition) attached to more than one network.

2. If you have a file server and some diskless nodes, run a name server on the file server to serve this group of machines.

3. Run name servers on large time-sharing machines. The users and their processes probably generate a lot of queries, and, as administrators, you will work harder to keep a multi-user host up.

4. Run one name server off-site. This makes your data available when your network isn't. You might argue that it's useless to look up an address when you can't reach the host. Then again, the off-site name server may be available if your network is reachable, but your name server is down.

Figure 8-1 shows a sample topology and a brief analysis to show you how this might work:

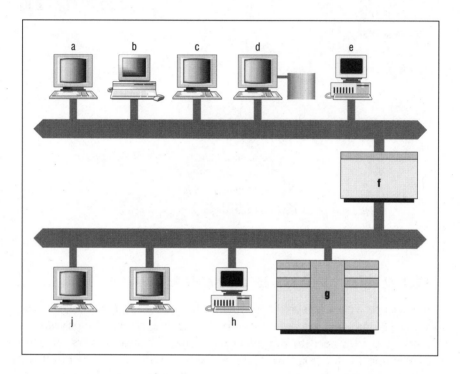

Figure 8.1: Sample network topology

Notice that if you follow our guidelines, there are still a number of places you could choose to run a name server. Host **d**, the file server for hosts **a**, **b**, **c**, and **e**, could run a name server. Host **g**, a big, multi-user host, is another good candidate. But probably the best choice is host **f**, the smaller multi-user system with interfaces on both networks. You'll only need to run one name server, instead of two, and it'll run on a closely-watched host. If you want more than one name server on either network, you can also run one on **d** or **g**.

Where Do I Put My Name Servers?

In addition to giving you a rough idea of how many name servers you'll need, these criteria should also help you decide *where* to run name servers (e.g., on file servers, large time-sharing machines). But there are other important considerations when choosing the right host.

Other factors to keep in mind are the host's connectivity, the software it runs (BIND and otherwise), and maintaining the homogeneity of your name servers:

Connectivity   It's important that name servers be well-connected. Having a name server running on the fastest, most reliable host on your network won't do you any good if the host is mired in some backwater subnet of your network behind a slow, flaky serial line. Try to find a host close to your link to the Internet (if you have one), or find a well-connected Internet host to act as a secondary for your domain. And on your own network, try to run name servers near your network hubs.

It's doubly important that your primary master name server be well-connected. The primary needs good connectivity to all the secondaries that update from it, for reliable zone transfers. And, like any name server, it'll benefit from fast, reliable networking.

Software   Another factor to consider in choosing a host for a name server is the software the host runs. Software-wise, the best candidate for a name server is a host running a vendor-supported version of 4.8.3 BIND or later and a robust implementation of TCP/IP (preferably based on 4.3 BSD UNIX's networking—we're Berkeley snobs). Compiling your own 4.8.3 BIND from the sources—while instructive—may not leave you with a particularly hardy product, and you'll probably have a tough time getting your vendor to support it. A reliable port of older BIND code, like 4.8 or 4.8.1, may not be as feature-rich as the latest bits, but if it's supported by your vendor, may be worth the sacrifice in functionality.

Homogeneity   One last thing to take into account is the homogeneity of your name servers. As much as you might believe in "open systems," hopping between different versions of UNIX can be frustrating and confusing. Avoid running

> name servers on lots of different platforms if you can.
> You can waste a lot of time porting your scripts (or ours!)
> from one operating system to another or looking for the
> location of *nslookup* or *named.boot* on three different
> UNIXes.

Though these are really secondary considerations—it's more important to
have a name server on a given subnet than to have it running on the perfect
host—do keep these criteria in mind when making a choice.

Capacity Planning

If you have heavily-populated networks, or users who do a lot of name-
server-intensive work, you may find you need more name servers than
what we've recommended to handle the load. Or our recommendations
may be fine for a little while, but as people add hosts to your nets or install
new name server-intensive programs, you may find your name servers
bogged down by queries.

Just which tasks are "name server-intensive"? Sending electronic mail,
especially to large mailing lists, can be name server-intensive. Programs
that make lots of remote procedure calls to different hosts can be name-
server-intensive. Even running certain graphical user environments can tax
your name server. X Window based user environments query the name
server to check access lists (among other things).

The astute (and precocious) among you may be asking, "But how do I
know when my name servers are overloaded? What do I look for?" An
excellent question!

One criterion you can use to measure the load on your name server is the
load the name server process places on the host's CPU. Programs like *top**
can help you characterize your name server's average CPU utilization.
Unfortunately, there are no absolute rules when it comes to acceptable CPU
utilization. We offer a rough rule of thumb, though: 5% average CPU utilization is probably acceptable; 10% is a bit high, unless the host is dedicated
to providing name service. Memory utilization is also important. *named*
can get very large on a name server authoritative for many domains. If
named's size, plus the size of the other processes you run, exceeds your

---

* *top* is a very handy program written by Bill LeFebvre that gives you a continuous report of
which processes are sucking up the most CPU time on your host. The most recent version of
top is available via anonymous *ftp* from **eecs.nwu.edu** as */pub/top/top-3.0.tar.Z*.

real memory, your host may swap furiously ("thrash") and not get anything done. Even if your host has more than enough memory to run all its processes, large name servers are slow to start and slow to spawn new *named* processes (e.g., to handle zone transfers). Another problem: since *named* creates new *named* processes to handle zone transfers, it's quite possible to have more than one *named* process running at one time: one answering queries, and one or more servicing zone transfers. If your master name server is already consumes five or ten megabytes of memory, count on two or three times that being used occasionally.

To get an idea of what normal figures are, here's what *top* might show for a relatively quiet name server:

```
last pid: 14299;  load averages: 0.11, 0.12, 0.12      18:19:08
68 processes: 64 sleeping, 3 running, 1 stopped
Cpu states: 11.3% usr, 0.0% nice, 15.3% sys, 73.4% idle, 0.0% intr, 0.0% ker
Memory: Real: 8208K/13168K act/tot Virtual: 16432K/30736K act/tot Free: 4224K

  PID USERNAME PRI NICE   SIZE   RES STATE  TIME  WCPU    CPU COMMAND
   89 root       1    0  2968K 2652K sleep  5:01 0.00%  0.00% named
```

Okay, that's *really* quiet. Here's what *top* shows on a busy (though not overloaded) name server:

```
load averages: 0.30, 0.46, 0.44                 system: relay 16:12:20
39 processes: 38 sleeping, 1 waiting
Cpu states: 4.4% user, 0.0% nice, 5.4% system, 90.2% idle, 0.0% unk5, 0.0%
unk6, 0.0% unk7, 0.0% unk8
Memory: 31126K (28606K) real, 33090K (28812K) virtual, 54344K free Screen #1/3

  PID USERNAME PRI NICE   SIZE   RES STATE  TIME  WCPU    CPU COMMAND
21910 root       1    0  2624K 2616K sleep 146:21 0.00%  1.42% /etc/named
```

Another statistic to look at is the number of queries the name server receives per minute (or second, if you have a busy name server). Again, there are no absolutes here: an HP9000 Model 750 can probably handle hundreds of queries per second without breaking into a sweat, while a '286 PC might have problems with more than a few queries a second.

To check the volume of queries your name server is receiving, it's easiest to look at the name server's internal statistics at regular intervals. (Recall from Chapter 7, *Maintaining BIND*, that to induce a name server to dump its current statistics, you send it the *ABRT* signal—that's *IOT* to you old timers.) For example, you might dump stats at 9 a.m. Monday and again at 10, and compare the number of queries received. (Monday morning is often busy, because many people like to respond to mail they've received over the weekend first-thing Monday.) This will give you the number of queries received in that hour. It'll also tell you the numbers of packets received and packets received and sent versus the corresponding 9 o'clock figures. This will tell you how much DNS traffic on your LAN is associated with this name server.

You might also want to take a sample starting just after lunch, when people are returning to their desks and getting back to work—all at about the same time. Of course, if your domain is spread across several timezones, you'll have to use your own good judgment to determine a busy time.

Here's how you might dump stats (and go out for a mocha in the meantime):

```
# at 9 am
kill -ABRT `cat /etc/named.pid`; sleep 2; mv /usr/tmp/named.stats \
/usr/tmp/named.stats.9; sleep 3600; kill -ABRT `cat /etc/named.pid`
^D
```

This will dump the name server's statistics to */usr/tmp/named.stats* at 9 a.m., wait a couple of seconds for the dump to complete, move that file aside, and dump the statistics again at 10. The number of queries received is dumped under `queries`, while the numbers of packets received and sent are `input packets` and `output packets`, respectively. To calculate the number of queries received in the hour, just subtract the 10 o'clock `queries` from the 9 o'clock number.

Even if your host is fast enough to handle the number of queries it receives, you should make sure the DNS traffic isn't placing undue load on your network. To estimate the volume of DNS traffic on your LAN, multiply the number of packets received plus the number of packets sent in an hour by 800 bits (100 bytes, a rough average size for a DNS packet), and divide by 3600 (seconds per hour) to find the bandwidth utilized. This should give you a feeling for how much of your network's bandwidth is being consumed by DNS traffic.

To give you an idea of what's normal, the NSFNET reports that DNS traffic currently constitutes less than 5% of the total traffic volume (in bytes) on their backbone. The NSFNET's figures are based upon actual traffic sampling, not calculations like ours using the name server's statistics. If you want to get a more accurate idea of the traffic your name server is receiving, you can always do your own traffic sampling with a LAN protocol analyzer.

Once you've found your name servers are overworked, what then? First, it's a good idea to make sure that your name servers aren't being bombarded with queries by a misbehaving program. To do that, you'll need to find out where all the queries are coming from.

The only way to find out which resolvers and name servers are sending all those darned queries is to turn on name server debugging. (We'll cover this in depth in the chapter on Chapter 11, *Reading BIND Debugging Output.*) All you're really interested in is the source IP addresses of the queries your name server is receiving. Here's a short *perl* script called *sum_debug* to help you summarize query activity in your debugging output:

```perl
#!/usr/bin/perl

# Usage:  sum_debug < named.run
#
# where named.run is your name server's debugging output.
# Be sure to turn off debugging before running sum_debug:
# it generates queries (and consequently debugging output) of its own!

require 'sys/socket.ph';

while (<>) {

    if (/^datagram from/) {

      split;
      if ($_[4] == 53)
      {
          $nsqueriers{$_[2]}++;
      }
      else
      {
          $resqueriers{$_[2]}++;
      }
    }

}

print "Name server queriers\n\n";

while (($ip, $count) = each(%nsqueriers)) {
    $addr = pack('C4', split(/\./, $ip));
    ($host, $rest) = gethostbyaddr($addr, &AF_INET);
    if ($host eq "")
    {
      printf "unknown (%s): %d queries\n", $ip, $count;
    } else {
      printf "%s (%s): %d queries\n", $host, $ip, $count;
    }
}

print "\nResolver queriers:\n\n";

while (($ip, $count) = each(%resqueriers)) {
    $addr = pack('C4', split(/\./, $ip));
    ($host, $rest) = gethostbyaddr($addr, &AF_INET);
```

```
if ($host eq "")
{
  printf "unknown (%s): %d queries\n", $ip, $count;
} else {
  printf "%s (%s): %d queries\n", $host, $ip, $count;
}
}
```

sum_debug will summarize the DNS activity in debugging output. It's up to you, however, to analyze it. Look for hosts sending repeated queries, especially for the same or similar information. That may indicate a misconfigured or buggy program running on the host, or a foreign name server pelting your name server with queries.

If all the queries appear to be legitimate, add a new name server. Don't put the name server just anywhere, though: use the information from the debugging output to help you decide where best to run one. In cases where DNS traffic is gobbling up your ethernet, it won't help to choose a host at random and create a name server there. You need to consider which hosts are sending all the queries, then figure out how to best provide them name service. Here are some hints to help you decide:

1. Look for queries from resolvers on hosts that share the same file server. You could run a name server on the file server.

2. Look for queries from resolvers on large, multi-user hosts. You could run a name server there.

3. Look for queries from resolvers on another subnet. Those resolvers should be configured to query a name server on their local subnet. If there isn't one, create one.

4. Look for queries from resolvers on the same bridged segment (assuming you use bridging). If you run a name server on the bridged segment, the traffic won't need to be bridged to the rest of the network.

5. Look for queries from hosts connected to each other via another, lightly-loaded network. You could run a name server on the other network.

Adding More Name Servers

When you need to create new name servers for your domain, the simplest recourse is to add secondaries. You already know how—we went over it in *Setting Up BIND*—and once you've set one secondary up, cloning it is a piece of cake. But you can run into trouble indiscriminately adding secondaries.

If you run a large number of secondary servers for a domain, the primary name server can take quite a beating just keeping up with the secondaries' polling to check that their data are current. There are a number of courses of action to take for this problem:

1. Make more primary name servers

2. Increase the refresh interval so secondaries don't check so often

3. Direct some of the secondary name servers to load from other secondary name servers

4. Create caching-only name servers (described below)

5. Create "partial-secondary" name servers (also described below)

Primary and Secondary Servers

Creating more primaries will mean extra work for you since you have to keep the db files synchronized manually. Whether or not this is preferable to your other alternatives is your call. You can use tools like *rdist* to simplify the process of distributing the files. A *distfile** to synchronize files between primaries might be as simple as:

Contents of file *distfile:*

```
dup-primary:

# copy named.boot file to dup'd primary

/etc/named.boot  -> wormhole
    install ;

# copy contents of /usr/local/named (db files, etc.) to dup'd primary

/usr/local/named -> wormhole
    install ;
```

or for multiple primaries:

```
dup-primary:

primaries =  ( wormhole carrie )
/etc/named.boot  -> ${primaries}
    install ;

/usr/local/named -> ${primaries}
    install ;
```

---

*The file *rdist* reads to find out which files to update.

You can even have *rdist* trigger your name server's reload using the *special* option by adding lines like:

```
special /usr/local/named/* "kill -HUP `cat /etc/named.pid`" ;
special /etc/named.boot "kill -HUP `cat /etc/named.pid`" ;
```

These tell *rdist* to execute the quoted command if any of the files change.

Increasing your name servers' refresh interval is another option. This slows down the propagation of new information, however. In some cases, this is not a problem. If you rebuild your DNS data with *h2n* only once each day at 1 a.m. (run from cron) and then allow six hours for the data to distribute, all the secondaries will be current by 7 a.m. That may be acceptable to your user population. See the section on "Changing Other SOA Values" later in this chapter for more detail.

You can even have some of your secondaries load from other secondaries. Secondary name servers *can* load zone data from another secondary name server instead of loading from a primary name server. The secondary name server can't tell if it is loading from a primary or a secondary. There's no trick to configuring this. Instead of specifying the IP address of the primary in the secondary's boot file, you simply specify the IP address of another secondary:

Contents of file *named.boot*:

```
; this secondary updates from wormhole, another secondary
secondary   movie.edu   192.249.249.1   db.movie
```

When you go to this "second level" of distribution though, it can take up to twice as long for the data to percolate from the primary name server to all the secondaries. Remember that the *refresh interval* is the period after which the secondary servers will check to make sure that their zone data are still current. Therefore, it can take the first-level secondary servers the entire refresh interval before they get their copy of the zone files from the primary server. Similarly, it can take the second-level servers the entire refresh interval to get their copy of the files from the first-level secondary servers. The propagation time from the primary servers to all of the secondary servers can therefore be twice the refresh interval.

If you decide to configure your network with two (or more) tiers of secondary servers, be careful to avoid updating loops. If we were to configure **wormhole** to update from **diehard**, and then accidentally configured **diehard** to update from **wormhole**, neither would ever get data from the primary. They would merely check their out-of-date serial numbers against each other, and perpetually decide that they were both up-to-date.

Caching-only Servers

Creating *caching-only name servers* is another alternative when you need more servers. Caching-only name servers are name servers not authoritative for any domains (except **0.0.127.in-addr.arpa**). The name doesn't imply that primary and secondary name servers don't cache—they do. The name means the *only* function this server performs is looking up data and caching them. As with primary and secondary name servers, a caching-only name server needs a *db.cache* file and a *db.127.0.0* file. The *named.boot* file for a caching-only server contains these lines:

Contents of file *named.boot*:

```
directory /usr/local/named  ; or your data directory

primary 0.0.127.in-addr.arpa  db.127.0.0  ; for loopback address
cache   .                     db.cache
```

A caching-only name server can look up names inside and outside your domain, as can primary and secondary name servers. The difference is that when a caching-only name server initially looks up a name within your domain, it ends up asking one of the primary or secondary name servers for your domain for the answer. A primary or secondary would answer the same question out of its authoritative data. Which primary or secondary does the caching-only server ask? As with name servers outside of your domain, it finds out which name servers serve your domain from the name server for your parent domain. Is there any way to prime a caching-only name server's cache so it knows which hosts run primary and secondary name servers for your domain? No, there isn't. You can't use *db.cache*—the *db.cache* file is only for *root* name server hints.

A caching-only name server's real value comes after it builds up its cache. Each time it queries an authoritative name server and receives an answer, it caches the records in the answer. Over time, the cache will grow to include the information most often requested by the resolvers querying the caching-only name server. And you avoid the overhead of zone transfers—a caching-only name server doesn't need to do them.

Partial-secondary Servers

In between a caching-only name server and a secondary name server is another variation: a name server secondary for only a few of the local domains. We call this a *partial-secondary name server* (and probably nobody else does). Suppose **movie.edu** had twenty class C networks (and a corresponding twenty **in-addr.arpa** domains). Instead of creating a secondary server for all 21 domains (all the **in-addr** domains plus movie.edu), we could create a partial-secondary server for **movie.edu** and only those **in-addr** domains the host itself is in. If the host had two network interfaces, then its name server would be a secondary for three domains: **movie.edu** and the two **in-addr.arpa** domains.

Let's say we scare up the hardware for another name server. We'll call the new host **zardoz.movie.edu**, with IP addresses 192.249.249.9 and 192.253.253.9. We'll create a partial-secondary name server on **zardoz**, with this *named.boot* file:

Contents of file *named.boot*:

```
directory    /usr/local/named
secondary    movie.edu                    192.249.249.3 db.movie
secondary    249.249.192.in-addr.arpa 192.249.249.3 db.192.249.249
secondary    253.253.192.in-addr.arpa 192.249.249.3 db.192.253.253
primary      0.0.127.in-addr.arpa         db.127.0.0
cache                                     db.cache
```

This server is a secondary for **movie.edu** and only two of the 20 **in-addr.arpa** domains. A "full" secondary would have 21 different *secondary* directives in *named.boot*.

What's so useful about a partial-secondary name server? They're not much work to administer, because their *named.boot* files don't change much. On a server authoritative for all the **in-addr.arpa** domains, we'd need to add and delete **in-addr.arpa** domains (and their corresponding entries in *named.boot*) as our network changed. That can be a surprising amount of work on a large network.

A partial-secondary can still answer most of the queries it receives, though. Most of these queries will be for data in the **movie.edu** and two **in-addr.arpa** domains. Why? Because most of the hosts querying the name server are on the two networks it's connected to, 192.249.249 and 192.253.253. And those hosts probably communicate primarily with other hosts on their own network. This generates queries for data within the **in-addr.arpa** domain corresponding to the local network.

Registering Name Servers

When you get around to setting up more and more name servers, a question may strike you—must *all* of the primary and secondary name servers be registered with the parent domain? No, only those servers you want to make available to servers outside of your domain need to be registered with the parent. For instance, if you run nine name servers within your domain, you may choose to tell the parent domain about only four of them. Within your domain, all nine servers are used. Five of those nine servers, however, are only queried by resolvers on hosts which are configured to query them (in *resolv.conf,* for example). Their parent name servers will never delegate to them, since they're not registered in the domain name space. Only the four servers registered with your parent domain are queried by other name servers, including caching-only and partial-secondary name servers within your domain. This setup is shown in Figure 8.2.

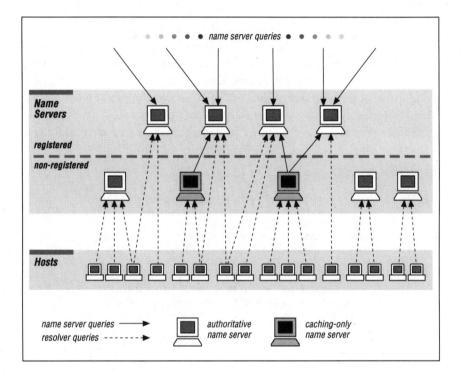

Figure 8.2: Registering only some of your name servers

Besides being able to pick and choose which of your name servers are hammered by outside queries, there's a technical motivation for registering only some of your domain's name servers: there is a limit to how many servers will fit in a UDP response packet. In practice, around ten name server records should fit. Depending on the data (how many servers are in the same domain), you could get more or fewer. There's not much point in registering more than ten servers, anyway—if none of the ten servers can be reached, it's unlikely the destination host can be reached.

If you've set up a new authoritative name server and decide it should be registered, make a list of the parents of the domains it's authoritative for. You'll need to contact the administrators for each of these parent domains. For example, let's say we want to register the name server we set up on **zardoz** above. In order to get this secondary registered in all the right domains, we'll need to contact the administrators of **edu** and **arpa**. (You might remember from Chapter 3, *Where Do I Start?*, that **arpa** is the parent domain for all **in-addr** domains corresponding to class A, B, and C networks.)

When you contact the administrators of a parent domain, be sure to give them the name of the domain the new name server is authoritative for. If the new name server is in the new domain, you'll also need to give them the IP address(es) of the new name server. In fact, it's often best just to send your parent the complete list of registered name servers for the domain, plus any addresses necessary, in data file format. That avoids any potential confusion. Our message to the administrator of **arpa** might read something like:

```
Howdy!

I've just set up a new secondary name server on
zardoz.movie.edu for the 249.249.192.in-addr.arpa
and 253.253.192.in-addr.arpa domains.  Would you
please add NS records for this name server to the
arpa domain?  That would make our delegation
information look like:

253.253.192.in-addr.arpa. 86400 IN NS terminator.movie.edu.
253.253.192.in-addr.arpa. 86400 IN NS wormhole.movie.edu.
253.253.192.in-addr.arpa. 86400 IN NS zardoz.movie.edu.

249.249.192.in-addr.arpa. 86400 IN NS terminator.movie.edu.
249.249.192.in-addr.arpa. 86400 IN NS wormhole.movie.edu.
249.249.192.in-addr.arpa. 86400 IN NS zardoz.movie.edu.

Thanks!

Albert LeDomaine
al@robocop.movie.edu
```

Notice we specified explicit TTLs on the NS and A records? That's because our parent name servers aren't authoritative for those records; *our* name servers are. By including them, we're indicating our choice of a TTL for your domain's delegation. Of course, our parent may have other ideas about what the TTL should be.

In this case, glue data—A records for each of the name servers—aren't necessary, since the addresses of the name servers aren't within the **in-addr.arpa** domains. They're within **movie.edu**, so a name server that was referred to **terminator** or **wormhole** could still find their addresses.

Is a partial-secondary name server a good name server to register with your parent domain? Actually, it's not *ideal*, because it's only authoritative for *some* of your **in-addr.arpa** domains. Administratively, it may be easier to register only servers backing up *all* the local domains; that way, you don't need to keep track of which name servers are authoritative for which domains. All of your parent domains can delegate to the same set of name servers: your primary and your "full" secondaries.

If you don't have many name servers, though, or if you're good at remembering which name servers are authoritative for what, go ahead and register a partial-secondary.

Caching-only name servers, on the other had, should *never* be registered. A caching-only name server rarely has complete information for any domain, just bits and pieces of it. If a parent name server were mistakenly to refer a foreign name server to a caching-only name server, the foreign name server would send the caching-only name server a non-recursive query. The caching-only name server might have the data cached, but then again might not. If it didn't have the data, it would refer the querier to the best name servers it knew (those closest to the domain in the query)—which might include the caching-only name server itself! The poor foreign name server might never get an answer.

Changing TTLs

An experienced domain administrator needs to know how to set the time to live on his zone's data to his best advantage. The *TTL* on a resource record, remember, is the time in seconds any server can cache that record. So if the TTL for a particular resource record is 3600 (seconds), and a server outside your domain caches that record, it will have to remove the entry from its cache after an hour. If it needs the same data after the hour is up, it'll have to query your name servers again.

When we introduced TTLs, we emphasized that your choice of a TTL would dictate how current you'd keep copies of your data, at the cost of increased load on your name servers. A low TTL would mean that name servers outside your domain would have to get data from your name servers often, and would therefore keep current. On the other hand, your name servers would be peppered by their queries.

You don't *have* to choose a TTL once and for all, though. You can—and experienced administrators do—change TTLs periodically to suit your needs.

Suppose we know that one of our hosts is about to be moved to another network. This host is the **movie.edu** film library. It houses a large collection of files our site makes available to hosts on the Internet. During normal operation, outside name servers cache the address of our host according to the minimum TTL in the SOA record. (We set the **movie.edu** TTL to be one day in our sample files.) A loss of connectivity for a day is unacceptable, though. What can we do to minimize the loss of connectivity? We can lower the TTL, so that outside servers cache the address record for a shorter period. By reducing the TTL, we force the outside servers to update their data more frequently, which means that any changes we make when we actually move the system will be propagated to the outside world quickly.

The easiest change is to lower the TTL in the SOA record in the *db.movie* file. If you don't place an explicit TTL on resource records in the db files, the name server applies this *minimum TTL* from the SOA record to each resource record. If you lower the minimum TTL field, though, the new, lower TTL applies to all addresses, not just the address of the host being moved. The drawback to this approach is that your name server will be answering a lot more queries since the querying servers will cache *all* the data in your zone for a shorter period. A better alternative is to put a different TTL only on the affected address record.

To add an explicit TTL on an individual resource record, place it before the IN in the class field. The TTL value is in seconds. Here's an example of an explicit TTL from *db.movie*:

```
cujo  3600 IN  A   192.253.253.5  ; explicit TTL:  cache for only 1 hour
```

If you're observant, you may have noticed a potential problem: the explicit TTL on **cujo**'s address is 3600 seconds, but the TTL field in the SOA record—ostensibly the *minimum* TTL for the zone—is *higher.* Which takes precedence?

If BIND followed the DNS RFCs, the TTL field in the SOA record would really define the minimum TTL value for all resource records in the zone. Thus, you could only specify TTLs larger than this minimum. BIND name servers don't work this way, though. In other words, in BIND, "minimum" is not really minimum. Instead, BIND implements the minimum TTL field in the SOA record as a "default" TTL. If there is no TTL on a record, the minimum applies. If there is a TTL on the resource record, BIND allows it even if it is smaller than the minimum.

You should also know that, when giving out answers, a secondary supplies the same TTL a primary does—that is, if a primary gives out a TTL of 86400 for a particular record, a secondary will, too. The secondary doesn't decrement the TTL according to how long it has been since it loaded the zone. So, if the TTL of a single resource record is set smaller than the SOA minimum, both the primary and secondary name servers give out the resource record with the same, smaller TTL. If the secondary name server has reached the expiration time for the zone, it expires the whole zone. It will never expire an individual resource record within a zone.

So BIND does allow you to put a small TTL on an individual resource record if you know the data is going to change shortly. Thus, any server caching that data only caches it for a brief time. Unfortunately, while BIND makes tagging records with a small TTL possible, most domain administrators don't spend the time to do it. When a host changes address, you often lose connectivity to it for a while.

More often than not, the host having its address changed is not one of the main hubs on the site, so the outage impacts few people. If one of the mail hubs or a major *ftp* repository—like the film library—is moving, though, a day's loss of connectivity may be unacceptable. In cases like this, the domain administrator should plan ahead and reduce the TTL on the data to be changed.

Remember that the TTL on the affected data will need to be lowered *before* the change takes place. Reducing the TTL on a workstation's address record and changing the workstation's address simultaneously may do you little or no good: the address record may have been cached minutes before you made the change, and may linger until the old TTL times out. *And* be sure to factor in the time it'll take your secondaries to load from your primary. For example, if your minimum TTL is 12 hours, and your refresh interval is three hours, be sure to lower the TTLs at least 15 hours ahead of time, so that by the time you move the host, all the long TTL records will have timed out.

Changing Other SOA Values

We briefly mentioned increasing the refresh interval as a way of offloading your primary name server. Let's discuss refresh in a little more detail and go over the remaining SOA values, too.

The *refresh* value, you'll remember, controls how often a secondary checks whether its data is up-to-date. The *retry* value then becomes the refresh time after the first failure to reach a master name server. The *expire* value determines how long data can be held before it's discarded when a master is unreachable. Finally, the *minimum TTL* sets how long domain information may be cached.

Suppose we've decided we want the secondaries to pick up new information every hour instead of every 3 hours. We change the refresh value to 3600 in each of the db files (or with the -o option to *h2n*). Since the retry is related to refresh, we should probably reduce retry, too—to every 15 minutes or so. Typically, the retry is less than the refresh, but that's not required. While lowering the refresh value will speed up the distribution of data, it will also increase the load on the server being loaded from since the secondaries will check more often. The added load isn't much, though: each secondary makes a single SOA query over a TCP connection during each zone's refresh interval to check the primary's copy of the zone. So with two secondary name servers, changing the refresh time from three hours to one hour will only generate four more queries (per zone) to the primary in any three hour span.

Some older versions of BIND secondaries stopped answering queries during a zone load. As a result, BIND was modified to spread out the zone loads, reducing the periods of unavailability. So, even if you set a low refresh interval, your secondaries may not check as often as you request. BIND attempts a certain number of zone loads and then waits 15 minutes before trying another batch.

Expiration times on the order of a week are common; longer if you frequently have problems reaching your updating source. The expiration time should always be much larger than the retry and refresh interval: if the expire time is smaller than the refresh interval, your secondaries will expire their data before trying to load new data.

If your data doesn't change much, you might consider raising the minimum TTL. The SOA's minimum TTL value is typically one day (86400 seconds), but you can make it longer. One week is about the longest value that makes sense for a TTL. Longer than that and you may find yourself unable to change bad, cached data in a reasonable amount of time.

Planning for Disasters

It's a fact of life on a network that things go wrong. Hardware fails, software has bugs, and people very occasionally make mistakes. Sometimes this results in minor inconvenience, like having a few users lose connections. Sometimes the results are catastrophic, and involve the loss of important data and valuable jobs.

Because the Domain Name System relies so heavily on the network, it is vulnerable to network outages. Thankfully, the design of DNS takes into account the imperfection of networks: it allows for multiple, redundant name servers, retransmission of queries, retrying zone transfers, and so on.

The Domain Name System doesn't protect itself from every conceivable calamity, though. There are types of network failure—some of them quite common—that DNS doesn't or can't protect against. But with a small investment of time and money, you can minimize the threat of these outages.

Outages

Power outages, for example, are relatively common in many parts of the world. In some parts of the U.S., thunderstorms or tornadoes may cause a site to lose power, or have only intermittent power, for an extended period. Elsewhere, typhoons, volcanoes or construction work may interrupt your electrical service.

If all your hosts are down, of course, you don't need name service. Quite often, however, sites have problems when power is *restored*. Following our recommendations, they run their name servers on file servers and big multi-user machines. And when the power comes up, those machines are naturally the last to boot—because all those disks need to be *fsck*'d first! Which means that all the hosts on-site that are quick to boot do so without the benefit of name service.

This can cause all sorts of wonderful problems, depending on how your hosts' startup files are written. UNIX hosts often execute some variant of:

```
/etc/ifconfig lan0 inet `hostname` netmask 255.255.128.0 up
/etc/route add default site-router 1
```

to bring up their network interface. Using host names in the commands (`hostname` expands to the local host name and site-router is the name of the local router) is admirable for two reasons:

1. It lets the administrators change the router's IP address without changing all the startup files on site.

2. It lets the administrators change the host's IP address by changing the IP address in only one file.

Unfortunately, the *route* command will fail without name service. The *ifconfig* command will fail only if the localhost's name and IP address don't appear in the host's */etc/hosts* file, so it's a good idea to leave at least that data in each host's */etc/hosts*.

By the time the startup sequence reaches the *route* command, the network interface will be up, and the host will use name service to map the name of the router to an IP address. And since the host has no default route until the *route* command is executed, the only name servers it can reach are those on the local subnet.

If the booting host can reach a working name server on its local subnet, it can execute the route command successfully. Quite often, however, one or more of the name servers it can reach aren't yet running. What happens then depends on the contents of *resolv.conf*.

In BIND 4.8.3, the resolver will only fall back to the host table if there is only one name server listed in *resolv.conf* (or if no name server is listed and the resolver defaults to using a name server on the local host). If only one name server is configured, the resolver will query it, and if the network returns an error each time the resolver sends a query, the resolver will fall back to searching the host table. The errors that cause the resolver to fall back include:

1. Receipt of an ICMP **port unreachable** message

2. Receipt of an ICMP **network unreachable** message

3. Inability to send the UDP packet (e.g., because networking is not yet running on the local host)*

If the host running the one configured name server isn't running at all, though, the resolver won't receive any errors. The name server is effectively a black hole. After about 75 seconds of trying, the resolver will just time out and return a null answer to the application which called it. Only if the name server host has actually started networking—but not yet started the name server—will the resolver get an error: an ICMP port unreachable message.

Overall, the single name server configuration works if you have name servers available on each net, but perhaps not as elegantly as we might like. If the local name server hasn't come up when a host on its network reboots, the *route* command will fail.

This may seem awkward, but it's not nearly as bad as what happens with multiple servers. With multiple servers listed in *resolv.conf*, BIND *never* falls back to the host table after the primary network interface has been *ifconfig*'d. The resolver simply loops through the name servers, querying them until one answers or the 75 second timeout is reached.

This is especially problematic during bootup. If none of the configured name servers are available, the resolver will time out without returning an IP address, and adding the default route will fail.

Recommendations

Our recommendation, as primitive as it sounds, is to hardcode the IP address of the default router into the startup file. This will ensure that your host's networking will start correctly.

An alternative is to list just a single, reliable name server on your host's local net in *resolv.conf*. This will allow you to use the name of the default router in the startup file, as long as you make sure that the router's name appears in */etc/hosts* (in case your reliable name server isn't running when the host reboots). Of course, if the host running the reliable name server isn't running when your host reboots, all bets are off. You won't fall back to */etc/hosts* because there won't be any networking running to return an error to your host.

---

*Check Chapter 6, *Configuring Hosts*, chapter for vendor-specific enhancements to and variants on this resolver algorithm.

If your vendor's version of BIND allows configuration of the order in which services are queried, or will fall back from DNS to */etc/hosts* if DNS doesn't find an answer, take advantage of it! In the former case, you can configure the resolver to check */etc/hosts* first, and then keep a "stub" */etc/hosts* file on each host, including the default router and the local host's name. In the latter situation, just make sure such a "stub" */etc/hosts* exists: no other configuration should be necessary.

A last, promising prospect is to do away with setting the default route altogether, by using Cisco Systems' *Gateway Discovery Protocol* (GDP) or the forthcoming *ICMP Router Discovery Protocol* (IRDP). These protocols use broadcast messages to dynamically discover or advertise routers on a network. Cisco routers support GDP, and a daemon which implements the host protocol is freely available from Cisco (currently on **ftp.cisco.com** as *gdpd.shar*). Implementations of the ICMP Router Discovery Protocol, which is on the Internet standards track, are available, too.

And what if your default route is added correctly, but the name servers still haven't come up? This can affect *sendmail,* NFS, and a slew of other services. Your *sendmail.cf* file may be frozen incorrectly without DNS, and your NFS mounts may fail.

The best solution to this problem is to run a name server on a host with uninterruptible power. If you rarely experience extended power loss, it could just have battery backup. If your outages are longer, and name service is critical to you, you should consider an uninterruptible power system (UPS) with a generator of some kind.

If you can't afford luxuries like these, you might just try to track down the fastest-booting host around and run a name server on it. Hosts with filesystem journaling should boot especially quickly, since they don't need to *fsck*. Hosts with small filesystems should boot quickly, too, since they don't have as much filesystem to check.

Once you've located the right host, you'll need to make sure the host's IP address appears in the *resolv.conf* files of all the hosts which need full-time name service. You'll probably want to list the backed-up host last, since during normal operation, hosts should use the name server closest to them. Then, after a power failure, your critical applications will still have name service, albeit at a small sacrifice in performance.

Coping with Disaster

When disaster strikes, it really helps to know what to do. Knowing to duck under a sturdy table or desk during an earthquake can save you from being pinned under a toppling monitor. Knowing how to turn off your gas can save your house from conflagration.

Likewise, knowing what to do in a network disaster (or even just a minor mishap) can help you keep your network running. Living out in California, as we do, we have some experience and some suggestions.

Short Outages (Hours)

If your network is cut off from the outside world (whether "the outside world" is the rest of the Internet or the rest of your company), your name servers may start to have trouble resolving names. For example, if your domain, **corp.acme.com**, is cut off from the rest of the Acme Internet, you may not have access to your parent (**acme.com**) name servers, or to the root name servers.

You'd think this wouldn't impact communication between hosts in your local domain, but it can. For example, if you type:

```
% telnet selma.corp.acme.com
```

the first domain name the resolver looks up will be **selma.corp.acme.com.corp.acme.com** (assuming your host is using the default search list—remember this from *Configuring Hosts*?). The local domain name server can tell that's not a kosher domain name. The following lookup, however, is for **selma.corp.acme.com.acme.com**. This prospective domain name is no longer in the **corp.acme.com** domain, so the query is sent to the **acme.com** name servers. Or rather your local name server *tries* to send the query there, and keeps retransmitting until it times out.

You can avoid this problem by making sure the first domain name the resolver looks up is the right one. Instead of typing:

```
% telnet selma.corp.acme.com
```

typing:

```
% telnet selma
```

or:

```
% telnet selma.corp.acme.com.
```

(note the trailing dot) will result in a lookup of **selma.corp.acme.com** first.

If you're running 4.8.3 BIND, you can also take advantage of the definable search list. You can use the *search* directive to define a search list which doesn't include your parent domain. For example, to work around the problem **corp.acme.com** is having, you could temporarily set your hosts' search lists to:

```
search corp.acme.com
```

Now, when a user types:

```
% telnet selma.corp.acme.com
```

the resolver looks up **selma.corp.acme.com.corp.acme.com** first (which the local name server can answer), then **selma.corp.acme.com**, the correct domain name. And:

```
% telnet selma
```

works fine, too.

Longer Outages (Days)

If you lose network connectivity for a long time, your name servers may have other problems. If they lose connectivity to the root name servers for an extended period, they'll stop resolving queries outside their authoritative data. If the secondaries can't reach the primary, sooner or later they'll expire the zone.

In case your name service really goes haywire because of the connectivity loss, it's a good idea to keep a site-wide or workgroup */etc/hosts* around. In times of dire need, you can move *resolv.conf* to *resolv.bak,* kill the local name server (if there is one), and just use */etc/hosts*. It's not flashy, but it'll get you by.

As for secondaries, you can reconfigure a secondary that can't reach its updating source to run as a primary. Just edit *named.boot* and change the *secondary* directives to *primary* directives and delete the IP address(es) to load from. If more than one secondary for the same domain are cut off, you can configure one as a primary temporarily and reconfigure the other to load from the temporary primary.

Really Long Outages (Weeks)

If an extended outage cuts you off from the Internet—say for a week or more—you may need to restore connectivity to root name servers artificially to get things working again. Every name server needs to talk to a root name server occasionally. It's a bit like therapy: the name server needs to contact the root to regain its perspective on the world.

To provide root name service during a long outage, you can set up your own root name servers, *but only temporarily*. Once you're reconnected to the Internet, you *must* shut off your temporary root servers. The most obnoxious vermin on the Internet are name servers that believe they're root name servers but don't know anything about most top-level domains. A close second is the Internet name server configured to query—and report—a false set of root name servers.

That said, and our alibis in place, here's what you have to do to configure your own root name server. First, you need to create a *db.root* file. The *db.root* file will delegate to the highest-level domain in your isolated network. For example, if **movie.edu** were to be segmented from the Internet, we might create a *db.root* file for **terminator** that looked like this:

Contents of file *db.root*:

```
. IN SOA terminator.movie.edu. al.robocop.movie.edu. (
                1       ; Serial
                10800   ; Refresh after 3 hours
                3600    ; Retry after 1 hour
                604800  ; Expire after 1 week
                86400   ; Minimum TTL of 1 day

; Refresh, retry and expire really don't matter, since all
; roots are primaries.  Minimum TTL could be longer, since
; the data is likely to be stable.

  IN NS terminator.movie.edu. ; terminator is the temp. root

; Our root only knows about movie.edu and our two
; in-addr.arpa domains

movie.edu. 86400 IN NS terminator.movie.edu.
           86400 IN NS wormhole.movie.edu.

249.249.192.in-addr.arpa. 86400 IN NS terminator.movie.edu.
                          86400 IN NS wormhole.movie.edu.

253.253.192.in-addr.arpa. 86400 IN NS terminator.movie.edu.
                          86400 IN NS wormhole.movie.edu.

terminator.movie.edu. 86400 IN A 192.249.249.3
```

```
wormhole.movie.edu.    86400 IN A 192.249.249.1
                       86400 IN A 192.253.253.1
```

Then we need to add the appropriate line to **terminator**'s *named.boot* file:

Contents of file *named.boot*:

```
; cache    .    db.cache   (comment out the cache directive)
primary  .    db.root
```

and update all of our name servers (except the new, temporary root) with a *db.cache* file that includes just the temporary root (best to move the old cache file aside—we'll need it later, once connectivity is restored):

Contents of file *db.cache*:

```
.  99999999  IN  NS  terminator.movie.edu.

terminator.movie.edu.  IN  A  192.249.249.3
```

That'll keep **movie.edu** name resolution going during the outage. Then, once Internet connectivity is restored, we can delete the primary directive from *named.boot* on **terminator**, and restore the original cache files on all our other name servers.

9

Parenting

The way Dinah washed her children's faces was this: first she held the poor thing down by its ear with one paw, and then with the other paw she rubbed its face all over, the wrong way, beginning at the nose: and just now, as I said, she was hard at work on the white kitten, which was lying quite still and trying to purr—no doubt feeling that it was all meant for its good.

Once your domain reaches a certain size, or you decide you need to distribute the management of parts of your domain to various entities within your organization, you'll want to divide the domain into subdomains. These subdomains will be the children of your current domain on the domain tree; your domain will be the parent. We like to call the management of your subdomains—your children—*parenting*.

Good parenting starts with carving up your domain sensibly and choosing appropriate names for your child domains. Responsible parents also work hard at maintaining the relationship between the name servers authoritative for their domain and its subdomains: they ensure that delegation from parent to child is current and correct.

Good parenting is vital to the success of your network, especially as name service becomes critical to navigating between sites. Incorrect delegation to a child domain's name servers can render a site effectively unreachable, while the loss of connectivity to the parent domain's name servers can leave a site unable to reach any hosts outside the local domain.

In this chapter we present our views on when to create subdomains, and go over how to create them in some detail. We also discuss management of the parent-child relationship and, finally, how to manage the process of carving up a large domain into smaller subdomains with a minimum of disruption and inconvenience.

When to Become a Parent

Far be it from us to *tell* you when you should become a parent, but we *will* be so bold as to offer you some guidelines. You may find some compelling reason to implement subdomains that isn't on our list, but some of the most common reasons are:

- A need to delegate or distribute management of the domain to a number of organizations
- The large size of your domain: dividing it would make it easier to manage and offload the name servers for the domain
- A need to distinguish hosts' organizational affiliation by including them in particular domains

Once you've decided to have children, the next question to ask yourself is, naturally, how many children to have.

How Many Children?

Of course, you won't simply say, "I want to create four subdomains." Deciding how many child domains to implement is really choosing the organizational affiliation of your subdomains. For example, if your company has four branch offices, you might decide to create four subdomains, each of which corresponds to a branch office.

Should you create subdomains for each site, for each division, or even for each department? You have a lot of latitude in your choice because of DNS's scalability. You can create a few large domains or many small domains. There are tradeoffs whichever you choose, though.

Delegating to a few large subdomains isn't much work for the parent domain, because there's not much delegation to keep track of. However, you wind up with larger subdomains, which require more memory and faster name servers, and administration isn't as distributed. If you implement site-level subdomains, for example, you may force autonomous or unrelated groups at a site to share a single name space and a single point of administration.

Delegating to many smaller subdomains can be a headache for the administrator of the parent domain. Keeping delegation data current involves keeping track of which hosts run name servers and which domains they're authoritative for. The data changes each time a subdomain adds a new name server, or when the address of a name server for the subdomain changes. If the subdomains are all administered by different people, that's more administrators to train, more relationships for the parent administrator to maintain and more overhead for the organization overall. On the other hand, the subdomains are smaller and easier to manage, and the administration is more widely distributed, allowing closer management of subdomain data.

Given the advantages and disadvantages of either alternative, it may seem difficult to make a choice. Actually, though, there's probably a natural division in your organization. Some companies manage computers and networks at the site-level; others have decentralized, relatively autonomous workgroups which manage everything themselves. Here are a couple of basic rules ·· help you find the right way to carve up your name space:

1. Don't shoe..orn v·ur organization into a weird or uncomfortable domain structure. Trying to fit 50 independent, unrelated U.S. divisions into four regional subdomains may save you work (as the administrator of the parent domain), but it won't help your reputation. Decentralized, autonomous operations demand different domains—that's the *raison d'etre* of the Domain Name System.

2. The structure of your domain should mirror the structure of your organization, especially your organization's *support* structure. If departments run networks, assign IP addresses, and manage hosts, then departments should manage domains.

What to Name Your Children

Once you've decided how many subdomains you'd like to create and what they correspond to, you should choose good names for them. Rather than unilaterally deciding on your subdomains' names, it's considered polite to involve your future subdomain administrators and their constituencies in the decision. In fact, you can leave the decision entirely to them, if you like.

This can lead to problems, though. It's nice to use a relatively consistent naming scheme across your subdomains: it makes it easier for users in one subdomain, or outside your domain entirely, to guess or remember your subdomain names, and to figure out in which domain a particular host or user lives.

Leaving the decision to the locals can result in naming chaos. Some will want to use geographical names, others will insist on organizational names. Some will want to abbreviate, others will want to use full names.

Therefore, it's often best to establish a naming convention before choosing subdomain names. Here are some suggestions from our experience:

- In a dynamic company, the names of organizations can change frequently. Naming subdomains organizationally in a climate like this can be disastrous. One month the Relatively Advanced Technology (RAT) group seems stable enough, the next month they've been merged into the Questionable Computer Systems organization, and the following quarter they're all sold to a German conglomerate. Meanwhile, you're stuck with well-known hosts in a subdomain whose name no longer has any meaning.

- Geographical names are more stable than organizational names, but sometimes not as well-known. You may know that your famous Software Evangelism Business Unit is in Poughkeepsie or Waukegan, but people outside your company may have no idea where it is (and might have trouble spelling either name).

- Don't sacrifice readability for convenience. Two-letter subdomain names may be easy to type, but impossible to recognize. Why abbreviate "Italy" to "it" and have it confused with your Information Technology organization when for a paltry three more letters you can use the full name and eliminate any ambiguity?

  Too many companies use cryptic, inconvenient domain names. The general rule seems to be: the larger the company, the more indecipherable the domain names. Buck the trend: make the names of your subdomains obvious!

- Don't use existing or reserved top-level domain names as subdomain names. It might seem sensible to use two-letter country abbreviations for your international subdomains, or to use organizational top-level domain names like **net** for your networking organization, but it can cause nasty problems. For example, naming your Communications department's subdomain **com** might impede your ability to communicate with hosts under the top-level **com** domain. Imagine the

administrators of your **com** subdomain naming their new Sun workstation **sun** and their new HP 9000/710 **hp** (they aren't the most imagina-
tive folks): users anywhere within your domain sending mail to friends
at **sun.com** or **hp.com** would have their letters end up in your **com** subdomain,* since your parent domain is (by default) in all of your hosts'
search lists.

How to Become a Parent: Creating Subdomains

Once you've decided on names, creating child domains is easy. But first,
you've got to decide how much autonomy you're going to give your subdomains. Odd that you have to decide that before you actually create
them . . .

Thus far, we've assumed that if you create a subdomain, you'll want to delegate it to another organization. Is this always true, though? Not necessarily.

Think carefully about how the computers and networks within a subdomain are managed when choosing whether or not to delegate it. It
doesn't make sense to delegate a subdomain to an entity which doesn't
manage its own hosts or nets. For example, in a large corporation, the personnel department probably doesn't run its own computers; the MIS (Management Information Systems) or IT (Information Technology—same ani-
mal as MIS) department manages them. So while you may want to create a
subdomain for personnel, delegating management for that subdomain to
them is probably wasted effort.

Creating a Subdomain in the Parent's Zone

You can *create* a subdomain without delegating it, however. How? By
creating resource records that refer to the subdomain within the parent's
zone. For example, **movie.edu** has a host that stores its complete database
of employee and student records, **brazil**. To put **brazil** in the **person-
nel.movie.edu** domain, we could add records to *db.movie:*

---

*Actually, not all mailers have this problem, but some popular versions of *sendmail* do. It all
depends on which form of canonicalization it does, as we discussed in the section entitled
"Electronic Mail" in Chapter 6, *Configuring Hosts.*

Partial contents of file *db.movie:*

```
brazil.personnel        IN  A      192.253.253.10
                        IN  MX     10 brazil.personnel.movie.edu.
                        IN  MX     100 postmanrings2x.movie.edu.
employeedb.personnel    IN  CNAME  brazil.personnel.movie.edu.
db.personnel            IN  CNAME  brazil.personnel.movie.edu.
```

Now users can log into **db.personnel.movie.edu** to get to the employee database. We could make this setup especially convenient for personnel department employees by adding **personnel.movie.edu** to their PCs' or workstations' search lists: they'd only need to type **telnet db** to get to the right host.

Notice there's no SOA record for **personnel.movie.edu**? There's no need for one, since the **movie.edu** SOA record indicates the start of authority for the entire **movie.edu** zone. Since there's no delegation to **personnel.movie.edu**, it's part of the **movie.edu** zone.

Creating and Delegating a Subdomain

If you decide to delegate your subdomains, to send your children out into the world, as it were, you'll need to do things a little differently. We're in the process of doing it now, so you can follow along with us.

We need to create a new domain for our special effects lab, and we've chosen the name **fx.movie.edu**—short, recognizable, unambiguous. The hosts **bladerunner** and **outland**, both within the special effects lab, will serve as the domain's name servers (**bladerunner** will serve as the primary master). We've chosen to run two name servers for the domain for redundancy—a single **fx.movie.edu** name server would be a single point of failure that could effectively isolate the entire special effects lab. Since there aren't many hosts in the lab, though, we feel two name servers should be enough.

The special effects lab is on **movie.edu**'s new 192.253.254 subnet:

Partial contents of */etc/hosts:*

```
192.253.254.1 movie-gw.movie.edu movie-gw
# fx primary
192.253.254.2 bladerunner.fx.movie.edu bladerunner br
# fx secondary
192.253.254.3 outland.fx.movie.edu outland
192.253.254.4 starwars.fx.movie.edu starwars
192.253.254.5 empire.fx.movie.edu empire
192.253.254.6 jedi.fx.movie.edu jedi
```

First, we create a data file that includes records for all the hosts that will live in **fx.movie.edu**:

Contents of file *db.fx:*

```
@   IN   SOA   bladerunner.fx.movie.edu. hostmaster.fx.movie.edu. (
                   1        ; serial
                   10800    ; refresh every 3 hours
                   3600     ; retry every hour
                   604800   ; expire after a week
                   86400 )  ; minimum TTL of 1 day

      IN   NS   bladerunner
      IN   NS   outland

      ; MX records for fx.movie.edu
      IN   MX   10 starwars
      IN   MX   100 wormhole.movie.edu.

; starwars handles bladerunner's mail
; wormhole is the movie.edu mail hub

bladerunner   IN   A    192.253.254.2
              IN   MX   10 starwars
              IN   MX   100 wormhole.movie.edu.

br            IN   CNAME    bladerunner

outland       IN   A    192.253.254.3
              IN   MX   10 starwars
              IN   MX   100 wormhole.movie.edu.

starwars      IN   A    192.253.254.4
              IN   MX   10 starwars
              IN   MX   100 wormhole.movie.edu.

empire        IN   A    192.253.254.5
              IN   MX   10 starwars
              IN   MX   100 wormhole.movie.edu.

jedi          IN   A    192.253.254.6
              IN   MX   10 starwars
              IN   MX   100 wormhole.movie.edu.
```

Then we create the *db.192.253.254* file:

```
@   IN   SOA   bladerunner.fx.movie.edu. hostmaster.fx.movie.edu. (
                   1        ; serial
                   10800    ; refresh every 3 hours
                   3600     ; retry every hour
                   604800   ; expire after a week
                   86400 )  ; minimum TTL of 1 day

      IN   NS    bladerunner.fx.movie.edu.
```

```
          IN    NS    outland.fx.movie.edu.

1         IN    PTR   movie-gw.movie.edu.
2         IN    PTR   bladerunner.fx.movie.edu.
3         IN    PTR   outland.fx.movie.edu.
4         IN    PTR   starwars.fx.movie.edu.
5         IN    PTR   empire.fx.movie.edu.
6         IN    PTR   jedi.fx.movie.edu.
```

Notice the PTR record for **1.254.253.192.in-addr.arpa** points to
movie-gw.movie.edu. That's intentional: the router connects to the other
movie.edu networks, so it really doesn't belong in the **fx.movie.edu**
domain, and there's no requirement that all the PTR records in
254.253.192.in-addr.arpa map into a single domain—though they should
correspond to the canonical names for those hosts.

Next, we create an appropriate *named.boot* file for the primary:

Contents of file *named.boot:*

```
directory      /usr/local/named

primary        0.0.127.in-addr.arpa        db.127.0.0  ; loopback
primary        fx.movie.edu                db.fx
primary        254.253.192.in-addr.arpa    db.192.253.254

cache                                      db.cache
```

Of course, if we'd used *h2n*, we could have just run:

```
% h2n -d fx.movie.edu -n 192.253.254 -s bladerunner -s outland \
-u hostmaster.fx.movie.edu -m 10:starwars -m 100:wormhole.movie.edu
```

and saved ourselves some typing. *h2n* would have created essentially the
same *db.fx, db.192.253.254*, and *named.boot* files.

Now we need to configure **bladerunner**'s resolver. Actually, this may not
require creating *resolv.conf*. If we set **bladerunner**'s *hostname* to its new
domain name, **bladerunner.fx.movie.edu**, the resolver can derive the local
domain from the fully-qualified domain name.

Next we start up the *named* process on **bladerunner** and check for *syslog*
errors. If *named* starts okay, and there are no *syslog* errors that need tending to, we'll use *nslookup* to look up a few hosts in **fx.movie.edu** and in
254.253.192.in-addr.arpa:

```
% nslookup
Default Server:  bladerunner.fx.movie.edu
Address:  192.253.254.2

> jedi
Server:  bladerunner.fx.movie.edu
```

```
Name:    jedi.fx.movie.edu
Address: 192.253.253.6

> set type=mx
> empire
Server: bladerunner.fx.movie.edu
Address: 192.253.254.2

empire.fx.movie.edu      preference = 10,
                         mail exchanger = starwars.fx.movie.edu
empire.fx.movie.edu      preference = 100,
                         mail exchanger = wormhole.movie.edu
starwars.fx.movie.edu    internet address = 192.253.254.4
> ls fx.movie.edu
[bladerunner.fx.movie.edu]
 fx.movie.edu.               server = bladerunner.fx.movie.edu
 bladerunner                 192.253.254.2
 fx.movie.edu.               server = outland.fx.movie.edu
 outland                     192.253.254.3
 jedi                        192.253.254.6
 starwars                    192.253.254.4
 bladerunner                 192.253.254.2
 empire                      192.253.254.5
> set q=ptr
> 192.253.254.3
Server: bladerunner.fx.movie.edu
Address: 192.253.254.2

3.254.253.192.in-addr.arpa      name = outland.fx.movie.edu

> ls 254.253.192.in-addr.arpa.
[bladerunner.fx.movie.edu]
 254.253.192.IN-ADDR.ARPA.      server = bladerunner.fx.movie.edu
 bladerunner.fx.movie.edu.      192.253.254.2
 254.253.192.IN-ADDR.ARPA.      server = outland.fx.movie.edu
 outland.fx.movie.edu.          192.253.254.3
 6                              host = jedi.fx.movie.edu
 1                              host = movie-gw.movie.edu
 2                              host = bladerunner.fx.movie.edu
 3                              host = outland.fx.movie.edu
 4                              host = starwars.fx.movie.edu
 5                              host = empire.fx.movie.edu
> ^D
```

The output looks reasonable, so it's safe to set up a secondary name server for **fx.movie.edu** and to delegate **fx.movie.edu** from **movie.edu**.

An fx.movie.edu Secondary

Setting up the secondary master name server for **fx.movie.edu** is simple: copy *named.boot, db.127.0.0* and *db.cache* over from **bladerunner** and edit *named.boot* and *db.127.0.0* according to the instructions in Chapter 4, *Setting Up BIND:*

Contents of file *named.boot:*

```
directory  /usr/local/named

primary    0.0.127.in-addr.arpa      db.127.0.0
secondary  fx.movie.edu              192.253.254.2  db.fx
secondary  254.253.192.in-addr.arpa  192.253.254.2  db.192.253.254

cache                                db.cache
```

Like **bladerunner**, **outland** really doesn't need a *resolv.conf* file, as long as its *hostname* is set to **outland.fx.movie.edu**.

Again, we start *named* and check for errors in the *syslog* output. If the *syslog* output is clean, we'll look up a few records in **fx.movie.edu**.

On the movie.edu Primary

All that's left now is to delegate the **fx.movie.edu** domain to the new **fx.movie.edu** name servers on **bladerunner** and **outland**. We add the appropriate NS records to *db.movie:*

Partial contents of file *db.movie:*

```
fx   86400   IN   NS   bladerunner.fx.movie.edu.
     86400   IN   NS   outland.fx.movie.edu.
```

This alone isn't enough, though. Do you see the problem? How can a name server outside of **fx.movie.edu** look up information within **fx.movie.edu**? Well, a **movie.edu** name server would refer it to the name servers authoritative for **fx.movie.edu**, right? That's true, but the NS records in *db.movie* only give the *names* of the **fx.movie.edu** name servers. The foreign name server needs the IP addresses of the **fx.movie.edu** name servers in order to send queries to them. Who can give it those addresses? Only the **fx.movie.edu** name servers. A real chicken-and-egg problem!

The solution is to include the addresses of the **fx.movie.edu** name servers in the *db.movie* file. While these aren't strictly part of the **movie.edu** domain, they're necessary for delegation to **fx.movie.edu** to work. Of course, if the name servers for **fx.movie.edu** weren't within **fx.movie.edu**, these addresses—called *glue records*—wouldn't be necessary. A foreign name server would be able to find the address it needed by querying other name servers.

So, with the glue records, the records added look like:

Partial contents of file *db.movie:*

```
fx     86400    IN    NS    bladerunner.fx.movie.edu.
       86400    IN    NS    outland.fx.movie.edu.

bladerunner.fx.movie.edu.    86400  IN  A  192.253.254.2
outland.fx.movie.edu.        86400  IN  A  192.253.254.3
```

One other thing that we might want to include are aliases for any hosts moving into **fx.movie.edu** from **movie.edu**. For example, if we were to move **plan9.movie.edu**, a server with an important library of public domain special effects algorithms, into **fx.movie.edu**, we should create an alias under **movie.edu** pointing the old name to the new one:

```
plan9          IN      CNAME    plan9.fx.movie.edu.
```

This will allow people outside of **movie.edu** to reach **plan9** even though they're using its old domain name, **plan9.movie.edu**.

Delegating an in-addr.arpa Domain

We almost forgot to delegate the **254.253.192.in-addr.arpa** domain! This is a little trickier than delegating **fx.movie.edu**, because we don't manage the parent domain.

The top-level **arpa** domain is **254.253.192.in-addr.arpa**'s parent domain. And, if you think about it, that makes some sense. There's no reason for the NIC to delegate **253.192.in-addr.arpa** or **192.in-addr.arpa** to a separate authority, because networks like 192.253.253 and 192.253.254 don't necessarily have anything in common with each other: they may be managed by totally unrelated organizations.

You might have remembered (distantly, from Chapter 8, *Growing Your Domain*) that the **arpa** domain is managed by the NIC—it's one of the original top-level organizational domains. Of course, if you didn't remember, you could always use *nslookup* to find the contact address in **arpa**'s SOA record. All that's left is for us to fill out *in-addr-template.txt* (there's a copy in Appendix E, *IN-ADDR.ARPA Registration*, and send it to the e-mail address **hostmaster@internic.net**.

Good Parenting

Now that the delegation to the **fx.movie.edu** name servers is in place, we—responsible parents that we are—should check that delegation using *check_del*. What? We haven't given you *check_del* yet? Unfortunately, *check_del* is too long to include in this book, but we've made it available via anonymous *ftp*. See the preface for details. Feel free to snatch the code there and compile it if you want to follow along.

check_del "knows" delegation. *check_del* reads NS records. For each NS record, *check_del* issues a query to the name server listed for the domain's SOA record. The query is non-recursive, so the name server queried doesn't query other name servers to find the SOA record. If the name server replies, *check_del* checks the reply to see whether the *aa*—authoritative answer—bit in the reply packet is set. If it is, the name server checks to make sure that the packet contains an answer. If both these criteria are met, the name server is flagged as authoritative for the domain. Otherwise, the name server is not authoritative and *check_del* reports an error.

Why all the fuss over bad delegation? Incorrect delegation can cause the propagation of old and erroneous root name server information. When a name server is queried for data in a domain it isn't authoritative for, it does its best to provide useful information to the querier. This "useful information" comes in the form of NS records for the closest ancestor domain the name server knows. (We mentioned this briefly in the Chapter 8, *Growing Your Domain*, when we discussed why you shouldn't register a caching-only name server.)

For example, say one of the **fx.movie.edu** name servers mistakenly receives an iterative query for the address of **carrie.horror.movie.edu**. It knows nothing about the **horror.movie.edu** domain (except for what it might have cached), but it likely has NS records for **movie.edu** cached, since those are its parent name servers. So it would return those records to the querier.

In that scenario, the NS records may help the querying name server get an answer. However, it's a fact of life on the Internet that not all administrators keep their cache files up-to-date. If one of your name servers follows a bad delegation and queries a remote name server for records it doesn't have, look what can happen:

```
% nslookup
Default Server: terminator.movie.edu
Address: 192.249.249.3

> set type=ns
> .
Server: terminator.movie.edu
Address: 192.249.249.3

Non-authoritative answer:
(root)   nameserver = NS.NIC.DDN.MIL
(root)   nameserver = AOS.BRL.MIL
(root)   nameserver = KAVA.NISC.SRI.COM
(root)   nameserver = C.NYSER.NET
(root)   nameserver = TERP.UMD.EDU
(root)   nameserver = NS.NASA.GOV
(root)   nameserver = NIC.NORDU.NET
```
(root)   nameserver = A.ISI.EDU   *--These three name*
(root)   nameserver = SRI-NIC.ARPA   *--servers are no longer*
(root)   nameserver = GUNTER-ADAM.ARPA   *--roots*

A remote name server tried to "help out" our local name server by sending it the current list of roots. Unfortunately, the remote name server was corrupt, and returned NS records that were incorrect. And our local name server, not knowing any better, cached that data.

Queries to misconfigured **in-addr.arpa** name servers often result in bad root NS records, because the **arpa** domain is the closest ancestor of most **in-addr.arpa** domains, and name servers very seldom cache **arpa**'s NS records. (The roots seldom give them out, since they delegate directly to lower-level domains.) Once your name server has cached bad root NS records, your name resolution may suffer.

Those root NS records may have your name server querying a root name server that is no longer at that IP address, or a root name server that no longer exists at all. If you're having an especially bad day, the bad root NS records may point to a real, non-root name server that is close to your network. Even though it won't return authoritative root data, your name server will favor it because of its proximity to your network.

Using check_del

If our little lecture has convinced you of the importance of maintaining correct delegation, you'll be eager to learn how to use *check_del* to ensure you don't join the ranks of the miscreants.

check_del usually takes two arguments: the name of a data file to check and the default origin in the data file. The default origin tells *check_del* which domain to append to relative names in the file. (When *named* reads the db file, it learns the default origin in the boot file: it's always the second field. *check_del* doesn't read the boot file, though, so you need to specify the domain on the command line. If it read the boot file, it'd be limited to checking only db files listed in it.)

To check whether the *db.movie* file contains proper delegation to **fx.movie.edu** (and any other subdomains), we'd run:

```
% check_del -o movie.edu -f db.movie
```

If the delegation is correct, we'd see this:

```
5 domains properly delegated
```

Actually, it's one domain delegated to three authoritative servers (**movie.edu** delegated to **terminator, wormhole** and **zardoz**) and one subdomain delegated to two authoritative servers (**fx.movie.edu** delegated to **bladerunner** and **outland**), but *check_del* doesn't know that. The point is that all the NS records in *db.movie* are correct.

If one of the **fx.movie.edu** name servers—say **outland**—were misconfigured, we'd see this:

```
Server outland.fx.movie.edu is not authoritative for fx.movie.edu

4 domains properly delegated
1 domains improperly delegated
```

Okay, *check_del* doesn't really understand plurals, either.

If one of the **fx.movie.edu** name servers weren't running at all, we'd see:

```
4 domains properly delegated
1 servers not running

Servers not running:
        outland.fx.movie.edu
```

In this case, not running really means that *check_del* tried to send the name server a query and got an ICMP port unreachable error back, which indicated that nothing was listening on the name server port.

And if the name server didn't answer in an acceptable amount of time, you'd see:

```
4 domains properly delegated
1 servers not responding

Servers not responding:
         outland.fx.movie.edu
```

Managing Delegation

If the special effects lab gets bigger, we may find that we need additional name servers. We dealt with setting up new name servers in Chapter 8, *Growing Your Domain*, and even went over what information to send to the parent domain. But we never explained what the parent needed to do.

It turns out that the parent's job is relatively easy, especially if the administrators of the subdomain send complete information. Imagine the special effects lab expands to a new network, 192.254.20. They have a passel of new, high-powered graphics workstations. One of them, **alien.fx.movie.edu**, will act as the network's name server.

The administrators of **fx.movie.edu** (we delegated it to the folks in the lab) send their parent domains' administrators (that's us) a short note:

```
Hi!

We've just set up alien.fx.movie.edu (192.254.20.3) as a name
server for fx.movie.edu.  Would you please update your
delegation information?  I've attached the NS records you'll
need to add.

Thanks,

Arty Segue
ajs@fx.movie.edu

----- cut here -----

fx.movie.edu.   86400  IN  NS  bladerunner.fx.movie.edu.
fx.movie.edu.   86400  IN  NS  outland.fx.movie.edu.
fx.movie.edu.   86400  IN  NS  alien.fx.movie.edu.

bladerunner.fx.movie.edu.   86400  IN  A  192.253.254.2
outland.fx.movie.edu.       86400  IN  A  192.253.254.3
alien.fx.movie.edu.         86400  IN  A  192.254.20.3
```

Our job as the **movie.edu** administrator is straightforward: add the NS and A records to *db.movie*.

What if we're using *h2n* to create our name server data? We can stick the delegation information into the *spcl.movie* file, which *h2n* $INCLUDEs at the end of the *db.movie* file it creates.

The final step for the **fx.movie.edu** administrator is to send a similar message to hostmaster@internic.net (administrator for the **arpa** domain), requesting that the **20.254.192.in-addr.arpa** domain be delegated to **alien.fx.movie.edu**, **bladerunner.fx.movie.edu**, and **outland.fx.movie.edu**.

Managing the Transition to Subdomains

We won't lie to you: the **fx.movie.edu** example we showed you was unrealistic for several reasons. The main one is the magical appearance of the special effects lab's hosts. In the real world, the lab would have started out with a few hosts, probably in the **movie.edu** domain. After a generous endowment, an NSF grant or a corporate gift, they might expand the lab a little and buy a few more computers. Sooner or later, the lab would have enough hosts to warrant the creation of a new subdomain. By that point, however, many of the original hosts would be well-known by their names under **movie.edu**.

We briefly touched on using CNAME records under the parent domain (in our **plan9.movie.edu** example) to help people adjust to a host's change of domain. But what happens when you move a whole network or subnet into a new subdomain?

The strategy we recommend uses CNAME records in much the same way, but on a larger scale. Using a tool like *h2n*, you can create CNAMEs for hosts *en masse*. This allows users to continue using the old domain names for any of the hosts that have moved. When they *telnet* or *ftp* (or whatever) to those hosts, however, the command will report that they're connected to a host in **fx.movie.edu**, though:

```
% telnet plan9
Trying...
Connected to plan9.fx.movie.edu.
Escape character is '^]'.

HP-UX plan9.fx.movie.edu B.08.00 B 9000/380 (ttyu1)

login:
```

Some users, of course, don't notice subtle changes like this, so you should also do some public relations work and notify folks of the change.

NOTE

On **fx.movie.edu** hosts running old versions of *sendmail*, we may also need to configure mail to accept mail addressed to the new domain names. Modern versions of *sendmail* canonicalize the host names in addresses in message headers using a name server before sending the messages. This will turn a **movie.edu** alias into a canonical name in **fx.movie.edu**. If, however, the *sendmail* on the receiving end is older and hard-codes the local host's domain name, we'd have to change the name to the new domain name by hand. This usually requires a simple change to class *w* or fileclass *w* in *sendmail.cf*; see "The MX Algorithm" section of Chapter 5, *DNS and Electronic Mail.*

How do you create all these aliases? You simply need to tell *h2n* to create the aliases for hosts on the **fx.movie.edu** networks (192.253.254 and 192.254.20), and indicate (in the */etc/hosts* file) what the new domain names for the hosts are. For example, using the **fx.movie.edu** host table, we could easily generate the aliases under **movie.edu** for all the hosts in **fx.movie.edu**:

Partial contents of */etc/hosts*:

```
192.253.254.1 movie-gw.movie.edu movie-gw
# fx primary
192.253.254.2 bladerunner.fx.movie.edu bladerunner br
# fx secondary
192.253.254.3 outland.fx.movie.edu outland
192.253.254.4 starwars.fx.movie.edu starwars
192.253.254.5 empire.fx.movie.edu empire
192.253.254.6 jedi.fx.movie.edu jedi
192.254.20.3  alien.fx.movie.edu alien
```

h2n's **-c** option takes a domain name as an argument. When *h2n* finds any hosts in that domain on networks it's building data for, it'll create aliases for them in the current domain. So by running:

```
% h2n -d movie.edu -n 192.253.254 -n 192.254.20 \
-c fx.movie.edu -f options
```

(where *options* contains other command line options for building data from other **movie.edu** networks) we could create aliases under **movie.edu** for all **fx.movie.edu** hosts.

Removing Parent Aliases

Although parent-level aliases are useful for minimizing the impact of moving your hosts, they're also a crutch of sorts. Like a crutch, they'll restrict your freedom: They'll clutter up your parent name space, when one of your motivations for implementing a subdomain may have been making the parent domain smaller. And they'll prevent you from using the names of hosts in the subdomain as names for hosts in the parent domain.

After a grace period—which should be well-advertised to users—you should remove all the aliases, with the possible exception of aliases for extremely well-known Internet hosts. During the grace period, users can adjust to the new domain names, modify scripts, *.rhosts* files, and the like. But don't get suckered into leaving all those aliases in the parent domain: they defeat part of the purpose of the DNS, because they prevent you and your subdomain administrator from naming hosts autonomously.

You might want to leave CNAME records for well-known Internet hosts or central network resources intact, because of the potential impact of a loss of connectivity. On the other hand, rather than moving the well-known host or central resource into a subdomain at all, it might be better to leave it at the parent domain level.

h2n gives you an easy way to delete the aliases you created so simply with the -c option, even if the records for the subdomain's hosts are mixed in the host table or on the same network as hosts in other domains. The -e option takes a domain as an argument, and tells *h2n* to exclude (hence -e) all records containing that domain name on networks it would otherwise create data for. This command line, for example, would delete all the CNAME records for **fx.movie.edu** hosts created earlier, while still creating an A record for **movie-gw** (which is on the 192.253.254 network):

```
% h2n -d movie.edu -n 192.253.254 -n 192.254.20 \
-e fx.movie.edu -f options
```

The Life of a Parent

That's a lot of parental advice to digest in one sitting, so let's recap the highlights of what we've talked about. The life cycle of a typical parent domain goes something like this:

1. You have a single domain, with all of your hosts in that domain.
2. You break your domain into a number of subdomains, some of them in the same zone as the parent, if necessary. You provide CNAME records

in the parent domain for well-known hosts that have moved into sub-domains.

3. After a grace period, you delete any remaining CNAME records.

Okay, now that you know all there is to parenting, let's go on to talk about some important troubleshooting tools. As a new parent, you might think of these as the DNS equivalent of a baby monitor: they'll tell you when something's gone wrong with the little ones.

10

nslookup

> *"Don't stand chattering to yourself like that," Humpty Dumpty said, looking at her for the first time, "but tell me your name and your business."*
>
> *"My name is Alice, but—"*
>
> *"It's a stupid name enough!" Humpty Dumpty interrupted impatiently. "What does it mean?"*
>
> *"Must a name mean something?" Alice asked doubtfully.*
>
> *"Of course it must," Humpty Dumpty said with a short laugh . . . "*

To be proficient at troubleshooting name server problems, you'll need a special tool to make DNS queries, one that gives you complete control. We'll cover *nslookup* in this chapter because it's distributed with BIND and with many vendors' systems. If you're the renegade type, you might check out *dig*; it provides similar functionality. You can pick up source for *dig* from isi.edu (among other places) in */pub/dig.2.0.tar.Z.*

Note that this chapter isn't comprehensive: there are aspects of *nslookup*—mostly obscure and seldom-used—that we won't cover. You can always consult the manual pages for those. And note, too, that your version of *nslookup* may not have all the functionality of the *nslookup* we describe (the *nslookup* shipped with 4.8.3 BIND). You can always compile your own *nslookup*, of course. The source to the 4.8.3 version of BIND is currently available via anonymous *ftp* from ftp.uu.net as part of */networking/ip/dns/bind/bind.4.8.3.tar.Z.* Instructions for compiling *nslookup* (on a Sun, anyway) are included as part of Appendix B.

Is nslookup a Good Tool?

Much of the time you'll use *nslookup* to make queries just like the resolver does. Sometimes, though, you'll use *nslookup* to query other name servers like a name server would, instead. Which one you emulate will depend on the problem you're trying to debug. You might wonder, "How accurately does *nslookup* emulate a resolver or a name server? Does *nslookup* actually use the BIND resolver library routines?" No, *nslookup* uses its own routines for querying name servers, but those routines are based on the resolver routines. Consequently, *nslookup*'s behavior is very similar to the resolver's behavior, but does differ slightly. We'll point out some of those differences. As for emulating name server behavior, *nslookup* allows us to query another server with the same query packet as a name server would use, but the retransmission scheme is quite different. Like a name server, though, *nslookup* can pull a copy of the zone data. So *nslookup* does not exactly emulate either the resolver or the name server, but it does emulate them well enough to make a good troubleshooting tool. Let's delve into those differences we alluded to.

Multiple Servers

nslookup only talks to one name server at a time. This is the biggest difference between *nslookup*'s behavior and the resolver's behavior. The resolver makes use of each *nameserver* entry in *resolv.conf.* If there are two *nameserver* lines in *resolv.conf,* the resolver tries the first name server, then the second, then the first, then the second, until it receives a response or it gives up. The resolver does this for every query. On the other hand, *nslookup* tries the first name server in *resolv.conf* and keeps retrying it. It will finally give up on the first name server and try the second. Once it gets a response, it locks onto that server and doesn't try the other. But, you *want* your troubleshooting tool to talk only with one name server because you can force that name server to look up whatever you want. You can even make that name server print out debugging information while you have it under the spotlight. If *nslookup* used more than one name server, you wouldn't have as much control over your troubleshooting session. So, talking to only one server is the right thing for a troubleshooting tool to do.

Timeouts

The *nslookup* timeouts match the resolver timeouts when the resolver is only querying one name server. A name server's timeouts, however, are based on how quickly the remote server answered the last query, a dynamic measure. *nslookup* will never match name server timeouts, but that's not a problem either. When you're querying remote name servers with *nslookup*, you probably only care *what* the response was, not how long it took.

Domain Searches

nslookup implements the search list just like the resolver code does. Name servers don't implement search lists, so, to act like a name server, the *nslookup* search function must be turned off—more on that later.

Zone Transfers

nslookup will do zone transfers just like a name server. Unlike the name server, *nslookup* does not check SOA serial numbers before pulling the zone data; you'll have to do that manually if you want. *nslookup* filters the zone data—by default, it only shows you the address and name server resource records even though *nslookup* processes all of the zone data. As you might expect, you can force *nslookup* to show you all the zone data.

Using NIS and /etc/hosts

This last point doesn't compare *nslookup* to the resolver or name server but to looking up names in general. *nslookup*, as distributed from Berkeley, only uses DNS; it won't use NIS or */etc/hosts*. Most applications will use DNS, NIS, or */etc/hosts*. Don't look to *nslookup* to help you find your lookup problem unless your host is really configured to use name servers.

Interactive Versus Non-interactive

Let's start our tutorial on *nslookup* by looking at how to start it and how to exit from it. *nslookup* can be run either interactively or non-interactively. If you only want to look up one piece of data, use the non-interactive form. If you plan on doing something more extensive, like changing servers or options, then use an interactive session.

To start an interactive session, just type **nslookup**:

```
% nslookup
Default Server: terminator.movie.edu
Address:  0.0.0.0

> ^D
```

If you need help, type **?** or **help**. When you want to exit, type **^D** (control-D). If you try to exit from *nslookup* by interrupting it, with **^C** (or whatever your interrupt character is), you won't get very far. *nslookup* catches the interrupt, stops whatever it is doing (like a zone transfer), and gives you the > prompt.

For a non-interactive lookup, include the name you are looking up on the command line:

```
% nslookup carrie
Server:  terminator.movie.edu
Address:  0.0.0.0

Name:    carrie.movie.edu
Address: 192.253.253.4
```

Option Settings

nslookup has its own set of dials and knobs, called option settings. All of the option settings can be changed. We'll discuss here what each of the options mean. We'll use the rest of the chapter to show you how to use them.

```
% nslookup
Default Server:  bladerunner.fx.movie.edu
Address:  0.0.0.0

> set all
Default Server:  bladerunner.fx.movie.edu
Address:  0.0.0.0

Set options:
    nodebug        defname        search         recurse
    nod2           novc           noignoretc     port=53
    querytype=A    class=IN       timeout=5      retry=4
    root=ns.nic.ddn.mil.
    domain=fx.movie.edu
    srchlist=fx.movie.edu/movie.edu

> ^D
```

Before we get into the options, we need to cover the introductory lines.

The default name server is **bladerunner.fx.movie.edu**. This means that every query sent by *nslookup* is going to be sent to **bladerunner**. The address 0.0.0.0 means "this host." When *nslookup* is using address 0.0.0.0 or 127.0.0.1 as its server, it is using the name server running on the local system, in this case, **bladerunner**.

The options come in two flavors: *boolean* and *value*. The options that do not have an "=" after them are boolean options. They have the interesting property of being either "on" or "off." The value options can take on different, well, values. How can we tell which boolean options are on and which are off? The option is *off* when a "no" precedes the option's name. *nodebug* means that debugging is off. As you might guess, the option *search* is on.

How you change boolean or value options depends on whether you are using *nslookup* interactively or not. In an interactive session, you change an option with the *set* command, as in **set debug** or **set domain=classics.movie.edu**. From the command line, you omit the word *set* and precede the option with a "–", as in **nslookup –debug** or **nslookup –domain=classics.movie.edu**. The options can be abbreviated to their shortest unique string—e.g., *nodeb* for *nodebug*. In addition to its abbreviation, the *querytype* option can also be called simply *type*.

Let's go through each of the options:

[no]debug   Debugging is turned off by default. If it is turned on, the name server shows timeouts and displays the response packets. See [no]d2 for a discussion of debug level 2.

[no]defname By default, *nslookup* adds the default domain name to names without a dot in them. Before search lists existed, the BIND resolver code would only add the default domain to names without *any* dots in them; this option reflects that behavior. *nslookup* can implement the pre-search list behavior (with search off and defname on), or it can implement the search list behavior (with search on).

[no]search   The search option "overshadows" the default domain name (defname) option. That is, defname only applies if search is turned off. By default, *nslookup* appends the domains in the search list (srchlist) to names that don't end in a dot.

[no]recurse *nslookup* requests recursive service by default. This turns on the recursion-desired bit in query packets. The BIND resolver

sends recursive queries in the same way. Name servers, however, send out non-recursive queries to other name servers.

[no]d2   Debugging at level 2 is turned off by default. If it is turned on, you see the query packets sent out in addition to the regular debugging output. Turning on *d2* also turns on *debug*. Turning off *d2* only turns off *d2*; *debug* is left on. Turning off *debug* turns off both *debug* and *d2*.

[no]vc   By default, *nslookup* makes queries using UDP packets instead of over a virtual circuit (TCP). Most BIND resolver queries are made with UDP, so the default *nslookup* behavior matches the resolver. As the resolver can be instructed to use TCP, so can *nslookup*.

[no]ignoretc   By default, *nslookup doesn't* ignore truncated packets. If a packet is received that has the "truncated" bit set—indicating that the name server couldn't fit all the important information in the UDP response packet—*nslookup* doesn't ignore it; it retries the query using a TCP connection instead of UDP. Again, this matches the BIND resolver behavior. The reason for retrying the query using a TCP connection is that TCP responses can be twice as large as UDP responses. TCP responses *could* be many times the size of a UDP response (a TCP connection can carry much more data than a single UDP packet), but the buffers BIND uses for a TCP query are only twice as large as the UDP buffers.

port=53   The DNS service is on port 53. You can start a name server on another port—for debugging purposes, for example—and *nslookup* can be directed to use that port.

querytype=A   By default, *nslookup* looks up address (A) resource record types. In addition, if you type in an IP address (and the *nslookup* query type is address or pointer), then *nslookup* will invert the address, append **in-addr.arpa**, and look up pointer (PTR) data instead.

class=IN   The only class that matters is *Internet*. Well, there is the *Hesiod* (HS) class too, if you are an MIT'er or run Ultrix.

timeout=5   If the name server doesn't respond within 5 seconds, *nslookup* resends the query and doubles the timeout (to 10, 20, and 40 seconds). The BIND resolver uses the same timeouts when querying a single name server.

retry=4   Send the query four times before giving up. After each retry, the timeout value is doubled. Again, this matches the BIND resolver.

root=ns.nic.ddn.mil.

There is a convenience command called **root** which switches your default server to the server named here. Executing the **root** command from a modern *nslookup*'s prompt is equivalent to executing **server ns.nic.ddn.mil.** Older versions use **nic.ddn.mil** (old) or even **sri-nic.arpa** (ancient) as the default root name server. You can change the default "root" server with **set root=**server.

domain=fx.movie.edu

This is the default domain appended if the `defname` option is on.

srchlist=fx.movie.edu/movie.edu

If `search` is on, these are the domains appended to names that do not end in a dot. The domains are listed in the order that they are tried, separated by a slash ("/").

The .nslookuprc File

You can set up new default *nslookup* options in an *.nslookuprc* file. *nslookup* will look for an *.nslookuprc* file in your home directory when it starts up, in both interactive and non-interactive modes. The *.nslookuprc* file can contain any legal **set** commands, one per line. This is useful, for example, if your old *nslookup* still thinks **sri-nic.arpa** is a root name server. You can set the default root name server to a real root with a line like this in your *.nslookuprc* file:

```
set root=ns.nic.ddn.mil.
```

You might also use *.nslookuprc* to set your search list to something other than your host's default search list, or to change the timeouts *nslookup* uses.

Avoiding the Search List

nslookup implements the search list like the resolver. When you are debugging, the search list can get in your way. Either you need to turn the search list off completely (**set nosearch**), or you need to add a trailing dot to the fully qualified domain name you are looking up. We prefer the latter, as you'll see in our examples.

Common Tasks

There are little chores you'll come to use *nslookup* for almost every day: finding out the IP address or MX records for a given domain name, or querying a particular name server for data. We'll cover these first, before moving on into the more occasional stuff.

Looking Up Different Data Types

By default, *nslookup* looks up the address for a name or the name for an address. You can look up any data type by changing the *querytype*, as we will show in this example:

```
% nslookup
Default Server: terminator.movie.edu
Address:  0.0.0.0

> misery                    --Look up address
Server:  terminator.movie.edu
Address:  0.0.0.0

Name:     misery.movie.edu
Address:  192.253.253.2

> 192.253.253.2             --Look up name
Server:  terminator.movie.edu
Address:  0.0.0.0

Name:     misery.movie.edu
Address:  192.253.253.2

> set q=mx                  --Look up MX data
> wormhole
Server:  terminator.movie.edu
Address:  0.0.0.0

wormhole.movie.edu        preference = 10, mail exchanger = wormhole.movie.edu
wormhole.movie.edu        internet address = 192.249.249.1
wormhole.movie.edu        internet address = 192.253.253.1

> set q=any                 --Look up data of any type
> diehard
Server:  terminator.movie.edu
Address:  0.0.0.0

diehard.movie.edu         internet address = 192.249.249.4
diehard.movie.edu         preference = 10, mail exchanger = diehard.movie.edu
diehard.movie.edu         internet address = 192.249.249.4
```

These are only a few of the valid DNS data types, of course. For the complete list, see Appendix A, *DNS Message Format and Resource Records*.

Authoritative Versus Non-authoritative Answers

If you've used *nslookup* before, you might have noticed something peculiar—the first time you look up a remote name, the answer is authoritative, but the second time you look up the same name it is non-authoritative. Here's an example:

```
% nslookup
Default Server:  relay.hp.com
Address:  15.255.152.2

> slate.mines.colorado.edu.
Server:  relay.hp.com
Address:  15.255.152.2

Name:    slate.mines.colorado.edu
Address:  138.67.1.3

> slate.mines.colorado.edu.
Server:  relay.hp.com
Address:  15.255.152.2

Non-authoritative answer:
Name:    slate.mines.colorado.edu
Address:  138.67.1.3
```

While this looks odd, it really isn't. What is happening is that the first time the local name server looks up **slate**, it contacts the name server for **mines.colorado.edu** and the **mines.colorado.edu** server responds with an authoritative answer. The local name server, in effect, passes the authoritative response directly back to *nslookup*. It also caches the response. The second time you look up **slate**, the name server answers out of its cache, which results in the answer being "non-authoritative."

Notice that we ended the domain name with a trailing dot each time we looked it up. The response would have been the same had we left the trailing dot off. There are times when it is critical that you use the trailing dot while debugging and times when it is not. Rather than stopping to decide if *this* name needs a trailing dot, we always add one if we know the name is fully qualified, except, of course, for the example where we turn off the search list.

Switching Servers

Sometimes you want to query another name server directly—you may
think it is misbehaving, for example. You can switch servers with *nslookup*
by using the *server* or *lserver* commands. The difference between *server*
and *lserver* is that *lserver* queries your "local" server—the one you started
out with—to get the address of the server you want to switch to; *server*
uses the default server instead of the local server. This difference is important to know because the server you just switched to may not be responding, as we'll show in this example:

```
% nslookup
Default Server:  relay.hp.com
Address:  15.255.152.2
```

When we start up, our first server, **relay.hp.com,** *becomes our* lserver. *This will matter
later on in this session.*

```
> server bors.cs.purdue.edu.
Default Server:  bors.cs.purdue.edu
Address:  128.10.2.48

> cs.purdue.edu.
Server:  bors.cs.purdue.edu
Address:  128.10.2.48

*** bors.cs.purdue.edu can't find cs.purdue.edu.: No response from server
```

*At this point we try to switch back to our original name server. But there is no name server
running on* **bors** *to look up* **relay** *'s address.*

```
> server relay.hp.com.
*** Can't find address for server relay.hp.com.: No response from server
```

Instead of being stuck, though, we use the lserver *command to have our local server look up*
relay *'s address.*

```
> lserver relay.hp.com.
Default Server:  relay.hp.com
Address:  15.255.152.2

>
```

Since the server on **bors** did not respond—it's not even running a name
server—it wasn't possible to look up the address of **relay** to switch back to
using **relay**'s name server. Here's where *lserver* comes to the rescue: the
local name server, **relay**, was still responding, so we used it. Instead of
using *lserver,* we could have recovered by using **relay**'s IP address
directly—**server 15.255.152.2.**

You can even change servers on a per-query basis. To specify that you'd like *nslookup* to query a particular server for information about a given domain name, you can specify the server as the second argument on the line, after the domain name to look up, like so:

```
% nslookup
Default Server:  relay.hp.com
Address:  15.255.152.2

> wintermute.central.sun.com. sun.com.
Name Server:  sun.com
Address:  192.9.9.1

Name:    wintermute.central.sun.com
Address:  129.152.4.7

> ^D
```

And, of course, you can change servers from the command line. You can specify the server to query as the argument after the domain name to look up, like this:

```
% nslookup -type=mx fisherking.movie.edu. terminator.movie.edu.
```

This instructs *nslookup* to query **terminator.movie.edu** for MX records for **fisherking.movie.edu**.

Finally, to specify an alternate default server and enter interactive mode, you can use a "-" in place of the domain name to look up:

```
% nslookup - terminator.movie.edu.
```

Less Common Tasks

These are tricks you'll probably have to use less often, but which are very handy to have in your repertoire. Most of these will be helpful when you're trying to troubleshoot a DNS or BIND problem: they'll enable you to grub around in the packets the resolver sees, and mimic a BIND name server querying another name server or transferring zone data.

Seeing the Query and Response Packets

If you need to, you can direct *nslookup* to show you the queries it sends out and the responses it receives. Turning on *debug* shows you the responses. Turning on *d2* shows you the queries as well. When you want to turn off debugging completely, you have to use **set nodebug** since **set nod2** only turns off level 2 debugging. After this trace, we'll explain some parts of the packet output. If you want, you can pull out your copy of RFC 1035, turn to page 25, and read along with our explanation.

```
% nslookup
Default Server: terminator.movie.edu
Address:  0.0.0.0

> set debug
> wormhole
Server:  terminator.movie.edu
Address:  0.0.0.0

------------
Got answer:
    HEADER:
          opcode = QUERY, id = 1, rcode = NOERROR
          header flags:  response, auth. answer, want recursion,
       recursion avail.  questions = 1,  answers = 2,
       authority records = 0,  additional = 0

    QUESTIONS:
          wormhole.movie.edu, type = A, class = IN
    ANSWERS:
    ->  wormhole.movie.edu
          internet address = 192.249.249.1
          ttl = 86400 (1 day)
    ->  wormhole.movie.edu
          internet address = 192.253.253.1
          ttl = 86400 (1 day)

------------
Name:     wormhole.movie.edu
Addresses:  192.249.249.1, 192.253.253.1

> set d2
> carrie.movie.edu.
Server:  terminator.movie.edu
Address:  0.0.0.0

------------
SendRequest(), len 34
    HEADER:
          opcode = QUERY, id = 2, rcode = NOERROR
          header flags:  query, want recursion
          questions = 1,  answers = 0,  authority records = 0,
       additional = 0

    QUESTIONS:
          carrie.movie.edu, type = A, class = IN

------------
------------
Got answer (50 bytes):
```

```
HEADER:
    opcode = QUERY, id = 2, rcode = NOERROR
    header flags:  response, auth. answer, want recursion,
  recursion avail.  questions = 1,  answers = 1,
  authority records = 0,  additional = 0

QUESTIONS:
    carrie.movie.edu, type = A, class = IN
ANSWERS:
-> carrie.movie.edu
    type = A, class = IN, dlen = 4
    internet address = 192.253.253.4
    ttl = 86400 (1 day)


------------
Name:    carrie.movie.edu
Address:  192.253.253.4


>
```

The text between the dashes is the query and response packets. As promised, we'll go through the packet contents. DNS packets are comprised of five sections:

1. Header section
2. Question section
3. Answer section
4. Authority section
5. Additional section

Header section

The header section is present in every query and response. The operation code is always QUERY. The only other opcodes are inverse query (IQUERY) and status (STATUS), but those aren't used. The id is used to associate a response with a query and to detect duplicate queries or responses. You have to look in the header flags to see which packets are queries and which are responses. The string want recursion means that the querier wants the name server to do all the work. The flag is parroted in the response. The string auth. answer means that this response is *authoritative*. In other words, the response is from the name server's authoritative data and not from its cache data. The response code, rcode, can be one of no error, server failure, name error (also known as "nxdomain" or "non-existent domain"), not implemented, or refused. The server failure, name error, not implemented and refused response codes cause the *nslookup* "Server failed," "Non-existent domain," "Not implemented," and "Query refused" errors, respectively. The last four entries in the header section are counters—they indicate how many resource records there are in each of the next four sections.

Question section

There is always *one* question in a DNS packet; it includes the name, and the requested data type and class. There is never more than one question in a DNS packet. The capability of handling more than one question in a DNS packet would require a redesign of the packet format. For one thing, the single authority bit would have to be changed because the answer section could contain a mix of authoritative answers and non-authoritative answers. In the present design, setting the authoritative answer bit means the name server is an authority for the domain name in the question section.

Answer section

This section contains the resource records that answer the question. There can be more than one resource record in the response. For example, if the host is multi-homed, there will be more than one address resource record.

Authority section

The authority section is where name server records are returned. When a response refers the querier to some other name servers, those name servers are listed here.

Additional section

The additional record section adds information that may complete information included in other sections. For instance, if a name server is listed in the authority section, the name server's address is added to the additional records section. After all, to contact the name server, you need to have its address.

Notice that our example above (the lookup of **carrie**) doesn't include either an additional record section or an authority section. The additional section is empty because name servers don't add any additional data when answering an address query. The authority section is empty because the name server we asked was authoritative for the domain name in the question.

For you sticklers for detail, there *is* a time when the number of questions in a query packet isn't one: in an inverse query, when it's zero. In an inverse query, there is one answer in the query packet and the question section is empty. The name server fills in the question. But, like we said, inverse queries are almost non-existent.

Querying Like a BIND Name Server

You can make *nslookup* send out the same query packet a name server would. Name server query packets are not much different from resolver packets. The primary difference in the query packets is that resolvers request recursive services and name servers seldom do. Recursion is the default with *nslookup*, so you have to explicitly turn it off. The difference in *operation* between a resolver and a name server is that the resolver implements the search list and the name server doesn't. By default, *nslookup* implements the search list, so that, too, has to be turned off. Of course, judicious use of the trailing dot will have the same effect.

In raw *nslookup* terms, this means that to query like a resolver, you use *nslookup*'s default settings. To query like a name server, **set norecurse** and **set nosearch**. On the command line, that's **nslookup -norecurse -nosearch**.

When a BIND name server gets a query, it looks for the answer in its cache. If it doesn't have the answer, and it is authoritative for the domain, the name server responds that the name doesn't exist or that there is no data for that type. If the name server doesn't have the answer, and it is *not* authoritative for the domain, it starts walking up the domain tree looking for NS records. There will always be NS records somewhere higher in the domain tree. As a last resort, it will use the NS records at the root domain, the highest level.

If the name server received a non-recursive query, it would respond to the querier giving the NS records that it had found. On the other hand, if the original query was a recursive query, the name server then queries the remote name servers in the NS records that it found. When the name server receives a response from one of the remote name servers, it caches the response, and repeats this process, if necessary. The remote server's response will either have the answer to the question, or it will contain a list of name servers lower in the domain tree and closer to the answer.

Let's assume for our example that we are trying to satisfy a recursive query and that we didn't find any NS records until we checked the root domain. That is, in fact, the case when we ask the name server on **relay.hp.com** about **skyler.mavd.honeywell.com**—it doesn't find any NS records until the root domain. From there we switch servers to a root name server and ask the same question. It directs us to the **honeywell.com** servers. We then switch to a **honeywell.com** name server and ask the same question.

```
% nslookup
Default Server:  relay.hp.com
Address:  15.255.152.2
```

> **set norec**	*--Query like a name server:*
	--turn off recursion
> **set nosearch**	*--turn off the search list*
> **skyler.mavd.honeywell.com**	*--(we don't need to dot-*
	--terminate since we've turned
	--search off

```
Server:  relay.hp.com
Address:  15.255.152.2
```

The blank lines after the IP addresses below aren't really blank lines; they just look that way. Instead, those lines list the domain the server is a name server for. Since these are root name servers and the root domain prints as an empty string, the line looks blank.

```
Name:    skyler.mavd.honeywell.com
Served by:
- NS.NIC.DDN.MIL
        192.112.36.4

- AOS.BRL.MIL
        128.63.4.82, 26.3.0.29, 192.5.25.82

- KAVA.NISC.SRI.COM
        192.33.33.24

- C.NYSER.NET
        192.33.4.12

- TERP.UMD.EDU
        128.8.10.90

- NS.NASA.GOV
        128.102.16.10, 192.52.195.10

- NIC.NORDU.NET
        192.36.148.17
```

Switch to a root name server. You may have to turn recursion back on temporarily if the name server doesn't have the address already cached. Since the server we are switching to is a root name server, the address will be cached. We chose this particular root because it happens to be close to us.

```
> server ns.nasa.gov
Default Server:  ns.nasa.gov
Addresses:  128.102.16.10, 192.52.195.10
```

Ask the same question of the root name server. It will refer us to name servers closer to our desired answer.

```
> skyler.mavd.honeywell.com
Server:  ns.nasa.gov
Addresses:  128.102.16.10, 192.52.195.10

Name:    skyler.mavd.honeywell.com
Served by:
- FISHERY.HONEYWELL.COM
          129.30.3.16
          HONEYWELL.COM
- SRC.HONEYWELL.COM
          129.235.16.32
          HONEYWELL.COM
- NIC.MR.NET
          137.192.240.5
          HONEYWELL.COM
```

Switch to a honeywell.com *name server--any of the three will do. Fortunately, the root name server has the address of the server we want to switch to, so we don't have to turn recursion on.*

```
> server src.honeywell.com
Default Server:  src.honeywell.com
Address:  129.235.16.32
```

Ask the same question of the honeywell.com *name server. The* honeywell.com *name server may refer us to the* mavd.honeywell.com *name servers or it may answer the question if it's also a* mavd.honeywell.com *name server. As luck would have it, the server answers the question.*

```
> skyler.mavd.honeywell.com
Server:  src.honeywell.com
Address:  129.235.16.32

Name:    skyler.mavd.honeywell.com
Address:  129.30.6.101
```

We hope this example gives you a feeling for how name servers look up names. If you need to refresh your understanding of what this looks like graphically, flip back to Figure 2.10.

Before we move on, notice that we asked each of the servers the very same question: "What's the address for **skyler.mavd.honeywell.com**?" What do you think would happen if the root name server had already cached **skyler**'s address itself? The root name server would have answered the question out of its cache instead of referring you to the **honeywell.com** name servers. Why is this significant? Suppose you messed up a particular host's address in your domain. Someone points it out to you and you clean up the problem. Even though your name server now has the correct data, some remote sites find the old, messed-up data when they look up the name. One of the name servers higher up in the domain tree, like a root name server, has cached the incorrect data; when it receives a query for that host's address, it returns the incorrect data instead of referring the querier to your name servers. What makes this problem hard to track down is that only one of the "higher up" name servers has cached the incorrect data, so only some of the remote lookups get the wrong answer—the ones that use this server. Fun, huh? Eventually, though, the "higher up" name server will time out the old record. If you're pressed for time, you can contact the administrators of the remote name server and ask them to kill and restart *named* to flush the cache.

Zone Transfers

nslookup can be used to transfer a whole zone using the *ls* command. This feature is useful for troubleshooting, or figuring out how to spell a remote host's name, or just to count how many hosts are in some remote domain. Since the output can be substantial, *nslookup* allows you to redirect the output to a file and view the file with *more*. If you want to bail out in the middle of a transfer, you can interrupt it by typing your interrupt character.

Beware: some hosts won't let you pull a copy of their zone either for security reasons or to limit the load on their name server host. The Internet is a friendly place, but administrators have to defend their turf. If you remember from earlier discussions, a name server spawns a child process to handle a zone transfer. If that name server is a very large process, the host's administrator won't want it spawning many children—the host will bog down. There is no mechanism to limit how many children a name server can start, so administrators instead limit which hosts can pull a copy of the zone data.

As we mentioned earlier, *nslookup* filters the zone data. It only shows you some of the zone unless you tell it otherwise. By default, you only see address and name server data. You will see all of the zone data if you tell *nslookup* to display data of *any* type. Since the zone data can produce many screens of output, you can redirect the output to a file. The *nslookup* manual page tells you all of the parameters to the *ls* command. We are only going to show you the –t parameter since the others can be emulated with –t. The –t takes one argument—the data type to filter on. So, to pull a copy of a zone and see all the *mx* data, use **ls –t mx** *domain*. Let's do some zone transfers.

```
% nslookup
Default Server:  terminator.movie.edu
Address:  0.0.0.0

> ls movie.edu.              --List NS and A records for movie.edu
[terminator.movie.edu]
 movie.edu.                      server = terminator.movie.edu
 terminator                      192.249.249.3
 movie.edu.                      server = wormhole.movie.edu
 wormhole                        192.249.249.1
 wormhole                        192.253.253.1
 robocop                         192.249.249.2
 shining                         192.253.253.3
 localhost                       127.0.0.1
 carrie                          192.253.253.4
 diehard                         192.249.249.4
 misery                          192.253.253.2
> ls -t mx movie.edu.       --List MX records
[terminator.movie.edu]
 wormhole                        10   wormhole.movie.edu
 robocop                         10   robocop.movie.edu
 shining                         10   shining.movie.edu
 terminator                      10   terminator.movie.edu
 carrie                          10   carrie.movie.edu
 diehard                         10   diehard.movie.edu
 misery                          10   misery.movie.edu
> ls -t any movie.edu > /tmp/movie   --List all data into /tmp/movie
[terminator.movie.edu]
Received 19 records.
> view /tmp/movie           --view also sorts the file
 carrie                    A    192.253.253.4
 carrie                    MX   10   carrie.movie.edu
 diehard                   A    192.249.249.4
 diehard                   MX   10   diehard.movie.edu
 localhost                 A    127.0.0.1
 misery                    A    192.253.253.2
 misery                    MX   10   misery.movie.edu
 movie.edu.                NS   terminator.movie.edu
 movie.edu.                NS   wormhole.movie.edu
 movie.edu.                SOA  terminator.movie.edu
(root.terminator.movie.edu. 1 10800 3600 604800 86400)
 movie.edu.                SOA  terminator.movie.edu
(root.terminator.movie.edu. 1 10800 3600 604800 86400)
 robocop                   A    192.249.249.2
 robocop                   MX   10   robocop.movie.edu
 shining                   A    192.253.253.3
 shining                   MX   10   shining.movie.edu
 terminator                A    192.249.249.3
 terminator                MX   10   terminator.movie.edu
 wormhole                  A    192.249.249.1
 wormhole                  A    192.253.253.1
 wormhole                  MX   10   wormhole.movie.edu
```

Troubleshooting nslookup Problems

The last thing you want is to have problems with your troubleshooting tool. Unfortunately, some types of failures render the troubleshooting tool mostly useless. Other types of *nslookup* failures are, at best, confusing because they don't give you any direct information to work with. While there may be a few problems with *nslookup* itself, most of the problems you encounter will be with name server configuration and operation. We'll cover a few odd problems here.

Looking Up the Right Data

This isn't really a problem, *per se*, but it can be awfully confusing. If you use *nslookup* to look up a type of data for a domain name, and the domain name exists, but no data of the type you're looking for exists, you'll get an error like this:

```
% nslookup
Default Server:  terminator.movie.edu
Address:  0.0.0.0

> movie.edu.

*** No address (A) records available for movie.edu.
```

So what types of records *do* exist? Just **set type=any** to find out:

```
> set type=any
> movie.edu.
Server:  terminator.movie.edu
Address:  0.0.0.0

movie.edu
        origin = terminator.movie.edu
        mail addr = al.robocop.movie.edu
        serial = 42
        refresh = 10800 (3 hours)
        retry   = 3600 (1 hour)
        expire  = 604800 (7 days)
        minimum ttl = 86400 (1 day)
movie.edu       nameserver = terminator.movie.edu
movie.edu       nameserver = wormhole.movie.edu
movie.edu       nameserver = zardoz.movie.edu
movie.edu       preference = 10, mail exchanger = postmanrings2x.movie.edu
postmanrings2x.movie.edu        internet address = 192.249.249.66
```

No Response from Server

What could have gone wrong if your server can't look up its own name?

```
% nslookup
Default Server: terminator.movie.edu
Address:  0.0.0.0

> terminator
Server: terminator.movie.edu
Address:  0.0.0.0

*** terminator.movie.edu can't find terminator: No response from server
```

The "no response from server" error message means exactly that: the name server didn't get a response back. *nslookup* doesn't necessarily look up anything when it starts up. If you see that the address of your server is 0.0.0.0, *nslookup* grabbed the system's host name (what the *hostname* command returns) for the server field and gave you its prompt. It is only when you try to look up something that you find out that there is no server responding. In this case, it is pretty obvious that there is no name server running—a name server ought to be able to look up its own name. If you are looking up some remote information, though, the name server could fail to respond because it is still trying to look up the item and *nslookup* gave up waiting. How can you tell the difference between a name server that isn't running and a name server that is running, but didn't respond? Use the *ls* command to point out the difference:

```
% nslookup
Default Server: terminator.movie.edu
Address:  0.0.0.0

> ls foo.      --Try to list a non-existent domain
*** Can't list domain foo.: No response from server
```

In this case, no name server is running. If the host couldn't be reached, the error would be "timed out." If a name server is running, you'll see the following error message:

```
% nslookup
Default Server: terminator.movie.edu
Address:  0.0.0.0

> ls foo.
[terminator.movie.edu]
*** Can't list domain foo.: No information
```

That is, unless there's a top-level **foo** domain in your world.

No PTR Data for Name Server's Address

Here is one of the most annoying problems: something went wrong and *nslookup* exited on startup.

```
% nslookup
*** Can't find server name for address 192.249.249.3: Non-existent domain
*** Default servers are not available
```

The "non-existent domain" means that the name **3.249.249.192.in-addr.arpa** doesn't exist. In other words, *nslookup* couldn't find the name for 192.249.249.3, its name server host. But didn't we just say that *nslookup* doesn't look up anything when it starts up? In the configuration presented before, *nslookup* didn't look up anything, but that's not a rule. If you create an *resolv.conf* that includes *nameserver* lines, *nslookup* looks up the address in order to get the name server's name. In the example above, there *is* a name server running on 192.249.249.3, but it said there is no PTR data for the address 192.249.249.3. Obviously, this name server's data is messed up, at least for the **249.249.192.in-addr.arpa** domain.

The "default servers are not available" message above is misleading. After all, there is a name server there to say the address doesn't exist. More often, you'll see the error "no response from server" if the name server isn't running on the host or the host can't be reached. Only then does the "default servers are not available" message makes sense.

First resolv.conf Name Server Not Responding

Here is another twist on the last problem:

```
% nslookup
*** Can't find server name for address 192.249.249.3: No response from server
Default Server:  wormhole.movie.edu
Address:  192.249.249.1
```

This time the first *nameserver* in *resolv.conf* did not respond. We had put a second *nameserver* line in *resolv.conf* and the second server did respond. From now on, *nslookup* will send queries only to **wormhole**; it won't try 192.249.249.3 again.

Finding Out What Is Being Looked Up

We've been waving our hands in the last examples, saying that *nslookup* was looking up the name server's address but not proving it. Here is our proof. This time when we started up *nslookup* we turned on *d2* debugging from the command line. This causes *nslookup* to print out the query packets it sent as well as printing out when the query times out and is retransmitted.

```
% nslookup -d2
------------
SendRequest(), len 44
    HEADER:
        opcode = QUERY, id = 1, rcode = NOERROR
        header flags:  query, want recursion
        questions = 1,  answers = 0,  authority records = 0,  additional = 0

    QUESTIONS:
        3.249.249.192.in-addr.arpa, type = PTR, class = IN

------------
timeout (5 secs)
timeout (10 secs)
timeout (20 secs)
timeout (40 secs)
SendRequest failed
*** Can't find server name for address 192.249.249.3: No response from server
*** Default servers are not available
```

As you can see by the timeouts, it took 75 seconds for *nslookup* to give up. Without the debugging output, you won't see anything printed to your screen for 75 seconds; it'll look like *nslookup* has hung.

Unspecified Error

You can run into a rather unsettling problem called "unspecified error." We have an example of this error here. We've only included the tail end of the output since we only want to talk about the error at this point. You'll find the whole *nslookup* session that produced this segment in Chapter 12, *Troubleshooting DNS and BIND*.

```
Authoritative answers can be found from:
(root)   nameserver = NS.NIC.DDN.MIL
(root)   nameserver = AOS.BRL.MIL
(root)   nameserver = KAVA.NISC.SRI.COM
(root)   nameserver = C.NYSER.NET
(root)   nameserver = TERP.UMD.EDU
(root)   nameserver = NS.NASA.GOV
(root)   nameserver =

*** Error: record size incorrect (1050690 != 65519)

*** relay.hp.com can't find .: Unspecified error
```

What happened here is that there was too much data to fit into a UDP
datagram. The name server stopped filling in the response when it ran out
of room. The name server *didn't* set the truncation bit in the response
packet or *nslookup* would have retried the query over a TCP connection;
the name server must have decided that enough of the "important" information fit. You won't see this kind of error very often. You'll see it if you create too many NS records for a domain, so don't create too many. (Advice
like this makes you wonder why you bought this book, right?) How many
is too many depends upon how well the names can be "compressed" in the
packet which, in turn, depends upon how many name servers share the
same domain in their domain name. As a rule of thumb, don't go over ten
NS records. As for what caused *this* error, you'll have to read Chapter 12,
Troubleshooting DNS and BIND. Those of you who just read Chapter 9,
Parenting, may know already.

11

Reading BIND Debugging Output

*"O Tiger-lily!" said Alice, addressing herself to one that was waving gracefully about in the wind, "I **wish** you could talk!"*

*"We **can** talk," said the Tiger-lily, "when there's anybody worth talking to."*

One of the tools in your troubleshooting toolchest is the name server's debugging output. As long as your name server has been compiled with DEBUG defined, you can get query-by-query reports of its internal operation. The messages you get are often quite cryptic; they were meant for someone who has the source code to follow. We'll explain some of the debugging output in this chapter. Our goal is to cover enough for you to follow what the name server is doing; we aren't trying to supply an exhaustive compilation of debugging messages.

As you read through the explanations here, think back to material covered in earlier chapters. Seeing this information again, in another context, should help you understand more fully how a name server works.

Debugging Levels

The amount of information the name server provides depends on the debugging level. The lower the debugging level, the less information you get. Higher debugging levels give you more information, but also fill up your disk faster. After you've read a lot of debugging output, you'll develop a feel for how much information you'll need to solve any particular problem. Of course, if you can easily recreate the problem, you can start at level one and increase the debugging level until you have enough information. For the most basic problem—why a name can't be looked up—level one will often suffice, so you should start there.

What Information Is at Each Level

Here is a list of the information that each debugging level will give. The debugging information is cumulative; for example, level two includes all level one's debugging information. The data is divided into the following basic areas: starting up, updating the database, processing queries, and maintaining zones. We won't cover updating the name server's internal database—problems always occur elsewhere. However, *what* the name server adds or deletes from its internal database can be a problem, as you'll see in Chapter 12, *Troubleshooting DNS and BIND*.

Level 1   The information at this level is necessarily brief. Name servers can process *lots* of queries, which can create *lots* of debugging output. Since the output is condensed, you can collect data over long periods. Use this debugging level for basic startup information and for watching query transactions. You'll see some errors logged at this level, including syntax errors and DNS packet formatting errors.

Level 2   Level 2 provides lots of useful stuff: it lists the IP addresses of remote name servers that are used during a lookup, along with their round trip time values; it calls out duplicate responses and bad responses (counted in the statistics); and it tags a response as to which type of query it is answering: a SYSTEM (sysquery) or a USER query. When tracking down a problem with a secondary server loading a zone, this level shows you the zone values—serial number, refresh time, retry time, expire time, and time left—as a secondary checks if it is up-to-date with its master.

Level 3   Level 3 debugging becomes much more verbose because it generates lots of messages about updating the name server database; make sure you have enough disk space if you are going to collect debugging output at level 3 or above. At level 3, you'll also see: duplicate queries called out, system queries generated (sysquery), the names of the remote name servers used during a lookup, the number of addresses found for each server, and the SOA response when a secondary checks if it is up-to-date with its master.

Level 4   Use level 4 debugging when you want to see the query and response packets *received* by the name server. The format of these packets is much like the *nslookup* output in *d2* (debugging level 2) mode.

Level 5   There are a variety of messages at level 5, but none of them are particularly useful to general debugging. This level includes some error messages, like when a *malloc* fails, and a message when the name server gives up on a query.

Level 6   There are only a couple of extra debugging messages at this level, and they are in seldom-traversed code.

Level 7   There is no additional debugging information at this level.

Level 8   There is no additional debugging information at this level.

Level 9   There is no additional debugging information at this level.

Level 10   Use level 10 debugging when you want to see the query and response packets *sent* by the name server. The format of these packets is the same format used in level 4. You wouldn't use this level very often since you can see the name server response packet with *nslookup*.

Level 11   There are only a couple of debugging messages at this level, and they are in seldom-traversed code.

Keep in mind that this *is* debugging information—it was used by the authors of BIND to debug the code, so it is not as readable as you might like. You can use it, too, to figure out why the name server isn't doing what you think it should be doing, or just to learn how the name server operates; but don't expect nicely-designed, carefully formatted output.

Turning on Debugging

Name server debugging can be started either from the command line or with signals. If you need to see the startup information to diagnose your current problem, you'll have to use the command line option. If you want to start debugging on a name server that is already running or to turn off debugging, you'll have to use signals. The name server writes its debugging output to */usr/tmp/named.run* (or */var/tmp/named.run*). When debugging is turned on, the debugging output file is truncated. If you want to save an old trace, you'll have to make a copy of it before you start your next debugging session.

Debugging Command Line Option

When troubleshooting, you sometimes need to see the sort list, or to know which interface a file descriptor is bound to, or to find out where in the initialization stage the name server was when it exited (if the syslog error message wasn't clear enough). To see this kind of debugging information, you'll have to start debugging with a command line option; by the time you send a signal, it will be too late. The command line option for debugging is -d *level.* When you use the command line option to turn on debugging, the name server will not go into the background as it does normally; you'll have to add the "&" at the end of your command line to get your shell prompt back. Here's how to start the name server at debugging level 1:

```
# /etc/named -d 1 &
```

Changing the Debugging Level with Signals

If you don't need to see the name server initialization, start your name server without the debugging command line option. You can later turn debugging on and off by sending the USR1 and USR2 signals to the name server process. The first USR1 signal causes *named* to start writing debugging output at level 1. Each subsequent USR1 signal increases the debugging level by 1. Send USR2 to turn off debugging. Below, we set debugging to level 3, then turn debugging off:

```
# kill -USR1 `cat /etc/named.pid`      level 1
# kill -USR1 `cat /etc/named.pid`      level 2
# kill -USR1 `cat /etc/named.pid`      level 3
# kill -USR2 `cat /etc/named.pid`      off
```

And, as you might expect, if you turn on debugging from the command line, you can still send USR1 and USR2 signals to the name server.

Reading Debugging Output

We'll cover six examples of debugging output. The first example shows the name server starting up. The next three examples show successful name lookups. The fifth example shows a secondary name server keeping its zone up-to-date. In the last example, we switch from showing you name server behavior to showing you resolver behavior: the resolver search algorithm. After each trace, except the last one, we killed the name server and started it again so that each trace started with a fresh, nearly empty cache.

You might wonder why we've chosen to show normal name server behavior for all our examples; after all, this chapter is about debugging. We are showing you normal behavior because you have to know what normal operation *is* before you track down abnormal operation. Another reason is to help you *understand* the concepts (retransmissions, round trip times, etc.) we have described in earlier chapters.

Name Server Startup (Debug Level 1)

We'll start the debugging examples by watching the name server initialize. We used **–d 1** on the command line and this is the */usr/tmp/named.run* output that resulted:

```
1)   Debug turned ON, Level 1
2)   Version = named 4.8.3 Tue Feb 26 19:36:53 GMT 1991
3)           bootfile = ./named.boot
4)   dqp->dq_addr 127.0.0.1 d_dfd 5
5)   loopback address: x7f000001
6)   dqp->dq_addr 192.249.249.3 d_dfd 6
7)   dqp->dq_addr 0.0.0.0 d_dfd 7
8)
9)   ns_init(./named.boot)
10)  zone origin 0.0.127.IN-ADDR.ARPA, source = db.127.0.0
11)  reloading zone
12)  db_load(db.127.0.0, 0.0.127.IN-ADDR.ARPA, 1, 0)
13)  zone[1] type 1: '0.0.127.IN-ADDR.ARPA' z_time 0, z_refresh 0
14)  zone origin ., source = db.cache
15)  reloading zone
16)  db_load(db.cache, , 0, 0)
17)  zone[0] type 3: '.' z_time 0, z_refresh 0
18)  exit ns_init(), need maintenance immediately
19)  Network and sort list:
20)  net xc0f9f900 mask xffffff00 my_addr xc0f9f903 192.249.249.3
21)  database initialized
22)  Ready to answer queries.
23)  prime_cache: priming = 0
24)  sysquery: send -> 192.33.33.24 7 (53), nsid=1 id=0 0ms
25)
26)  ns_maint(); now Sat Feb 15 13:13:04 1992
27)  sched_maint: Next interrupt in 0 sec
28)  exit ns_maint()
29)
30)  datagram from 192.33.33.24 port 53, fd 6, len 361
31)  7 root servers
```

We added the line numbers to the debugging output; you won't see them in yours. Lines 2 and 3 give the version of BIND you are running and the name of the boot file. This name server is vintage 1991 BSD: full-bodied, somewhat fruity. Version 4.8.3 was released by Berkeley in mid-1990. This server probably has a few defects fixed since it was compiled some months later. We used the boot file in the current directory, *./named.boot*, for this run.

Lines 4 through 7 show the initialization of file descriptors. (In this case, they're really socket descriptors.) File descriptor 5 is bound to 127.0.0.1, the loopback address. File descriptor 6 is bound to the 192.249.249.3 interface. File descriptor 7 is bound to 0.0.0.0, the wildcard address. Most network daemons use only one socket bound to the wildcard address, not sockets bound to individual interfaces. The wildcard address picks up packets sent to any interface on the host. Let's digress for a moment to explain why *named* uses both a socket bound to the wildcard address and sockets bound to specific interfaces.

When *named* receives a request from an application or from another name server it will receive the request on one of the sockets bound to a specific interface. If *named* did not have sockets bound to specific interfaces, it would receive the requests on the socket bound to the wildcard address. When *named* sends back a response, it uses the same socket descriptor that the request came in on. Why does *named* do this? When responses are sent out the socket bound to the wildcard address, the kernel fills in the sender's address with the address of the interface the response was actually sent out on. This address may or may not be the same address as the request was sent to. When responses are sent out the socket bound to a specific address, the kernel fills in the sender's address with that specific address—the same address the request was sent to. Remember in Chapter 7, *Maintaining BIND*, when we talked about the martian responses statistic? If the name server gets a response from an IP address it didn't know about, the response is tagged a "martian" and discarded. *named* tries to avoid martian responses by sending its responses on descriptors bound to specific interfaces, so the sender's address is the same address the request was sent to. However, when *named* sends out *queries*, it uses the wildcard descriptor since there is no need to force a specific IP address.

Lines 9 through 18 show BIND reading the boot file and the db files. This name server is a caching-only name server—the only files read are *db.127.0.0* (lines 10-12) and *db.cache* (lines 14-16). The zone origin came from the second field of the boot file *primary* line. The source is the third field. On lines 13 and 17, z_time is the time to check when this zone is up-to-date; z_refresh is the zone refresh time. These values only matter when the server is a secondary server for the zone. On line 18, the name server notes that it should check that all of its zones are up-to-date.

Line 20 shows the sort list. This name server's sort list contains only the network number 192.249.249.0, which it found by grubbing through the kernel's network interface list; there is no *sortlist* entry in our boot file. If you don't see 192.249.249.0 there, but you do see 192.249.249.3, look at the hex net and mask to the left of the IP address—xc0f9f900 is hex for 192.249.249.0.

Have you ever written a program that needed to know all of a host's network interfaces, as well as each interface's address? We bet you found out that nothing documents how do this *programmatically*. The next best thing to documentation (maybe even better) is to "borrow" some code from a program that does what you want. *netstat* has this code and so does *named*. We've taken the section of code from *named* that rummages through the kernel's network interfaces and used it in several local system administration tools. Remember that it is there—you might find it handy to use some day too.

Lines 23 through 31 show the name server sending out a system query to find out which name servers are currently serving the root domain. This is known as "priming the cache." The first server queried sent a response that included seven name servers. Ignore the messages about maintenance (ns_maint and sched_maint); secondaries use the maintenance routines to keep their zones up-to-date and this server isn't a secondary.

The name server is now initialized and it is ready to answer queries.

A Successful Lookup (Debug Level 1)

Suppose you want to watch the name server look up a name. Your name server wasn't started with debugging. Send a USR1 signal to turn on debugging, look up the name, and send a USR2 signal to turn off debugging like this:

```
# kill -USR1 `cat /etc/named.pid`
# /etc/ping bors.cs.purdue.edu.
# kill -USR2 `cat /etc/named.pid`
```

We did this; here's the resulting */usr/tmp/named.run* file:

```
Debug turned ON, Level 1

datagram from 192.249.249.3 port 2403, fd 6, len 36
req: nlookup(bors.cs.purdue.edu) id 1 type=1

req: found 'bors.cs.purdue.edu' as 'edu' (cname=0)
forw: forw -> 128.63.4.82 7 (53) nsid=2 id=1 0ms retry 4 sec
```

```
datagram from 128.63.4.82 port 53, fd 6, len 202
resp: nlookup(bors.cs.purdue.edu) type=1
resp: found 'bors.cs.purdue.edu' as 'cs.purdue.edu' (cname=0)
resp: forw -> 128.42.5.4 7 (53) nsid=3 id=1 0ms

datagram from 128.42.5.4 port 53, fd 6, len 52
send_msg -> 192.249.249.3 (UDP 6 2403) id=1
Debug turned OFF
```

First, notice that IP addresses are logged and not names—odd for a *name* server, don't you think? It's not that odd, though. If you are trying to debug a problem looking up names, you don't want the name server looking up additional names just to make the debugging output more readable—the extra queries would interfere with the debugging. None of the debugging levels translate IP addresses into names. You'll have to use a tool (like the one we provide later) to convert them for you.

Let's go through this debugging output line-by-line. This detailed approach is important if you want to understand what each line means: if you turn on debugging, you're probably trying to find out why some name can't be looked up, and you're going to have to figure out what the trace means. You've got to crawl before you can walk, and we are going to crawl through this trace.

```
datagram from 192.249.249.3 port 2403, fd 6, len 36
```

A datagram came from the host with IP address 192.249.249.3 (**terminator**). You may see the datagram come from 127.0.0.1 if the sender is on the same host as the name server. The sending application used port 2403. The name server received the datagram on file descriptor (`fd`) 6. The startup debugging output, like the one shown earlier, will tell you which interface file descriptor 6 is bound to. The length (`len`) of the datagram was 36 bytes. We know that this datagram was a query from an application because the datagram was not from port 53 (the **domain** service). All name servers send queries and responses from port 53.

```
req: nlookup(bors.cs.purdue.edu) id 1 type=1
```

Since the next debugging line starts with `req`, we know the datagram was a *request*. The name looked up in the request was **bors.cs.purdue.edu**. The request id is 1—the first query from this application. The `type=1` means the request is for *address* information. You will find a complete list of query types in the header file */usr/include/arpa/nameser.h*. Heard of RTFM? This is RTFHF (where HF stands for "header file").

```
req: found 'bors.cs.purdue.edu' as 'edu' (cname=0)
```

The name server database contains the name edu, but the debugging information doesn't state *what* information was found at **edu**. We have to figure out what was found at **edu** by looking at what the name server does next. Okay, so we have to look at the next debugging line, but what *was* at **edu** anyway?

To explain that, we have to give you some details about the name server's internal representation of its database. When the name server primed its cache, it cached the address of **terp.umd.edu**, one of the root name servers. This created an entry in the name server's database under the root domain called **edu**. Under **edu** it created a subdomain called **umd**. Under **umd** it created a subdomain called **terp**. This entry was assigned the address resource record for **terp.umd.edu**. As you can see, a database entry can have resource record entries *and* linkage to a subdomain. Leaf-level domain names, like **terp**, will only have resource records attached to them. Interior-level domain names, like **edu**, will have subdomain data and may also have resource records. Back to the original question about what was found at **edu**. The **edu** database entry has subdomain data for the subdomain **umd**. It could also have resource records: NS or SOA records.

The cname=0 means the name server has not encountered a CNAME record. If it does see a CNAME record, the canonical name is looked up instead of the original name, and cname will be non-zero.

```
forw: forw -> 128.63.4.82 7 (53) nsid=2 id=1 0ms retry 4 sec
```

The query was forwarded to the name server (port 53) on host 128.63.4.82 (**aos.brl.mil**). Since this host is a name server for the root domain, we speculate that no NS records were found at edu; the name server went up a level (to the root domain) to find name servers. (Level 3 debugging output would prove this.) The name server used file descriptor 7 (which is the wildcard address) to send the query. The name server tagged this query with ID number 2 (nsid=2) so that it can match the response to the original question. (Priming the cache was name server ID 1.) The application used ID number 1 (id=1), as you saw on the nlookup line. Since this server has not been contacted before—you can tell from the 0ms—the name server will wait 4 seconds before trying the next name server.

```
datagram from 128.63.4.82 port 53, fd 6, len 202
```

The name server on **aos.brl.mil** responded. We have to look at what happens next to figure out the content of this response.

```
resp: nlookup(bors.cs.purdue.edu) type=1
```

After caching the information in the response packet, the name is looked up again. As mentioned earlier, `type=1` means the name server is looking for *address* information.

```
resp: found 'bors.cs.purdue.edu' as 'cs.purdue.edu' (cname=0)
```

This time there is some information at the **cs.purdue.edu** level. The previous response probably included a list of name servers for **purdue.edu**; root name servers usually don't have NS information three levels down in the tree. We can verify this with *nslookup*:

```
% nslookup
Default Server:  relay.hp.com
Address:  15.255.152.2

> server aos.brl.mil.              --query aos
Default Server:  aos.brl.mil
Addresses:  128.63.4.82, 26.3.0.29, 192.5.25.82

> set norec                        --turn off recursion
> bors.cs.purdue.edu.              --look up the name
Server:  aos.brl.mil
Addresses:  128.63.4.82, 26.3.0.29, 192.5.25.82

Name:     bors.cs.purdue.edu
Served by:
- PENDRAGON.CS.PURDUE.EDU
        128.10.2.5
        PURDUE.EDU
- MOE.RICE.EDU
        128.42.5.4
        PURDUE.EDU
- MENTOR.CC.PURDUE.EDU
        128.210.10.8
        PURDUE.EDU
- ZOO.ECN.PURDUE.EDU
        128.46.129.78
        PURDUE.EDU
```

This is the same response that **aos** sent to the name server and, as we speculated, it has a list of **purdue.edu** name servers. One of the name servers for **purdue.edu** is **pendragon.cs.purdue.edu**. When the name server caches this name, it creates an entry for **cs.purdue.edu** for storing subdomain data. Like the previous case with **edu**, the name server finds **cs.purdue.edu** in its database, but it has to go up a level, to **purdue.edu**, to find the next name server to query.

```
resp: forw -> 128.42.5.4 7 (53) nsid=3 id=1 0ms
```

A query was sent to the name server on 128.42.5.4—**moe.rice.edu**, an off-site name server for **purdue.edu**. There is no special reason that the off-site name server was tried first; it just happened. This time the name server ID is 3.

```
datagram from 128.42.5.4 port 53, fd 6, len 52
```

The name server on **moe.rice.edu** responded. Again, we have to look at what happens next to figure out the contents of this response.

```
send_msg -> 192.249.249.3 (UDP 6 2403) id=1
```

The last response must have contained the address requested since the name server responded to the application (which used port 2403, if you look back at the original query). The response was in a UDP packet (as opposed to a TCP connection) and it used file descriptor 6.

This name server was "quiet" when we did this trace; it wasn't handling other queries at the same time. When you do a trace on an active name server you won't be so lucky. You'll have to sift through the output and patch together those pieces that pertain to the lookup in which you are interested. It's not that hard, though. Start up your favorite editor, search for the nlookup line with the name you looked up and trace the entries with the same nsid. You'll see how to follow the nsid in the next trace.

A Successful Lookup with Retransmissions (Debug Level 1)

Not all lookups are as "clean" as the last one—sometimes the query must be retransmitted. The user doesn't see any difference so long as the lookup succeeds, although the query involving retransmissions will take longer. Below is a trace where there are retransmissions. We converted the IP addresses to names after the trace was done. Notice how much easier it is to read with names!

```
1)  Debug turned ON, Level 1
2)
3)  datagram from terminator.movie.edu port 3397, fd 6, len 35
4)  req: nlookup(ucunix.san.uc.edu) id 1 type=1
5)  req: found 'ucunix.san.uc.edu' as 'edu' (cname=0)
6)  forw: forw -> aos.brl.mil 7 (53) nsid=2 id=1 0ms retry 4 sec
7)
8)  datagram from aos.brl.mil port 53, fd 6, len 240
9)  resp: nlookup(ucunix.san.uc.edu) type=1
10) resp: found 'ucunix.san.uc.edu' as 'san.uc.edu' (cname=0)
11) resp: forw -> uceng.uc.edu 7 (53) nsid=3 id=1 0ms
```

```
12) resend(addr=1 n=0) -> ucbeh.san.uc.edu 7 (53) nsid=3 id=1 0ms
13)
14) datagram from terminator.movie.edu port 3397, fd 6, len 35
15) req: nlookup(ucunix.san.uc.edu) id 1 type=1
16) req: found 'ucunix.san.uc.edu' as 'san.uc.edu' (cname=0)
17) resend(addr=2 n=0) -> uccba.uc.edu 7 (53) nsid=3 id=1 0ms
18) resend(addr=3 n=0) -> mail.cis.ohio-state.edu 7 (53) nsid=3 id=1 0ms
19)
20) datagram from mail.cis.ohio-state.edu port 53, fd 6, len 51
21) send_msg -> terminator.movie.edu (UDP 6 3397) id=1
```

This trace starts out like the last trace (lines 1-11): the name server receives a query for **ucunix.san.uc.edu**, sends the query to a root name server (**aos.brl.mil**), receives a response that includes a list of name servers for **uc.edu**, and sends the query to one of the **uc.edu** name servers (**uceng.uc.edu**).

What is new in this trace are the resend lines (lines 12, 17, and 18). The forw on line 11 counts as "resend(addr=0 n=0)"—CS dweebs always start counting with zero. Since **uceng.uc.edu** didn't respond, the name server went on to try **ucbeh** (line 12), **uccba** (line 17), and **mail** (line 18). The off-site name server on **mail.cis.ohio-state.edu** finally responded (line 20). Notice that you can track all of the retransmissions by searching for nsid=3; that's important to know because lots of other queries can be wedged between these.

Also, notice the second datagram from **terminator** (line 14). It has the same port, file descriptor, length, id, and type as the query on line 3. The application didn't receive a response in time, so it retransmitted its original query. Since the name server is still working on the first one transmitted, this one is a duplicate. It doesn't say so in this output, but the name server detected the duplicate and dropped it. We can tell because there is no forw: line after the req: lines like there was on lines 4 through 6.

Can you guess what this output might look like if the name server was having trouble looking up a name? You'd see a lot of retransmissions as the name server kept trying to look up the name (which you could track by matching the nsid= lines). You'd see the application send a couple more retransmissions thinking the name server hadn't received the application's first query. Eventually the name server would give up, usually after the application itself gave up.

And now for the domain name trivia question: "Who owns the domain **uc.edu**?" The University of California? The University of Colorado? The University of Cincinnati? The school for Unelected Congress-critters? You'll find the answer at the end of this chapter.

A Successful Lookup with Retransmissions (Debug Level 3)

Let's try this lookup again, but at debugging level 3. We don't want you to get the idea that we are picking on this site because the last trace and this one look up the same name. We latched on to this name after trying 40 to 50 other names we got from Usenet postings that didn't cause what we wanted to show: the retransmissions. The Internet has become much more reliable—a few years ago, by the time we had tried a half-dozen names, we would have had a good trace with retransmissions. Don't be put off by the length of this trace—it goes on for a couple of pages. At this debugging level (and above), you have to skim through the data because there is much more information than you need.

```
1)   Debug turned ON, Level 1
2)   Debug turned ON, Level 2
3)   Debug turned ON, Level 3
4)
5)   datagram from terminator.movie.edu port 3395, fd 6, len 35
6)   req: nlookup(ucunix.san.uc.edu) id 1 type=1
7)   req: found 'ucunix.san.uc.edu' as 'edu' (cname=0)
8)   findns: using cache
9)   findns: 7 NS's added for ''
10)  ns_forw()
11)  nslookup(nsp=xffeff794,qp=x1c67c)
12)  nslookup: NS NS.NIC.DDN.MIL c1 t2 (x0)
13)  nslookup: 1 ns addrs
14)  nslookup: NS AOS.BRL.MIL c1 t2 (x0)
15)  nslookup: 4 ns addrs
16)  nslookup: NS KAVA.NISC.SRI.COM c1 t2 (x0)
17)  nslookup: 5 ns addrs
18)  nslookup: NS C.NYSER.NET c1 t2 (x0)
19)  nslookup: 6 ns addrs
20)  nslookup: NS TERP.UMD.EDU c1 t2 (x0)
21)  nslookup: 7 ns addrs
22)  nslookup: NS NS.NASA.GOV c1 t2 (x0)
23)  nslookup: 9 ns addrs
24)  nslookup: NS NIC.NORDU.NET c1 t2 (x0)
25)  nslookup: 10 ns addrs
26)  nslookup: 10 ns addrs total
```

With the additional information in this trace, there is less that we have to deduce about what happens. Start with line 7: although this says the name server found 'edu' in its database, lines 9 through 26 show the name server collecting NS records for the root domain (the ' '); this means there was an entry in the database for **edu**, but no NS records. The name server then looks for NS records at the next level up from **edu**—in this case, the

root domain. A healthy name server will always find NS records for the
root.

```
27)  forw: forw -> aos.brl.mil 7 (53) nsid=2 id=1 0ms retry 4 sec
28)
29)  datagram from aos.brl.mil port 53, fd 6, len 240
30)  USER response nsid=2 id=1
31)  stime 698193318/767256  now 698193319/118952 rtt 352
32)  NS #0 addr aos.brl.mil used, rtt 352
33)  NS #1 aos.brl.mil rtt now 0
34)  NS #2 aos.brl.mil rtt now 0
35)  NS #3 kava.nisc.sri.com rtt now 0
36)  NS #4 ns.nic.ddn.mil rtt now 0
37)  NS #5 c.nyser.net rtt now 0
38)  NS #6 nic.nordu.net rtt now 0
39)  NS #7 terp.umd.edu rtt now 0
40)  NS #8 norad.arc.nasa.gov rtt now 0
41)  NS #9 norad.arc.nasa.gov rtt now 0
```

The datagram from **aos.brl.mil** (line 29) is a response to a USER query (line
30), not a SYSTEM query (sysquery). Lines 32 through 41 show the newly
adjusted name server round trip time (rtt) values. Those name servers that
haven't been queried still have an rtt of zero. The next time the name
server contacts a root name server, it will use one of those servers with an
rtt of zero. (Zero *is* the lowest rtt value, no?) Because of this, each interface on each name server will be queried once—to initialize its rtt—before
the name server starts preferring one server over another.

```
42)  resp: ancount 0, aucount 5, arcount 5
43)  doupdate(zone 0, savens ffefef7c, flags 19)
44)  doupdate: dname UC.EDU type 2 class 1 ttl 172800
45)  db_update(UC.EDU, 0x1b6b4, 0x1b6b4, 031, 0x1c160)
46)  db_update: adding 1b6b4
47)  doupdate(zone 0, savens ffefef7c, flags 19)
48)  doupdate: dname UC.EDU type 2 class 1 ttl 172800
49)  db_update(UC.EDU, 0x1b730, 0x1b730, 031, 0x1c160)
50)  db_update: adding 1b730
51)  doupdate(zone 0, savens ffefef7c, flags 19)
52)  doupdate: dname UC.EDU type 2 class 1 ttl 172800
53)  db_update(UC.EDU, 0x1b76c, 0x1b76c, 031, 0x1c160)
54)  db_update: adding 1b76c
55)  doupdate(zone 0, savens ffefef7c, flags 19)
56)  doupdate: dname UC.EDU type 2 class 1 ttl 172800
57)  db_update(UC.EDU, 0x1b7a8, 0x1b7a8, 031, 0x1c160)
58)  db_update: adding 1b7a8
59)  doupdate(zone 0, savens ffefef7c, flags 19)
60)  doupdate: dname UC.EDU type 2 class 1 ttl 172800
61)  db_update(UC.EDU, 0x1b7e8, 0x1b7e8, 031, 0x1c160)
62)  db_update: adding 1b7e8
```

As you can see in lines 43 through 62, the response contained NS records
(type 2) for **UC.EDU** (dname UC.EDU) with a TTL of 172800 (2 days).

The class 1 is the IN class.

```
63)  doupdate(zone 0, savens ffefef7c, flags 19)
64)  doupdate: dname UCBEH.SAN.UC.EDU type 1 class 1 ttl 172800
65)  db_update(UCBEH.SAN.UC.EDU, 0x1b830, 0x1b830, 031, 0x1c160)
66)  db_update: adding 1b830
67)  doupdate(zone 0, savens ffefef7c, flags 19)
68)  doupdate: dname UCENG.UC.EDU type 1 class 1 ttl 172800
69)  db_update(UCENG.UC.EDU, 0x1c960, 0x1c960, 031, 0x1c160)
70)  db_update: adding 1c960
71)  doupdate(zone 0, savens ffefef7c, flags 19)
72)  doupdate: dname UCCBA.UC.EDU type 1 class 1 ttl 172800
73)  db_update(UCCBA.UC.EDU, 0x1ca00, 0x1ca00, 031, 0x1c160)
74)  db_update: adding 1ca00
75)  doupdate(zone 0, savens ffefef7c, flags 19)
76)  doupdate: dname UCGCCD.SAN.UC.EDU type 1 class 1 ttl 172800
77)  db_update(UCGCCD.SAN.UC.EDU, 0x1caa0, 0x1caa0, 031, 0x1c160)
78)  db_update: adding 1caa0
79)  doupdate(zone 0, savens ffefef7c, flags 19)
80)  doupdate: dname MAIL.CIS.OHIO-STATE.EDU type 1 class 1 ttl 172800
81)  db_update(MAIL.CIS.OHIO-STATE.EDU, 0x1cb40, 0x1cb40, 031, 0x1c160)
82)  db_update: adding 1cb40
```

Lines 63 through 82 show that the response also contained address records (type 1) for the name servers listed in the NS records. You can see the names for the name servers in these lines.

```
83)  resp: nlookup(ucunix.san.uc.edu) type=1
84)  resp: found 'ucunix.san.uc.edu' as 'san.uc.edu' (cname=0)
85)  findns: 5 NS's added for 'UC'
86)  nslookup(nsp=xffeff4ec,qp=x1c67c)
87)  nslookup: NS UCBEH.SAN.UC.EDU c1 t2 (x0)
88)  nslookup: 1 ns addrs
89)  nslookup: NS UCENG.UC.EDU c1 t2 (x0)
90)  nslookup: 2 ns addrs
91)  nslookup: NS UCCBA.UC.EDU c1 t2 (x0)
92)  nslookup: 3 ns addrs
93)  nslookup: NS UCGCCD.SAN.UC.EDU c1 t2 (x0)
94)  nslookup: 4 ns addrs
95)  nslookup: NS MAIL.CIS.OHIO-STATE.EDU c1 t2 (x0)
96)  nslookup: 5 ns addrs
97)  nslookup: 5 ns addrs total
```

Line 84 shows the name server finding 'san.uc.edu' in its database. However, when it looked for name servers to query, it found NS records at the **uc.edu** level, not at the **san.uc.edu** level. Lines 85 through 97 show the name server collecting the NS records for **uc.edu**.

```
98)  resp: forw -> uceng.uc.edu 7 (53) nsid=3 id=1 0ms
99)  resp: Query sent.
100) resend(addr=1 n=0) -> ucbeh.san.uc.edu 7 (53) nsid=3 id=1 0ms
101)
102) datagram from terminator.movie.edu port 3395, fd 6, len 35
```

```
103) req: nlookup(ucunix.san.uc.edu) id 1 type=1
104) req: found 'ucunix.san.uc.edu' as 'san.uc.edu' (cname=0)
105) findns: 5 NS's added for 'UC'
106) ns_forw()
107) forw: dropped DUP id=1
108) resend(addr=2 n=0) -> uccba.uc.edu 7 (53) nsid=3 id=1 0ms
109) resend(addr=3 n=0) -> mail.cis.ohio-state.edu 7 (53)
        nsid=3 id=1 0ms
110)
111) datagram from mail.cis.ohio-state.edu port 53, fd 6, len 51
112) USER response nsid=3 id=1
113) stime 698193331/783312  now 698193331/935808 rtt 152
114) NS #3 addr mail.cis.ohio-state.edu used, rtt 152
115) NS #0 uceng.uc.edu rtt now 182
116) NS #1 ucbeh.san.uc.edu rtt now 182
117) NS #2 uccba.uc.edu rtt now 182
118) NS #4 ucgccd.san.uc.edu rtt now 0
```

Line 102 shows the query that was retransmitted from the application and line 107 shows the name server detecting that this is a duplicate and dropping it. Line 111 shows that a response that was received. Lines 114 through 118 show the new rtt values for the **uc.edu** name servers; the ones that didn't respond are given a higher value than the server that did respond. These higher values "decay" when **uc.edu** name servers are queried again, so the servers will be given another chance later on. Failing to respond to one query doesn't mean that a remote name server is locked out for eternity.

```
119) resp: ancount 1, aucount 0, arcount 0
120) doupdate(zone 0, savens ffefef7c, flags 19)
121) doupdate: dname ucunix.san.uc.edu type 1 class 1 ttl 86400
122) db_update(ucunix.san.uc.edu, 0x1cca0, 0x1cca0, 031, 0x1c160)
123) db_update: adding 1cca0
124) resp: got as much answer as there is
125) send_msg -> terminator.movie.edu (UDP 6 3395) id=1
```

The response is cached and sent to the application.

Is it worthwhile to trace lookups at debugging level 3? As you can see, you have much more information. But once you know how the name server operates, you can trace at level 1 and mentally fill in the missing parts. The same holds true for higher levels of debugging data. Do some tracing at various debugging levels all the way up to level 10. Figure out how the name server operates—the higher debugging levels are mostly adding details to what you already know—so that when you are tracking down a problem, you can confidently read a debugging level 1 trace.

A Secondary Name Server Checking Its Zone (Debug Level 1)

In addition to tracking down problems with name server lookups, you may have to track down why a secondary server is not loading from its master. Tracking down this problem can often be done by simply comparing the domain's SOA serial numbers on the two servers using *nslookup* or *dig* as we'll show in Chapter 12, *Troubleshooting DNS and BIND*. If your problem is more elusive, you may have to resort to looking at the debugging information. We'll show you what the debugging information should look like if your server is running normally.

This debugging output was on a "quiet" name server—one not receiving any queries—to show you exactly which lines pertain to zone maintenance. If you remember, a secondary name server uses a child process to transfer the zone data to the local disk before reading it in. While the secondary logs its debugging information to */usr/tmp/named.run*, the secondary's child process logs its debugging information to */usr/tmp/xfer.ddt.PID*. The *PID* suffix, by default the process id of the child process, may be changed to ensure that the filename is unique. Beware—turning on debugging on a secondary name server will leave *xfer.ddt.PID* files laying around even if you are only trying to trace a lookup. Our trace is at debugging level 1. Debug level 3 gives you more information, more than you may want if a transfer actually occurs—a debugging level 3 trace of a zone transfer of several hundred resource records can create an *xfer.ddt.PID* file several megabytes large.

```
1)  Debug turned ON, Level 1
2)
3)  ns_maint(); now Thu Feb 20 22:48:02 1992
4)  startxfer() movie.edu
5)  started xfer child 20189
6)  sched_maint: Next interrupt in 7200 sec
7)  exit ns_maint()
8)
9)  endxfer: child 20189 zone movie.edu returned status=0 termsig=0
10) sched_maint: Next interrupt in 10800 sec
11)
12) ns_maint(); now Fri Feb 21 01:48:05 1992
13) startxfer() movie.edu
14) started xfer child 20196
15) sched_maint: Next interrupt in 7200 sec
16) exit ns_maint()
17)
18) endxfer: child 20196 zone movie.edu returned status=1 termsig=0
19) sched_maint: no schedule change
20) loadxfer() 'movie.edu'
```

```
21) db_load(db.movie, movie.edu, 2, 0)
22) sched_maint: Next interrupt in 10799 sec
```

This server is a secondary for a single zone, **movie.edu**. Line four shows that it is time to check with the master server. Just because this trace says `startxfer()`, it doesn't mean that a transfer actually takes place; the child process, not the parent, compares zone serial numbers and pulls the zone, and the child hasn't been started yet. The child process ID is 20189 (line 5) and an alarm is set to go off in 7200 seconds, or two hours (line 6). The alarm in two hours is to kill off a child process that has apparently hung; two hours is plenty of time to transfer a zone. On line 9, you see the exit status of the child process. The status of zero indicates the zone data are current. If `termsig` is non-zero, the server was terminated by a signal. Maintenance is scheduled for 10800 seconds—three hours (line 10)—the zone's *refresh* interval.

Three hours later (compare the time stamps), the secondary checks whether **movie.edu** is up-to-date. This time, the child process exits with a status of one (line 18). The zone data had expired, so the child retrieved a new copy of the database. The secondary server reads in the file *db.movie* (lines 20 and 21) and the next maintenance is scheduled for three hours later.

These are the two debugging files left by the child processes:

Contents of file *xfer.ddt.a20189*:

```
1) domain 'movie.edu' file 'db.movie' ser no 1363
2) zone found (2): 'movie.edu', source = db.movie
3)   (addrcnt) = 1
4) getzone() movie.edu
5) zone up-to-date, serial 1363
```

Contents of file *xfer.ddt.a20196*:

```
1) domain 'movie.edu' file 'db.movie' ser no 1363
2) zone found (2): 'movie.edu', source = db.movie
3)   (addrcnt) = 1
4) getzone() movie.edu
5) need update, serial 1364
```

The *xfer.ddt.a20189* file was the debug file when the zone data was current—it says so on line 5. Notice that 20189—the child process ID—is in the filename.

The *xfer.ddt.a20196* file was the debug file when new zone data was pulled. At debugging level 3, this file would have showed you the SOA record fields nicely formatted and it would have showed you *every* resource record transferred (several lines per resource record), which can result in a huge file.

The Resolver Search Algorithm (Debug Level 1)

Let's change our focus for this last trace. Up to now, we have been showing you the name server's behavior. This time we are going to show you name server debugging output, but it points out a particular resolver behavior—its search algorithm. If you look back at the second trace we did, we *ping*'ed **bors.cs.purdue.edu.**, a name ending with a dot. The "trailing dot" told the resolver that the name was already fully qualified and to skip using its search algorithm. In the trace we are about to show you, we omitted the trailing dot. Check out the difference:

```
1)  datagram from cujo.horror.movie.edu port 1351, fd 6, len 48
2)  req: nlookup(bors.cs.purdue.edu.horror.movie.edu) id 4 type=1
3)  req: found 'bors.cs.purdue.edu.horror.movie.edu' as
                              'horror.movie.edu' (cname=0)
4)  forw: forw -> carrie.horror.movie.edu 7 (53) nsid=10 id=4 0ms
                                        retry 4 sec
5)
6)  datagram from carrie.horror.movie.edu port 53, fd 6, len 110
7)  send_msg -> cujo.horror.movie.edu (UDP 6 1351) id=4
8)
9)  datagram from cujo.horror.movie.edu port 1353, fd 6, len 43
10) req: nlookup(bors.cs.purdue.edu.movie.edu) id 5 type=1
11) req: found 'bors.cs.purdue.edu.movie.edu' as 'movie.edu' (cname=0)
12) forw: forw -> wormhole.movie.edu 7 (53) nsid=11 id=5 0ms retry 4 sec
13)
14) datagram from wormhole.movie.edu port 53, fd 6, len 102
15) send_msg -> cujo.horror.movie.edu (UDP 6 1353) id=5
16)
17) datagram from cujo.horror.movie.edu port 1355, fd 6, len 36
18) req: nlookup(bors.cs.purdue.edu) id 6 type=1
19) req: found 'bors.cs.purdue.edu' as 'bors.cs.purdue.edu' (cname=0)
20) req: answer -> cujo.horror.movie.edu 6 (1355) id=6 Local
```

The first name looked up (line 2) is in the domain of the sender, **horror.movie.edu**. The next name looked up (line 10) is in the parent domain of the sender, **movie.edu**. The last name looked up (line 18) is the one we typed in. We had already looked up this name before and so the name server answered out of its cache.

The resolver search algorithm does "extra" work to make domain names easier for us to use. We can type in a partial domain name, like **carrie** or **carrie.horror**, and the resolver "completes" the name by appending domains until the lookup succeeds. Most of the time, this happens very

quickly and users are happy that they get by typing in a shorter name. But
sometimes the lookup takes longer than it should. In our domain, failing to
reach the **movie.edu** server (a "mid-level" domain) would result in a long
delay—a minute or so—as the name server tries to look up a name in
movie.edu like on line 10. You can tell when the delay is being caused by
the interaction between the resolver search algorithm and the loss of connectivity to a mid-level domain server by looking at a debugging trace. But
the trace only shows you what is causing the problem, not how to deal with
it. If you want ideas on how to deal with the problem, check out Chapter
8, *Growing Your Domain*.

Tools and Trivia

Let's wrap up a few loose ends. We told you about a tool to convert IP
addresses to names so that your debugging output is easier to read. Here is
such a tool written in *perl*:

```
#!/usr/bin/perl

require 'sys/socket.ph';

while(<>){
    if(/\b([0-9]+\.[0-9]+\.[0-9]+\.[0-9]+)\b/){
        $addr = pack('C4', split(/\./, $1));
        ($name, $rest) = gethostbyaddr($addr, &AF_INET);
        if($name) {s/$1/$name/;}
    }
    print;
}
```

It's best not to pipe *named.run* output into this script with debugging on,
because the script will generate its own queries to the name server.

If you do any significant amount of name server debugging, you'll want a
tool to turn debugging on and off. This *perl* script will do that for you:

```
#!/usr/bin/perl
#
# Turn name server debugging on or off.
#
# To turn off debugging, use "binddebug 0"
# To turn on debugging to level 3, use "binddebug 3"

# Find the process ID in /etc/named.pid.
open(PID, "/etc/named.pid") || die "Can\'t open /etc/named.pid\n";
$pid = <PID>;
chop($pid);
$pid || die "No process ID in /etc/named.pid\n";
```

```
# Get the debugging level from the command line.
$savelevel = $level = $ARGV[0];
$level =~ /^[0-9]+$/ || die "Integer argument required\n";

# Turn off debugging if it is on.
if(!kill 'USR2', $pid){ die "Kill of process ID $pid failed.\n"; }

if($level == 0){
  print "Debugging turned off.\n";
} else {
  while($level-- > 0) {
    select(undef, undef, undef, 0.25);  # spread out signals
    kill 'USR1', $pid;
  }
  printf "Name server now at debugging level $savelevel.\n";
}
```

And last, the answer to the trivia question: **uc.edu** is the University of Cincinnati.

12

Troubleshooting DNS and BIND

"Of course not," said the Mock Turtle. "Why, if a fish came to me, and told me he was going a journey, I should say 'With what porpoise?'"

"Don't you mean 'purpose'?" said Alice.

"I mean what I say," the Mock Turtle replied, in an offended tone. And the Gryphon added "Come, let's hear some of your adventures."

In the last two chapters we've demonstrated how to use *nslookup* and how to read the name server's debugging information. In this chapter, we'll show you how to use these tools—plus traditional UNIX networking tools like trusty ol' *ping*—to troubleshoot real-life problems with DNS and BIND.

Troubleshooting, by its nature, is a tough subject to teach. You start with any of a world of symptoms and try to work your way back to the cause. We can't cover the whole gamut of problems you may encounter on the Internet, but we will certainly do our best to show you how to diagnose the most common of them. And along the way, we hope to teach you troubleshooting techniques that will be valuable in tracking down more obscure problems that we don't document.

Is NIS Really Your Problem?

Before we launch into a discussion of how to troubleshoot a DNS or BIND problem, we should make sure you know how to tell whether a problem is caused by DNS and not NIS. On hosts running NIS, figuring out whether the culprit is DNS or NIS can be difficult. The stock BSD *nslookup*, for example, doesn't pay any attention to NIS. You can run *nslookup* on a Sun and query the name server 'til the cows come home, while all the other services are using NIS.

How do you know where to put the blame? Some vendors have modified *nslookup* to use NIS for name service if NIS is configured. The HP-UX *nslookup*, for example, will report that it's querying an NIS server when it starts up:

```
% nslookup
Default NIS Server:  terminator.movie.edu
Address:  192.249.249.3

>
```

On hosts with vanilla versions of *nslookup*, you can often use *ypmatch* to determine whether you're using DNS or NIS. *ypmatch* will print a blank line after the host information if it received the data from a name server. So in this example the answer came from NIS:

```
% ypmatch ruby hosts
140.186.65.25   ruby ruby.ora.com
%
```

While in this example the answer came from a name server:

```
% ypmatch harvard.harvard.edu hosts
128.103.1.1     harvard.harvard.edu

%
```

Note that this works now (with SunOS 4.1.1), but is not guaranteed to work on every future version of SunOS. For all we know this is a bug-cum-feature that may disappear in the next release.

A more sure-fire way to decide whether an answer came from NIS is to use *ypcat* to list the hosts database. For example, to find out whether **andrew.cmu.edu** is in your NIS hosts map, you could execute:

```
% ypcat hosts | grep andrew.cmu.edu
```

If you find the answer in NIS (and you know NIS is being consulted first), you've found the cause of the problem.

These hints should help you identify the guilty party, or at least exonerate one. If you narrow down the suspects and DNS is still implicated, you'll just have to read this chapter.

Troubleshooting Tools and Techniques

We went over *nslookup* and the name server's debugging output in the last two chapters. Before we go on, let's introduce two new tools that can be useful in troubleshooting: *named-xfer* and name server database dumps.

How to Use named-xfer

named-xfer is the program *named* starts to perform zone transfers. *named-xfer* checks whether the secondary's copy of the zone data is up-to-date, and transfers a new zone, if necessary.

In Chapter 11, *Reading BIND Debugging Output*, we showed you the debugging information left behind by *named-xfer* when it was started by a *named* process with debugging on. We didn't tell you, however, that you can also start *named-xfer* manually, instead of waiting for *named* to start it, and that you can tell it to produce debugging output independently of *named*.

This can be useful if you're tracking down a problem with zone transfers but don't want to wait for *named* to schedule one. To test a zone transfer manually, you need to specify a number of command-line options:

```
% /etc/named-xfer
Usage: xfer
        -z zone_to_transfer
        -f db_file
        -s serial_no
        [-d debug_level]
        [-l debug_log_file (default /usr/tmp/xfer.ddt.XXXXXX)]
        [-t trace_file]
        [-p port]
        servers...
```

When *named* starts *named-xfer*, it specifies the -z option (the zone *named* wants to check), the -f option (the name of the db file that corresponds to the zone, from *named.boot*), the -s option (the zone's serial number on the secondary, from the current SOA record) and the addresses of the servers the secondary was instructed to load from (the IP addresses from the sec- ondary line in *named.boot*). If *named* is running in debug mode, it also specifies the debug level for *named-xfer* with the -d option.

When you run *named-xfer* manually, you can also specify the debug level on the command line with -d. (Don't forget, though, that debug levels above three will produce tons of debugging output if the transfer succeeds!) You can also specify an alternate filename for the debug file with the -l option. And you can specify the name of the host to load from, instead of its IP address.

For example, you could check to see whether zone transfers from **termina-tor** were working with the following command line:

```
% /etc/named-xfer -z movie.edu -f /tmp/db.movie -s 0 terminator
% echo $?
1
```

In this command, we specified a serial number of zero because we wanted to force *named-xfer* to attempt a zone transfer, even if it wasn't needed. Zero will certainly be less than the zone file's serial number. Also, we told *named-xfer* to put the new zone file in */tmp*, rather than overwriting the zone's working data file.

We can tell if the transfer succeeded by looking at *named-xfer*'s return value, which has four possible values:

0   means the zone data is up-to-date and that no transfer was needed

1   indicates a successful transfer

2   means that the host(s) *named-xfer* queried can't be reached, or that an error occurred and *named-xfer* didn't log a corresponding error message

3   means that an error occurred, and that *named-xfer* logged an error message

How to Read a Database Dump

Poring over a dump of the name server's internal database—including cached information—can also help you track down problems. The INT signal causes *named* to dump its authoritative data, cache data, and hints data to */usr/tmp/named_dump.db* (or */var/tmp/named_dump.db*). Below is an example of a *named_dump.db* file. The authoritative data and cache entries, mixed together, appear first in the file. At the end of the file are the hints data.

```
; Dumped at Thu Jan 16 21:36:28 1992
; --- Cache & Data ---
$ORIGIN .
.        518364      IN    NS    NS.NIC.DDN.MIL.
         518364      IN    NS    AOS.BRL.MIL.
         518364      IN    NS    KAVA.NISC.SRI.COM.
         518364      IN    NS    C.NYSER.NET.
         518364      IN    NS    TERP.UMD.EDU.
         518364      IN    NS    NS.NASA.GOV.
         518364      IN    NS    NIC.NORDU.NET.
```

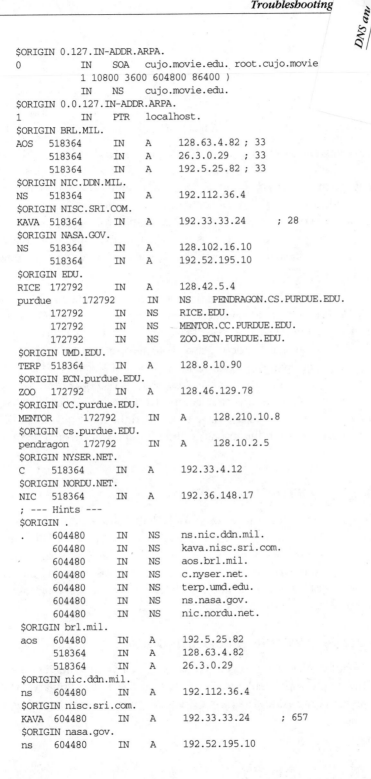

```
$ORIGIN 0.127.IN-ADDR.ARPA.
0           IN     SOA    cujo.movie.edu. root.cujo.movie
            1 10800 3600 604800 86400 )
            IN     NS     cujo.movie.edu.
$ORIGIN 0.0.127.IN-ADDR.ARPA.
1           IN     PTR    localhost.
$ORIGIN BRL.MIL.
AOS   518364      IN     A      128.63.4.82 ; 33
      518364      IN     A      26.3.0.29   ; 33
      518364      IN     A      192.5.25.82 ; 33
$ORIGIN NIC.DDN.MIL.
NS    518364      IN     A      192.112.36.4
$ORIGIN NISC.SRI.COM.
KAVA  518364      IN     A      192.33.33.24       ; 28
$ORIGIN NASA.GOV.
NS    518364      IN     A      128.102.16.10
      518364      IN     A      192.52.195.10
$ORIGIN EDU.
RICE  172792      IN     A      128.42.5.4
purdue      172792       IN     NS     PENDRAGON.CS.PURDUE.EDU.
      172792      IN     NS     RICE.EDU.
      172792      IN     NS     MENTOR.CC.PURDUE.EDU.
      172792      IN     NS     ZOO.ECN.PURDUE.EDU.
$ORIGIN UMD.EDU.
TERP  518364      IN     A      128.8.10.90
$ORIGIN ECN.purdue.EDU.
ZOO   172792      IN     A      128.46.129.78
$ORIGIN CC.purdue.EDU.
MENTOR      172792       IN     A      128.210.10.8
$ORIGIN cs.purdue.EDU.
pendragon   172792       IN     A      128.10.2.5
$ORIGIN NYSER.NET.
C     518364      IN     A      192.33.4.12
$ORIGIN NORDU.NET.
NIC   518364      IN     A      192.36.148.17
; --- Hints ---
$ORIGIN .
.     604480      IN     NS     ns.nic.ddn.mil.
      604480      IN     NS     kava.nisc.sri.com.
      604480      IN     NS     aos.brl.mil.
      604480      IN     NS     c.nyser.net.
      604480      IN     NS     terp.umd.edu.
      604480      IN     NS     ns.nasa.gov.
      604480      IN     NS     nic.nordu.net.
$ORIGIN brl.mil.
aos   604480      IN     A      192.5.25.82
      518364      IN     A      128.63.4.82
      518364      IN     A      26.3.0.29
$ORIGIN nic.ddn.mil.
ns    604480      IN     A      192.112.36.4
$ORIGIN nisc.sri.com.
KAVA  604480      IN     A      192.33.33.24       ; 657
$ORIGIN nasa.gov.
ns    604480      IN     A      192.52.195.10
```

```
        518364      IN    A     128.102.16.10
$ORIGIN umd.edu.
terp  604480      IN    A     128.8.10.90
$ORIGIN nyser.net.
c     604480      IN    A     192.33.4.12
$ORIGIN nordu.net.
nic   604480      IN    A     192.36.148.17
```

It's easy to tell which data come from the cache. Cache data have a TTL on each resource record; the authoritative data have no TTLs. The name server that created this *named_dump.db* file was authoritative only for **0.0.127.in-addr.arpa**. In the hints section, most of the hints are from the *db.cache* file—the ones with the 604480 TTL. In the process of priming the cache (i.e., looking up the NS records for "."), the hints section was also updated and a few new resource records were added—the ones with the 518364 TTL.

Notice that the TTLs on the hints from the *db.cache* file are not the 99999999s we inserted. The name server clips the TTL to 604800 (1 week) and starts decrementing its value. The TTL of the hints data may go to zero, but the hints are never discarded. Also, note that many of the resource records are followed by a semicolon (the comment character) and a number. You will only see these on the *address* records of *name servers*. The number is a round trip time (rtt) calculation that the name server keeps so that it knows which name servers have responded the most quickly in the past; the name server with the lowest round trip time will be tried first the next time.

Potential Problem List

Now that we've given you a nice set of tools, let's talk about how you can use them to diagnose real problems. There are some problems that are easy to recognize and correct. We should cover these as a matter of course—they're some of the most common problems because they're caused by some of the most common mistakes. Here are the contestants, in no particular order. We call 'em our "Dirty Dozen."

1. Forget to Increment Serial Number

The main symptom of this problem is that secondary name servers don't pick up any changes you make to the zone's db file on the primary. The secondaries think the zone data hasn't changed, since the serial number is still the same.

How do you check whether or not you remembered to increment the serial number? Unfortunately, that's not so easy. If you don't remember what the old serial number was, there's no direct way to tell whether it's changed. When you signal the primary, it will load the updated zone file regardless of whether you've changed the serial number: it will check the file's time stamp, see that it's been modified since it last loaded the data, and read the file.

About the best you can do is to use *nslookup* to compare the data returned by the primary and a secondary. If they return different data, you probably forgot to increment the serial number. If you remember a recent change you made, you can look for that data. If you can't remember a recent change, you could try transferring the zone from a primary and from a secondary, sorting the results, and using *diff* to compare them.

The good news is that, although determining whether the zone was transferred is tricky, making sure the zone is transferred is simple. Just increment the serial number on the primary's copy of the db file and signal the primary to reload. The secondaries should pick up the new data within their refresh interval. If you want to make sure the secondaries can transfer the new data, you can execute *named-xfer* by hand (on the secondaries, naturally):

```
# /etc/named-xfer -z movie.edu -f db.movie -s 0 terminator
# echo $?
```

If *named-xfer* returns 1, the zone was transferred successfully. Other return values indicate that no zone was transferred, either because of an error, or because the secondary thought the zone was up-to-date. (See the section earlier in this chapter on "How to Use named-xfer" for more detail.)

There's another variation on the "forgot to increment the serial number" line we see in environments where administrators use tools like *h2n* to create db files from the host table. With scripts like *h2n*, it's temptingly easy to delete old db files and create them from scratch. Some administrators do this occasionally because they mistakenly believe that data in the old db files can creep into the new ones. The problem with deleting the db files is that, without the old db file to read for the current serial number, *h2n* starts over at serial number 1. If your primary's serial number rolls all the way back to 1 from 598 or 92042001 or what-have-you, the secondaries don't complain; they just figure they're all caught up and don't need zone transfers. So if the serial number on the primary looks suspiciously low, check the serial number on the secondaries, too, and compare them:

```
% nslookup
Default Server:  terminator.movie.edu
Address:   192.249.249.3

> set q=soa
> movie.edu.
Server:  terminator.movie.edu
Address:   192.249.249.3

movie.edu
        origin = terminator.movie.edu
        mail addr = al.robocop.movie.edu
        serial = 1
        refresh = 10800 (3 hours)
        retry   = 3600 (1 hour)
        expire  = 604800 (7 days)
        minimum ttl = 86400 (1 day)
> server wormhole.movie.edu.
Default Server:  wormhole.movie.edu
Addresses:   192.249.249.1, 192.253.253.1

> movie.edu.
Server:  wormhole.movie.edu
Addresses:   192.249.249.1, 192.253.253.1

movie.edu
        origin = terminator.movie.edu
        mail addr = al.robocop.movie.edu
        serial = 112
        refresh = 10800 (3 hours)
        retry   = 3600 (1 hour)
        expire  = 604800 (7 days)
        minimum ttl = 86400 (1 day)
```

wormhole, as a **movie.edu** secondary, should never have a larger serial number than the primary, so clearly something's amiss.

This problem is really easy to spot, by the way, with the tool we'll write in Chapter 13, *Programming with the Resolver Library Routines*, coming up next.

2. Forget to Signal Primary

Occasionally, you may forget to signal your primary name server after making a change to the boot file or to the db file. The name server won't know to load the new data—it doesn't automatically check the timestamp of the file and notice that it changed. Consequently, any changes you've made won't be reflected in the name server's data: new zones won't be loaded, and new records won't percolate out to the secondaries.

To check when you last signaled the name server to reload, scan the *syslog* output for the last entry like this:

```
Mar  8 17:22:08 terminator named[22317]: reloading nameserver
```

This is the last time you sent a HUP signal to the name server. If you killed and then restarted the name server, you'll see an entry like this:

```
Mar  8 17:22:08 terminator named[22317]: restarted
```

If the time of the restart doesn't correlate with when you made the last change, signal the name server to reload its data again. And check that you incremented the serial numbers on db files you changed, too.

3. Secondary Can't Load Zone Data

If a secondary name server can't load the zone from another name server, it'll log a message like the following via *syslog*:

```
Mar  3 8:19:34 wormhole named[22261]: zoneref: Masters for secondary
     zone movie.edu unreachable
```

If you let this problem fester, the secondary will expire the zone:

```
Mar  8 17:12:43 wormhole named[22261]: secondary zone
     "movie.edu" expired
```

Once the zone has expired, you'll start getting SERVFAIL errors when you query the name server for data in the zone:

```
% nslookup robocop wormhole.movie.edu.
Server:  wormhole.movie.edu
Addresses:  192.249.249.1, 192.253.253.1

*** wormhole.movie.edu can't find robocop.movie.edu: Server failed
```

There are two leading causes of this problem: a loss in connectivity to the master server due to network failure, and an incorrect IP address in the boot file. First check the boot file's entry for the zone and see what IP address the secondary is attempting to load from:

```
secondary        movie.edu        192.249.249.3        db.movie
```

Make sure that's really the IP address of the master name server. If it is, check connectivity to that IP address:

```
% ping 192.249.249.3 -n 10
PING 192.249.249.3: 64 byte packets

----192.249.249.3 PING Statistics----
10 packets transmitted, 0 packets received, 100% packet loss
```

If the master server isn't reachable, make sure that the server's host is really running (i.e., is powered on, etc.), or look for a network problem. If the server is reachable, make sure *named* is running on the host, and that you can manually transfer the zone:

```
# named-xfer -z movie.edu -f /tmp/db.movie -s 0 192.249.249.3
# echo $?
```

4. Add Name to Database File, but Forget to Add PTR Record

Because the mappings from host names to IP addresses are disjoint from the mappings from IP addresses to host names in DNS, it's easy to forget to add a PTR record for a new host. Adding the A record is intuitive, but many people who are used to host tables assume that adding an address record takes care of the reverse mapping, too. That's not true: you need to add a PTR record for the host to the appropriate **in-addr.arpa** domain.

Forgetting to add the PTR record for a host usually causes that host to fail authentication checks. For example, users on the host won't be able to */login* to other hosts without specifying a password, and *rsh* or *rcp* to other hosts simply won't work. These commands need to be able to map the connection's IP address to a domain name to check *.rhosts* and *hosts.equiv*. These users' connections will cause entries like this to be *syslog*'d:

```
Aug 15 17:32:36 terminator inetd[23194]: login/tcp:
    Connection from unknown (192.249.249.23)
```

Also, many large *ftp* archives, including **ftp.uu.net**, refuse anonymous *ftp* access to hosts whose IP addresses don't map back to domain names. **ftp.uu.net**'s *ftp* server emits a message that reads, in part:

```
530- Sorry, we're unable to map your IP address 140.186.66.1 to a hostname
530- in the DNS. This is probably because your nameserver does not have a
530- PTR record for your address in its tables, or because your reverse
530- nameservers are not registered. We refuse service to hosts whose
530- names we cannot resolve.
```

That makes the reason you can't use anonymous *ftp* pretty evident. Other *ftp* sites, however, don't bother printing informative messages and simply deny service.

nslookup is handy for checking whether you've forgotten the PTR record or not:

```
% nslookup
Default Server: terminator.movie.edu
Address:  192.249.249.3

> beetlejuice       --Check for a hostname-to-address mapping
Server:  terminator.movie.edu
Address:  192.249.249.3

Name:     beetlejuice.movie.edu
Address:  192.249.249.23

> 192.249.249.23   --Now check for a corresponding address-to-hostname mapping
Server:  terminator.movie.edu
Address:  192.249.249.3

*** terminator.movie.edu can't find 192.249.249.23: Non-existent domain
```

On the primary for **249.249.192.in-addr.arpa**, a quick check of the *db.192.249.249* file will tell you if the PTR record hasn't been added to the db file yet, or if the name server hasn't been signaled to load the file. If the name server having trouble is a secondary for the domain, check that the serial number was incremented on the primary and that the secondary has had enough time to load the zone.

5. Syntax Error in the Boot File or DNS Database File

Syntax errors in the boot file and in database files are also relatively common (more or less, depending on the experience of the administrator). Generally, an error in the boot file will cause the name server to fail to load one or more zones. A typo in the `directory` line will cause the name server to fail to start at all, and log an error like this via *syslog*:

```
Apr  9 21:38:59 terminator named[29049]: directory /usr/name:
    No such file or directory
```

Note that you won't see an error message when you try to start *named* on the command line, but *named* won't stay running for long.

If the syntax error is in a less important line in the boot file, say in a `primary` or `secondary` line, only that zone will be affected. Usually, the name server will not be able to load the zone at all (say you misspell "primary" or the name of the data file). This would produce *syslog* output like:

```
Apr  9 21:40:02 terminator named[29055]: /etc/named.boot:
        line 28: unknown field 'primray'
```

If a db file contains a syntax error, yet the name server succeeds in loading the zone, it will either answer as "non-authoritative" for *all* data in the zone or will return a SERVFAIL error for lookups in the zone:

```
% nslookup carrie
Server:  terminator.movie.edu
Address: 192.249.249.3

Non-authoritative answer:
Name:    carrie.movie.edu
Address: 192.253.253.4
```

Here's the *syslog* message produced by the syntax error that caused this problem:

```
Mar  8 16:13:03 terminator named[22076]: db.movie: line 9:
        database format error ()
```

Note that unless you correlate the lack of authority (when you expect the name server to be authoritative) with a problem, or scan your *syslog* file assiduously, you might never notice the syntax error!

6. Missing Dot at the End of a Name in a DNS Database File

It's *very* easy to leave off trailing dots when editing a db file. Since the rules for when to use them change so often (*don't* use them in the boot file, *don't* use them in *resolv.conf, do* use them in db files to override $ORIGIN . . .), it's hard to keep them straight. These resource records:

```
zorba         in    mx    10 zelig.movie.edu
movie.edu     in    ns    terminator.movie.edu
```

really don't look that odd to the untrained eye, but they probably don't do what they're intended to. In the *db.movie* file, they'd be equivalent to:

```
zorba.movie.edu.        in    mx    10 zelig.movie.edu.movie.edu.
movie.edu.movie.edu.    in    ns    terminator.movie.edu.movie.edu.
```

unless the origin were explicitly changed.

If you omit a trailing dot after a domain name in the resource record's data (as opposed to leaving off a trailing dot in the resource record's *name*), you usually end up with wacky NS or MX records:

```
% nslookup -type=mx zorba.movie.edu.
Server:  terminator.movie.edu
Address:  192.249.249.3

zorba.movie.edu        preference = 10, mail exchanger
                       = zelig.movie.edu.movie.edu
zorba.movie.edu        preference = 50, mail exchanger
                       = postmanrings2x.movie.edu.movie.edu
```

The cause of this should be fairly clear from the *nslookup* output. But if you forget the trailing dot on the domain name field in a record (like in the **movie.edu** NS record above), spotting your mistake might not be as easy. If you try to look up the record with *nslookup*, you won't find it under the name you thought you used. Dumping your name server's database may help you root it out:

```
$ORIGIN edu.movie.edu.
movie   IN   NS   terminator.movie.edu.movie.edu.
```

The $ORIGIN line looks odd enough to stand out.

7. Missing Cache Data

If, for some reason, you forget to install a cache file on your host, or if you accidentally delete it, your name server will be unable to resolve names outside of its authoritative data. This behavior is easy to recognize using *nslookup*, but be careful to use full, dot-terminated domain names, or else the search list may cause misleading failures.

```
% nslookup
Default Server:  terminator.movie.edu
Address:  192.249.249.3

> ftp.uu.net.     --A lookup of a name outside your name server's authoritative
                    data causes a SERVFAIL error...
Server:  terminator.movie.edu
Address:  192.249.249.3

*** terminator.movie.edu can't find ftp.uu.net.: Server failed
```

while a lookup of a name in your name server's authoritative data returns a response:

```
> wormhole.movie.edu.
Server:  terminator.movie.edu
Address:  192.249.249.3

Name:     wormhole.movie.edu
Addresses:  192.249.249.1, 192.253.253.1

> ^D
```

To confirm your suspicion that the cache data is missing, check the *syslog* output for an error like this:

```
Mar  8 17:21:04 terminator named[22317]:
    No root nameservers for class 1
```

Class 1, you'll remember, is the IN, or Internet, class. This error indicates that because no cache data were available, no root name servers were found.

8. Loss of Network Connectivity

Though the Internet is more reliable today than it was back in the wild and wooly days of the ARPANET, network outages are still relatively common. Without "lifting the hood" and poking around in debugging output, these failures usually look like poor performance:

```
% nslookup nisc.sri.com.
Server:  terminator.movie.edu
Address: 192.249.249.3

*** Request to terminator.movie.edu timed out ***
```

If you turn on name server debugging, though, you'll see that *your* name server, anyway, is healthy. It received the query from the resolver, sent the necessary queries, and waited patiently for a response. It just didn't get one. Here's what the debugging output might look like:

```
Debug turned ON, Level 1
```

Here nslookup sends the first query to our local name server, for the IP address of nisc.sri.com. You can tell it's not another name server because the query is received from a port other than 53, the name server's port. Notice that the query is forwarded to another name server, and when no answer is received, resent to a different name server:

```
datagram from 192.249.249.3 port 2375, fd 6, len 30
req: nlookup(nisc.sri.com) id 4 type=1
req: found 'nisc.sri.com' as 'com' (cname=0)
forw: forw -> 128.102.16.10 7 (53) nsid=3352 id=4 30ms retry 4 sec
resend(addr=1 n=0) -> 192.52.195.10 7 (53) nsid=3352 id=4 36ms
```

Now nslookup is getting impatient, and queries our local name server again. Notice that it uses the same port. The local name server tries forwarding the query two more times:

```
datagram from 192.249.249.3 port 2375, fd 6, len 30
req: nlookup(nisc.sri.com) id 4 type=1
req: found 'nisc.sri.com' as 'com' (cname=0)
resend(addr=2 n=0) -> 192.33.33.24 7 (53) nsid=3352 id=4 121ms
resend(addr=3 n=0) -> 128.8.10.90 7 (53) nsid=3352 id=4 140ms
```

nslookup queries the local name server again, and the name server fires off four more queries:

```
datagram from 192.249.249.3 port 2375, fd 6, len 30
req: nlookup(nisc.sri.com) id 4 type=1
req: found 'nisc.sri.com' as 'com' (cname=0)
resend(addr=4 n=0) -> 192.33.4.12 7 (53) nsid=3352 id=4 623ms
resend(addr=5 n=0) -> 192.36.148.17 7 (53) nsid=3352 id=4 721ms
resend(addr=0 n=1) -> 128.102.16.10 7 (53) nsid=3352 id=4 30ms
resend(addr=1 n=1) -> 192.52.195.10 7 (53) nsid=3352 id=4 36ms
```

nslookup queries one last time, and the local name server sends five queries out but still doesn't receive an answer:

```
datagram from 192.249.249.3 port 2375, fd 6, len 3(
req: nlookup(nisc.sri.com) id 4 type=1
req: found 'nisc.sri.com' as 'com' (cname=0)
resend(addr=2 n=1) -> 192.33.33.24 7 (53) nsid=3352 id=4 121ms
resend(addr=3 n=1) -> 128.8.10.90 7 (53) nsid=3352 id=4 140ms
resend(addr=4 n=1) -> 192.33.4.12 7 (53) nsid=3352 id=4 623ms
resend(addr=5 n=1) -> 192.36.148.17 7 (53) nsid=3352 id=4 721ms
resend(addr=0 n=2) -> 128.102.16.10 7 (53) nsid=3352 id=4 30ms
Debug turned OFF
```

From the debugging output, you can extract a list of the IP addresses of the name servers that your name server tried to query, and then check your connectivity to them. Odds are, *ping* won't have much better luck than your name server did. If it does, you should check that the remote name servers are really running.

```
% ping 128.102.16.10 -n 10  --ping first name server queried
PING 128.102.16.10: 64 byte packets

----128.102.16.10 PING Statistics----
10 packets transmitted, 0 packets received, 100% packet loss
% ping 192.52.195.10 -n 10  --ping second name server queried
PING 192.52.195.10: 64 byte packets

----192.52.195.10 PING Statistics----
10 packets transmitted, 0 packets received, 100% packet loss
```

Now all that's left is to locate the break in the network. Utilities like *traceroute* and *ping*'s record route option can be very helpful in determining whether the problem is on your network, the destination network, or somewhere in the middle.

You should also use your own common sense when tracking down the break. In this trace, for example, the remote name servers your name server tried to query are all root name servers. (You might have had their PTR records cached somewhere, so you could find out their domain names.) Now it's not very likely that each root's local network went down, nor is it likely that the NSFNET backbone collapsed entirely. Occam's razor says that the simplest condition that could cause this behavior—namely, the loss of *your* network's link to the Internet—is the most likely cause.

9. Missing Subdomain Delegation

Even though the NIC does its best to process your requests as quickly as possible, it may take a week or two for your domain's delegation to appear in the root name servers. If the NIC doesn't manage your parent domain, your mileage may vary. Some parents are quick and responsible, others are slow and inconsistent. Just like in real life, though, you're stuck with them.

Until your delegation data appear in your parent domain's name servers, your name servers will be able to look up data in the Internet domain name space, but no one else on the Internet (outside of your domain) will know how to look up data in *your* name space.

That means that even though you can send mail outside of your domain, the recipients won't be able to reply to it. Furthermore, no one will be able to *telnet* to, *ftp* to, or even *ping* your hosts by name.

To determine whether or not your domain's delegation has made it into your parent domain's name servers, query a root name server for the NS records for your domain. If the root name server can find the data, any name server on the Internet can:

```
% nslookup
Default Server:  terminator.movie.edu
Address:  192.249.249.3

> server ns.nasa.gov.    --Query a root name server
Default Server:  ns.nasa.gov
Addresses:  128.102.16.10, 192.52.195.10

> set norecurse          --Instruct the server to answer out of its own data
> set type=ns            --and to look for NS records
> movie.edu.             --for movie.edu
Server:  ns.nasa.gov
Addresses:  128.102.16.10, 192.52.195.10

*** ns.nasa.gov can't find movie.edu.: Non-existent domain
```

Here, the delegation clearly hasn't been added yet. You can either wait patiently, or if an unreasonable amount of time has passed since you requested delegation from your parent, contact your parent and ask what's up.

10. Incorrect Subdomain Delegation

Incorrect subdomain delegation is another familiar problem on the Internet. Keeping delegation up-to-date requires human intervention—informing your parent domain's administrator of changes to your set of authoritative name servers. Consequently, delegation information often becomes inaccurate as domain administrators make changes without letting their parents know. Far too many administrators believe that setting up delegation is a one-shot deal: they let their parents know which name servers are authoritative once, when they set up your domain, and then they never talk to them again. They don't even call on Mother's Day.

An administrator may add a new name server, decommission another, and change the IP address of a third, all without telling the parent domain's administrator. Gradually, the number of name servers correctly delegated to by the parent domain dwindles. In the best case, this leads to long resolution times, as querying name servers struggle to find an authoritative name server for the domain. If the delegation information becomes badly out of date, and the last authoritative name server host is brought down for maintenance, the information within the domain will be inaccessible.

If you suspect bad delegation, from your parent to your domain, from your domain to one of your subdomains, or from a remote domain to one of its subdomains, you can check with *nslookup*:

```
% nslookup
Default Server:  terminator.movie.edu
Address:  192.249.249.3

> server ns.nasa.gov.        --Set server to the parent name server you suspect has
                             --bad delegation
Default Server:  ns.nasa.gov
Addresses:  128.102.16.10, 192.52.195.10

> set type=ns               --Look for NS records
> hp.com.                   --for the domain in question
Server:  ns.nasa.gov
Addresses:  128.102.16.10, 192.52.195.10

Non-authoritative answer:
hp.com          nameserver = RELAY.HP.COM
hp.com          nameserver = HPLABS.HPL.HP.COM
hp.com          nameserver = NNSC.NSF.NET
hp.com          nameserver = HPSDLO.SDD.HP.COM

Authoritative answers can be found from:
hp.com          nameserver = RELAY.HP.COM
hp.com          nameserver = HPLABS.HPL.HP.COM
```

```
hp.com              nameserver = NNSC.NSF.NET
hp.com              nameserver = HPSDLO.SDD.HP.COM
RELAY.HP.COM        internet address = 15.255.152.2
HPLABS.HPL.HP.COM        internet address = 15.255.176.47
NNSC.NSF.NET        internet address = 128.89.1.178
HPSDLO.SDD.HP.COM        internet address = 15.255.160.64
HPSDLO.SDD.HP.COM        internet address = 15.26.112.11
```

Let's say you suspect that the delegation to hpsdlo.sdd.hp.com *is incorrect. You now query* hpsdlo *for data in the* hp.com *zone and check the answer:*

```
> server hpsdlo.sdd.hp.com.
Default Server:  hpsdlo.sdd.hp.com
Addresses:  15.255.160.64, 15.26.112.11

> set norecurse
> set type=soa
> hp.com.
Server:  hpsdlo.sdd.hp.com
Addresses:  15.255.160.64, 15.26.112.11

Non-authoritative answer:
hp.com
        origin = relay.hp.com
        mail addr = hostmaster.hp.com
        serial = 1001462
        refresh = 21600 (6 hours)
        retry   = 3600 (1 hour)
        expire  = 604800 (7 days)
        minimum ttl = 86400 (1 day)

Authoritative answers can be found from:
hp.com              nameserver = RELAY.HP.COM
hp.com              nameserver = HPLABS.HPL.HP.COM
hp.com              nameserver = NNSC.NSF.NET
RELAY.HP.COM        internet address = 15.255.152.2
HPLABS.HPL.HP.COM        internet address = 15.255.176.47
NNSC.NSF.NET        internet address = 128.89.1.178
```

If **hpsdlo** really were authoritative, it would have responded with an authoritative answer. The administrator of the **hp.com** domain can tell you whether **hpsdlo** should be an authoritative name server for **hp.com**, so that's who you should contact.

11. Syntax Error in resolv.conf

Despite the *resolv.conf* file's simple syntax, people do occasionally make mistakes when editing it. And, unfortunately, lines with syntax errors in *resolv.conf* are silently ignored by the resolver. The result is usually that some part of your intended configuration doesn't take effect: either your domain or search list isn't set correctly, or the resolver won't query one of the name servers you configured it to query. Commands that rely on the search list won't work, or your resolver won't query the right name server(s), or it won't query a name server at all.

The easiest way to check whether your *resolv.conf* file is having the intended effect is to run *nslookup*. *nslookup* will kindly report the default domain and search list it derives from *resolv.conf*, plus the name server it's querying, when you type **set all**, like we showed you back in Chapter 10, *nslookup*:

```
% nslookup
Default Server:  terminator.movie.edu
Address:  192.249.249.3

> set all
Default Server:  terminator.movie.edu
Address:  192.249.249.3

Set options:
  nodebug        defname        search         recurse
  nod2           novc           noignoretc     port=53
  querytype=A    class=IN       timeout=5      retry=4
  root=ns.nic.ddn.mil.
  domain=movie.edu
  srchlist=movie.edu

>
```

Check that the output of **set all** is what you expect, given your *resolv.conf* file. For example, if you'd set domain fx.movie.edu in *resolv.conf*, you'd expect to see:

```
domain=fx.movie.edu
srchlist=fx.movie.edu/movie.edu
```

in the output. If you don't see what you're expecting, look carefully at *resolv.conf*. If you don't see anything obvious, look for non-printing characters (with *vi*'s **set list** command, for example). Watch out for trailing spaces, especially: a trailing space after the domain name will set the default domain to include a space. No real domain names actually end with spaces, so all of your non-dot-terminated lookups will fail.

12. Default Domain Not Set

Failing to set your default domain is another old standby. You can set it implicitly, by setting your *hostname* to your host's fully-qualified domain name, or explicitly, in *resolv.conf*. The characteristics of an unset default domain are straightforward: folks who use single-label names (or abbreviated domain names) in commands get no joy:

```
% telnet br
br: No address associated with name
% telnet br.fx
br.fx: No address associated with name
% telnet br.fx.movie.edu
Trying...
Connected to bladerunner.fx.movie.edu.
Escape character is '^]'.

HP-UX bladerunner.fx.movie.edu A.08.07 A 9000/730 (ttys1)
login:
```

You can use *nslookup* to check this one, much as you do when you suspect a syntax error in *resolv.conf*:

```
% nslookup
Default Server:  terminator.movie.edu
Address:  192.249.249.3

> set all
Default Server:  terminator.movie.edu
Address:  192.249.249.3

Set options:
  nodebug        defname        search         recurse
  nod2           novc           noignoretc     port=53
  querytype=A    class=IN       timeout=5      retry=4
  root=ns.nic.ddn.mil.
  domain=
  srchlist=
```

Notice neither the local domain nor the searchlist is set. You can also track this down by enabling debugging on the name server. (This, of course, requires access to the name server, which may not be running on the host the problem's affecting.) Here's how the debugging output might look after trying those **telnet** commands:

```
Debug turned ON, Level 1

req: nlookup(br) id 1 type=1
req: missed 'br' as '' (cname=0)
forw: forw -> 192.33.33.24 7 (53) nsid=1670 id=1 53890ms retry 45 sec

datagram from 192.33.33.24 port 53, fd 6, len 20
send_msg -> 192.249.249.3 (UDP 6 1494) id=1

datagram from 192.249.249.3 port 1496, fd 6, len 23
req: nlookup(br.fx) id 1 type=1
req: missed 'br.fx' as '' (cname=0)
forw: forw -> 192.33.33.24 7 (53) nsid=1671 id=1 37730ms retry 45 sec
```

```
datagram from 192.33.33.24 port 53, fd 6, len 23
send_msg -> 192.249.249.3 (UDP 6 1496) id=1

datagram from 192.249.249.3 port 1500, fd 6, len 33
req: nlookup(br.fx.movie.edu) id 1 type=1
req: found 'br.fx.movie.edu' as 'br.fx.movie.edu' (cname=0)
req: nlookup(bladerunner.fx.movie.edu) id 1 type=1
req: found 'bladerunner.fx.movie.edu' as 'bladerunner.fx.movie.edu'
    (cname=1)
req: answer -> 192.249.249.3 6 (1500) id=1 Local
Debug turned OFF
```

Contrast this with the debugging output produced by the application of the search list in Chapter 11, *Reading BIND Debugging Output.* The only names looked up here are exactly what the user typed, with no domains appended at all. Clearly the search list isn't being applied.

Problem Symptoms

Some problems, unfortunately, aren't as easy to identify as the ones we listed. You'll experience some misbehavior but won't be able to attribute it directly to the cause, often because any of a number of problems may cause the symptoms you see. In cases like this, we'll suggest some of the common causes of these symptoms and how to isolate them.

Local Name Can't Be Looked Up

The first thing to do when a program like *telnet* or *ftp* can't look up a local name is to use *nslookup* to try to look up the same name. When we say "the same name," we mean *literally* the same name: don't add a domain and a trailing dot if the user didn't type either one. Don't query a different name server than the user did.

As often as not, the user mistyped the name, or doesn't understand how the search list works, and just needs direction. Occasionally, you'll turn up real host configuration errors:

- Syntax errors in *resolv.conf* (problem 11, above), or
- An unset default domain (problem 12).

You can check for either of these using *nslookup*'s **set all** command.

If *nslookup* points to a problem with the name server, rather than with the host configuration, check the problems appropriate for the type of name server. Is the name server the primary master for the zone, but doesn't respond with data you think it should? On a primary:

- Check that the db file contains the data in question, and that the name server has been signaled to reload it (problem 2).
- Check the boot file and the pertinent db file for syntax errors (problem 5).
- Ensure that the records have trailing dots, if they require them (problem 6).

If the name server is a secondary server, you should first check whether or not the primary has the correct data. If it does, and the secondary doesn't:

- Make sure you've incremented the serial number on the primary (problem 1).
- Look for a problem on the secondary in updating the zone (problem 3).

If the primary *doesn't* have the correct data, of course, diagnose the problem on the primary.

If the problem server is a caching-only name server:

- Make sure it has its cache data (problem 7).
- Check that your parent domain's delegation to your domain exists and is correct (problems 9 and 10). Remember that to a caching-only server, your domain looks just like any other remote domain. Even though the host it runs on may be inside your domain, the caching-only name server must be able to locate an authoritative server for your domain from your parent domain's servers.

Remote Names Can't Be Looked Up

If your local lookups succeed, but you can't look up names outside your local domains, there are a different set of problems to check:

- First, did you just set up your servers? You might have omitted the cache data (problem 7).
- Can you *ping* the remote domain's name servers? Maybe you can't reach the remote domain's servers because of connectivity loss (problem 8).
- Is the remote domain new? Maybe its delegation hasn't yet appeared (problem 9). Or the delegation information for the remote domain may be wrong or out-of-date, due to neglect (problem 10).

Wrong or Inconsistent Answer

If you get the wrong answer when looking up a local name, or an inconsistent answer, depending on which name server you ask or when you ask, first check the synchronization between your name servers.

- Are they all holding the same serial number for the zone? Did you forget to increment the serial number on the primary after you made a change (problem 1)? If you did, the name servers may all have the same serial number, but answer differently out of their authoritative data.

- Did you roll the serial number back to one (problem 1, again)? Then the primary's serial number will appear much lower than the secondaries' serial numbers.

- Did you forget to signal the primary (problem 2)? Then the primary will return (via *nslookup*, for example) a different serial number than the serial number in the data file.

- Are the secondaries having trouble updating from the primary (problem 3)? If so, they should have *syslog*'d appropriate error messages.

If you get these results when looking up a name in a remote domain, you should check whether the remote domain's name servers have lost synchronization. You can use tools like *nslookup* to determine whether the remote domain's administrator has forgotten to increment the serial number, for example. If the name servers answer differently from their authoritative data but show the same serial number, the serial number probably wasn't incremented. If the primary's serial number is much lower than the secondaries', the primary's serial number was probably accidentally reset. We usually assume a domain's primary name server is running on the host listed as the origin in the SOA record.

You probably can't determine conclusively that the primary hasn't been signaled, though. It's also difficult to pin down updating problems between remote name servers. In cases like this, if you've determined that the remote name servers are giving out incorrect data, contact the domain administrator and (gently) relay what you've found. This will help the administrator track down the problem on the remote end.

If you can determine that a parent server—a remote domain's parent, your domain's parent, or even your domain—is giving out a bad answer, check whether this is coming from old delegation information. Sometimes, this will require contacting both the administrator of the remote domain and the administrator of its parent to compare the delegation and the current, correct list of authoritative name servers.

Lookups Take a Long Time

Long name resolution is usually due to one of two problems:

- Connectivity loss (problem 8), which you can diagnose with name server debugging output and tools like *ping*.
- Incorrect delegation information (problem 10), which points to the wrong name servers or the wrong IP addresses.

Usually, going over the debugging output and sending a few *ping*s will point to one or the other: either you can't reach the name servers at all, or you can reach the hosts but the name servers aren't responding.

Sometimes, though, the results are inconclusive: the parent name servers delegate to a set of name servers that don't respond to *ping*s or queries, but connectivity to the remote network seems all right (a *traceroute*, for example, will get you to the remote network's "doorstep": the last router between you and the host). Is the delegation information so badly out of date that the name servers have long since moved to other addresses? Are the hosts simply down? Or is there really a remote network problem? Usually, finding out will require a call or a message to the administrator of the remote domain. (And remember, *whois* gives you phone numbers!)

rlogin and rsh to Host Fails Access Check

This is a problem you expect to see right after you set up your name servers. Users who are unaware of the change from the host table to domain name service won't know to update their *.rhosts* files. (We covered what needs to be updated in Chapter 6, *Configuring Hosts.*) Consequently, *rlogin* or *rsh*'s access check will fail and deny the user access.

Other causes of this problem are missing or incorrect **in-addr.arpa** delegation (problems 9 and 10), or forgetting to add a PTR record for the client host (problem 4). Any of these will result in the same behavior:

```
% rlogin wormhole
Password:
```

In other words, the user is prompted for a password despite having set up password-less access with *.rhosts* or *hosts.equiv.* If you were to look at the *syslog* file on the destination host (**wormhole**, in this case), you'd probably see something like:

```
May  4 18:06:22 wormhole inetd[22514]: login/tcp: Connection
      from unknown (192.249.249.213)
```

You can tell which problem it is by stepping through the resolution process with *nslookup*. First query one of your **in-addr.arpa** domain's parent name servers for NS records for your **in-addr** domain. If these are correct, query the name servers listed for the PTR record corresponding to the IP address of the *rlogin* or *rsh* client. Make sure they all have the PTR record, and that the record maps to the right domain name. If not all the name servers have the record, check for a loss of synchronization between the primary and the secondaries (problems 1 and 3).

Access to Services Denied

Sometimes *rlogin* and *rsh* aren't the only services to go. Occasionally you'll install DNS on your server and your diskless hosts won't boot, and hosts won't be able to mount disks from the server, either.

If this happens, make sure the case of the names your name servers return agrees with the case your previous name service returned. For example, if you had been running NIS, and your NIS hosts maps contained only lower-case names, you should make sure your name servers also return lowercase names. Some programs are case sensitive, and will fail to recognize names in a different case in a data file, such as */etc/bootparams* or */etc/exports*.

Name Server is Infected with Bogus Root Server Data

Here's a problem that'll be familiar to anyone who's run a name server on the Internet for any length of time:

```
% nslookup
Default Server: terminator.movie.edu
Address:  192.249.249.3

> set type=ns
> .
Server:  terminator.movie.edu
Address:  192.249.249.3

Non-authoritative answer:
(root)  nameserver = NS.NIC.DDN.MIL
(root)  nameserver = AOS.BRL.MIL
(root)  nameserver = KAVA.NISC.SRI.COM
```

```
(root)   nameserver = C.NYSER.NET
(root)   nameserver = TERP.UMD.EDU
(root)   nameserver = NS.NASA.GOV
(root)   nameserver = NIC.NORDU.NET
(root)   nameserver = hpfcsx.fc.hp.com
(root)   nameserver = hp-pcd.cv.hp.com
(root)   nameserver = hp-ses.sde.hp.com
(root)   nameserver = hpsatc1.gva.hp.com
(root)   nameserver = named_master.ch.apollo.hp.com
(root)   nameserver = A.ISI.EDU
(root)   nameserver = SRI-NIC.ARPA
(root)   nameserver = GUNTER-ADAM.ARPA

Authoritative answers can be found from:
(root)   nameserver = NS.NIC.DDN.MIL
(root)   nameserver = AOS.BRL.MIL
(root)   nameserver = KAVA.NISC.SRI.COM
(root)   nameserver = C.NYSER.NET
(root)   nameserver = TERP.UMD.EDU
(root)   nameserver = NS.NASA.GOV
(root)   nameserver =

*** Error: record size incorrect (1050690 != 65519)

*** terminator.movie.edu can't find .: Unspecified error
```

Whoa! Where in the heck did all those root name servers come from? And why is the record size messed up?

If you look carefully, you'll notice that most of those records are bogus. **SRI-NIC.ARPA**, for example, is the original name of **nic.ddn.mil**, from the days when all ARPANET hosts lived under the top-level **ARPA** domain. Moreover, even the name server on **nic.ddn.mil** was decommissioned as a root some time ago, replaced by a new root on **ns.nic.ddn.mil** (and *that* name server moved from the old NIC at SRI to the new one at GSI . . .).

The name servers in **hp.com** aren't Internet roots, and haven't *ever* been. So how did these get into our cache? Here's how:

Remember when we described what a name server does when queried for a name it isn't authoritative for? It does its best to provide information that will be helpful to the querier: NS records that are as close as possible to the domain name the querier is after. Sometimes, the queried name server can only get as close as the root name servers. And sometimes, the name server has the *wrong* list of roots, either deliberately (because of incorrect configuration) or because no one went to the effort to keep the cache file up-to-date.

So what does that have to do with caching? Well, say your name server queries what it thinks is a **10.in-addr.arpa** name server and the name server turns out to know nothing about **10.in-addr.arpa**. The name server, trying to be helpful, sends along its current list of root name servers in a response packet, but the list is wrong. BIND, trusting as a newborn, gratefully caches all this useless information.

Why did *nslookup* return a record size error when we looked up your name server's list of root servers? The list of roots exceeded the size of a UDP response packet, but was truncated to fit into a response. The length field in the response indicated that more data was included, though, so *nslookup* complained.

This infection can spread if the bogus NS records point to real—but non-root—name servers. If these name servers give out more bogus data, your name server's cache may become polluted by more and more erroneous records.

The only ways to track down the source of these bogus roots are to turn name server debugging way up (to level four or above) and watch for the receipt of these records, or to patch your name server to report receiving bad root information. Even when you think you've found the culprit, though, you may have only discovered another name server that was corrupted before yours, not the original source of the corruption. To uncover the original sinner, you often have to work backwards, together with other administrators, to discover who made the first gaffe.

Name Server Keeps Loading Old Data

Here's a weird class of problems related to the previous cache corruption problem. Sometimes, after decommissioning a name server, or changing a name server's IP address, you'll find the old address record lingering around. An old record may show up in a name server's cache or in a db files weeks, or even months later. The record clearly should have timed out of any caches by now. So why's it still there? Well, there are a few reasons this happens. We'll describe the simpler cases first.

Old Delegation Information

The first (and simplest) case can occur if a parent domain doesn't keep up with its children, or if the children don't inform the parent of changes to the authoritative name servers for the zone. If the **edu** administrators have this old delegation information for **movie.edu**:

```
$ORIGIN movie.edu.
@    86400    in    ns    terminator
     86400    in    ns    wormhole
terminator   86400  in    a     192.249.249.3
wormhole     86400  in    a     192.249.249.254 ; wormhole's former
                                                ; IP address
```

then the **edu** name servers will give out the bogus old address for **wormhole**.

This is easily corrected once it's isolated to the parent name servers: just contact the parent domain's administrator and ask to have the delegation information updated. If any of the child domain's servers have cached the bad data, kill them (to clear out their caches), delete any data files which contain the bad data, then restart them.

Unnecessary Glue Data

When *named-xfer* pulls zone data over from a master server, it transfers more than it strictly needs. This is arguably a bug in BIND. The main excess baggage *named-xfer* retrieves is the addresses of name servers for the zone, when those servers are outside of the zone. If the name servers are in the zone, their addresses are necessary as glue data. But if they're not in the zone, they don't belong in the zone's data file. So, for example, in a backup file for **movie.edu**, you'd find:

Partial contents of file *db.movie*:

```
$ORIGIN edu.
movie          IN     NS       terminator.movie.edu.
$ORIGIN movie.edu.
terminator     IN     A        192.249.249.3
$ORIGIN edu.
movie          IN     NS       wormhole.movie.edu.
$ORIGIN movie.edu.
wormhole       IN     A        192.249.249.1
               IN     A        192.253.253.1
               IN     A        192.249.249.254
```

But you'd also find similar records in *db.192.249.249* and *db.192.253.253*:

Partial contents of file *db.192.249.249*:

```
$ORIGIN 249.192.in-addr.arpa.
249            IN     NS       terminator.movie.edu.
$ORIGIN movie.edu.
terminator     56422  IN     A        192.249.249.3
$ORIGIN 249.192.in-addr.arpa.
249            IN     NS       wormhole.movie.edu.
```

```
$ORIGIN movie.edu.
wormhole          56422   IN      A       192.249.249.1
                  56422   IN      A       192.253.253.1
                  56422   IN      A       192.249.249.254
```

The last of **wormhole**'s addresses is **wormhole**'s former address.

There's no reason to include the address records for **terminator** or **wormhole** in either **in-addr** backup file. They *should* be listed in *db.movie*, but since they're not necessary as glue in either **in-addr** domain, they shouldn't appear in *db.192.249.249* or *db.192.253.253*.

When the secondary loads the **in-addr** backup file, it also loads the address records for **terminator** and **wormhole**. If the address is old, then the name server loads—and gives out—the wrong address:

```
% nslookup wormhole
Server:  wormhole.movie.edu
Address:  192.249.249.1

Name:    wormhole.movie.edu
Address:  192.249.249.1, 192.253.253.1, 192.249.249.254
```

You might think, "If I clean the old address out of *db.movie* (you can think in italics), the secondaries will time it out of the **in-addr.arpa** domains. After all, there's a TTL on the address records."

Unfortunately, the secondary servers don't age those records. They're given out with the TTL in the data file, but the secondary never decrements the TTL or times out the record. So the old address could linger as long as the **in-addr** backup files remain unchanged. And **in-addr.arpa** domains are very stable if no one's adding new hosts to the network or shuffling IP addresses. There's no need to increment their serial numbers and have them reloaded by the secondaries.

The secret is to increment *all* of the zones' serial numbers at once when you make a change affecting the zones' authoritative name servers. That way, you flush out any old, stale records and ensure that the secondaries all load up-to-date glue.

Mutual Infection

There's one more scenario we're familiar with that can cause these symptoms. This one doesn't require old data in files at all—just two secondary name servers. BIND can run into problems when two name servers act as secondaries for each other, and when one zone is the child of the other; for example, when name server A loads **movie.edu** from name server B, and B loads **fx.movie.edu** from A.

In these cases, certain data can float back and forth between the two name servers indefinitely. In particular, the name servers can pass delegation data, which is really part of the "child" zone, back and forth.

How does this work? Say **terminator.movie.edu** is the primary master **movie.edu** server and it backs up **fx.movie.edu** from **bladerunner**. **bladerunner** is the primary master **fx.movie.edu** name server and backs up **movie.edu** from **terminator**. Then suppose you change **bladerunner**'s IP address. You remember to change *named.boot* on **terminator** to load **fx.movie.edu** from **bladerunner**'s new IP address, and you change the IP address in *db.fx*. You even update the **fx** domain's delegation data in *db.movie* on the primary to reflect the address change. Isn't that enough?

Nope. Here's why: **terminator** still has **bladerunner**'s old IP address in the backup file *db.fx*, and **bladerunner** still has its own old address in its backup copy of *db.movie* (a glue record in the **fx** delegation).

Now let's say you delete *db.fx* on **terminator** and kill and restart its name server. Won't that suffice? No, because **bladerunner** still has the old address and will pass it along to **terminator** in the next **fx.movie.edu** zone transfer. If you delete *db.movie* on **bladerunner** and kill and restart the name server, something similar will happen: **bladerunner** will get the old record back with the next **movie.edu** zone transfer.

That's a little complicated to follow—for us, too—so here's Figure 12.1 to help you picture what's going on.

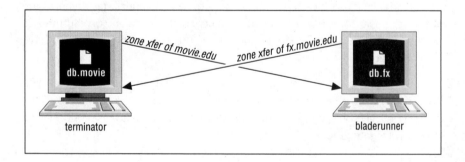

Figure 12.1: Infection through zone transfer

You need to rid both name servers of the old record simultaneously. Our solution to this problem is to bring both name servers down at the same time, clean out any backup files, and start them both up again. That way, the caches can't re-infect each other.

What Have I Got?

How do you determine which of these problems is ailing you? Pay attention to which name servers are distributing the old data, and which domains the data relates to:

- Is the name server your parent name server? Check the parent for either old delegation information, or for parent-child infection.
- Are both a name server and its parent affected? Then check for parent-child infection.
- Are secondaries affected, but not the primary? Check for stale data in backup files.

That's about all we can think to cover. It's certainly less than a comprehensive list, but we hope it'll help you solve the more common problems you encounter with DNS, and give you ideas about how to approach the rest. Boy, if we'd only had a troubleshooting guide when *we* started!

In this chapter:
• Shell Script
  Programming with
  nslookup
• C Programming
  with the Resolver
  Library Routines

13
Programming with
the Resolver
Library Routines

"I know what you're thinking about," said Tweedledum; "but it isn't so, nohow."

"Contrariwise," continued Tweedledee, "if it was so, it might be; and if it were so, it would be; but as it isn't, it ain't. That's logic."

I bet you think resolver programming is hard. Contrariwise! It isn't very hard, really. The format of DNS packets is quite straightforward—you don't have to deal with ASN.1* at all, like you have to with SNMP. And you have nifty library routines to make parsing DNS packets easy. There are even a couple of useful resolver routines waiting to be discovered by those of us who read the source code; we'll tell you about them in this chapter. We've included portions of RFC 1035 in *Appendix A*. However, you might find it handy to have a copy of RFC 1035 to look at while we are going through this chapter; at least, have a copy of it nearby when you write your own DNS program.

Shell Script Programming with nslookup

Before you go off and write a C program to do your DNS chore, you should write the program as a shell script using *nslookup*. There are good reasons to start with a shell script:

• You'll write the shell script much faster than you'll write the C program.

• If you are not comfortable with DNS, you can work out the muck in your program's logic with a quick shell script prototype. When you

---

*ASN.1 stands for Abstract Syntax Notation. ASN.1 is a language for encoding object types, accepted as an international standard by the International Organization for Standards.

finally write the C program, you can focus on the additional control you have with C rather than spending your time reworking the basic functionality.

- You might find out that the shell script version does your task well enough so that you don't have to write the C program after all. Not only is the coding time shorter, but shell scripts are easier to maintain if you stick with them for the long run.

A Typical Problem

Before you write a program, you have to have a problem to solve. Let's suppose you want your network management system to watch over your primary and secondary name servers. You want it to notify you of several problems: a name server that is not running (it might have died), a name server that is not authoritative for a domain that it is supposed to be authoritative for (the boot file might have been messed up), or a name server that has fallen behind in updating its data (the primary's serial number might have been decreased accidentally).

Each of these problems is easily detectable. If a name server is not running on a host, the host will send back an ICMP port unreachable message. You can find this out with both *nslookup* and the resolver routines. Checking if a name server is authoritative for a domain is easy: ask it for the domain's SOA record. If the answer is non-authoritative or the name server does not have the SOA record, there is a problem. You'll have to ask for the SOA record in a *non-recursive* query so that the name server doesn't go off and look up the SOA record from another server. Once you have the SOA record, you can extract the serial number.

Solving this Problem with a Script

This problem requires a program that takes a single domain as an argument, looks up the name servers for that domain, and then queries each of those name servers for the SOA record for the domain. The response will show if the server is authoritative and it will show the domain's serial number. If there is no response, the program needs to determine if a name server is even running on the host. Once this program is written, it needs to be called for every domain you want to watch over. Since this program looks up the name servers (by looking up the NS records for the domain), we assume that you have listed all your name servers in NS records in your zone data. If that is not the case, then you will have to change this program to take a list of name servers from the command line.

Let's write the basic program as a shell script that uses *nslookup*. First, we must figure out what the output of *nslookup* looks like so that we can parse it with UNIX tools. We'll look up NS records to find out which servers are supposed to be authoritative for a domain, both when the server is authoritative for the NS records and when it isn't:

```
% nslookup
Default Server: relay.hp.com
Address:  15.255.152.2

> set type=ns
```

Find out what the response looks like when the server is not authoritative for the NS records.

```
> mit.edu.
Server:  relay.hp.com
Address:  15.255.152.2

Non-authoritative answer:
mit.edu nameserver = STRAWB.MIT.EDU
mit.edu nameserver = W20NS.MIT.EDU
mit.edu nameserver = BITSY.MIT.EDU
mit.edu nameserver = LITHIUM.LCS.MIT.EDU

Authoritative answers can be found from:
MIT.EDU nameserver = STRAWB.MIT.EDU
MIT.EDU nameserver = W20NS.MIT.EDU
MIT.EDU nameserver = BITSY.MIT.EDU
MIT.EDU nameserver = LITHIUM.LCS.MIT.EDU
STRAWB.MIT.EDU   internet address = 18.71.0.151
W20NS.MIT.EDU    internet address = 18.70.0.160
BITSY.MIT.EDU    internet address = 18.72.0.3
LITHIUM.LCS.MIT.EDU    internet address = 18.26.0.121
```

Find out what the response looks like when the server is authoritative for the NS records.

```
> server strawb.mit.edu.
Default Server: strawb.mit.edu
Address:  18.71.0.151

> mit.edu.
Server:  strawb.mit.edu
Address:  18.71.0.151

mit.edu nameserver = BITSY.MIT.EDU
mit.edu nameserver = LITHIUM.LCS.MIT.EDU
mit.edu nameserver = STRAWB.MIT.EDU
mit.edu nameserver = W20NS.MIT.EDU
BITSY.MIT.EDU    internet address = 18.72.0.3
```

```
LITHIUM.LCS.MIT.EDU      internet address = 18.26.0.121
STRAWB.MIT.EDU  internet address = 18.71.0.151
W20NS.MIT.EDU   internet address = 18.70.0.160
```

You can see from this output that we can grab the name server names by looking for the lines that contain `nameserver` and saving the last field. When the server was not authoritative for the NS records, it printed them twice, so we'll have to weed out duplicates.

Next, look up the SOA record for the domain, both when the server is authoritative for the SOA record and when it isn't. We turn off *recurse* so the name server doesn't go off and query an authoritative name server for the SOA.

```
% nslookup
Default Server:  relay.hp.com
Address:  15.255.152.2

> set type=soa
> set norecurse
```

Find out what the response looks like when the server does not have the SOA record.

```
> mit.edu.
Server:  relay.hp.com
Address:  15.255.152.2

Authoritative answers can be found from:
MIT.EDU nameserver = STRAWB.MIT.EDU
MIT.EDU nameserver = W20NS.MIT.EDU
MIT.EDU nameserver = BITSY.MIT.EDU
MIT.EDU nameserver = LITHIUM.LCS.MIT.EDU
STRAWB.MIT.EDU  internet address = 18.71.0.151
W20NS.MIT.EDU   internet address = 18.70.0.160
BITSY.MIT.EDU   internet address = 18.72.0.3
LITHIUM.LCS.MIT.EDU      internet address = 18.26.0.121
```

Find out what the response looks like when the server is authoritative for the domain.

```
> server strawb.mit.edu.
Default Server:  strawb.mit.edu
Address:  18.71.0.151

> mit.edu.
Server:  strawb.mit.edu
Address:  18.71.0.151

mit.edu
        origin = BITSY.MIT.EDU
        mail addr = NETWORK-REQUEST.BITSY.MIT.EDU
        serial = 378
        refresh = 3600 (1 hour)
```

```
retry   = 300 (5 mins)
expire  = 3600000 (41 days 16 hours)
minimum ttl = 21600 (6 hours)
```

When the name server was not authoritative for the domain, it returned references to other name servers. If the name server had previously looked up the SOA record and cached it, the name server would have returned the SOA record and said it was "non-authoritative." We need to check for both cases. When the name server returns the SOA record and it is authoritative, we can grab the serial number from the line that contains `serial`.

Now, we need to see what *nslookup* returns when no name server is running on a host. We'll change servers to a host that does not normally run a name server and look up an SOA record:

```
% nslookup
Default Server:  relay.hp.com
Address:  15.255.152.2

> server bors.cs.purdue.edu.
Default Server:  bors.cs.purdue.edu
Address:  128.10.2.48

> set type=soa
> mit.edu.
Server:  bors.cs.purdue.edu
Address:  128.10.2.48

*** bors.cs.purdue.edu can't find mit.edu.: No response from server
```

Last, we need to see what *nslookup* returns if a host is not responding. We can test this by switching servers to an unused IP address on our LAN:

```
% nslookup
Default Server:  relay.hp.com
Address:  15.255.152.2

> server 15.255.152.100
Default Server:  [15.255.152.100]
Address:  15.255.152.100

> set type=soa
> mit.edu.
Server:  [15.255.152.100]
Address:  15.255.152.100

*** Request to [15.255.152.100] timed-out
```

In the last two error cases, the error message was written to *stderr*. We can make use of that fact when writing our shell script. Now we are ready to compose the shell script. We'll call it *check_soa*.

```
#!/bin/sh
if test "$1" = ""
then
     echo usage: $0 domain
     exit 1
fi
DOMAIN=$1
#
# Use nslookup to discover the nameservers for this domain ($1).
# Use awk to grab the name server names from the nameserver lines.
# (The names are always in the last field.)  Use sort -u to weed out
# duplicates; we don't actually care about collation.
#
SERVERS=`nslookup -type=ns $DOMAIN |\
                 awk '/nameserver/ {print $NF}' | sort -u`
if test "$SERVERS" = ""
then
     #
     # Didn't find any servers.  Just quit silently; nslookup will
     # have detected this error and printed a message.  That will
     # suffice.
     #
     exit 1
fi
#
# Check each server's SOA serial number.  The output from
# nslookup is saved in two tmp files: nso.$$ (standard output)
# and nse.$$ (standard error).  These files are rewritten on
# every iteration.  Turn off defname and search since we
# should be dealing with fully qualified names.
#
# NOTE: this loop is rather long; don't be fooled.
#
for i in $SERVERS
do
  nslookup >/tmp/nso.$$ 2>/tmp/nse.$$ <<-EOF
     server $i
     set nosearch
     set nodefname
     set norecurse
     set q=soa
     $DOMAIN
EOF
  #
  # Does this response indicate that the current server ($i) is
  # authoritative?  The server is NOT authoritative if (a) the
  # response says so, or (b) the response tells you to find
  # authoritative info elsewhere.
  #
  if egrep "Non-authoritative|Authoritative answers can be" \
                                  /tmp/nso.$$ >/dev/null
  then
     echo $i is not authoritative for $DOMAIN
     continue
```

```
        fi
        #
        # We know the server is authoritative; extract the serial number.
        #
        SERIAL=`cat /tmp/nso.$$ | grep serial | sed -e "s/.*= //"`
        if test "$SERIAL" = ""
        then
            #
            # We get here if SERIAL is null.  In this case, there should
            # be an error message from nslookup; so cat the "standard
            # error" file.
            #
            cat /tmp/nse.$$
        else
            #
            # Report the server's name and its serial number.
            #
            echo $i has serial number $SERIAL
        fi
done    # end of the "for" loop
#
# Delete the temporary files.
#
rm -f /tmp/nso.$$ /tmp/nse.$$
```

Here is what the output looks like:

```
% check_soa mit.edu
BITSY.MIT.EDU has serial number 378
LITHIUM.LCS.MIT.EDU has serial number 378
STRAWB.MIT.EDU has serial number 378
W20NS.MIT.EDU has serial number 378
```

If you are pressed for time, this short tool will solve your problem and you can go on to other work. If you find that you are checking lots of domains and that this tool is too slow, you'll want to convert it to a C program. Also, if you want more control over the error messages—rather than relying on *nslookup* for error messages—then you'll have to write a C program. We'll do just that, later on in this chapter.

C Programming with the Resolver Library Routines

Before writing any code, though, you need to be familiar with the DNS packet format and the resolver library routines. In the shell script we just wrote, *nslookup* parsed the DNS packet. In a C program, you have to do the parsing. Let's start this section on programming by looking at the DNS packet format.

DNS Packet Format

You've seen the DNS packet format before, in Chapter 10, *nslookup*. It looks like this:

1. Header section
2. Question section
3. Answer section
4. Authority section
5. Additional section

The format of the header section is described in RFC 1035 on pages 26-28 and in *Appendix A*. When you write a C program to parse a DNS packet, you'll need a data structure to embody the header section. There is a header section data structure that you can use already defined in the include file *arpa/nameser.h*:

```
typedef struct {
    u_short id;         /* query identification number */
        /* fields in third byte */
    u_char  qr:1;       /* response flag */
    u_char  opcode:4;   /* purpose of message */
    u_char  aa:1;       /* authoritative answer */
    u_char  tc:1;       /* truncated message */
    u_char  rd:1;       /* recursion desired */
        /* fields in fourth byte */
    u_char  ra:1;       /* recursion available */
    u_char  pr:1;       /* primary server required (non standard) */
    u_char  unused:2;   /* unused bits */
    u_char  rcode:4;    /* response code */
        /* remaining bytes */
    u_short qdcount;    /* number of question entries */
    u_short ancount;    /* number of answer entries */
    u_short nscount;    /* number of authority entries */
    u_short arcount;    /* number of resource entries */
} HEADER;
```

You'll also find opcode, response code, type, and class values defined in *arpa/nameser.h*.

Notice that the pr bit is labeled "non standard." That's because that bit is not part of the DNS protocol. It's defined in the header, but BIND doesn't implement the feature.

The question section is described on pages 28-29 of RFC 1035. It looks like this:

```
domain name (variable length)
query type (2 octets)
query class (2 octets)
```

The answer, authority, and additional sections are described on pages 29-30 of RFC 1035. These sections are comprised of some number of resource records that look like this:

```
domain name (variable length)
type (2 octets)
class (2 octets)
TTL (4 octets)
resource data length (2 octets)
resource data (variable length)
```

The header section contains a count of how many of these resource records are in each section.

Domain Name Storage

As you can see, the names stored in the DNS packet are variable length. Unlike C, the names are not stored as null-terminated strings. Domain names are stored as a series of length/value pairs ending with a zero length octet. Each label in a domain name is comprised of a length octet and the label. A name like **venera.isi.edu** is stored as:

```
6 venera 3 isi 3 edu 0
```

You can imagine how much of a DNS packet would be devoted to storing names. The DNS authors recognized this, and came up with a simple way to compress domain names.

Domain Name Compression

Often an entire domain name or, at least, the trailing labels of a domain name, match a name already stored in the response. Domain name compression eliminates the repetition of domain names by storing a pointer to the earlier occurrence of the name instead of inserting the name again. This is how it works. Suppose a response packet already contains the name **venera.isi.edu**. If the name **vaxa.isi.edu** is added to the response, the label **vaxa** is stored and then a pointer to the earlier occurrence of **isi.edu** is added. So how are pointers implemented?

The first two bits of the length octet indicate whether or not a length/label pair follows, or a pointer to a length/label pair follows. If the first two bits are zero, then the length and label follow. As you may have read else-where, a label is limited to 63 characters. That's because the length field has only the remaining six bits for the length of the label—enough to rep-resent the lengths 0-63. If the first two bits of the length octet are ones, then what follows is not a length, but a pointer. The pointer is the last six bits of the length octet *and* the next octet—14 bits total. The pointer is an offset from the start of the DNS packet. Now, when **vaxa.isi.edu** is com-pressed into a buffer containing only **venera.isi.edu**, this is what results:

```
byte offset: 0 123456 7 890 1 234 5 6 7890 1    2
             -------------+--------------+--------
pkt contents: 6 venera 3 isi 3 edu 0 4 vaxa 0xC0 7
```

The 0xC0 is a byte with the high two bits one and the rest of the bits zero. Since the high two bits are ones, this is a pointer instead of a length. The pointer value is seven—the last six bits of the first octet are zero and the second octet is seven. At offset seven in this buffer, you find the rest of the **vaxa** domain name: **isi.edu**.

In this example, we only showed compressing two names in a buffer, not a whole DNS packet. A DNS packet would have had a header as well as other fields. This example was only to give you an idea of how the domain name compression works. Now the good news: you don't care how names are compressed, as long as the library routines do it properly. What you need to know is how parsing a DNS response can get messed up if you are off by one byte. For example, try to expand the name starting with byte two instead of byte one. You'll discover that "v" doesn't make a very good length octet or a very good pointer.

The Resolver Library Routines

The first thing you need to know about the resolver library routines is that there are more resolver library routines than are on the 4.8.3 manual page. Maybe you can get by with what is documented. If you do, then you've probably re-implemented undocumented routines. As you'll see in our C code example, there are a couple of extra library calls that help get you through a DNS packet. We'll start with the routines from the manual page.

Here are the header files you must include:

```
#include <sys/types.h>
#include <netinet/in.h>
#include <arpa/nameser.h>
#include <resolv.h>
```

These are the documented resolver library routines:

```
int res_search(dname, class, type, answer, anslen)
char *dname;
int class, type;
u_char *answer;
int anslen;
```

res_search is the "highest" level resolver routine. It is called by *gethost-byname*. *res_search* implements the search algorithm on the domain name passed to it; that is, it takes the domain name it receives (*dname*), "completes" the name (if it's not fully-qualified) by adding the various "extensions" from the resolver search list, and calls *res_query* until it receives a successful response, indicating that it found a valid, fully qualified name. In addition to implementing the search algorithm, *res_search* looks in the file referenced by your HOSTALIASES environment variable. (The HOSTALIASES variable was described in Chapter 6, *Configuring Hosts*.) So it also takes care of any "private" host aliases you might have.

Therefore, the only parameter that's really of interest to *res_search* is *dname*; the others are just passed to *res_query* and the other resolver routines. The other arguments are:

class   The "address type" of the data you're looking up. This is almost always the constant C_IN, which requests an "internet class" address. These constants are defined in *arpa/nameser.h*.

type   The type of request that you're making. Again, this is a constant defined in *arpa/nameser.h*. A typical value would be T_NS, to retrieve a name server record; or T_MX, to retrieve an MX record.

answer   A buffer in which *res_search* will place the response packet. Its size should be at least PACKETSZ (from *arpa/nameser.h*) bytes.

anslen   The size of the *answer* buffer (e.g., PACKETSZ).

res_search returns the size of the response, or –1 if there was an error.

```
int res_query(dname, class, type, answer, anslen)
char *dname;
int class, type;
u_char *answer;
int anslen;
```

res_query is one of the "mid-level" resolver routines. It does all the real work in looking up the domain name; it makes a query packet by calling *res_mkquery*, sends the query by calling *res_send*, and looks at enough of the response to determine if your question was answered. In many cases, *res_query* is called by *res_search*, which just feeds it the different domain names to look up. As you'd expect, these two functions have the same arguments. *res_query* returns the size of the response, or it fills in *h_errno* and returns –1 if there was an error or the answer count is zero. (*h_errno* is like *errno*, but for DNS lookups.)

```
int res_mkquery(op, dname, class, type, data, datalen, newrr, buf, buflen)
int op;
char *dname;
int class, type;
char *data;
int datalen;
struct rrec *newrr;
char *buf;
int buflen;
```

res_mkquery makes the query packet. It fills in all the header fields, compresses the domain name into the question section, and fills in the other question fields. The *dname*, *class*, and *type* arguments are the same as for *res_search* and *res_query*. The remaining arguments are:

op   The "operation" to be performed. This is normally QUERY, but it can be IQUERY (inverse query). However, as we've explained before, IQUERY is seldom used.

data A buffer containing the data for inverse queries. It is NULL when *op* is QUERY.

datalen The size of the *data* buffer. If *data* is NULL, then *datalen* is zero.

newrr A buffer used for the experimental dynamic update code (a topic not covered in this book). Unless you are playing with this feature, it is always NULL.

buf   A buffer in which *res_mkquery* makes the query packet. It should be PACKETSZ or larger, just like the answer buffer in *res_search* and *res_query*.

buflen The size of the *buf* buffer (e.g., PACKETSZ).

res_mkquery returns the size of the query packet, or –1 if there was an error.

```
int res_send(msg, msglen, answer, anslen)
char *msg;
int msglen;
char *answer;
int anslen;
```

res_send implements the retry algorithm. It sends the query packet, *msg*, in a UDP packet, but it can also send it over a TCP stream. The response packet is stored in *answer*. This routine, of all the resolver routines, is the only one to use black magic (unless you know all about connected datagram sockets). You've seen these arguments before in the other resolver routines:

msg   The buffer containing the DNS query packet.

msglen   The size of the *msg* buffer.

answer   The buffer to store the DNS response packet.

anslen   The size of the *answer* buffer.

res_send returns the size of the response, or –1 if there was an error. If this routine returns –1 and *errno* is ECONNREFUSED, then there is no name server running on the target name server host.

You can look at *errno* to see if it is ECONNREFUSED after calling *res_search* or *res_query*. (*res_search* calls *res_query* which calls *res_send*.) If you want to check *errno* after calling *res_query*, then clear *errno* first. That way, you know the current call to *res_send* was the one that set *errno*. However, you don't have to clear *errno* before calling *res_search*. *res_search* clears *errno* itself before calling *res_query*.

```
int res_init()
```

res_init reads *resolv.conf* and initializes a data structure called *_res* (more about that later). All of the previously discussed routines will call *res_init*, if they detect that it hasn't been called previously. Or you can call it on your own; this is useful if you want to change some of the defaults before calling the first resolver library routine. If there are any lines in *resolv.conf* that *res_init* doesn't understand, it ignores them. *res_init* always returns zero, even if the manual page reserves the right to return –1.

```
int dn_comp(exp_dn, comp_dn, length, dnptrs, lastdnptr)
char *exp_dn, *comp_dn;
int length;
char **dnptrs, **lastdnptr;
```

dn_comp compresses a domain name. You won't normally call this routine yourself—you'll let *res_mkquery* do it for you. However, if you need to compress a name for some reason, this is the tool to do it. The arguments are:

exp_dn   The "expanded" domain name that you supply; i.e., a normal null-terminated string containing a fully qualified domain name.

comp_dn   The place where *dn_comp* will store the compressed domain name.

length   The size of the *comp_dn* buffer.

dnptrs   An array of pointers to previously compressed domain names. *dnptrs[0]* points to the beginning of the message; the list ends with a NULL pointer. After you've initialized *dnptrs[0]* to the beginning of the message and *dnptrs[1]* to NULL, *dn_comp* updates the list each time you call it.

lastdnptr   A pointer to the end of the *dnptrs* array. *dn_comp* needs to know where the end of the array is, so it doesn't overrun it.

If you want to use this routine, look at how it is used in *res/res_mkquery.c* from the BIND source. It's often easier to see how to use a routine from an example rather than from an explanation. *dn_comp* returns the size of the compressed name or −1 if there was an error.

```
int dn_expand(msg, eomorig, comp_dn, exp_dn, length)
char *msg, *eomorig, *comp_dn, exp_dn;
int  length;
```

dn_expand expands a "compressed" domain name. You will use this routine if you parse a name server response, as we do in the example below. The arguments are:

msg   A pointer to the beginning of your response packet (message).

eomorig   A pointer to the first byte after the message. It is used to make sure that *dn_expand* doesn't go past the end of the message.

comp_dn   A pointer to the compressed domain name within the message.

exp_dn   The place where *dn_expand* will store the expanded name. You should always allocate an array of MAXDNAME characters for the expanded name.

length   The size of the *exp_dn* buffer.

dn_expand returns the size of the compressed name or −1 if there was an error. You might wonder why *dn_expand* returns the size of the *compressed* name and not the size of the *expanded* name. It does this because when you call *dn_expand*, you are parsing a DNS packet and need to know how much space the compressed name took in the packet so that you can skip over it.

```
extern int h_errno;

int herror(s)
char *s;
```

herror is a routine like *perror*, except that it prints out a string based on the value of the external variable *h_errno* instead of *errno*. The only argument is:

s   A string used to identify the error message. If a string *s* is supplied, it is printed first, followed by ": " and then a string based on the value of *h_errno*.

Here are the possible values of *h_errno*:

HOST_NOT_FOUND
            The domain name does not exist. The return code in the name server response was NXDOMAIN.

TRY_AGAIN   Either the name server is not running or the name server returned SERVFAIL.

NO_RECOVERY Either the domain name could not be compressed because it was an invalid domain name (e.g., a name missing a label—**movie..edu**) or the name server returned FORMERR, NOTIMP, or REFUSED.

NO_DATA   The domain name exists, but there is no data of the requested type.

The Undocumented Library Routines

If you spend any time reading through the resolver source code, you'll see some handy undocumented routines:

```
u_short _getshort(msgp)
u_char *msgp;
```

The DNS packets have fields that are unsigned short integer—type, class, and data length, to name a few. This routine returns the unsigned short integer pointed to by *msgp*.

```
u_long _getlong(msgp)
u_char *msgp;
```

This routine is like *_getshort*, except that it deals with an unsigned long integer instead of an unsigned short integer. The TTL field (time to live) of a resource record is a long integer.

```
int dn_skipname(comp_dn, eom)
u_char *comp_dn, *eom;
```

This routine is like *dn_expand*, except that it skips over the domain name instead of expanding it out for you. This is a handy way for moving around within a response packet; you'll see it used in our sample program. The arguments are:

comp_dn   A pointer to the compressed domain name.

eom   The first location after the message.

dn_skipname returns the size of the compressed name, or −1 if there was an error (like running past the end of the packet).

```
int p_query(msg)
char *msg;
```

This routine prints the packet contents to *stdout* in a format similar to the debug output of *nslookup*. On older versions of BIND, you may need to compile *res/res_debug.c* with DEBUG defined; otherwise, *p_query* might not do anything. *p_query* doesn't return a specific value. The only argument is:

msg   A pointer to the DNS packet.

The _res Structure

Each of the resolver routines (i.e., each routine whose name starts with *res_*) makes use of a common data structure called *_res*. You can change the behavior of the resolver routines by changing *_res*. If you want to change the number of times *res_send* retries a query, you can change the

value of the *retry* field. If you want to turn off the resolver search algorithm, you turn off the RES_DNSRCH bit from the *options* mask. You'll find
the all-important *_res* structure in *resolv.h*:

```
struct state {
    int     retrans;   /* retransmission time interval */
    int     retry;     /* number of times to retransmit */
    long    options;   /* option flags - see below. */
    int     nscount;   /* number of name servers */
    struct  sockaddr_in nsaddr_list[MAXNS]; /* address of name server */
#define nsaddr  nsaddr_list[0]    /* for backward compatibility */
    u_short id;                   /* current packet id */
    char    defdname[MAXDNAME];   /* default domain */
    char    *dnsrch[MAXDNSRCH+1]; /* components of domain to search */
};
```

The *options* field is a simple bit mask of the enabled options. To turn on a
feature, turn on the corresponding bit in the options field. Bit masks for
each of the options are defined in *resolv.h*; the options are:

RES_INIT   If this bit is on, then *res_init* has been called.

RES_DEBUG   This bit causes resolver debugging messages to be printed,
                if the resolver routines were compiled with DEBUG, that is.
                Off by default.

RES_AAONLY   Require the answer to be authoritative, not from a name
                server's cache. It's too bad this isn't implemented; it would
                be a useful feature. With the BIND resolver design, this
                feature would have to be implemented in the name server
                and it's not.

RES_PRIMARY   Query the primary server only—again, not implemented.
                This option turns on the pr bit in the HEADER structure
                shown earlier, but, if you remember, the pr bit is not part
                of the DNS protocol and is not implemented by BIND.

RES_USEVC   Turn this bit on if you'd like the resolver to make its
                queries over a virtual circuit (TCP) connection instead of
                with UDP packets. As you might guess, there is a perfor-
                mance penalty for setting up and tearing down a TCP con-
                nection. Off by default.

RES_STAYOPEN   If you are making your queries over a TCP connection,
                turning this bit on causes the connection to be left open.
                Otherwise, the connection is torn down after the query has
                been answered. Off by default.

RES_IGNTC   If the name server response has the truncation bit set, then the default resolver behavior is to retry the query using TCP. If this bit is turned on, then the truncation bit in the response packet is ignored and the query is not retried using TCP. Off by default.

RES_RECURSE The default behavior for the BIND resolver is to make recursive queries. Turning this bit off turns off the recursion desired bit in the query packet. On by default.

RES_DEFNAMES The default behavior for the BIND resolver is to append the default domain to names that do not have a dot in them. Turning this bit off turns off appending the default domain. On by default.

RES_DNSRCH   The default behavior for the BIND resolver is to append each entry in the search list to a name that does not end in a dot. Turning this bit off turns off the search list function. On by default.

Parsing DNS Responses

The easiest way to learn how to parse a DNS packet is to look at code that already does it. Assuming that you have the DNS source code, the best file to look through is *res/res_debug.c.* This file has *fp_query*, the routine that prints out the DNS packets in the name server debugging output. Another place to look is *res/named/gethostnamadr.c* where you'll find *getanswer*, the routine that is used by *gethostbyname*. Our sample program traces its parentage to code from these two files.

You won't always want to parse the DNS response manually. An "intermediate" way to parse the response is to call *p_query*, which calls *fp_query*, to print out the DNS packet. Then use basic UNIX tools, like *perl* or *awk*, to grab what you need. Cricket's been known to wimp out this way.

A Sample Program: check_soa

Here is a C program to solve the same problem that we earlier wrote a shell script for.

```
/****************************************************************
 * check_soa -- Retrieve the SOA record from each name server   *
 *      for a given domain and print out the serial number.     *
 *                                                              *
 * usage: check_soa domain                                      *
 *                                                              *
 * The following errors are reported:                           *
 *      o There is no address for a server.                     *
 *      o There is no server running on this host.              *
 *      o There was no response from a server.                  *
 *      o The server is not authoritative for the domain.       *
 *      o The response had an error response code.              *
 *      o The response had more than one answer.                *
 *      o The response answer did not contain an SOA record.    *
 *      o The expansion of a compressed domain name failed.     *
 ****************************************************************/

/* Various header files */
#include <sys/types.h>
#include <sys/socket.h>
#include <netinet/in.h>
#include <netdb.h>
#include <stdlib.h>
#include <stdio.h>
#include <errno.h>
#include <arpa/inet.h>
#include <arpa/nameser.h>
#include <resolv.h>
#include <string.h>

/* Error variables */
extern int h_errno;   /* for resolver errors */
extern int errno;     /* general system errors */

/* Our own routines; code included later in this chapter */
void nsError();            /* report resolver errors */
void findNameServers();    /* find a domain's name servers */
void queryNameServers();   /* grab SOA records from servers */
void returnCodeError();    /* report response packet errors */
int  skipToData();         /* skip to the resource record data */
int  skipName();           /* skip a compressed name */

/* Maximum number of name servers we will check */
#define NSLIMIT 20
```

Here are the header files that are needed, the declarations for external variables, and the declarations of functions. Notice that we use both *h_errno* (for the resolver routines) and *errno*. We've set a limit of 20 name servers that this program will check. You will rarely see a domain with more than 10 name servers, so an upper limit of 20 should suffice.

```
main(argc, argv)
int argc;
char *argv[];
{
    char *nsList[NSLIMIT]; /* list of name servers */
    int  nsNum = 0;         /* number of name servers in list */

    /* sanity check: one (and only one) argument? */
    if(argc != 2){
        (void) fprintf(stderr, "usage: %s domain\n", argv[0]);
        exit(1);
    }

    (void) res_init();

    /*
     * Find the name servers for the domain.
     * The name servers are written into nsList.
     */
    findNameServers(argv[1], nsList, &nsNum);

    /*
     * Query each name server for the domain's SOA record.
     * The name servers are read from nsList.
     */
    queryNameServers(argv[1], nsList, nsNum);

    exit(0);
}
```

The main body of the program is small. We have an array of string pointers, *nsList*, to store the names of the name servers for the domain. We call the resolver function *res_init* to initialize the *_res* structure. It wasn't necessary for this program to call *res_init* explicitly, since it would have been called by the first resolver routine that used the *_res* structure. However, if we had wanted to modify the value of any of the *_res* fields before calling the first resolver routine, we would have made the modifications right after calling *res_init*. Next, the program calls *findNameServers* to find all the name servers for the domain referenced in *argv[1]* and store them in *nsList*. Last, the program calls *queryNameServers* to query each of the name servers in *nsList* for the SOA record for the domain.

The routine *findNameServers* follows. This routine queries the local name server for the NS records for the domain. It parses the response packet and stores away all the name servers it finds. The header files, *arpa/nameser.h* and *resolv.h*, contain declarations we make extensive use of.

```
/***************************************************************
 * findNameServers -- find all of the name servers for the     *
 *      given domain and store their names in nsList. nsNum is  *
 *      the number of servers in the nsList array.              *
 ***************************************************************/
void
findNameServers(domain, nsList, nsNum)
char *domain;
char *nsList[];
int  *nsNum;
{
    union {
        HEADER hdr;            /* defined in resolv.h */
        u_char buf[PACKETSZ]; /* defined in arpa/nameser.h */
    } response;                /* response buffers */
    int responseLen;          /* buffer length */

    u_char  *cp;        /* character pointer to parse DNS packet */
    u_char  *endOfMsg; /* need to know the end of the message */
    u_short class;      /* classes defined in arpa/nameser.h */
    u_short type;       /* types defined in arpa/nameser.h */
    u_long  ttl;        /* resource record time to live */
    u_short dlen;       /* size of resource record data */

    int i, count, dup; /* misc variables */

    /*
     * Look up the NS records for the given domain name.
     * We expect the domain to be a fully qualified name, so
     * we use res_query().  If we wanted the resolver search
     * algorithm, we would have used res_search() instead.
     */
    if((responseLen =
            res_query(domain,       /* the domain we care about    */
                    C_IN,           /* Internet class records      */
                    T_NS,           /* Look up name server records */
                    (u_char *)&response,        /*response buffer  */
                    sizeof(response)))          /*buffer size      */
                                < 0){   /*If negative              */
        nsError(h_errno, domain); /* report the error              */
        exit(1);                      /* and quit                  */
    }

    /*
     * Keep track of the end of the message so we don't
     * pass it while parsing the response.  responseLen is
     * the value returned by res_query.
     */
    endOfMsg = response.buf + responseLen;

    /*
     * Set a pointer to the start of the question section,
     * which begins immediately AFTER the header.
     */
```

```
cp = response.buf + sizeof(HEADER);

/*
 * Skip over the whole question section.  The question
 * section is comprised of a name, a type, and a class.
 * QFIXEDSZ (defined in arpa/nameser.h) is the size of
 * the type and class portions, which is fixed.  Therefore,
 * we can skip the question section by skipping the
 * name (at the beginning) and then advancing QFIXEDSZ.
 * After this calculation, cp points to the start of the
 * answer section, which is a list of NS records.
 */
cp += skipName(cp, endOfMsg) + QFIXEDSZ;

/*
 * Create a list of name servers from the response.
 * NS records may be in the answer section and/or in the
 * authority section depending on the DNS implementation.
 * Walk through both.  The name server addresses may be in
 * the additional records section, but we will ignore them
 * since it is much easier to call gethostbyname() later
 * than to parse and store the addresses here.
 */
count = ntohs(response.hdr.ancount) +
        ntohs(response.hdr.nscount);
while (    (--count >= 0)         /* still more records    */
        && (cp < endOfMsg)       /* still inside the packet*/
        && (*nsNum < NSLIMIT)) { /* still under our limit  */

    /* Skip to the data portion of the resource record */
    cp += skipToData(cp, &type, &class, &ttl, &dlen, endOfMsg);

    if (type == T_NS) {

        /*
         * Allocate storage for the name.  Like any good
         * programmer should, we test malloc's return value,
         * and quit if it fails.
         */
        nsList[*nsNum] = (char *) malloc (MAXDNAME);
        if(nsList[*nsNum] == NULL){
            (void) fprintf(stderr, "malloc failed\n");
            exit(1);
        }

        /* Expand the name server's name */
        if (dn_expand(response.buf, /* Start of the packet  */
                    endOfMsg,       /* End of the packet    */
                    cp,             /* Position in the packet*/
                    (u_char *)nsList[*nsNum], /* Result     */
                    MAXDNAME)       /* size of nsList buffer */
                          < 0) { /* Negative: error    */
                (void) fprintf(stderr, "dn_expand failed\n");
                exit(1);
```

```
        }

        /*
         * Check the name we've just unpacked and add it to
         * the list of servers if it is not a duplicate.
         * If it is a duplicate, just ignore it.
         */
        for(i = 0, dup=0; (i < *nsNum) && !dup; i++)
            dup = !strcasecmp(nsList[i], nsList[*nsNum]);
        if(dup)
            free(nsList[*nsNum]);
        else
            (*nsNum)++;
    }

    /* Advance the pointer over the resource record data */
    cp += dlen;

} /* end of while */
}
```

Notice that we don't explicitly check for finding zero name server records. We don't need to check because *res_query* flags that case as an error; it returns −1 and sets *herrno* to NO_DATA. If *res_query* returns −1, we call our own routine, *nsError*, to print out an error string from *h_errno* instead of using *herror*. The *herror* routine isn't a good fit for our program because its messages assume you are looking up address data. (E.g., if *h_errno* is NO_DATA, the error message is "No address associated with name.")

The next routine queries each name server that we've found for an SOA record. In this routine, we change the value of several of the *_res* structure fields. By changing the *nsaddr_list* field, we change which server *res_send* queries. We disable the search list by turning off bits in the *options* field—all the names that this program handles are fully qualified.

```
/****************************************************************
 * queryNameServers -- Query each of the name servers in nsList *
 *      for the SOA record of the given domain.  Report any     *
 *      errors encountered.  (E.g., a name server not running or *
 *      the response not being an authoritative response.)  If   *
 *      there are no errors, print out the serial number for the *
 *      domain.                                                 *
 ****************************************************************/
void
queryNameServers(domain, nsList, nsNum)
char *domain;
char *nsList[];
int nsNum;
{
    union {
        HEADER hdr;             /* defined in resolv.h */
```

```
              u_char buf[PACKETSZ];   /* defined in arpa/nameser.h */
        } query, response;           /* query and response buffers */
        int responseLen, queryLen; /* buffer lengths */

        u_char  *cp;         /* character pointer to parse DNS packet */
        u_char  *endOfMsg; /* need to know the end of the message */
        u_short class;       /* classes defined in arpa/nameser.h */
        u_short type;        /* types defined in arpa/nameser.h */
        u_long  ttl;         /* resource record time to live */
        u_short dlen;        /* size of resource record data */

        struct in_addr saveNsAddr[MAXNS];  /* addrs saved from _res */
        int nsCount;               /* count of addresses saved from _res */
        struct hostent *host; /* structure for looking up ns addr */
        int i;                 /* counter variable */

        /*
         * Save the _res name server list since
         * we will need to restore it later.
         */
        nsCount = _res.nscount;
        for(i = 0; i < nsCount; i++)
          saveNsAddr[i] = _res.nsaddr_list[i].sin_addr;

        /*
         * Turn off the search algorithm and turn off appending
         * the default domain before we call gethostbyname(); the
         * name server names will be fully qualified.
         */
        _res.options &= ~(RES_DNSRCH | RES_DEFNAMES);

        /*
         * Query each name server for an SOA record.
         */
        for(nsNum-- ; nsNum >= 0; nsNum--){

            /*
             * First, we have to get the IP address of every server.
             * So far, all we have are names.  We use gethostbyname
             * to get the addresses, rather than anything fancy.
             * But first, we have to restore certain values in _res
             * because _res affects gethostbyname().  (We altered
             * _res in the previous iteration through the loop.)
             *
             * We can't just call res_init() again to restore
             * these values since some of the _res fields are
             * initialized when the variable is declared, not when
             * res_init() is called.
             */
            _res.options |= RES_RECURSE;  /* recursion on (default) */
            _res.retry = 4;                /* 4 retries (default)    */
            _res.nscount = nsCount;        /* original name servers  */
            for(i = 0; i < nsCount; i++)
                _res.nsaddr_list[i].sin_addr = saveNsAddr[i];
```

```
/* Look up the name server's address */
host = gethostbyname(nsList[nsNum]);
if (host == NULL) {
    (void) fprintf(stderr,"There is no address for %s\n",
                                    nsList[nsNum]);
    continue; /* nsNum for-loop */
}

/*
 * Now get ready for the real fun.  host contains IP
 * addresses for the name server we're testing.
 * Store the first address for host in the _res
 * structure.  Soon, we'll look up the SOA record...
 */
(void) memcpy((void *)&_res.nsaddr_list[0].sin_addr,
    (void *)host->h_addr_list[0], (size_t)host->h_length);
_res.nscount = 1;

/*
 * Turn off recursion.  We don't want the name server
 * querying another server for the SOA record; this name
 * server ought to be authoritative for this data.
 */
_res.options &= ~RES_RECURSE;

/*
 * Reduce the number of retries.  We may be checking
 * several name servers, so we don't want to wait too
 * long for any one server.  With two retries and only
 * one address to query, we'll wait at most 15 seconds.
 */
_res.retry = 2;

/*
 * We want to see the response code in the next
 * response, so we must make the query packet and
 * send it ourselves instead of having res_query()
 * do it for us.  If res_query() returned -1, there
 * might not be a response to look at.
 *
 * There is no need to check for res_mkquery()
 * returning -1.  If the compression was going to
 * fail, it would have failed when we called
 * res_query() earlier with this domain name.
 */
queryLen = res_mkquery(
            QUERY,             /* regular query         */
            domain,            /* the domain to look up */
            C_IN,              /* Internet type         */
            T_SOA,             /* Look up an SOA record */
            (char *)NULL,      /* always NULL           */
            0,                 /* length of NULL        */
            (struct rrec *)NULL, /* always NULL         */
            (char *)&query,    /* buffer for the query  */
```

```
                                sizeof(query));  /* size of the buffer    */

        /*
         * Send the query packet.  If there is no name server
         * running on the target host, res_send() returns -1
         * and errno is ECONNREFUSED.  First, clear out errno.
         */
        errno = 0;
        if((responseLen = res_send((char *)&query, /* the query    */
                                    queryLen,       /* true length */
                                    (char *)&response, /*buffer    */
                                    sizeof(response))) /*buf size */
                                      < 0){            /* error    */
            if(errno == ECONNREFUSED) { /* no server on the host   */
                (void) fprintf(stderr,
                    "There is no name server running on %s\n",
                    nsList[nsNum]);
            } else {                      /* anything else: no response */
                (void) fprintf(stderr,
                    "There was no response from %s\n",
                    nsList[nsNum]);
            }
            continue; /* nsNum for-loop */
        }

        /*
         * Set up the pointers to parse the response.
         * We set up two pointers: one to the end of the message
         * (so we can test for overruns) and one to the question
         * section (which we'll move as we parse the response).
         */
        endOfMsg = response.buf + responseLen;
        cp = response.buf + sizeof(HEADER);

        /*
         * If the response reports an error, issue a message
         * and proceed to the next server in the list.
         */
        if(response.hdr.rcode != NOERROR){
            returnCodeError((int)response.hdr.rcode,
                                        nsList[nsNum]);
            continue; /* nsNum for-loop */
        }

        /*
         * Did we receive an authoritative response?  Check the
         * authoritative answer bit.  If the server isn't
         * authoritative, report it, and go on to the next server.
         */
        if(!response.hdr.aa){
            (void) fprintf(stderr,
                "%s is not authoritative for %s\n",
                nsList[nsNum], domain);
            continue; /* nsNum for-loop */
```

```
    }

    /*
     * The response should only contain one answer; if more,
     * report the error, and proceed to the next server.
     */
    if(ntohs(response.hdr.ancount) != 1){
        (void) fprintf(stderr,
            "%s: expected 1 answer, got %d\n",
            nsList[nsNum], ntohs(response.hdr.ancount));
        continue; /* nsNum for-loop */
    }

    /*
     * Skip the question section (we know what we asked,
     * don't we?). cp now points to the answer section.
     */
    cp += skipName(cp, endOfMsg) + QFIXEDSZ;

    /*
     * cp is now pointing at a resource record in the answer
     * section. Skip to the data portion of this record;
     * in the process, extract the type, class, etc.
     */
    cp += skipToData(cp, &type, &class, &ttl, &dlen, endOfMsg);

    /*
     * We asked for an SOA record; if we got something else,
     * report the error and proceed to the next server.
     */
    if (type != T_SOA) {
        (void) fprintf(stderr,
            "%s: expected answer type %d, got %d\n",
            nsList[nsNum], T_SOA, type);
        continue; /* nsNum for-loop */
    }

    /*
     * Skip the SOA origin and mail address, which we don't
     * care about. Both are standard "compressed names."
     */
    cp += skipName(cp, endOfMsg);
    cp += skipName(cp, endOfMsg);

    /* cp now points to the serial number; print it. */
    (void) printf("%s has serial number %d\n",
        nsList[nsNum], _getlong(cp));

    } /* end of nsNum for-loop */
}
```

Notice that we use recursive queries when we call *gethostbyname*, but use non-recursive queries when we look up the SOA record. *gethostbyname* may need to query other servers to find the host's address. But we don't want the name server querying another server when we ask it for the SOA record—it's *supposed* to be authoritative for this domain after all. Allowing the name server to ask another server for the SOA record would defeat the error check.

The next routine provides a "wrapper" around *dn_skipname*. It checks the return value of *dn_skipname* and exits if there was an error. If we messed up parsing the response, this routine gives us immediate feedback.

```
/***************************************************************
 * skipName -- This routine skips over a domain name.  If the   *
 *     domain name expansion fails, it reports an error and      *
 *     exits.  dn_skipname() is probably not on your manual      *
 *     page; it is similar to dn_expand() except that it just    *
 *     skips over the name.  dn_skipname() is in res_comp.c if   *
 *     you need to find it.                                      *
 ***************************************************************/
int
skipName(cp, endOfMsg)
u_char *cp;
u_char *endOfMsg;
{
    int n;

    if((n = dn_skipname(cp, endOfMsg)) < 0){
        (void) fprintf(stderr, "dn_skipname failed\n");
        exit(1);
    }
    return(n);
}
```

The next routine skips to the data portion of a resource record from the answer, authority, or additional sections of a DNS packet. It fills in the type, class, TTL, and data length variables. We skip over the resource record name because it will be the same name we looked up. That wouldn't be the case, though, if our program looked at the additional records section of the DNS packet.

```
/***************************************************************
 * skipToData -- This routine advances the cp pointer to the    *
 *     start of the resource record data portion.  On the way,  *
 *     it fills in the type, class, TTL, and data length         *
 ***************************************************************/
int
skipToData(cp, type, class, ttl, dlen, endOfMsg)
u_char  *cp;
u_short *type;
u_short *class;
u_long  *ttl;
u_short *dlen;
```

```
u_char   *endOfMsg;
{
     u_char *tmp_cp = cp;   /* temporary version of cp */

     /* Skip the domain name; it matches the name we looked up */
     tmp_cp += skipName(tmp_cp, endOfMsg);

     /*
      * Grab the type, class, and TTL.  The routines called
      * _getshort() and _getlong() are also resolver routines
      * you may not find in a manual page.  They are in
      * res_comp.c if you want to see them.
      */
     *type = _getshort(tmp_cp);
     tmp_cp += sizeof(u_short);
     *class = _getshort(tmp_cp);
     tmp_cp += sizeof(u_short);
     *ttl = _getlong(tmp_cp);
     tmp_cp += sizeof(u_long);
     *dlen = _getshort(tmp_cp);
     tmp_cp += sizeof(u_short);

     return(tmp_cp - cp);
}
```

The next two routines print out error messages.

```
/******************************************************************
 * nsError -- Print an error message from h_errno for a failure *
 *      looking up NS records.  res_query() converts the DNS    *
 *      packet return code to a smaller list of errors and      *
 *      places the error value in h_errno.  There is a routine  *
 *      called herror() for printing out strings from h_errno   *
 *      like perror() does for errno.  Unfortunately, the       *
 *      herror() messages assume you are looking up address     *
 *      records for hosts.  In this program, we are looking up  *
 *      NS records for domains, so we need our own list of error*
 *      strings.                                                *
 ******************************************************************/
void
nsError(error, domain)
int error;
char *domain;
{
     switch(error){
          case HOST_NOT_FOUND:
             (void) fprintf(stderr, "Unknown domain: %s\n", domain);
             break;
          case NO_DATA:
             (void) fprintf(stderr, "No NS records for %s\n", domain);
             break;
          case TRY_AGAIN:
             (void) fprintf(stderr, "No response for NS query\n");
             break;
```

```
                default:
                  (void) fprintf(stderr, "Unexpected error\n");
                  break;
        }
}

/****************************************************************
 * returnCodeError -- print out an error message from a DNS    *
 *      response return code.                                   *
 ****************************************************************/
void
returnCodeError(rcode, nameserver)
int rcode;
char *nameserver;
{
    (void) fprintf(stderr, "%s: ", nameserver);
    switch(rcode){
        case FORMERR:
          (void) fprintf(stderr, "FORMERR response\n");
          break;
        case SERVFAIL:
          (void) fprintf(stderr, "SERVFAIL response\n");
          break;
        case NXDOMAIN:
          (void) fprintf(stderr, "NXDOMAIN response\n");
          break;
        case NOTIMP:
          (void) fprintf(stderr, "NOTIMP response\n");
          break;
        case REFUSED:
          (void) fprintf(stderr, "REFUSED response\n");
          break;
        default:
          (void) fprintf(stderr, "unexpected return code\n");
          break;
    }
}
```

To compile this program using the resolver routines in *libc.a*:

```
% cc -o check_soa check_soa.c
```

Or, if you've newly ported the BIND code like we describe in *Appendix B, Compiling and Installing BIND on a Sun*, and want to use the 4.8.3 header files and resolver library:

```
% cc -o check_soa -I/tmp/include check_soa.c \
            /tmp/res/libresolv.a
```

Here is what the output looks like:

```
% check_soa mit.edu
LITHIUM.LCS.MIT.EDU has serial number 378
BITSY.MIT.EDU has serial number 378
W20NS.MIT.EDU has serial number 378
STRAWB.MIT.EDU has serial number 378
```

If you look back at the shell script output, it looks the same except the shell script's output is sorted by the name server's name. What you can't see is that the C program ran much faster.

Now that you've seen a program that uses the resolver library routines, it shouldn't be as hard to create one of your own.

14

Miscellaneous

'The time has come,' the Walrus said,
'To talk of many things:
Of shoes—and ships—and sealing-wax—
Of cabbages—and kings—
And why the sea is boiling hot—
And whether pigs have wings.'

It's time we tied up loose ends. We've already covered the mainstream of DNS and BIND, but there are a handful of interesting niches we haven't explored. Some of these may actually be useful to you, like instructions on how to set up DNS on a network without Internet connectivity; others may just be interesting. We can't in good conscience send you out into the world without completing your education!

CNAMEs

We talked about CNAME resource records in Chapter 4, *Setting Up BIND*. We didn't tell you all about CNAME records though; we saved that for this chapter. When you set up your first name servers, you didn't care about the subtle nuances of the magical CNAME record. Maybe you didn't realize there was more than we explained, maybe you didn't care. Some of this trivia is interesting, some is arcane. We'll let you decide which is which.

CNAMEs Pointing to Interior Nodes

If you've ever renamed your domain because of a company re-org, you may have considered creating a single CNAME record that pointed from the old domain to the new domain. For instance, if the **fx.movie.edu** domain were renamed to **magic.movie.edu**, we'd be tempted to create a single CNAME record to map all the old names to the new names:

```
fx.movie.edu.   IN  CNAME  magic.movie.edu.
```

With this in place, you'd expect a lookup of **empire.fx.movie.edu** to result in a lookup of **empire.magic.movie.edu**. Unfortunately, this doesn't work—you *can't* have CNAME records pointing to interior nodes. CNAME records must have "leaf" nodes as the canonical name. So, instead of a single CNAME record to rename a complete domain, you'll have to do it the old fashioned way—a CNAME record for each individual host within the domain:

```
empire.fx.movie.edu.       IN  CNAME  empire.magic.movie.edu.
bladerunner.fx.movie.edu.  IN  CNAME  bladerunner.magic.movie.edu.
```

Hopefully, the tool you use to manage your DNS database files will handle creating CNAME records for you. (*h2n*, which was introduced in *Chapter 4*, does.)

CNAMEs Pointing to CNAMEs

We've often wondered whether it was possible to have an alias (CNAME record) pointing to another alias. This might be useful in situations where an alias points from a domain name outside of your domain to a domain name inside your domain. You may not have any control over the alias outside of your domain. What if you want to change the domain name it points to? Can you simply add another CNAME record?

We weren't able to find this in the RFCs, so we enlisted the help of a local DNS expert. She produced this copy of a previous correspondence (our apologies to Judith Martin*):

---

*Author of *Miss Manners' Guide to Excruciatingly Correct Behavior* (Galahad Books, NY: 1982) and *Miss Manners' Guide to Rearing Perfect Children* (Atheneum, NY: 1984).

Dear Miss DNS Manners:

Our parent domain's administrator has finally agreed to provide a CNAME record in our parent domain that points to our mail hub's new name in our subdomain. We just moved our mail hub, *ZYZZYVA*, from our parent domain to our subdomain and everyone still knows it by its old name in the parent domain. Boy, the arm twisting it took to get a measly CNAME record installed!

The problem is that now we want to rename the host, since we've already stirred up the waters by changing domains (and people are expecting changes). Folks have complained that the name is too hard to remember. But the clod who runs our parent domain will only create a CNAME record that points to the same, old, hard-to-remember name in our subdomain. He says that is all his automated tool can handle. (I think he's holding out for a bribe.) What can we do?

Gentle Administrator:

Clod or not, one must respect the wishes of one's parent domain administrator. Parenting is a difficult and unrewarding job. When was the last time you thanked your parent domain administrator when she had you correct an error in your domain? If your parent has limited resources with which to run your domain family, then you must make do with what you get. But by all means, replace that "charming" host name that no one can remember.

Miss DNS Manners suggests that you consider creating a second CNAME resource record, one that points from the misguided name in your subdomain to its inspired replacement. For instance, if your parent domain has the following:

```
ZYZZYVA.SCRABBLE.NET.  IN CNAME ZYZZYVA.ADV.SCRABBLE.NET.
```

then, you create:

```
ZZYZZYVA.ADV.SCRABBLE.NET. IN CNAME BUCKINGHAM.ADV.SCRABBLE.NET.
```

(Miss DNS Manners recommends well-established British names, by the way.)

With this solution, you satisfy your needs while not imposing on your parent administrator. Miss DNS Manners cautions prankish administrators against creating CNAME "chains" that are too long. Name servers guard themselves from harm (CNAME loops) by limiting CNAME "chains" to eight CNAMES.

CNAMEs in the Resource Record Data

For any other record besides a CNAME record, you must have the canonical name in the resource record data. Applications and name servers won't operate correctly otherwise. As we mentioned back in Chapter 5, *DNS and Electronic Mail*, for example, *sendmail* only recognizes the canonical name of the local host on the right side of an MX record. If *sendmail* doesn't recognize the local host name, it won't strip the right MX records out when paring down the MX list, and may deliver mail to itself or less-preferred hosts, causing mail to loop.

Looking Up CNAMEs

At times you may want to look up a CNAME record itself, not data for the canonical name. With *nslookup*, this is easy to do. You can either set the query type to *cname* or you can set query type to *any* and then look up the name.

```
% nslookup
Default Server:  wormhole
Address:  0.0.0.0

> set query=cname
> bigt
Server:  wormhole
Address:  0.0.0.0

bigt.movie.edu  canonical name = terminator.movie.edu
> set query=any
> bigt
Server:  wormhole
Address:  0.0.0.0

bigt.movie.edu  canonical name = terminator.movie.edu
```

Finding Out a Host's Aliases

One thing you can't easily do with DNS is find out a host's aliases. With the host table, it's easy to find both the canonical name of a host and any aliases, no matter which you look up: they're all there, together, on the same line.

```
% grep terminator /etc/hosts
192.249.249.3  terminator.movie.edu terminator bigt
```

With DNS, however, if you look up the cano_{...}

canonical name. There's no easy way for the n_{...}
tion to know whether aliases exist for that canonic_{...}

```
% nslookup
Default Server:  wormhole
Address:  0.0.0.0

> terminator
Server:  wormhole
Address:  0.0.0.0

Name:     terminator.movie.edu
Address:  192.249.249.3
```

If you use *nslookup* to look up an alias, you'll see that alias and the canonical name. *nslookup* reports both the alias and the canonical name in the packet. But you won't see any other aliases that might point to that canonical name.

```
% nslookup
Default Server:  wormhole
Address:  0.0.0.0

> bigt
Server:  wormhole
Address:  0.0.0.0

Name:     terminator.movie.edu
Address:  192.249.249.3
Aliases:  bigt.movie.edu
```

About the only way to find out all the CNAMEs for a host is to transfer the whole zone and pick out the CNAME records where that host is the canonical name. You can have *nslookup* filter on CNAME records:

```
% nslookup
Default Server:  wormhole
Address:  0.0.0.0

> ls -t cname movie.edu
[wormhole]
 bigt                        terminator.movie.edu
 wh                          wormhole.movie.edu
 dh                          diehard.movie.edu
```

Even this method will only show you the aliases within that zone—there could be aliases in a different zone, pointing to canonical names in this zone.

Something else we haven't covered yet are DNS *wildcards*. There are times when you want a single resource record to cover any possible name, rather than creating zillions of resource records which are all the same except for the domain name to which they apply. DNS reserves a special character, *, to be used in a DNS database file as a wildcard name. It will match any number of labels in a name, as long as there isn't an exact match with a name already in the DNS database.

Most often, you'd use wildcards to forward mail to non-Internet connected networks. Suppose your site is not connected to the Internet, but you have a host that will relay mail between the Internet and your network. You could create a wildcard MX record for Internet consumption that points all your mail to the relay. Here is an example:

```
*.movie.edu.  IN  MX  10 movie-relay.nea.gov.
```

Since the wildcard matches one or more labels, this resource record would apply to names like **terminator.movie.edu**, **empire.fx.movie.edu**, or **casablanca.bogart.classics.movie.edu**. The danger with wildcards is that they clash with search lists. This wildcard also matches **cujo.movie.edu.movie.edu**, making wildcards useless within your domain data. Remember that some versions of *sendmail* apply the search list when looking up MX records:

```
% nslookup
Default Server:  wormhole
Address:  0.0.0.0

> set type=mx      --Look up MX records
> cujo.movie.edu   --for cujo
Server:  wormhole
Address:  0.0.0.0

cujo.movie.edu.movie.edu    --This isn't a real host's name!
        preference = 10, mail exchanger = movie-relay.nea.gov
```

What are the limitations of wildcards? Wildcards do not match names for which there is already data. Suppose you *did* use wildcards within your domain data:

```
*.movie.edu.   IN  MX  10 mail-hub.movie.edu.
et.movie.edu.  IN  MX  10 et.movie.edu.
jaws.movie.edu IN  A   192.253.253.113
```

Mail to **terminator.movie.edu** will be sent to **mail-hub**, but mail to **et.movie.edu** will be sent directly to **et**. An MX lookup of **jaws.movie.edu** would result in a response that said there was no MX data for that name. The wildcard doesn't apply because an A record exists. Can you use wildcards safely within your domain? Yes. We'll cover that case a little further in this chapter.

A Limitation of MX Records

While we are on the topic of MX records, let's talk about how they may result in mail taking a longer path than necessary. The MX records are a list of data returned when a name is looked up. The list is not ordered by what exchanger might be closest to the sender. Here is an example of this problem. Your non-Internet connected network has two hosts capable of relaying Internet mail to your network. One host is in the U.S. and one host is in France. Your network is in Greece. Most of your mail comes from the U.S., so you have someone maintain your domain and install two wildcard MX records—the highest preference to the U.S. relay and a lower preference to the France relay. Since the U.S. relay is at a higher preference, *all* mail will go through that relay (as long as it is reachable). If someone in France sends you a letter, it will travel across the Atlantic to the U.S. and back, because there is nothing in the MX list to indicate that the French relay is closer.

Non-Internet Connected Domains

Way back in Chapter 5, *DNS and Electronic Mail*, we went over how to create MX lists that will let users on the Internet send mail to users in your domain, even if most of your network is hidden behind a security firewall. That's only half of the picture, though. The solution we described will allow your domain's users to receive mail from the Internet, but doesn't let them send mail back. Since most users probably won't be satisfied with half-duplex communication, we feel obliged to provide the other half of the solution.

There's one major DNS problem to contend with on a network without direct Internet connectivity: BIND name servers need to communicate with root name servers. Even a slave name server using a remote forwarder needs to talk to a root name server at startup. If a name server can't reach a root, it can't resolve names outside its own authority.

This gives you two choices:

1. Run all your name servers *on* your firewall (i.e., on hosts with direct Internet connectivity)

2. Set up internal root name servers for your network.

If you have *no* Internet connectivity, you have no choice: you've got to run your own root name servers.

Firewall Name Servers Only

If you run a small network, running name servers only on firewall hosts might be okay. You won't need to configure and manage internal roots, and you can point all your "non-Internet"* hosts' resolvers to the name servers on the firewall hosts. Any host on your network will be able to find information about any other host on your network, and in fact, even non-Internet hosts will be able to look up information about Internet hosts—even though they can't reach them. Giving non-Internet hosts access to information they can't use can cause problems, though. Imagine what would happen if a user sent mail from an non-Internet host to, say, a friend on **sun.com**. The mail would cause an MX lookup on name server on a firewall host. That would return:

```
% nslookup -type=mx sun.com.
Server:  terminator.movie.edu
Address:  192.249.249.3

sun.com preference = 10, mail exchanger = Sun.COM
Sun.COM internet address = 192.9.9.1
```

The non-Internet host, not realizing it can't reach **Sun.COM**, would try to connect there. The connection would time out, and the mailer would queue the message. After the queue timeout, the mailer would return the message to the sender.

To deal with this problem, you'll need to configure your mailer to send mail addressed to Internet destinations to a firewall host first, and then let the firewall host forward it. In a *sendmail.cf* file, that's usually an easy modification. Unfortunately, most *sendmail.cf* files differ so much that we can't really tell you exactly what to change. The change usually involves scanning destination mail addresses for your local domain in the ruleset that resolves the delivery agent, destination host and user triple. If the address

---

*We'll call a host a "non-Internet" host if it can't reach the Internet's root name servers.

doesn't contain your local domain, change the destination host to a firewall mail relay. If the address contains your local domain, send the mail directly. Here's what that might look like in a **movie.edu** host's *sendmail.cf*:

```
# try to connect directly to hosts for user@localdomain
R$+<@$+.movie.edu>      $#tcp$@$2$:$1<@$2>
# forward user@remotedomain to postmanrings2x
R$+<@$+>                $#tcp$@postmanrings2x.movie.edu$:$1<@$2>
```

Unfortunately, running only firewall name servers won't work on large networks. On a large network with only a few hosts with direct Internet access, you won't have enough name servers to handle all the name resolution on the network.

Internal Roots

On a large network, or a network with no Internet connectivity, you'll need to set up internal root name servers. An internal root delegates directly to any domains you administer. For example, on the **movie.edu** network, the root database file would contain:

```
movie.edu.   86400   IN   NS   terminator.movie.edu.
             86400   IN   NS   wormhole.movie.edu.
             86400   IN   NS   zardoz.movie.edu.

terminator.movie.edu.   86400   IN   A   192.249.249.3
wormhole.movie.edu.     86400   IN   A   192.249.249.1
                        86400   IN   A   192.253.253.1
zardoz.movie.edu.       86400   IN   A   192.249.249.9
                        86400   IN   A   192.253.253.9
```

Normally, this information would appear in the **edu** name servers' databases. On the **movie.edu** network, of course, there aren't any **edu** name servers, so you delegate directly to **movie.edu** from the root.

Notice this doesn't contain delegation to **fx.movie.edu** or any other subdomain of **movie.edu**: the **movie.edu** name servers know which name servers are authoritative for all **movie.edu** subdomains, and all queries for information in those subdomains will pass through the **movie.edu** name servers, so there's no need to delegate them here.

in-addr.arpa Delegation

You'll also need to delegate from the internal roots to the **in-addr.arpa** domains that correspond to the network numbers **movie.edu** uses:

```
249.249.192.in-addr.arpa.   86400   IN   NS   terminator.movie.edu.
                            86400   IN   NS   wormhole.movie.edu.
                            86400   IN   NS   zardoz.movie.edu.
253.253.192.in-addr.arpa.   86400   IN   NS   terminator.movie.edu.
                            86400   IN   NS   wormhole.movie.edu.
                            86400   IN   NS   zardoz.movie.edu.
254.253.192.in-addr.arpa.   86400   IN   NS   bladerunner.fx.movie.edu.
                            86400   IN   NS   outland.fx.movie.edu.
                            86400   IN   NS   alien.fx.movie.edu.
20.254.192.in-addr.arpa.    86400   IN   NS   bladerunner.fx.movie.edu.
                            86400   IN   NS   outland.fx.movie.edu.
                            86400   IN   NS   alien.fx.movie.edu.
```

Now, notice that we *did* include delegation for the **254.253.192.in-addr.arpa** and **20.254.192.in-addr.arpa** domains, even though they correspond to the **fx.movie.edu** domain. We didn't need to delegate to **fx.movie.edu**, because we'd already delegated to its parent. The **movie.edu** name servers delegate to **fx.movie.edu**, so by transitivity, the roots delegate to **fx.movie.edu**. Since neither of the other **in-addr.arpa** domains are parents of **254.253.192.in-addr.arpa** or **20.254.192.in-addr.arpa**, we needed to delegate both domains from the root. As we've covered earlier, we don't need to add address records for the three name servers in **fx.movie.edu** name servers because a remote name server can already find that information by following the delegation to **movie.edu**.

The db.root File

Now all that's left is to add an SOA record for the root domain and NS records for this internal root and any others:

```
.   IN   SOA   rainman.movie.edu.   hostmaster.movie.edu.   (
                1        ; serial
                86400    ; refresh
                3600     ; retry
                608400   ; expire
                86400 )  ; minimum

    IN   NS   rainman.movie.edu.
    IN   NS   awakenings.movie.edu.

rainman.movie.edu.      86400   IN   A   192.249.249.254
awakenings.movie.edu.   86400   IN   A   192.253.253.254
```

rainman.movie.edu and **awakenings.movie.edu** are hosts running root name servers without direct Internet connectivity—internal roots. We shouldn't run an internal root on an Internet (firewall) host, because if a remote name server accidentally queries it for data it's not authoritative for, the internal root will respond with its list of roots—all internal!

So the whole *db.root* file (by convention, we call the root domain's db file *db.root*) looks like:

```
.   IN  SOA  rainman.movie.edu.  hostmaster.movie.edu.  (
                 1        ; serial
                 86400    ; refresh
                 3600     ; retry
                 608400   ; expire
                 86400 )  ; minimum

     IN  NS   rainman.movie.edu.
     IN  NS   awakenings.movie.edu.

rainman.movie.edu.     604800  IN  A  192.249.249.254
awakenings.movie.edu.  604800  IN  A  192.253.253.254

movie.edu.  86400  IN  NS  terminator.movie.edu.
            86400  IN  NS  wormhole.movie.edu.
            86400  IN  NS  zardoz.movie.edu.

terminator.movie.edu.  86400  IN  A  192.249.249.3
wormhole.movie.edu.    86400  IN  A  192.249.249.1
                       86400  IN  A  192.253.253.1
zardoz.movie.edu.      86400  IN  A  192.249.249.9
                       86400  IN  A  192.253.253.9

249.249.192.in-addr.arpa.  86400  IN  NS  terminator.movie.edu.
                           86400  IN  NS  wormhole.movie.edu.
                           86400  IN  NS  zardoz.movie.edu.
253.253.192.in-addr.arpa.  86400  IN  NS  terminator.movie.edu.
                           86400  IN  NS  wormhole.movie.edu.
                           86400  IN  NS  zardoz.movie.edu.
254.253.192.in-addr.arpa.  86400  IN  NS  bladerunner.fx.movie.edu.
                           86400  IN  NS  outland.fx.movie.edu.
                           86400  IN  NS  alien.fx.movie.edu.
20.254.192.in-addr.arpa.   86400  IN  NS  bladerunner.fx.movie.edu.
                           86400  IN  NS  outland.fx.movie.edu.
                           86400  IN  NS  alien.fx.movie.edu.
```

The *named.boot* file on both of the internal root name servers, **rainman** and **awakenings**, needs to contain the line:

```
primary    .   db.root
```

This replaces the *cache* directive: a root name server doesn't need a cache file to tell it where the other roots are; it can find that in *db.root*.

Did we really mean that *each* root name server is a primary for the root domain? Yes. Unfortunately, there's no such thing (yet!) as a secondary root name server. Each root loads the root database from *db.root*, so you need to keep the *db.root* files synchronized yourself.

Configuring Other Non-Internet Name Servers

Once you've set up internal root name servers, you can set up name servers on hosts anywhere in your network. Hosts with direct connectivity to the Internet should list the Internet roots in their cache files. Hosts without direct connectivity should list the internal roots:

```
; Internal db.cache file, for movie.edu hosts without direct
; Internet connectivity.
;
; Don't use this cache file on a host with Internet connectivity!
;

.  99999999  IN  NS  rainman.movie.edu.
   99999999  IN  NS  awakenings.movie.edu.

rainman.movie.edu.     99999999  IN  A  192.249.249.254
awakenings.movie.edu.  99999999  IN  A  192.253.253.254
```

Name servers on non-Internet hosts will be able to resolve names in **movie.edu** and in Movie U.'s **in-addr.arpa** domains, but not outside of those domains. More importantly, they'll *run*, since they have connectivity to (internal) root name servers.

Mail from Non-Internet Connected Hosts

But wait! Didn't we promise to show you how to configure the name servers to allow users to mail from non-Internet hosts? So we did.

Wildcard records are the key to getting mail to work; specifically, wildcard MX records. Let's say we'd like mail to the Internet to be forwarded through **postmanrings2x.movie.edu**, which has Internet connectivity. Then adding these records to *db.root*:

```
*       IN    MX     5 postmanrings2x.movie.edu.
*.edu.  IN    MX    10 postmanrings2x.movie.edu.
```

will get the job done. We need the ***.edu** MX record in addition to the ***** record because of the DNS wildcard production rules we described earlier in the chapter. Since there is explicit data for **movie.edu** in the domain, the first wildcard won't match **movie.edu** or any other subdomains of **edu**. We need another, explicit wildcard record for **edu** to match these domains.

Now mailers on non-Internet **movie.edu** hosts will send mail addressed to
Internet domains to **postmanrings2x** for forwarding. For example, mail
addressed to **nic.ddn.mil** will match the first wildcard MX record:

```
% nslookup -type=mx nic.ddn.mil.
Server:  rainman.movie.edu
Address:  192.249.249.19

nic.ddn.mil
      preference = 5, mail exchanger = postmanrings2x.movie.edu
postmanrings2x.movie.edu    internet address = 192.249.249.20
```

while mail addressed to **vangogh.cs.berkeley.edu** will match the second
MX record:

```
% nslookup -type=mx vangogh.cs.berkeley.edu.
Server:  rainman.movie.edu
Address:  192.249.249.19

vangogh.cs.berkeley.edu
      preference = 10, mail exchanger = postmanrings2x.movie.edu
postmanrings2x.movie.edu    internet address = 192.249.249.20
```

Once the mail reaches **postmanrings2x**, a firewall host, **postmanrings2x**'s
mailer will look up the MX records for these addresses itself. Since
postmanrings2x uses the Internet root name servers instead of the internal
roots, it will find the real MX records for the destination domain and deliver
the mail. No changes to *sendmail.cf* are necessary.

Forwarding Mail to External Domains

One nice perk of this internal root scheme is that it gives you the ability to
forward mail addressed to certain domains through particular mail relays.
We can choose, for example, to send all mail addressed to **uk** domain recipients to our host in London first, and then out onto the Internet. This can
be very useful if our internal network's connectivity or reliability is better
than the U.K.'s section of the Internet.

Let's say **movie.edu** has an X.400 gateway to our sister university in London
near Pinewood Studios. As it turns out, sending mail across the X.400 link,
and possibly through the Pinewood host to other users in other domains in
the U.K., is more reliable than sending it directly across the Internet. So we
add the following wildcard records to *db.root*:

```
; holygrail has the Movie U. end of the U.K. X.400 link
*.uk.  IN   MX   10 holygrail.movie.edu.
```

Now, mail addressed to users in subdomains of **uk** will be forwarded to **holygrail.movie.edu**, which presumably has facilities to forward that mail across its X.400 connection.

Name Server Corruption

The one major drawback of internal root name servers is the possibility of corrupting your name servers with bad data. With the internal root scheme, you divide your name servers into two classes: those that *must* use the Internet roots, because they have Internet connectivity; and those that *must* use the internal roots, because they lack Internet connectivity. When data meant for one set of name servers finds its way into a name server in the other set, the name server may start returning data inappropriate for the class of hosts it serves.

You need to make sure that neither set of name servers caches root NS records meant for the other. If an Internet name server caches internal root NS records and then queries the internal roots, it won't be able to find anything but wildcard MX information from those internal roots. Address resolution will fail, as will **in-addr.arpa** lookups. Only when the Internet name server happens to use the real Internet roots will it successfully resolve Internet domain names. And, unfortunately, since the Internet name server is on the same network as the internal roots, it will probably start to favor the internal roots after a few queries due to their low roundtrip times.

Non-Internet name servers wouldn't have quite the same problems, but might waste a lot of time sending queries to Internet roots they had no connectivity to.

Besides making sure your name servers are configured with the appropriate *db.cache* file, the best way to avoid corruption is to make sure delegation information for your domains is up-to-date. In Chapter 12, *Troubleshooting DNS and BIND*, we showed how following incorrect delegation can cause name servers to cache bogus root NS records. If there's any chance one of your Internet name servers could query an non-Internet name server for data, you need to make sure the non-Internet name server is authoritative for the data in question. If it isn't, it may return its list of internal roots, which the Internet name server will cache.

Network Names and Numbers

The original DNS definitions didn't provide the ability to look up network names based on a network number, a feature that was provided by the original HOSTS.TXT file. More recently, a procedure for storing network names has been defined; this procedure also works for subnets and subnet masks, so it goes significantly beyond HOSTS.TXT. Moreover, it doesn't require any modification to the DNS server software at all; it's based entirely on the clever use of pointer and address records.

If you remember, to map an IP address to a name in DNS, you reverse the IP address, append **in-addr.arpa**, and look up PTR data. This same technique is used to map a network number to a network name. To look up the network number, include the trailing zeroes to make it four bytes and look up PTR data just as you did with a host's IP address. For example, to find the network name for the old ARPANET, network 10, look up PTR data for **0.0.0.10.in-addr.arpa**. You'd get back an answer like **ARPANET.ARPA**.

If network 10 were subnetted, you'd also find address data at **0.0.0.10.in-addr.arpa**. The address data would be the subnet mask, 255.255.0.0, for instance. If you were interested in the subnet name instead of the network name, you'd apply the mask to the IP address and look up the subnet number.

This technique allows you to map the network number to a name. To provide a complete solution, there must be a way to map a network name to its network number. This, again, is accomplished with PTR records. The network name has PTR data that points to the network number (reversed with **in-addr.arpa** appended).

Let's see what the data might look like in HP's db files (HP is network number 15) and step through mapping a network number to a network name.

Part of file *db.hp*:

```
;
; Map HP's network name to 15.0.0.0.
;
hp-net.hp.com.              IN  PTR 0.0.0.15.in-addr.arpa.
```

Part of file *db.corp*:

```
;
; Map corp's subnet name to 15.1.0.0.
;
corp-subnet.corp.hp.com.  IN  PTR 0.0.1.15.in-addr.arpa.
```

Part of file *db.15*:

```
;
; Map 15.0.0.0 to hp-net.hp.com.
; HP's subnet mask is 255.255.248.0.
;
0.0.0.15.in-addr.arpa.    IN  PTR hp-net.hp.com.
                          IN  A   255.255.248.0
```

Part of file *db.15.1*:

```
;
; Map the 15.1.0.0 back to its subnet name.
;
0.0.1.15.in-addr.arpa.    IN  PTR corp-subnet.corp.hp.com.
```

Here's the procedure to look up the subnet name for the IP address 15.1.0.1:

1. Apply the default network mask for the address's class. Address 15.1.0.1 is a class A address, so the mask is 255.0.0.0. Applying the mask to the IP address makes the network number 15.

2. Send a query (**type=a** or **type=any**) for **0.0.0.15.in-addr.arpa**.

3. The query response contains address data. Since there is address data at **0.0.0.15.in-addr.arpa** (the subnet mask—255.255.248.0), apply the subnet mask to the IP address. This yields 15.1.0.0.

4. Send a query (**type=a** or **type=any**) for **0.0.1.15.in-addr.arpa**.

5. The query response does not contain address data, so 15.1.0.0 is not further subnetted.

6. Send a PTR query for **0.0.1.15.in-addr.arpa**.

7. The query response contains the network name for 15.1.0.1: **corp-subnet.corp.hp.com**.

In addition to mapping between network names and numbers, you can also list all the networks for your domain with PTR records:

```
movie.edu.  IN  PTR  0.249.249.192.in-addr.arpa.
            IN  PTR  0.253.253.192.in-addr.arpa.
```

Now for the bad news: despite the fact that RFC 1101 contains everything you need to know to set this up, there's no software we know of (yet) that actually *uses* this type of network name encoding, and very few administrators go to the trouble to add this information. But does that mean you shouldn't add the network information for your domain? Heck, no. If all your friends jumped off a cliff, would you? (Come to think of it . . . .) Buck

the trend and add the data! Chances are, it'll be useful to you—or someone—someday.

RFC 1183 (New RR Types)

RFC 1183, *New DNS RR Definitions*, introduced five new DNS types for
experimental purposes. Although we don't know of any BIND implementations that support these new record types yet, support for at least a few of
the types—particularly AFSDB—should be along shortly. We'll describe
them here to give you a little head start in getting used to them.

AFSDB

The first of these types, AFSDB, has a syntax like that of the MX record and
semantics a bit like that of the NS record. An AFSDB record gives either the
location of an AFS cell database server, or of a DCE cell's authenticated
name server. The type of server the record points to, and the name of the
host running the server, are contained in the record-specific data portion of
the record.

So what's an AFS cell database server? Or AFS, for that matter? AFS originally stood for the Andrew File System, designed by the good folks at Car-
negie-Mellon as part of the Andrew Project. (It's now a registered trade-
mark of Transarc Corporation, which sells AFS as a product.) AFS is a network filesystem, like NFS, but which handles the latency of wide-area networks much better than NFS does, and which provides local caching of files
to enhance performance. An AFS cell database server runs the process
responsible for tracking the location of filesets (groups of files) on various
AFS fileservers within a cell (a logical group of hosts). So being able to find
the AFS cell database server is the key to finding any file in the cell.

And what's an authenticated name server? It holds location information
about all sorts of services available within a DCE cell. A DCE cell? That's a
logical group of hosts that share services offered by the Open Software
Foundation's Distributed Computing Environment (DCE).

And now, back to our story. To access another cell's AFS or DCE services
across a network, you must first find out where that cell's cell database
servers or authenticated name servers are. Hence the new record type.
The domain name the record is attached to gives the name of the cell the
server knows about. Cells are often named after DNS domains, so this
usually doesn't look at all odd.

As we said, the AFSDB record's syntax is like the MX record's syntax. In place of the preference value, you specify the number 1 or 2:

1   For an AFS cell database server

2   For a DCE authenticated name server

In place of the mail exchanger host, you specify the name of the host running the server. Simple!

Say an **fx.movie.edu** systems administrator sets up a DCE cell (which includes AFS services) because she wants to experiment with distributed processing to speed up graphics rendering. She runs both an AFS cell database server and a DCE name server on **bladerunner.fx.movie.edu**, another cell database server on **empire**, and another DCE name server on **aliens**. She should set up the AFSDB records as follows:

```
; Our DCE cell is called fx.movie.edu, same as the domain

fx.movie.edu.   IN   AFSDB   1 bladerunner.fx.movie.edu.
                IN   AFSDB   2 bladerunner.fx.movie.edu.
                IN   AFSDB   1 empire.fx.movie.edu.
                IN   AFSDB   2 aliens.fx.movie.edu.
```

RP

Domain administrators will undoubtedly develop a love/hate relationship with this record: the Responsible Person, or RP, record. The RP record can be attached to any domain name, internal or leaf, and indicates who is responsible for that host or domain. This will enable you to locate the miscreant responsible for the host peppering you with DNS queries, for example. But it will also lead people to you when one of your hosts acts up.

The record takes two arguments as its record-specific data: an electronic mail address, in domain name format, and a domain name, which points to additional data about the contact. The electronic mail address is in the same format the SOA record uses: it substitutes a "." for the "@". The next argument is a domain name, which must have a TXT record associated with it. The TXT record then contains free-format information about the contact, like full name and phone number. You can omit either field, and specify the root domain (".") as a placeholder instead.

You can specify as many Responsible People for a given domain name as you want, but you should make sure that RP records for the same domain name share the same TTL, so some aren't timed out of a cache before others.

Here are some RP (and associated) records taken from the **fx.movie.edu** domain:

```
; The current origin is fx.movie.edu

@           IN  RP   ajs.fx.movie.edu.      ajs.fx.movie.edu.
bladerunner IN  RP   root.fx.movie.edu.     hotline.fx.movie.edu.
            IN  RP   richard.fx.movie.edu.  rb.fx.movie.edu.
ajs         IN  TXT  "Arty Segue, (415) 555-3610"
hotline     IN  TXT  "Movie U. Network Hotline, (415) 555-4111"
rb          IN  TXT  "Richard Boisclair, (415) 555-9612"
```

Note that TXT records for **root.fx.movie.edu** and **richard.fx.movie.edu** aren't necessary, since they're only the domain name encoding of electronic mail addresses, not real domain names.

X25, ISDN, and RT

These three record types were created specifically in support of research on next-generation internets. Two of the records, X25 and ISDN, are simply address records specific to X.25 and ISDN networks, respectively. Both take arguments (record-specific data) appropriate to the type of network. The X25 record type uses an X.121 address (X.121 is the ISO standard that specifies the format of addresses used in X.25 networks). The ISDN record type uses an ISDN address.

ISDN stands for Integrated Services Digital Network. Telephone companies around the world have proposed using ISDN protocols to allow their telephone networks to carry both voice and data, creating an integrated network. Although ISDN's availability is spotty throughout the U.S., it's catching on quickly in some international markets. Since ISDN uses the telephone companies' networks, an ISDN address is just a phone number, and in fact consists of a country code, followed by an area code or city code, then a local phone number. Sometimes there are a few extra digits you wouldn't see in a phone number at the end, called a subaddress. The subaddress is specified in a separate field in the record-specific data.

Examples of the X25 and ISDN record types are:

```
relay.pink.com.  IN  X25   31105060845

delay.hp.com.    IN  ISDN  141555514539488
hep.hp.com.      IN  ISDN  141555514539488 004
```

These records are intended for use in conjunction with the Route Through (RT) record type. RT is syntactically and semantically similar to the MX record type: it specifies an intermediate host that will route *packets* (instead of mail) to a destination host. So now, instead of only being able to route mail to a host that isn't directly connected to the Internet, you can route any kind of IP datagram to that host by using another host as a forwarder. The datagram could be part of a *telnet* or *ftp* session, or perhaps even a DNS query!

Like MX, RT includes a preference value, which indicates how desirable delivery to a particular host is. For example, the records:

```
housesitter.movie.edu.  IN  RT  10 relay.pink.com.
                        IN  RT  20 delay.hp.com.
```

instruct hosts to route datagrams bound for **housesitter** through **relay.pink.com** (the first choice) or through **delay.hp.com** (the second choice).

The way RT works with X25 and ISDN (and even A) records is like this:

1. Internet host A wants to send a datagram to host B, which is not connected to the Internet.
2. Host A looks up host B's RT records. This search also returns all address records (A, X25 *and* ISDN) for each intermediate host.
3. Host A sorts the list of intermediate hosts and looks for its own domain name. If it finds it, it removes it and all intermediate hosts at higher preference values. This is analogous to *sendmail*'s "paring down" a list of mail exchangers.
4. Host A examines the address record(s) for the most-preferred intermediate host that remains. If host A is attached to a network that corresponds to the type of address record, it uses that network to send the datagram to the intermediate host. For example, if host A were trying to send a datagram through **relay.pink.com**, it would need connectivity to an X.25 network.
5. If host A lacks appropriate connectivity, it tries the next intermediate host specified by the RT records. For example, if host A lacked X.25 connectivity, it might fall back to delivering via ISDN to **delay.hp.com**.

This process continues until the datagram is routed to the most-preferred intermediate host. The most-preferred intermediate host may then deliver the datagram directly to the destination host's address (which may be A, X25, or ISDN).

Negative Caching

A couple of years ago, there was much discussion on the name server related mailing lists about negative caching and how it would reduce the number of Internet DNS queries or, at least, improve response time. Briefly, negative caching means that the name server "remembers" that a name doesn't exist or a particular data type for a name doesn't exist. Current name server implementations only cache answers that have data with them—the address or MX record looked up, for instance. If the name doesn't exist, the name server tells that to the querier and then "forgets" about it. If another querier asks the same question, the name server goes through all the work again of finding out that the name doesn't exist, even though it just found that out moments ago.

It's obvious that caching a negative response would reduce queries to remote servers. What isn't necessarily obvious is what it would help out the most—the resolver search list. If you've watched the queries a name server receives for any length of time, you'll see quite a number of queries for names like **foo.bar.widget.com.widget.com**. If the **widget.com** name server is not local, then your **bar.widget.com** name server has to send the query off-site to find out that this name does not exist. This can be quite a performance hit if the **widget.com** name server is across a slow link or if the link is down. If the local name server cached that the name doesn't exist—negative caching—it would reduce the dependence on the **widget.com** name server.

Why hasn't negative caching been implemented? We can only guess. Probably the most difficult implementation aspect is keeping the name server from growing to be a huge process—it would be caching failures as well as successful lookups and that could use up lots of memory. However, negative caching isn't the only way to reduce DNS traffic. The search list can be made more "intelligent" to reduce the number of useless queries. Already, BIND 4.8.3 allows you to manually control the search list, so you can remove your parent domain from the search if you want. Further improvements may follow. For example, the search list algorithm *could* be enhanced to avoid appending any domain that is already on the right-most side of the name being looked up. This would stop **bar.widget.com** and **widget.com** from being appended to **foo.bar.widget.com**.

DNS Versus X.500

X.500 is an ISO (International Standards Organization) standard distributed directory system that's sometimes seen as a "competitor" to DNS. X.500 does, indeed, include some of the same functionality DNS does. For example, you can use X.500 to retrieve address information for a particular host. And in some ways, the two are similar: X.500 directories store data in hierarchical name spaces, and use recursion and iteration (well, ISO calls them "chaining" and "referral"). While we can hardly claim to be experts on X.500, we can make some general comparisons between DNS and X.500:

- X.500 is a full-blown distributed database meant to be used for a wide variety of applications. You can store the phone book in an X.500 database. You can store location data in an X.500 database. You can store information about all sorts of network devices and their attributes. DNS, on the other hand, is a relatively simple distributed database meant to solve a particular problem—an intractable HOSTS.TXT database.

- X.500 has security features involving credentials and the support of multiple encryption types; DNS is not secure.

- X.500 has a dynamic update capability—you can update individual records in the database over the network. DNS has a read-only database—you can't update individual records over the network. (Well, there is experimental dynamic update code in BIND, but without security, you wouldn't want to use it.)

Anyway, you get the idea. X.500 is rich in capabilities and will be extremely useful when it is completely defined, implemented, and optimized. DNS provides a few, critical functions. It is, for the most part, fully implemented and it will continue to evolve and improve.

Don't let this turn you off to DNS, though. The Domain Name System really is admirably good at its job, and it does it much faster than X.500 does. True, X.500 offers richer functionality, but it may never usurp DNS's position as the Internet's directory system of choice.

The Relationship Between NetBIOS and DNS

Those of you involved with PC networking using NetBIOS may have noticed that NetBIOS, when running over TCP/UDP, uses DNS-compatible names. That's intentional. In RFC 1001, *PROTOCOL STANDARD FOR A Net-BIOS SERVICE ON A TCP/UDP TRANSPORT: CONCEPTS AND METHODS*, the authors state that the NetBIOS Name Server (NBNS) design tries to align itself with DNS:

> *First, the NetBIOS names are encoded in a form acceptable to the domain name system.*
>
> *Second, a scope identifier is appended to each NetBIOS name. This identifier meets the restricted character set of the domain system and has a leading period. This makes the NetBIOS name, in conjunction with its scope identifier, a valid domain system name.*
>
> *Third, the negotiated responsibility mechanisms permit the NBNS to be used as a simple bulletin board on which are posted (name,address) pairs. This parallels the existing domain system query service.*

But DNS would need to be extended before it could function as a NetBIOS Name Server. It would have to offer:

- *Dynamic addition of entries*
- *Dynamic update of entry data*
- *Support for multiple instance (group) entries*
- *Support for entry time-to-live values and the ability to accept refresh messages to restart the time-to-live period*
- *New entry attributes*

Despite the close alignment between DNS and NetBIOS, we haven't heard of any efforts to extend DNS to accommodate NetBIOS over TCP/UDP.

A

DNS Message Format and Resource Records

This appendix outlines the format of DNS messages and enumerates all the resource record types. The resource records are shown in their textual format, as you would specify them in a DNS database file, and in their binary format, as they appear in DNS messages. You'll find a few resource records here that we didn't cover in the book because they are experimental or obsolete.

We've directly included the portions of RFC 1035, written by Paul Mockapetris, that deal with the textual format of master files (what we called *db files* or *DNS database files* in the book) or the DNS message format (for those of you who need to parse DNS packets).

Master File Format
(from RFC 1035, pages 33-35)

The format of these files is a sequence of entries. Entries are predominantly line-oriented, though parentheses can be used to continue a list of items across a line boundary, and text literals can contain CRLF within the text. Any combination of tabs and spaces act as a delimiter between the separate items that make up an entry. The end of any line in the master file can end with a comment. The comment starts with a ";".

The following entries are defined:

```
<blank>[<comment>]

$ORIGIN <domain-name> [<comment>]

$INCLUDE <file-name> [<domain-name>] [<comment>]

<domain-name><rr> [<comment>]

<blank><rr> [<comment>]
```

Blank lines, with or without comments, are allowed anywhere in the file.

Two control entries are defined: $ORIGIN and $INCLUDE. $ORIGIN is followed by a domain name, and resets the current origin for relative domain names to the stated name. $INCLUDE inserts the named file into the current file, and may optionally specify a domain name that sets the relative domain name origin for the included file. $INCLUDE may also have a comment. Note that a $INCLUDE entry never changes the relative origin of the parent file, regardless of changes to the relative origin made within the included file.

The last two forms represent RRs. If an entry for an RR begins with a blank, then the RR is assumed to be owned by the last stated owner. If an RR entry begins with a <domain-name>, then the owner name is reset.

<rr> contents take one of the following forms:

```
[<TTL>] [<class>] <type> <RDATA>

[<class>] [<TTL>] <type> <RDATA>
```

The RR begins with optional TTL and class fields, followed by a type and RDATA field appropriate to the type and class. Class and type use the standard mnemonics, TTL is a decimal integer. Omitted class and TTL values are default to the last explicitly stated values. Since type and class mnemonics are disjoint, the parse is unique. (Note that this order is different from the order used in examples and the order used in the actual RRs; the given order allows easier parsing and defaulting.)

<domain-name>s make up a large share of the data in the master file. The labels in the domain name are expressed as character strings and separated by dots. Quoting conventions allow arbitrary characters to be stored in domain names. Domain names that end in a dot are called absolute, and are taken as complete. Domain names which do not end in a dot are called relative; the actual domain name is the concatenation of the relative part with an origin specified in a $ORIGIN, $INCLUDE, or as an argument to the master file loading routine. A relative name is an error when no origin is available.

<character-string> is expressed in one or two ways: as a contiguous set of characters without interior spaces, or as a string beginning with a " and ending with a ". Inside a " delimited string any character can occur, except for a " itself, which must be quoted using "\".

Because these files are text files, several special encodings are necessary to allow arbitrary data to be loaded. In particular:

Of the root.

@	A free standing @ is used to denote the current origin.
\X	Where X is any character other than a digit (0-9), is used to quote that character so that its special meaning does not apply. For example, "\." can be used to place a dot character in a label.*
\DDD	Where each D is a digit is the octet corresponding to the decimal number described by DDD. The resulting octet is assumed to be text and is not checked for special meaning.†
( )	Parentheses are used to group data that crosses a line boundary. In effect, line terminations are not recognized within parentheses.‡
;	Semicolon is used to start a comment; the remainder of the line is ignored.

Character Case
(from RFC 1035, page 9)

For all parts of the DNS that are part of the official protocol, all comparisons between character strings (e.g., labels, domain names, etc.) are done in a case-insensitive manner. At present, this rule is in force throughout the domain system without exception. However, future additions beyond current usage may need to use the full binary octet capabilities in names, so attempts to store domain names in 7-bit ASCII or use of special bytes to terminate labels, etc., should be avoided.

Types

Here is a complete list of resource record types. The textual representation is used in master files. The binary representation is used in DNS queries and responses. These resource records are described on pages 13-21 of RFC 1035.

---

*Not implemented by BIND 4.8.3.

†Not implemented by BIND 4.8.3.

‡BIND 4.8.3 only allows parentheses on SOA and WKS resource records.

A

(from RFC 1035, page 20)

Textual Representation:
```
<owner> <class> <ttl> A <address>
```

Example:
```
localhost.movie.edu.    IN A 127.0.0.1
```

Binary Representation:
```
Address type code: 1

    +--+--+--+--+--+--+--+--+--+--+--+--+--+--+--+--+
    |                  ADDRESS                      |
    +--+--+--+--+--+--+--+--+--+--+--+--+--+--+--+--+
```

where:

```
ADDRESS          A 32 bit Internet address.
```

CNAME:

(from RFC 1035, page 14)

Textual Representation:
```
<owner> <class> <ttl> CNAME <canonical-dname>
```

Example:
```
wh.movie.edu.  IN  CNAME  wormhole.movie.edu.
```

Binary Representation:
```
CNAME type code: 5

    +--+--+--+--+--+--+--+--+--+--+--+--+--+--+--+--+
    /                   CNAME                       /
    /                                               /
    +--+--+--+--+--+--+--+--+--+--+--+--+--+--+--+--+
```

where:

```
CNAME            A <domain-name> which specifies the canonical
                 or primary name for the owner.  The owner name is
                 an alias.
```

HINFO
(from RFC 1035, page 14)

Textual Representation:
```
<owner> <class> <ttl> HINFO <cpu> <os>
```

Example:
```
grizzly.movie.edu.  IN  HINFO  VAX-11/780 UNIX
```

Binary Representation:
HINFO type code: 13

```
+--+--+--+--+--+--+--+--+--+--+--+--+--+--+--+--+
/                      CPU                      /
+--+--+--+--+--+--+--+--+--+--+--+--+--+--+--+--+
/                      OS                       /
+--+--+--+--+--+--+--+--+--+--+--+--+--+--+--+--+
```

where:

CPU   A <character-string> which specifies the CPU type.

OS   A <character-string> which specifies the
           operating system type.

MB
(from RFC 1035, page 14)

Textual Representation:
```
<owner> <class> <ttl> MB <mbox-dname>
```

Example:
```
al.movie.edu.  IN  MB  robocop.movie.edu.
```

Binary Representation:
MB type code: 7

```
+--+--+--+--+--+--+--+--+--+--+--+--+--+--+--+--+
/                    MADNAME                    /
/                                               /
+--+--+--+--+--+--+--+--+--+--+--+--+--+--+--+--+
```

where:

MADNAME   A <domain-name> which specifies a host which has
              the specified mailbox.

MD

MD has been replaced with MX.

MF

MF has been replaced with MX.

MG
(from RFC 1035, page 16)

Textual Representation:
```
<owner> <class> <ttl> MG <mgroup-dname>
```

Example:
```
admin.movie.edu.  IN  MG  al.movie.edu.
                  IN  MG  ed.movie.edu.
                  IN  MG  jc.movie.edu.
```

Binary Representation:
```
MG type code: 8
```

```
+--+--+--+--+--+--+--+--+--+--+--+--+--+--+--+--+
/                    MGMNAME                     /
/                                                /
+--+--+--+--+--+--+--+--+--+--+--+--+--+--+--+--+
```

```
where:
```

```
MGMNAME          A <domain-name> which specifies a mailbox which
                 is a member of the mail group specified by the
                 domain name.
```

MINFO
(from RFC 1035, page 16)

Textual Representation:
```
<owner> <class> <ttl> MINFO <resp-mbox> <error-mbox>
```

Example:
```
admin.movie.edu.  IN  MINFO  al.movie.edu. al.movie.edu.
```

Binary Representation:
```
MINFO type code: 14
```

```
+--+--+--+--+--+--+--+--+--+--+--+--+--+--+--+--+
/                    RMAILBX                     /
+--+--+--+--+--+--+--+--+--+--+--+--+--+--+--+--+
/                    EMAILBX                     /
+--+--+--+--+--+--+--+--+--+--+--+--+--+--+--+--+
```

where:

RMAILBX   A \<domain-name> which specifies a mailbox which
               is responsible for the mailing list or mailbox.
               If this domain name names the root, the owner of
               the MINFO RR is responsible for itself. Note
               that many existing mailing lists use a mailbox
               X-request for the RMAILBX field of mailing list
               X, e.g., Msgroup-request for Msgroup. This field
               provides a more general mechanism.

EMAILBX   A \<domain-name> which specifies a mailbox which is
               to receive error messages related to the mailing
               list or mailbox specified by the owner of the
               MINFO RR (similar to the ERRORS-TO: field which has
               been proposed). If this domain name names the root,
               errors should be returned to the sender of the
               message.

MR
(from RFC 1035, page 17)

Textual Representation:
    <owner> <class> <ttl> MR <new-mbox>

Example:
    eddie.movie.edu. IN MR eddie.bornagain.edu.

Binary Representation:
    MR type code: 9

```
    +--+--+--+--+--+--+--+--+--+--+--+--+--+--+--+--+
    /                    NEWNAME                    /
    /                                               /
    +--+--+--+--+--+--+--+--+--+--+--+--+--+--+--+--+
```

where:

NEWNAME   A \<domain-name> which specifies a mailbox which
               is the proper rename of the specified mailbox.

MX
(from RFC 1035, page 17)

Textual Representation:
    <owner> <class> <ttl> MX <preference> <exchange-dname>

Example:
    ora.com. IN MX 0   ora.ora.com.
              IN MX 10 ruby.ora.com.
              IN MX 10 opal.ora.com.

Binary Representation:
```
MX type code: 15
```
```
        +--+--+--+--+--+--+--+--+--+--+--+--+--+--+--+--+
        |                     PREFERENCE                |
        +--+--+--+--+--+--+--+--+--+--+--+--+--+--+--+--+
        /                      EXCHANGE                 /
        /                                               /
        +--+--+--+--+--+--+--+--+--+--+--+--+--+--+--+--+
```

where:

PREFERENCE   A 16 bit integer which specifies the preference given to this RR among others at the same owner. Lower values are preferred.

EXCHANGE   A <domain-name> which specifies a host willing to act as a mail exchange for the owner name.

NS
(from RFC 1035, page 18)

Textual Representation:
```
<owner> <class> <ttl> NS <name-server-dname>
```

Example:
```
movie.edu.      IN NS terminator.movie.edu
```

Binary Representation:
```
NS type code: 2
```
```
        +--+--+--+--+--+--+--+--+--+--+--+--+--+--+--+--+
        /                      NSDNAME                  /
        /                                               /
        +--+--+--+--+--+--+--+--+--+--+--+--+--+--+--+--+
```

where:

NSDNAME   A <domain-name> which specifies a host which should be authoritative for the specified class and domain.

NULL
(from RFC 1035, page 17)

Binary Representation:
```
NULL type code: 10
```

```
+--+--+--+--+--+--+--+--+--+--+--+--+--+--+--+--+
/                    <anything>                  /
/                                                /
+--+--+--+--+--+--+--+--+--+--+--+--+--+--+--+--+
```

Anything at all may be in the RDATA field so long as it is 65535 octets or less.

NULL is not implemented by BIND.

PTR

(from RFC 1035, page 18)

Textual Representation:

```
<owner> <class> <ttl> PTR <dname>
```

Example:

```
1.249.249.192.in-addr.arpa.  IN PTR wormhole.movie.edu.
```

Binary Representation:

PTR type code: 12

```
+--+--+--+--+--+--+--+--+--+--+--+--+--+--+--+--+
/                    PTRDNAME                    /
+--+--+--+--+--+--+--+--+--+--+--+--+--+--+--+--+
```

where:

PTRDNAME   A <domain-name> which points to some location in the domain name space.

SOA

(from RFC 1035, pages 19-20)

Textual Representation:

```
<owner> <class> <ttl> SOA <source-dname> <mbox> (
        <serial> <refresh> <retry> <expire> <minimum> )
```

Example:

```
movie.edu. IN SOA terminator.movie.edu. al.robocop.movie.edu. (
                        1        ; Serial
                        10800    ; Refresh after 3 hours
                        3600     ; Retry after 1 hour
                        604800   ; Expire after 1 week
                        86400 )  ; Minimum TTL of 1 day
```

Binary Representation:

SOA type code: 6

```
+--+--+--+--+--+--+--+--+--+--+--+--+--+--+--+--+
/                     MNAME                     /
/                                               /
+--+--+--+--+--+--+--+--+--+--+--+--+--+--+--+--+
/                     RNAME                     /
+--+--+--+--+--+--+--+--+--+--+--+--+--+--+--+--+
|                     SERIAL                    |
|                                               |
+--+--+--+--+--+--+--+--+--+--+--+--+--+--+--+--+
|                     REFRESH                   |
|                                               |
+--+--+--+--+--+--+--+--+--+--+--+--+--+--+--+--+
|                     RETRY                     |
|                                               |
+--+--+--+--+--+--+--+--+--+--+--+--+--+--+--+--+
|                     EXPIRE                    |
|                                               |
+--+--+--+--+--+--+--+--+--+--+--+--+--+--+--+--+
|                     MINIMUM                   |
|                                               |
+--+--+--+--+--+--+--+--+--+--+--+--+--+--+--+--+
```

where:

MNAME   The <domain-name> of the name server that was the original or primary source of data for this zone.

RNAME   A <domain-name> which specifies the mailbox of the person responsible for this zone.

SERIAL   The unsigned 32 bit version number of the original copy of the zone. Zone transfers preserve this value. This value wraps and should be compared using sequence space arithmetic.

REFRESH   A 32 bit time interval before the zone should be refreshed.

RETRY   A 32 bit time interval that should elapse before a failed refresh should be retried.

EXPIRE   A 32 bit time value that specifies the upper limit on the time interval that can elapse before the zone is no longer authoritative.

MINIMUM   The unsigned 32 bit minimum TTL field that should be exported with any RR from this zone.

TXT
(from RFC 1035, page 20)

Textual Representation:
```
<owner> <class> <ttl> TXT <txt-strings>
```

Example:
```
cujo.movie.edu.  IN  TXT  "Location: machine room dog house"
```

Binary Representation:
```
TXT type code: 16

    +--+--+--+--+--+--+--+--+--+--+--+--+--+--+--+--+
    /                     TXT-DATA                  /
    +--+--+--+--+--+--+--+--+--+--+--+--+--+--+--+--+

where:

TXT-DATA        One or more <character-string>s.
```

WKS
(from RFC 1035, page 21)

Textual Representation:
```
<owner> <class> <ttl> WKS <address> <protocol> <service-list>
```

Example:
```
terminator.movie.edu.  IN  WKS 192.249.249.3  TCP ( telnet smtp
                                                     ftp shell domain )
```

Binary Representation:
```
WKS type code: 11

    +--+--+--+--+--+--+--+--+--+--+--+--+--+--+--+--+
    |                     ADDRESS                   |
    +--+--+--+--+--+--+--+--+--+--+--+--+--+--+--+--+
    |     PROTOCOL      |                           |
    +--+--+--+--+--+--+--+                          |
    |                                               |
    /                     <BIT MAP>                 /
    /                                               /
    +--+--+--+--+--+--+--+--+--+--+--+--+--+--+--+--+

where:

ADDRESS         An 32 bit Internet address

PROTOCOL        An 8 bit IP protocol number

<BIT MAP>       A variable length bit map.  The bit map must
                be a multiple of 8 bits long.
```

New Types from RFC 1183

AFSDB

Textual Representation:
```
<owner> <ttl> <class> AFSDB <subtype> <hostname>
```

Example:
```
fx.movie.edu.   IN  AFSDB  1 bladerunner.fx.movie.edu.
                IN  AFSDB  2 bladerunner.fx.movie.edu.
                IN  AFSDB  1 empire.fx.movie.edu.
                IN  AFSDB  2 aliens.fx.movie.edu.
```

Binary Representation:
AFSDB type code: 18

```
+--+--+--+--+--+--+--+--+--+--+--+--+--+--+--+--+
|                    SUBTYPE                    |
+--+--+--+--+--+--+--+--+--+--+--+--+--+--+--+--+
/                    HOSTNAME                   /
/                                               /
+--+--+--+--+--+--+--+--+--+--+--+--+--+--+--+--+
```

where:

SUBTYPE   Subtype 1 is an AFS cell database server. Subtype 2
            is a DCE authenticated name server.

HOSTNAME   A <domain-name> which specifies a host that has a
            server for the cell named by the owner of the RR.

ISDN

Textual Representation:
```
<owner> <ttl> <class> ISDN <ISDN-address> <sa>
```

Example:
```
delay.hp.com.   IN  ISDN  141555514539488
hep.hp.com.     IN  ISDN  141555514539488 004
```

Binary Representation:
ISDN type code: 20

```
+--+--+--+--+--+--+--+--+--+--+--+--+--+--+--+--+
/                  ISDN ADDRESS                 /
+--+--+--+--+--+--+--+--+--+--+--+--+--+--+--+--+
/                   SUBADDRESS                  /
+--+--+--+--+--+--+--+--+--+--+--+--+--+--+--+--+
```

where:

ISDN ADDRESS   A <character-string> which identifies the ISDN number
                      of <owner> and DDI (Direct Dial In) if any.

SUBADDRESS   An optional <character-string> specifying the
                      subaddress.

RP

Textual Representation:
    <owner> <ttl> <class> RP <mbox-dname> <txt-dname>

Example:
    ; The current origin is fx.movie.edu

    @   IN   RP   ajs.fx.movie.edu.   ajs.fx.movie.edu.
    bladerunner   IN   RP   root.fx.movie.edu.   hotline.fx.movie.edu.
                   IN   RP   richard.fx.movie.edu.   rb.fx.movie.edu.
    ajs   IN   TXT   "Arty Segue, (415) 555-3610"
    hotline   IN   TXT   "Movie U. Network Hotline, (415) 555-4111"
    rb   IN   TXT   "Richard Boisclair, (415) 555-9612"

Binary Representation:
    RP type code: 17

```
        +--+--+--+--+--+--+--+--+--+--+--+--+--+--+--+--+
        /                    MAILBOX                    /
        /                                               /
        +--+--+--+--+--+--+--+--+--+--+--+--+--+--+--+--+
        /                    TXTDNAME                   /
        /                                               /
        +--+--+--+--+--+--+--+--+--+--+--+--+--+--+--+--+
```

where:

MAILBOX   A <domain-name> that specifies the mailbox for
                      the responsible person.

TXTDNAME   A <domain-name> for which TXT RR's exist. A
                      subsequent query can be performed to retrieve
                      the associated TXT resource records at
                      <txt-dname>

RT

Textual Representation:
    <owner> <ttl> <class> RT <preference> <intermediate-host>

Example:
```
sh.prime.com.  IN  RT   2   Relay.Prime.COM.
               IN  RT  10   NET.Prime.COM.
```

Binary Representation:
```
RT type code: 21

        +--+--+--+--+--+--+--+--+--+--+--+--+--+--+--+--+
        |                  PREFERENCE                   |
        +--+--+--+--+--+--+--+--+--+--+--+--+--+--+--+--+
        /                  INTERMEDIATE                 /
        /                                               /
        +--+--+--+--+--+--+--+--+--+--+--+--+--+--+--+--+
```

where:

PREFERENCE   A 16 bit integer which specifies the preference given to this RR among others at the same owner. Lower values are preferred.

EXCHANGE   A <domain-name> which specifies a host which will serve as an intermediate in reaching the host specified by <owner>.

X25

Textual Representation:
```
<owner> <ttl> <class> X25 <PSDN-address>
```

Example:
```
relay.pink.com.  IN  X25   31105060845
```

Binary Representation:
```
X25 type code: 19

        +--+--+--+--+--+--+--+--+--+--+--+--+--+--+--+--+
        /                  PSDN ADDRESS                 /
        +--+--+--+--+--+--+--+--+--+--+--+--+--+--+--+--+
```

where:

PSDN ADDRESS   A <character-string> which identifies the PSDN (Public Switched Data Network) address in the X.121 numbering plan associated with <owner>.

Classes
(from RFC 1035, page 13)

CLASS fields appear in resource records. The following CLASS mnemonics and values are defined:

IN: 1 the Internet.

CS: 2 the CSNET class (Obsolete - used only for examples in some obsolete RFCs)

CH: 3 the CHAOS class.

HS: 4 the Hesiod class.

DNS Message

In order to write programs that parse DNS packets, you need to understand the message format. DNS queries and responses are most often contained within UDP packets. Each message is fully contained within a UDP packet. If the query and response are sent over TCP, then they are prefixed with a two-byte value indicating the length of the query or response, excluding the two-byte length. The format and content of the DNS packet are as follows.

Format
(from RFC 1035, page 25)

All communications inside of the domain protocol are carried in a single format called a message. The top level format of message is divided into 5 sections (some of which are empty in certain cases) shown below:

```
+--------------------+
|       Header       |
+--------------------+
|      Question      | the question for the name server
+--------------------+
|       Answer       | RRs answering the question
+--------------------+
|      Authority     | RRs pointing toward an authority
+--------------------+
|      Additional    | RRs holding additional information
+--------------------+
```

The header section is always present. The header includes fields that specify which of the remaining sections are present, and also specify whether the message is a query or a response, a standard query or some other opcode, etc.

The names of the sections after the header are derived from their use in standard queries. The question section contains fields that describe a question to a name server. These fields are a query type (QTYPE), a query class (QCLASS), and a query domain name (QNAME). The last three sections have the same format: a possibly empty list of concatenated resource records (RRs). The answer section contains RRs that answer the question; the authority section contains RRs that point toward an authoritative name server; the additional records section contains RRs which relate to the query, but are not strictly answers for the question.

Header Section Format
(from RFC 1035, pages 26-28)

```
                                    1 1 1 1 1 1
      0  1  2  3  4  5  6  7  8  9  0  1  2  3  4  5
    +--+--+--+--+--+--+--+--+--+--+--+--+--+--+--+--+
    |                      ID                       |
    +--+--+--+--+--+--+--+--+--+--+--+--+--+--+--+--+
    |QR|   Opcode  |AA|TC|RD|RA|   Z    |   RCODE   |
    +--+--+--+--+--+--+--+--+--+--+--+--+--+--+--+--+
    |                    QDCOUNT                     |
    +--+--+--+--+--+--+--+--+--+--+--+--+--+--+--+--+
    |                    ANCOUNT                     |
    +--+--+--+--+--+--+--+--+--+--+--+--+--+--+--+--+
    |                    NSCOUNT                     |
    +--+--+--+--+--+--+--+--+--+--+--+--+--+--+--+--+
    |                    ARCOUNT                     |
    +--+--+--+--+--+--+--+--+--+--+--+--+--+--+--+--+
```

where:

ID   A 16 bit identifier assigned by the program that
                generates any kind of query. This identifier is copied
                the corresponding reply and can be used by the requester
                to match up replies to outstanding queries.

QR   A one bit field that specifies whether this message is a
                query (0), or a response (1).

OPCODE   A four bit field that specifies kind of query in this
                message. This value is set by the originator of a query
                and copied into the response. The values are:

                0   a standard query (QUERY)

                1   an inverse query (IQUERY)

                2   a server status request (STATUS)

                3-15   reserved for future use

AA   Authoritative Answer - this bit is valid in responses, and specifies that the responding name server is an authority for the domain name in question section.

Note that the contents of the answer section may have multiple owner names because of aliases. The AA bit corresponds to the name which matches the query name, or the first owner name in the answer section.

TC   TrunCation - specifies that this message was truncated due to length greater than that permitted on the transmission channel.

RD   Recursion Desired - this bit may be set in a query and is copied into the response. If RD is set, it directs the name server to pursue the query recursively. Recursive query support is optional.

RA   Recursion Available - this bit is set or cleared in a response, and denotes whether recursive query support is available in the name server.

Z   Reserved for future use. Must be zero in all queries and responses.

RCODE   Response code - this 4 bit field is set as part of responses. The values have the following interpretation:

         0   No error condition

         1   Format error - The name server was unable to interpret the query.

         2   Server failure - The name server was unable to process this query due to a problem with the name server.

         3   Name Error - Meaningful only for responses from an authoritative name server, this code signifies that the domain name referenced in the query does not exist.

         4   Not Implemented - The name server does not support the requested kind of query.

5	Refused - The name server refuses to perform the specified operation for policy reasons. For example, a name server may not wish to provide the information to the particular requester, or a name server may not wish to perform a particular operation (e.g., zone transfer) for particular data.
6-15	Reserved for future use.

QDCOUNT

an unsigned 16 bit integer specifying the number of entries in the question section.

ANCOUNT

an unsigned 16 bit integer specifying the number of resource records in the answer section.

NSCOUNT

an unsigned 16 bit integer specifying the number of name server resource records in the authority records section.

ARCOUNT

an unsigned 16 bit integer specifying the number of resource records in the additional records section.

Question Section Format
(from RFC 1035, pages 28-29)

The question section is used to carry the "question" in most queries, i.e., the parameters that define what is being asked. The section contains QDCOUNT (usually 1) entries, each of the following format:

```
                                    1  1  1  1  1  1
      0  1  2  3  4  5  6  7  8  9  0  1  2  3  4  5
    +--+--+--+--+--+--+--+--+--+--+--+--+--+--+--+--+
    |                                               |
    /                     QNAME                     /
    /                                               /
    +--+--+--+--+--+--+--+--+--+--+--+--+--+--+--+--+
    |                     QTYPE                      |
    +--+--+--+--+--+--+--+--+--+--+--+--+--+--+--+--+
    |                     QCLASS                     |
    +--+--+--+--+--+--+--+--+--+--+--+--+--+--+--+--+
```

where:

QNAME

a domain name represented as a sequence of labels, where each label consists of a length octet followed by that number of octets. The domain name terminates with the zero length octet for the null label of the root. Note that this field may be an odd number of octets; no padding is used.

QTYPE   a two octet code which specifies the type of the query.
                  The values for this field include all codes valid for a
                  TYPE field, together with some more general codes which
                  can match more than one type of RR.

QCLASS   a two octet code that specifies the class of the query.
                  For example, the QCLASS field is IN for the Internet.

QCLASS Values
(from RFC 1035, page 13)

QCLASS fields appear in the question section of a query. QCLASS values are
a superset of CLASS values; every CLASS is a valid QCLASS. In addition to
CLASS values, the following QCLASSes are defined:

*:   255 any class.

QTYPE Values
(from RFC 1035, pages 12-13)

QTYPE fields appear in the question part of a query. QTYPES are a superset
of TYPEs, hence all TYPEs are valid QTYPEs. In addition, the following
QTYPEs are defined:

AXFR: 252 A request for a transfer of an entire zone.

MAILB: 253 A request for mailbox-related records (MB, MG or MR).

MAILA: 254 A request for mail agent RRs (Obsolete - see MX).

*:   255 A request for all records.

Answer, Authority, and Additional Section Format
(from RFC 1035, pages 29-30)

The answer, authority, and additional sections all share the same format: a
variable number of resource records, where the number of records is specified in the corresponding count field in the header. Each resource record
has the following format:

```
                                1  1  1   1  1  1
            0  1  2  3  4  5  6  7  8  9  0  1  2  3  4  5
          +--+--+--+--+--+--+--+--+--+--+--+--+--+--+--+--+
          |                                               |
          /                                               /
          /                    NAME                       /
          |                                               |
          +--+--+--+--+--+--+--+--+--+--+--+--+--+--+--+--+
          |                    TYPE                       |
          +--+--+--+--+--+--+--+--+--+--+--+--+--+--+--+--+
          |                    CLASS                      |
          +--+--+--+--+--+--+--+--+--+--+--+--+--+--+--+--+
          |                    TTL                        |
          |                                               |
          +--+--+--+--+--+--+--+--+--+--+--+--+--+--+--+--+
          |                  RDLENGTH                     |
          +--+--+--+--+--+--+--+--+--+--+--+--+--+--+--+--|
          /                   RDATA                       /
          /                                               /
          +--+--+--+--+--+--+--+--+--+--+--+--+--+--+--+--+
```

where:

NAME   a domain name to which this resource record pertains.

TYPE   two octets containing one of the RR type codes. This
                field specifies the meaning of the data in the RDATA
                field.

CLASS   two octets which specify the class of the data in the
                RDATA field.

TTL   a 32 bit unsigned integer that specifies the time
                interval (in seconds) that the resource record may be
                cached before it should be discarded. Zero values are
                interpreted to mean that the RR can only be used for the
                transaction in progress, and should not be cached.

RDLENGTH   an unsigned 16 bit integer that specifies the length in
                octets of the RDATA field.

RDATA   a variable length string of octets that describes the
                resource. The format of this information varies
                according to the TYPE and CLASS of the resource record.
                For example, the if the TYPE is A and the CLASS is IN,
                the RDATA field is a 4 octet ARPA Internet address.

Data Transmission Order
(from RFC 1035, pages 8-9)

The order of transmission of the header and data described in this document is resolved to the octet level. Whenever a diagram shows a group of octets, the order of transmission of those octets is the normal order in which they are read in English. For example, in the following diagram, the octets are transmitted in the order they are numbered.

```
    0                   1
    0 1 2 3 4 5 6 7 8 9 0 1 2 3 4 5
   +-+-+-+-+-+-+-+-+-+-+-+-+-+-+-+-+
   |       1       |       2       |
   +-+-+-+-+-+-+-+-+-+-+-+-+-+-+-+-+
   |       3       |       4       |
   +-+-+-+-+-+-+-+-+-+-+-+-+-+-+-+-+
   |       5       |       6       |
   +-+-+-+-+-+-+-+-+-+-+-+-+-+-+-+-+
```

Whenever an octet represents a numeric quantity, the left most bit in the diagram is the high order or most significant bit. That is, the bit labeled 0 is the most significant bit. For example, the following diagram represents the value 170 (decimal).

```
    0 1 2 3 4 5 6 7
   +-+-+-+-+-+-+-+-+
   |1 0 1 0 1 0 1 0|
   +-+-+-+-+-+-+-+-+
```

Similarly, whenever a multi-octet field represents a numeric quantity the left most bit of the whole field is the most significant bit. When a multi-octet quantity is transmitted the most significant octet is transmitted first.

Resource Record Data

Data Format

In addition to two and four octet integer values, resource record data can contain *domain names* or *character strings*.

Domain Name
(from RFC 1035, page 10)

Domain names in messages are expressed in terms of a sequence of labels. Each label is represented as a one octet length field followed by that number of octets. Since every domain name ends with the null label of the root, a domain name is terminated by a length byte of zero. The high order two bits of every length octet must be zero, and the remaining six bits of the length field limit the label to 63 octets or less.

Message Compression
(from RFC 1035, page 30)

In order to reduce the size of messages, the domain system utilizes a compression scheme which eliminates the repetition of domain names in a message. In this scheme, an entire domain name or a list of labels at the end of a domain name is replaced with a pointer to a prior of the same name.

The pointer takes the form of a two octet sequence:

```
+--+--+--+--+--+--+--+--+--+--+--+--+--+--+--+--+
| 1  1|                OFFSET                   |
+--+--+--+--+--+--+--+--+--+--+--+--+--+--+--+--+
```

The first two bits are ones. This allows a pointer to be distinguished from a label, since the label must begin with two zero bits because labels are restricted to 63 octets or less. (The 10 and 01 combinations are reserved for future use.) The OFFSET field specifies an offset from the start of the message (i.e., the first octet of the ID field in the domain header). A zero offset specifies the first byte of the ID field, etc.

Character String
(from RFC 1035, page 13)

Character string is a single length octet followed by that number of characters. *Character string* is treated as binary information, and can be up to 256 characters in length (including the length octet).

B

Compiling and Installing BIND on a Sun

The version of BIND shipped with SunOS 4.1.1 is based on the 4.8.1 release of BIND—a tad stale. Solaris 2.0 will include a brand-new BIND based on 4.8.3, but by the time Solaris 2.0 is out, BIND 4.9 may be out, too. Luckily, compiling BIND from the sources on a Sun is relatively easy, because SunOS is based on BSD UNIX, and BIND was originally written for BSD UNIX. Here are instructions on how to compile and install 4.8.3 BIND on your SunOS host.

Get the Source Code

First, you've got to get the source code. There's a copy on **ftp.uu.net**, available for anonymous *ftp*:

```
% cd /tmp
% ftp ftp.uu.net.
Connected to ftp.uu.net.
220 ftp.UU.NET FTP server (Version 6.29 Mon Jul 13 17:26:39 EDT 1992) ready.
Name (ftp.uu.net.:user): ftp
331 Guest login ok, send e-mail address as password.
Password:
```

Now you need to find the right file:

```
ftp> cd networking/ip/dns/bind
250 CWD command successful.
ftp> binary
200 Type set to I.
ftp> get bind.4.8.3.tar.Z
200 PORT command successful.
150 Opening BINARY mode data connection for bind.4.8.3.tar.Z (447001 bytes).
226 Transfer complete.
447001 bytes received in 25.89 seconds (16.86 Kbytes/s)
ftp> quit
221 Goodbye.
```

Unpack the Source Code

Now you've got the compressed *tar* file that contains the BIND source. Just use *zcat* to uncompress it, then un*tar* it:

```
% zcat bind.4.8.3.tar.Z | tar xvf -
```

This will create several subdirectories under the current directory: *bin, doc, include, man, master, named, res* and *tools*. They contain:

bin   Shell scripts used by the current Berkeley (BSD) makefiles.

doc   A copy of the BIND Operations Guide and the DNS RFCs (but not this book).

include   Copies of include files referenced by the BIND code. You should use these to build your 4.8.3 BIND instead of the ones shipped with your system since they were modified between releases.

man   Manual pages for BIND programs like *named, nslookup*, and for the resolver library.

master   Sample db files, boot files, and a cache file. Note that the cache file is out-of-date.

named   Source code for the *named* program.

res   Source code for the resolver library.

tools   Source code for *nslookup* and two other programs, *nstest* and *nsquery*, which are considerably less useful than *nslookup*.

Build the Resolver Library

In order to build *named* and *nslookup* (don't bother with *nstest* or *nsquery*), you'll first need to compile the resolver library. To do that:

```
% cd res
% chmod +w Makefile
% vi Makefile
```

Now add **-I../include -DBSD=43** to the line which reads

```
CFLAGS= -O ${DEFS}
```

And run **make**:

```
% make
```

The resolver library should build without errors. Then run *ranlib* on the newly-created *libresolv.a*:

```
% ranlib libresolv.a
```

Build the Name Server

Next, you compile the name server, *named*:

```
% cd ../named
% chmod +w Makefile
% vi Makefile
```

Again, add **-I../include -DBSD=43** to the CFLAGS line. Also add **../res/libresolv.a** after RES=.

Now edit *pathnames.h* to look for *named-xfer* in */usr/etc*. Change the line that reads:

```
#define _PATH_XFER      "/usr/libexec/named-xfer"
```

to read:

```
#define _PATH_XFER      "/usr/etc/in.named-xfer"
```

Now run **make**:

```
% make
```

The source code should compile without any errors. Next install the new *named* and *named-xfer* into */usr/etc*. You'll need to become root to do this. Beware! On SunOS, they're called *in.named* and *in.named-xfer*, respectively.

```
# mv named /usr/etc/in.named
# mv named-xfer /usr/etc/in.named-xfer
```

Compile nslookup

All that's left is to compile and install *nslookup*:

```
% cd ../tools/nslookup
% chmod +w Makefile
% vi Makefile
```

As always, add `-I../../include  -DBSD=43` to the CFLAGS line. Also add `../../res/libresolv.a` to the line that starts RES=. Then type

```
% make
```

nslookup should compile without any errors. To install the program, type:

```
% mv nslookup /usr/bin
```

That's all there is!

C

Top-level Domains

This table lists all top-level domains known on the Internet. More domains are being added all the time, as new countries join the Internet. Given the rate at which the world and the Internet have been changing, this list is already out of date and will only get more so with time. In particular, new top-level domains will probably be created for the countries formed from the old Soviet republics and from the former Czechoslovakia and Yugoslavia.

Domain	Country or Organization	Domain	Country or Organization
AG	Antigua and Barbuda	EC	Ecuador
AL	Albania	EDU	Education
AQ	Antarctica	EG	Egypt
AR	Argentina	ES	Spain
ARPA	ARPA Internet	FI	Finland
AT	Austria	FR	France
AU	Australia	GB	United Kingdom
BB	Barbados	GOV	government
BE	Belgium	GR	Greece
BG	Bulgaria	HK	Hong Kong
BO	Bolivia	HU	Hungary
BR	Brazil	IE	Ireland
BS	Bahamas	IL	Israel
BZ	Belize	IN	India
CA	Canada	INT	international entities
CH	Switzerland	IS	Iceland
CL	Chile	IT	Italy
CN	China	JM	Jamaica
CO	Colombia	JP	Japan

Domain	Country or Organization	Domain	Country or Organization
KM	Comoros	SG	Singapore
CR	Costa Rica	SR	Suriname
CS	Czechoslovakia	TW	Taiwan
DE	Germany	TH	Thailand
DK	Denmark	TN	Tunisia
LU	Luxembourg	TR	Turkey
DM	Dominica	TT	Trinidad and Tobago
DO	Dominican Republic	UK	United Kingdom
KN	Saint Kitts and Nevis	SU	USSR
KR	Korea, Republic of	US	United States
LC	Saint Lucia	UY	Uruguay
LK	Sri Lanka	VE	Venezuela
MIL	military	VC	Saint Vincent and the Grenadines
MY	Malaysia	YU	Yugoslavia
MX	Mexico	ZA	South Africa
NA	Namibia	ZW	Zimbabwe
NATO	North Atlantic Treaty Organization		
NET	network entities		
NI	Nicaragua		
NL	Netherlands		
NO	Norway		
NZ	New Zealand		
ORG	organizations		
PE	Peru		
PG	Papua New Guinea		
PH	Philippines		
PL	Poland		
PR	Puerto Rico		
PT	Portugal		
PY	Paraguay		
KN	Saint Kitts and Nevis		
SE	Sweden		

D

Domain Registration Form

This appendix contains the form used to register the name of your domain
with the Network Information Center.

[NETINFO:DOMAIN-TEMPLATE.TXT]   [04/93]

```
To establish a domain, the following information must be sent to
the InterNIC Domain Registrar (HOSTMASTER@INTERNIC.NET). Questions
may be addressed to the Hostmaster by electronic mail at the
above address, or by phone at (703) 742-4777 or (800) 444-4345.

NOTE: The key people must have electronic mailboxes and
"handles," unique NIC database identifiers. If you have access to
"WHOIS", please check to see if you are registered and if so, make
sure the information is current. Include only your handle and any
changes (if any) that need to be made in your entry. If you do not
have access to "WHOIS", please provide all the information indicated
and a handle will be assigned.

(1) The name of the top-level domain to join
    (EDU, COM, MIL, GOV, NET, ORG).

   1.  Top-level domain:

(2) The name of the domain (up to 12 characters). This is the name
that will be used in tables and lists associating the domain with the
domain server addresses. [While, from a technical standpoint, domain
names can be quite long we recommend the use of shorter, more user-
friendly names.]

   2.  Complete Domain Name:

(3) The name and address of the organization establishing the domain.

   3a.  Organization name:

   3b.  Organization address:


(4) The date you expect the domain to be fully operational.

   4.  Date operational:
```

(5) The handle of the administrative head of the organization --
or this person's name, mailing address, phone number, organization,
and network mailbox. This is the contact point for administrative
and policy questions about the domain. In the case of a research
project, this should be the principal investigator.

NOTE: Both the Administrative and the Technical/Zone contact of a
domain MUST have a network mailbox, even if the mailbox is to be
within the proposed domain.

     Administrative Contact

  5a. Handle (if known) :
  5b. Name (Last, First) :
  5c. Organization:
  5d. Mail Address:

  5e. Phone Number:
  5f. Net Mailbox :

(6) The handle of the technical contact for the domain -- or
the person's name, mailing address, phone number, organization,
and network mailbox. This is the contact point for
problems concerning the domain or zone, as well as for updating
information about the domain or zone.

     Technical and Zone Contact

  6a. Handle (if known):
  6b. Name (Last, First) :
  6c. Organization:
  6d. Mail Address:

  6e. Phone Number:
  6f. Net Mailbox :

(7) Domains must provide at least two independent servers
    on Government-sponsored networks that provide the domain
    service for translating names to addresses for hosts in
    this domain.

* If you are applying for a domain and a network number assignment
simultaneously and a host on your proposed network will be used
as a server for the domain, you must wait until you receive your
network number assigment and have given the server(s) a netaddress
before sending in the domain application. Sending in the domain
application without complete information in Sections 7 and 8 of
this template will result in the delay of the domain registration.

Also, establishing the servers in physically separate locations
and on different PSNs and/or networks is strongly recommended.

NOTE: All new hosts acting as servers will appear in the DNS root
      servers but will not apppear in the HOSTS.TXT file
      unless otherwise requested.

Primary Server: HOSTNAME, NETADDRESS, HARDWARE, SOFTWARE

7a.   Primary Server Hostname:
7b.   Primary Server Netaddress:
7c.   Primary Server Hardware:
7d.   Primary Server Software:

(8) The Secondary server information.

8a.   Secondary Server Hostname:
8b.   Secondary Server Netaddress:
8c.   Secondary Server Hardware:
8d.   Secondary Server Software:

(9) If any currently registered hosts will be renamed into the new
    domain, please specify old hostname, netaddress, and new hostname.

For example:

    BAR-FOO2.XYZ.COM (26.8.0.193) -> FOO2.BAR.COM
    BAR-FOO3.XYZ.COM (192.7.3.193) -> FOO3.BAR.COM
    BAR-FOO4.ARPA (34.6.0.193) -> FOO4.BAR.COM

(10) Please describe your organization briefly.

For example: Our Corporation is a consulting
organization of people working with UNIX and the C language in an
electronic networking environment. It sponsors two technical
conferences annually and distributes a bimonthly newsletter.

For further information contact InterNIC Registration Services:

    Via electronic mail: HOSTMASTER@INTERNIC.NET
    Via telephone: (800) 444-4345 or (703) 742-4777
    Via postal mail: Network Solutions
                          InterNIC Registration Services
                          505 Huntmar Park Drive
                          Herndon, VA 22070

RECOMMENDED READING

Feinler, E.J.; Jacobsen, O.J.; Stahl, M.K.; Ward, C.A., eds. DDN
   Protocol Handbook: Menlo Park, CA: SRI International, DDN Network
   Information Center; 1985 December; NIC 50004 and NIC 50005 and NIC
   50006. 2749 p.

Garcia-Luna-Aceves, J.J.; Stahl, M.K.; Ward, C.A., eds. Internet
   Protocol Handbook: The Domain Name System (DNS) Handbook. Menlo Park,
   CA: SRI International, Network Information Systems Center; 1989
   August; 219 p. AD A214 698.

Postel, J.B.; Reynolds, J.K. Domain Requirements. Marina del Rey, CA:
   University of Southern California, Information Sciences Inst.; 1984
   October; RFC 920. 14 p. (RS.INTERNIC.NET POLICY RFC920.TXT).

Harrenstien, K.; Stahl, M.K.; Feinler, E.J. DoD Internet Host Table
   Specification. Menlo Park, CA: SRI International, DDN Network
   Information Center; 1985 October; RFC 952. 6 p. (RS.INTERNIC.NET
     POLICY RFC952.TXT). Obsoletes: RFC 810

Harrenstien, K.; Stahl, M.K.; Feinler, E.J. Hostname Server. Menlo
   Park, CA: SRI International, DDN Network Information Center; 1985
   October; RFC 953. 5 p. (NIC.DDN.MIL RFC:RFC953.TXT).
     Obsoletes: RFC 811

Partridge, C. Mail Routing and the Domain System. Cambridge, MA: BBN
   Labs., Inc.; 1986 January; RFC 974. 7 p. (RS.INTERNIC.NET
     POLICY RFC974.TXT).

Lazear, W.D. MILNET Name Domain Transition. McLean, VA: MITRE Corp.;
   1987 November; RFC 1031. 10 p. (RS.INTERNIC.NET POLICY RFC1031.TXT).

Stahl, M.K. Domain Administrators Guide. Menlo Park, CA: SRI
   International, DDN Network Information Center; 1987 November; RFC
   1032. 14 p. (RS.INTERNIC.NET POLICY RFC1032.TXT).

Lottor, M. Domain Administrators Operations Guide. Menlo Park, CA:
   SRI International, DDN Network Information Center; 1987 November; RFC
   1033. 22 p. (RS.INTERNIC.NET POLICY RFC1033.TXT).

Mockapetris, P. Domain Names - Concepts and Facilities. Marina del
   Rey, CA: University of Southern California, Information Sciences
   Inst.; 1987 November; RFC 1034. 55 p. (RS.INTERNIC.NET
   POLICY RFC1034.TXT). Updated-by: RFC 1101
     Obsoletes: RFC 973; RFC 882; RFC 883

Mockapetris, P. Domain names - Implementation and Specification.
   Marina del Rey, CA: University of Southern California, Information
   Sciences Inst.; 1987 November; RFC 1035. 55 p. (RS.INTERNIC.NET
     POLICY RFC1035.TXT). Updated-by: RFC 1101
     Obsoletes: RFC 973; RFC 882; RFC 883

Mockapetris, P. DNS Encoding of Network Names and Other Types. Marina
   del Rey, CA: University of Southern California, Information Sciences
   Inst.; 1989 April; RFC 1101. 14 p. (RS.INTERNIC.NET POLICY RFC1101.TXT).
     Updates: RFC 1034; RFC 1035

E

IN-ADDR.ARPA Registration

This appendix contains the form used to register your "reverse domain" (the **in-addr.arpa** domain) with the Network Information Center.

[netinfo/in-addr-template.txt]   [04/93]

The Internet uses a special domain to support gateway location and Internet address to host mapping. The intent of this domain is to provide a guaranteed method to perform host address to host name mapping, and to facilitate queries to locate all gateways on a particular network in the Internet.

                    IN-ADDR.ARPA Registration

The following information is needed for delegation of registered networks in your domain for inclusion in the IN-ADDR.ARPA zone files:

        * the IN-ADDR.ARPA domain
        * the Network name
        * the Hostnames of the two hosts on networks
                that will be acting as IN-ADDR servers

IN-ADDR domains are represented using the network number in reverse. For example, network 123.45.67.0's IN-ADDR domain is represented as 67.45.123.IN-ADDR.ARPA.

        For example:

        IN-ADDR domain   Network Name   IN-ADDR Servers
                                                    (Hostname)
                                                    (NetAddress)
                                                    (CPUType/OpSys)

        41.192.IN-ADDR.ARPA   NET-TEST-ONE   BAR.FOO.EDU
                                                    123.45.67.89
                                                    VAX-II/VMS
                                                    ONE.ABC.COM
                                                    98.76.54.32
                                                    SUN/UNIX

- -

NOTE: Unless specified, new hosts registered as IN-ADDR servers will
be registered in the root servers only and will not appear in the
HOSTS.TXT file.

Please have the Network Coordinator complete and return the following
information for those networks needing IN-ADDR registration.

      IN-ADDR domain   Network Name   IN-ADDR Servers
      ==============   ============   ===============

- -

Completed templates and questions can be directed to Hostmaster at
HOSTMASTER@INTERNIC.NET, or mailed to:

   Network Solutions
      InterNIC Registration Service
      505 Huntmar Park Drive
      Herndon, VA 22070

Index

C

ca domains, 42
cache data, 65-67
  missing, 261
caching data, 36-38
  negative caching, 333
  time limits on, 37
caching-only name servers,
  167, 171
canonical name records, 58,
  61, 313-317, 340
canonicalization, 112
case sensitivity, of DNS lookups, 58, 339
CH class, 351
Chaosnet, 20
check_del, 194-195
classes, 59, 351
class option, nslookup, 208
CNAME resource records, 58,
  61, 313-317, 340
  and subdomains, 198, 314
  in the resource record data,
    316
  looking up, 316
  pointing to CNAMEs, 314
  queries, 155
com (commercial) domain,
  21
comments, in db files, 58
configuring hosts, 101-124
**connectivity of name servers,
  159**
**conventions used in this
  book, xxii**
CPU utilization, 160
CS class, 351

D

d2 option, nslookup, 208
  translating host tables to,
    57-67
  (see also db files)
data files, (see db files)

database dumps, how to read,
  252
database format error,
  259-260
  error message, 74
db files, 28, 57-58
  adding and deleting hosts
    from, 128
  case sensitivity in, 58, 339
  comments in, 58
  control entries, 136-137
  example, 63, 69
  instructing name servers to
    read, 67
  rereading, 74
  resource record order in, 58
  syntax errors in, 259
  updating, 128-136
db.127.0.0, 57, 64-65
db.ADDR files, 57, 64
db.cache, 57, 65-66
  and caching-only name
    servers, 167
  updating, 134-136
db.DOMAIN, 57
db.root, 322
DCE cells, 329
debug option, nslookup, 207
debugging, 227-247
  command line option, 230
  levels, 227-229
  name servers, 163
  reading output, 230-246
  turning on, 229-230
  with signals, 230
decimal serial numbers, 130
DEC's Ultrix resolver, 121
default domains
  failing to set, 267
  initializing, 75, 102
defname option, nslookup,
  207
delegating domains, 24-25, 27,
  183-201
  checking, 194
  managing, 197
dig, tool for DNS queries, 203

About the Authors

Cricket Liu started working for Hewlett-Packard's Corporate Network Services right after graduating from U.C. Berkeley in 1988. He began managing the hp.com domain after the Loma Prieta earthquake forcibly moved the management of the hp.com domain to Corporate and rudely interrupted his first World Series game.

Currently, Cricket is investigating the deployment of the OSF's Distributed Computing Environment on the HP Internet. He also consults on network security issues and keeps his eyes open for interesting new networking technologies.

Cricket has had his nickname since he was a baby and his dad decided he looked like Jiminy Cricket. His real name is a pain to pronounce. He and his wife Paige live in 480 square feet in Palo Alto, California.

Paul Albitz is a software engineer at Hewlett-Packard. Paul earned a Bachelor of Science degree from the University of Wisconsin, LaCrosse, and a Master of Science degree from Purdue University.

Paul worked on BIND for the HP-UX 7.0 and 8.0 releases. During this time Paul developed the tools used to run the hp.com domain. More recently he has been involved in networking HP's DesignJet plotter. Before joining HP, Paul was a system administrator in the CS Department of Purdue University. As system administrator, Paul ran versions of BIND before BIND's initial release with 4.3 BSD. Paul and his wife Katherine live in San Diego, CA.

Colophon

Our look is the result of reader comments, our own experimentation, and distribution channels.

Distinctive covers complement our distinctive approach to technical topics, breathing personality and life into potentially dry subjects. UNIX and its attendant programs can be unruly beasts. Nutshell Handbooks help you tame them.

The insects featured on the cover of *DNS and BIND* are grasshoppers. Grasshoppers are found all over the globe. Of over 5000 species, 100 different grasshopper species are found in North America. Grasshoppers are greenish-brown, and range in length from a half inch to four inches, with wingspans of up to six inches. Their bodies are divided into three sections: the head, thorax, and abdomen, with three pairs of legs and two pairs of wings.

Male grasshoppers use their hind legs and forewings to produce a "chirping" sound. Their hind legs have a ridge of small pegs which are rubbed across a hardened vein in the forewing, causing an audible vibration much like a bow being drawn across a string.

Grasshoppers are major crop pests, particularly when they collect into swarms. A single grasshopper can consume 30 mg of food a day. In collections of 50 or more grasshoppers per square yard—a density often reached during grasshopper outbreaks—grasshoppers consume as much as a cow would, per acre. In addition to consuming foliage, grasshoppers damage plants by attacking plants at vulnerable points and causing the stems to break off.

Edie Freedman designed this cover and the entire UNIX bestiary that appears on other Nutshell Handbooks. The beasts themselves are adapted from 19th-century engravings from the Dover Pictorial Archive. The cover layout was produced with Quark XPress 3.1 using the ITC Garamond font.

The inside layout was formatted in sqtroff by Lenny Muellner and Kismet McDonough using ITC Garamond Light and ITC Garamond Book fonts, and was designed by Edie Freeman. The figures were created in Aldus Freehand 3.1 by Chris Reilley.

SYSTEM ADMINISTRATION

Books from O'Reilly & Associates, Inc.

Fall/Winter 1995-96

"Good reference books make a system administrator's job much easier. However, finding useful books about system administration is a challenge, and I'm constantly on the lookout. In general, I have found that almost anything published by O'Reilly & Associates is worth having if you are interested in the topic."

—*Dinah McNutt*, UNIX Review

INTERNET TOOLS

CP/IP Network Administration

By Craig Hunt
1st Edition August 1992
502 pages, ISBN 0-937175-82-X

TCP/IP Network Administration is a complete guide to setting up and running a TCP/IP network for administrators of networks of systems or lone home systems that access the Internet. It starts with the fundamentals: what the protocols do and how they work, how to request a network address and a name (the forms needed are included in an appendix), and how to set up your network. Beyond basic setup, the book discusses how to configure important network applications, including sendmail, the r* commands, and some simple setups for NIS and NFS. There are also chapters on troubleshooting and security. In addition, this book covers several important packages that are available from the Net (such as *gated*). Covers BSD and System V TCP/IP implementations.

"Whether you're putting a network together, trying to figure out why an existing one doesn't work, or wanting to understand the one you've got a little better, *TCP/IP Network Administration* is the definitive volume on the subject."
—Tom Yager, *Byte*

Networking Personal Computers with TCP/IP

By Craig Hunt
1st Edition July 1995
408 pages, ISBN 1-56592-123-2

If you're like most network administrators, you probably have several networking "islands": a TCP/IP-based network of UNIX systems (possibly connected to the Internet), plus a separate Netware or NetBIOS network for your PCs. Perhaps even separate Netware and NetBIOS networks in different departments, or at different sites. And you've probably dreaded the task of integrating those networks into one.

If that's your situation, you need this book! When done properly, integrating PCs onto a TCP/IP-based Internet is less threatening than it seems; long term, it gives you a much more flexible and extensible network. Craig Hunt, author of the classic *TCP/IP Network Administration*, tells you how to build a maintainable network that includes your PCs. Don't delay; as Craig points out, if you don't provide a network solution for your PC users, someone else will.

Covers: DOS, Windows, Windows for Workgroups, Windows NT, and Novell Netware; Chameleon (NetManage), PC/TCP (FTP Software), LAN WorkPlace (Novell), Super TCP, and Trumpet; Basic Network setup and configuration, with special attention given to email, network printing, and file sharing.

Managing Internet Information Services

By Cricket Liu, Jerry Peek, Russ Jones,
Bryan Buus & Adrian Nye
1st Edition December 1994
668 pages, ISBN 1-56592-062-7

This comprehensive guide describes how to set up information services and make them available over the Internet. It discusses why a company would want to offer Internet services, provides complete coverage of all popular services, and tells how to select which ones to provide. Most of the book describes how to set up Gopher, World Wide Web, FTP, and WAIS servers and email services.

"*Managing Internet Information Services* has long been needed in the Internet community, as well as in many organizations with IP-based networks. Although many on the Internet are quite savvy when it comes to administering these types of tools, *MIIS* will allow a much larger community to join in and perhaps provide more diverse information. This book will be a welcome addition to my Internet shelf."
—Robert H'obbes' Zakon, MITRE Corporation

Getting Connected: The Internet at 56K and Higher

By Kevin Dowd
1st Edition February 1996 (est.)
450 pages (est.), ISBN 1-56592-154-2

A complete guide for businesses, schools, and other organizations who want to connect their computers to the Internet. This book covers everything you need to know to make informed decisions, from helping you figure out which services you really need to providing down-to-earth explanations of telecommunication options, such as frame relay, ISDN, and leased lines. Once you're online, it shows you how to set up basic Internet services, such as a World Wide Web server. Tackles issues for the PC, Macintosh, and UNIX platforms.

DNS and BIND

By Paul Albitz & Cricket Liu
1st Edition October 1992
418 pages, ISBN 1-56592-010-4

DNS and BIND contains all you need to know about the Internet's Domain Name System (DNS) and the Berkeley Internet Name Domain (BIND), its UNIX implementation. The Domain Name System is the Internet's "phone book"; it's a database that tracks important information (in particular, names and addresses) for every computer on the Internet. If you're a system administrator, this book will show you how to set up and maintain the DNS software on your network.

sendmail

By Bryan Costales, with Eric Allman & Neil Rickert
1st Edition November 1993
830 pages, ISBN 1-56592-056-2

This Nutshell Handbook® is far and away the most comprehensive book ever written on sendmail, the program that acts like a traffic cop in routing and delivering mail on UNIX-based networks. Although sendmail is used on almost every UNIX system, it's one of the last great uncharted territories—and most difficult utilities to learn—in UNIX system administration. This book provides a complete sendmail tutorial, plus extensive reference material on every aspect of the program. It covers IDA sendmail, the latest version (V8) from Berkeley, and the standard versions available on most systems.

Using and Managing UUCP

By Tim O'Reilly, Dale Dougherty, Grace Todino & Ed Ravin
1st Edition March 1996 (est.)
350 pages (est.), ISBN 1-56592-153-4

Using and Managing UUCP describes, in one volume, this popular communications and file transfer program. UUCP is very attractive to computer users with limited resources, a small machine, and a dial-up connection. This book covers Taylor UUCP, the latest versions of HoneyDanBer UUCP, and the specific implementation details of UUCP versions shipped by major UNIX vendors.

Computer Crime

By David Icove, Karl Seger & William VonStorch
1st Edition August 1995
464 pages, ISBN 1-56592-086-4

Computer crime is a growing threat. Attacks on computers, networks, and data range from terrorist threats to financial crimes to pranks. *Computer Crime: A Crimefighter's Handbook* is aimed at those who need to understand, investigate, and prosecute computer crimes of all kinds.

This book discusses computer crimes, criminals, and laws, and profiles the computer criminal (using techniques developed for the FBI and other law enforcement agencies). It outlines the the risks to computer systems and personnel, operational, physical, and communications measures that can be taken to prevent computer crimes. It also discusses how to plan for, investigate, and prosecute computer crimes, ranging from the supplies needed for criminal investigation, to the detection and audit tools used in investigation, to the presentation of evidence to a jury.

Contains a compendium of computer-related federal statutes, all statutes of individual states, a resource summary, and detailed papers on computer crime.

Computer Security Basics

By Deborah Russell & G.T. Gangemi Sr.
1st Edition July 1991
464 pages, ISBN 0-937175-71-4

There's a lot more consciousness of security today, but not a lot of understanding of what it means and how far it should go. This handbook describes complicated concepts, such as trusted systems, encryption, and mandatory access control, in simple terms. For example, most U.S. government equipment acquisitions now require "Orange Book" (Trusted Computer System Evaluation Criteria) certification. A lot of people have a vague feeling that they ought to know about the Orange Book, but few make the effort to track it down and read it. *Computer Security Basics* contains a more readable introduction to the Orange Book—why it exists, what it contains, and what the different security levels are all about—than any other book or government publication.

PGP: Pretty Good Privacy

By Simson Garfinkel
1st Edition December 1994
430 pages, ISBN 1-56592-098-8

PGP is a freely available encryption program that protects the privacy of files and electronic mail. It uses powerful public key cryptography and works on virtually every platform. This book is both a readable technical user's guide and a fascinating behind-the-scenes look at cryptography and privacy. It describes how to use PGP and provides background on cryptography, PGP's history, battles over public key cryptography patents and U.S. government export restrictions, and public debates about privacy and free speech.

Building Internet Firewalls

By D. Brent Chapman & Elizabeth D. Zwicky
1st Edition September 1995
544 pages, ISBN 1-56592-124-0

Everyone is jumping on the Internet bandwagon, despite that fact that the security risks associated with connecting to the Net have never been greater. This book is a practical guide to building firewalls on the Internet. It describes a variety of firewall approaches and architectures and discusses how you can build packet filtering and proxying solutions at your site. It also contains a full discussion of how to configure Internetservices (e.g., FTP, SMTP, Telnet) to work with a firewall, as well as a complete list of resources, including the location of many publicly available firewall construction tools.

Practical UNIX and Internet Security

By Simson Garfinkel & Gene Spafford
2nd Edition February 1996 (est.)
800 pages (est.), ISBN 1-56592-148-8

A complete revision of the first edition, this new guide spells out the threats, system vulnerabilities, and counter-measures you can adopt to protect your UNIX system, network, and Internet connection. It's complete—covering both host and network security—and doesn't require that you be a programmer or a UNIX guru to use it. This edition contains hundreds of pages of new information on Internet security, including new security tools and approaches. Covers many platforms, both System V and Berkeley-based, including Sun, DEC, HP, IBM, SCO, NeXT, Linux, and other UNIX systems.

Essential System Administration

By Æleen Frisch
2nd Edition September 1995
788 pages, ISBN 1-56592-127-5

Essential System Administration takes an in-depth look at the fundamentals of UNIX system administration in a real-world, heterogeneous environment. Whether you are a beginner or an experienced administrator, you'll quickly be able to apply its principles and advice to your everyday problems.

The book approaches UNIX systems administration from the perspective of your job—the routine tasks and troubleshooting that make up your day. Whether you're dealing with frustrated users, convincing an uncomprehending management that you need new hardware, rebuilding the kernel, or simply adding new users, you'll find help in this book. You'll also learn about back up and restore and how to set up printers, secure your system, and perform many other systems administration tasks. But the book is not for full-time systems administrators alone. Linux users and others who administer their own systems will benefit from its practical, hands-on approach.

This second edition has been updated for the latest versions of all major UNIX platforms, including Sun OS 4.1, Solaris 2.3, AIX 4.1, Linux 1.1, Digital UNIX OSF/1, SCO UNIX version 3, HP/UX versions 9 and 10, and IRIX version 6. The entire book has been thoroughly reviewed and tested on all of the platforms covered. In addition, networking, electronic mail, security, and kernel configuration topics have been expanded.

Managing NFS and NIS

By Hal Stern
1st Edition June 1991
436 pages, ISBN 0-937175-75-7

Managing NFS and NIS is for system administrators who need to set up or manage a network filesystem installation. NFS (Network Filesystem) is probably running at any site that has two or more UNIX systems. NIS (Network Information System) is a distributed database used to manage a network of computers. The only practical book devoted entirely to these subjects, this guide is a "must-have" for anyone interested in UNIX networking.

Linux Network Administrator's Guide

By Olaf Kirch
1st Edition January 1995
370 pages, ISBN 1-56592-087-2

A UNIX-compatible operating system that runs on personal computers, Linux is a pinnacle within the free software movement. It is based on a kernel developed by Finnish student Linus Torvalds and is distributed on the Net or on low-cost disks, along with a complete set of UNIX libraries, popular free software utilities, and traditional layered products like NFS and the X Window System. Networking is a fundamental part of Linux. Whether you want a simple UUCP connection or a full LAN with NFS and NIS, you are going to have to build a network.

Linux Network Administrator's Guide by Olaf Kirch is one of the most successful books to come from the Linux Documentation Project. It touches on all the essential networking software included with Linux, plus some hardware considerations. Topics include serial connections, UUCP, routing and DNS, mail and News, SLIP and PPP, NFS, and NIS.

System Performance Tuning

By Mike Loukides
1st Edition November 1990
336 pages, ISBN 0-937175-60-9

System Performance Tuning answers the fundamental question: How can I get my computer to do more work without buying more hardware? Some performance problems do require you to buy a bigger or faster computer, but many can be solved simply by making better use of the resources you already have.

termcap & terminfo

By John Strang, Linda Mui & Tim O'Reilly
3rd Edition April 1988
270 pages, ISBN 0-937175-22-6

For UNIX system administrators and programmers. This handbook provides information on writing and debugging terminal descriptions, as well as terminal initialization, for the two UNIX terminal databases.

The Computer User's Survival Guide

By Joan Stigliani
1st Edition October 1995
296 pages, ISBN 1-56592-030-9

The bad news: You can be hurt by working at a computer. The good news: Many of the factors that pose a risk are within your control. *The Computer User's Survival Guide* looks squarely at all the factors that affect your health on the job, including positioning, equipment, work habits, lighting, stress, radiation, and general health. It is not a book of gloom and doom. It is a guide to protecting yourself against health risks from your computer, while boosting your effectiveness and making your work more enjoyable.

This guide will teach you what's going on "under the skin" when your hands and arms spend much of the day mousing and typing, and what you can do to prevent overuse injuries. You'll learn various postures to help reduce stress; what you can do to prevent glare from modern office lighting; simple breathing techniques and stretches to keep your body well oxygenated and relaxed; and how to reduce eye strain. Also covers radiation issues and what electrical equipment is responsible for the most exposure.

The Future Does Not Compute

By Stephen L. Talbott
1st Edition May 1995
502 pages, ISBN 1-56592-085-6

This book explores the networked computer as an expression of the darker, dimly conscious side of the human being. What we have been imparting to the Net—or what the Net has been eliciting from us—is a half-submerged, barely intended logic, contaminated by wishes and tendencies we prefer not to acknowledge. The urgent necessity is for us to wake up to what is most fully human and unmachinelike in ourselves, rather than yield to an ever more strangling embrace with our machines. The author's thesis is sure to raise a controversy among the millions of users now adapting themselves to the Net.

Volume 8: X Window System Administrator's Guide

By Linda Mui & Eric Pearce
1st Edition October 1992
372 pages, ISBN 0-937175-83-8

As X moves out of the hacker's domain and into the "real world," users can't be expected to master all the ins and outs of setting up and administering their own X software. That will increasingly become the domain of system administrators. Even for experienced system administrators, X raises many issues, both because of subtle changes in the standard UNIX way of doing things and because X blurs the boundaries between different platforms. Under X, users can run applications across the network on systems with different resources (including fonts, colors, and screen size). Many of these issues are poorly understood, and the technology for dealing with them is in rapid flux.

This book is the first and only book devoted to the issues of system administration for X and X-based networks, written not just for UNIX system administrators, but for anyone faced with the job of administering X (including those running X on stand-alone workstations).

Note: The CD that used to be offered with this book is now sold separately, allowing system administrators to purchase the book and the CD-ROM in quantities they choose.

The X Companion CD for R6

By O'Reilly & Associates
1st Edition January 1995
(Includes CD-ROM plus 126-page guide)
ISBN 1-56592-084-8

The X CD-ROM contains precompiled binaries for X11, Release 6 (X11 R6) for Sun4, Solaris, HP-UX on the HP700, DEC Alpha, DEC ULTRIX, and IBM RS6000. It includes X11 R6 source code from the "core" and "contrib" directories and X11 R5 source code from the "core" directory. The CD also provides examples from O'Reilly and Associates X Window System series books and *The X Resource* journal.

The package includes a 126-page book describing the contents of the CD-ROM, how to install the R6 binaries, and how to build X11 for other platforms. The book also contains the X Consortium release notes for Release 6.

At Your Fingertips—
A COMPLETE GUIDE TO O'REILLY'S ONLINE SERVICES

O'Reilly & Associates offers extensive product and customer service information online. We invite you to come and explore our little neck-of-the-woods.

For product information and insight into new technologies, visit the O'Reilly Resource Center

Most comprehensive among our online offerings is the O'Reilly Resource Center. You'll find detailed information on all O'Reilly products, including titles, prices, tables of contents, indexes, author bios, software contents, and reviews. You can also view images of all our products. In addition, watch for informative articles that provide perspective on the technologies we write about. Interviews, excerpts, and bibliographies are also included.

After browsing online, it's easy to order, too by sending email to **order@ora.com**. The O'Reilly Resource Center shows you how. Here's how to visit us online:

☞*Via the World Wide Web*

If you are connected to the Internet, point your Web browser (e.g., **mosaic, netscape,** or **lynx**) to:

http://www.ora.com/

For the plaintext version, **telnet** to:
www.ora.com (login: **oraweb**)

☞*Via Gopher*

If you have a Gopher program, connect your **gopher** to: **gopher.ora.com**

Or, point your Web browser to:
gopher://gopher.ora.com/

Or, you can **telnet** to: **gopher.ora.com** (login: **gopher**)

A convenient way to stay informed: email mailing lists

An easy way to learn of the latest projects and products from O'Reilly & Associates is to subscribe to our mailing lists. We have email announcements and discussions on various topics. Subscribers receive email as soon as the information breaks.

☞*To join a mailing list:*

Send email to:

listproc@online.ora.com

Leave the message "subject" empty if possible.

If you know the name of the mailing list you want to subscribe to, put the following information on the first line of your message: **subscribe** "listname" "your name" **of** "your company."

For example: **subscribe ora-news Kris Webber of Fine Enterprises**

If you don't know the name of the mailing list, listproc will send you a listing of all the mailing lists. Put this word on the first line of the body: **lists**

To find out more about a particular list, send a message with this word as the first line of the body: **info** "listname"

For more information and help, send this message: **help**

For specific help, email to:
   listmaster@online.ora.com

The complete O'Reilly catalog is now available via email

You can now receive a text-only version of our complete catalog via email. It contains detailed information about all our products, so it's mighty big: over 200 kbytes, or 200,000 characters.

To get the whole catalog in one message, send an empty email message to: **catalog@online.ora.com**

If your email system can't handle large messages, you can get the catalog split into smaller messages. Send email to: **catalog-split@online.ora.com**

To receive a print catalog, send your snail mail address to: **catalog@ora.com**

Check out Web Review, our new publication on the Web

Web Review is our new magazine that offers fresh insights into the Web. The editorial mission of Web Review is to answer the question: How and where do you BEST spend your time online? Each issue contains reviews that look at the most interesting and creative sites on the Web. Visit us at **http://gnn.com/wr/**

Web Review is the product of the recently formed Songline Studios, a venture between O'Reilly and America Online.

Get the files you want with FTP

We have an archive of example files from our books, the covers of our books, and much more available by anonymous FTP.

ftp to:

ftp.ora.com (login: **anonymous** – use your email address as the password.)

Or, if you have a WWW browser, point it to:

ftp://ftp.ora.com/

FTPMAIL

The ftpmail service connects to O'Reilly's FTP server and sends the results (the files you want) by email. This service is for people who can't use FTP—but who can use email.

For help and examples, send an email message to:

ftpmail@online.ora.com
(In the message body, put the single word: **help**)

Helpful information is just an email message away

Many customer services are provided via email. Here are a few of the most popular and useful:

info@online.ora.com
    For a list of O'Reilly's online customer services.

info@ora.com
    For general questions and information.

bookquestions@ora.com
    For technical questions, or corrections, concerning book contents.

order@ora.com
    To order books online and for ordering questions.

catalog@online.ora.com
    To receive an online copy of our catalog.

catalog@ora.com
    To receive a free copy of *ora.com*, our combination magazine and catalog. Please include your snail mail address.

international@ora.com
    Comments or questions about international ordering or distribution.

xresource@ora.com
    To order or inquire about *The X Resource* journal.

proposals@ora.com
    To submit book proposals.

O'Reilly & Associates, Inc.

103A Morris Street, Sebastopol, CA 95472
Inquiries: **707-829-0515, 800-998-9938**
Credit card orders: **800-889-8969**
(Weekdays 6 A.M.- 5 P.M. PST)

FAX: **707-829-0104**

O'Reilly & Associates—
LISTING OF TITLES

INTERNET

CGI Scriptin on the World Wide Web (Winter '95-96 est.)

Connecting to the Internet: An O'Reilly Buyer's Guide

Getting Connected (Winter '95-96 est.)

Smileys

The USENET Handbook

The Whole Internet User's Guide & Catalog

The Whole Internet for Windows 95

Web Design for Designers (Winter '95-96 est.)

The World Wide Web Journal (Winter '95-96 est.)

SOFTWARE

Internet In A Box™

WebSite™

WHAT YOU NEED TO KNOW SERIES

Bandits on the Information Superhighway (Winter '95-96 est.)

Marketing on the Internet (Winter '95-96 est.)

Using Email Effectively

When You Can't Find Your System Administrator

HEALTH, CAREER & BUSINESS

Building a Successful Software Business

The Computer User's Survival Guide (Fall '95 est.)

Dictionary of Computer Terms (Winter '95-96 est.)

The Future Does Not Compute

Love Your Job!

TWI Day Calendar - 1996

USING UNIX

BASICS

Learning GNU Emacs

Learning the bash Shell

Learning the Korn Shell

Learning the UNIX Operating System

Learning the vi Editor

MH & xmh: Email for Users & Programmers

SCO UNIX in a Nutshell

UNIX in a Nutshell: System V Edition

Using and Managing UUCP (Winter '95-96 est.)

Using csh and tcsh

ADVANCED

Exploring Expect

The Frame Handbook

Learning Perl

Making TeX Work

Programming perl

Running Linux

Running Linux Companion CD-ROM (Winter '95-96 est.)

sed & awk

UNIX Power Tools (with CD-ROM)

SYSTEM ADMINISTRATION

Building Internet Firewalls

Computer Crime: A Crimefighter's Handbook

Computer Security Basics

DNS and BIND

Essential System Administration

Linux Network Administrator's Guide

Managing Internet Information Services

Managing NFS and NIS

Managing UUCP and Usenet

Networking Personal Computers with TCP/IP

Practical UNIX and Internet Security (Winter '95-96 est.)

PGP: Pretty Good Privacy

sendmail

System Performance Tuning

TCP/IP Network Administration

termcap & terminfo

Volume 8 : X Window System Administrator's Guide

The X Companion CD for R6

PROGRAMMING

Applying RCS and SCCS

C++: The Core Language

Checking C Programs with lint

DCE Security Programming

Distributing Applications Across DCE and Windows NT

Encyclopedia of Graphics File Formats

Guide to Writing DCE Applications

High Performance Computing

lex & yacc

Managing Projects with make

Microsoft RPC Programming Guide

Migrating to Fortran 90

Multi-Platform Code Management

ORACLE Performance Tuning

ORACLE PL/SQL Programming

Porting UNIX Software

POSIX Programmer's Guide

POSIX.4: Programming for the Real World

Power Programming with RPC

Practical C Programming

Practical C++ Programming

Programming with curses

Programming with GNU Software (Winter '95-96 est.)

Programming with Pthreads (Winter '95-96 est.)

Software Portability with imake

Understanding and Using COFF

Understanding DCE

Understanding Japanese Information Processing

UNIX Systems Programming for SVR4 (Winter '95-96 est.)

BERKELEY 4.4 SOFTWARE DISTRIBUTION

4.4BSD System Manager's Manual

4.4BSD User's Reference Manual

4.4BSD User's Supp. Documents

4.4BSD Programmer's Reference Manual

4.4BSD Programmer's Supplementary Documents

4.4BSD-Lite CD Companion

4.4BSD-Lite CD Companion: International Version

X WINDOW SYSTEM

Volume 0: X Protocol Reference Manual

Volume 1: Xlib Programming Manual

Volume 2: Xlib Reference Manual:

Volume 3: X Window System User's Guide

Volume. 3M: X Window System User's Guide, Motif Ed

Volume. 4: X Toolkit Intrinsics Programming Manual

Volume 4M: X Toolkit Intrinsics Programming Manual, Motif Ed.

Volume 5: X Toolkit Intrinsics Reference Manual

Volume 6A: Motif Programming Manual

Volume 6B: Motif Reference Manual

Volume 6C: Motif Tools

Volume 8 : X Window System Administrator's Guide

Volume 9: X Window Window Programming Extentions (Winter '95-96 est.)

Programmer's Supplement for Release 6

The X Companion CD for R6

X User Tools (with CD-ROM)

The X Window System in a Nutshell

THE X RESOURCE

A QUARTERLY WORKING JOURNAL FOR X PROGRAMMERS

The X Resource: Issues 0 through 16

TRAVEL

Travelers' Tales France

Travelers' Tales Hong Kong (1/96est.)

Travelers' Tales India

Travelers' Tales Mexico

Travelers' Tales Spain

Travelers' Tales Thailand

Travelers' Tales: A Woman's World

O'Reilly & Associates—
INTERNATIONAL DISTRIBUTORS

Customers outside North America can now order O'Reilly & Associates books through the following distributors. They offer our international customers faster order processing, more bookstores, increased representation at tradeshows worldwide, and the high-quality, responsive service our customers have come to expect.

EUROPE, MIDDLE EAST, AND AFRICA
(except Germany, Switzerland, and Austria)

INQUIRIES
International Thomson Publishing Europe
Berkshire House
168-173 High Holborn
London WC1V 7AA, United Kingdom
Telephone: 44-71-497-1422
Fax: 44-71-497-1426
Email: itpint@itps.co.uk

ORDERS
International Thomson Publishing Services, Ltd.
Cheriton House, North Way
Andover, Hampshire SP10 5BE, United Kingdom
Telephone: 44-264-342-832 (UK orders)
Telephone: 44-264-342-806 (outside UK)
Fax: 44-264-364418 (UK orders)
Fax: 44-264-342761 (outside UK)

GERMANY, SWITZERLAND, AND AUSTRIA

International Thomson Publishing GmbH
O'Reilly-International Thomson Verlag
Königswinterer Straße 418
53227 Bonn, Germany
Telephone: 49-228-97024 0
Fax: 49-228-441342
Email: anfragen@ora.de

ASIA *(except Japan)*
INQUIRIES
International Thomson Publishing Asia
221 Henderson Road
#08-03 Henderson Industrial Park
Singapore 0315
Telephone: 65-272-6496
Fax: 65-272-6498

ORDERS
Telephone: 65-268-7867
Fax: 65-268-6727

JAPAN
O'Reilly & Associates, Inc.
103A Morris Street
Sebastopol, CA 95472 U.S.A.
Telephone: 707-829-0515
Telephone: 800-998-9938 (U.S. & Canada)
Fax: 707-829-0104
Email: order@ora.com

AUSTRALIA
WoodsLane Pty. Ltd.
7/5 Vuko Place, Warriewood NSW 2102
P.O. Box 935, Mona Vale NSW 2103
Australia
Telephone: 02-970-5111
Fax: 02-970-5002
Email: woods@tmx.mhs.oz.au

NEW ZEALAND
WoodsLane New Zealand Ltd.
21 Cooks Street (P.O. Box 575)
Wanganui, New Zealand
Telephone: 64-6-347-6543
Fax: 64-6-345-4840
Email: woods@tmx.mhs.oz.au

THE AMERICAS
O'Reilly & Associates, Inc.
103A Morris Street
Sebastopol, CA 95472 U.S.A.
Telephone: 707-829-0515
Telephone: 800-998-9938 (U.S. & Canada)
Fax: 707-829-0104
Email: order@ora.com

O'Reilly & Associates—
LISTING OF TITLES

INTERNET

!%@:: A Directory of Electronic Mail Addressing & Networks

Connecting to the Internet: An O'Reilly Buyer's Guide

The Mosaic Handbook for Microsoft Windows

The Mosaic Handbook for the Macintosh

The Mosaic Handbook for the X Window System

Smileys

The Whole Internet User's Guide & Catalog

SOFTWARE

Internet In A Box™

WebSite™

WHAT YOU NEED TO KNOW SERIES

Using Email Effectively

Marketing on the Internet (Fall '95 est.)

When You Can't Find Your System Administrator

HEALTH, CAREER & BUSINESS

Building a Successful Software Business

The Computer User's Survival Guide (Fall '95 est.)

The Future Does Not Compute

Love Your Job!

TWI Day Calendar - 1996

AUDIOTAPES

INTERNET TALK RADIO'S "GEEK OF THE WEEK" INTERVIEWS

The Future of the Internet Protocol

Global Network Operations

Mobile IP Networking

Networked Information and Online Libraries

Security and Networks

European Networking

NOTABLE SPEECHES OF THE INFORMATION AGE

John Perry Barlow

USING UNIX

BASICS

Learning GNU Emacs

Learning the Korn Shell

Learning the UNIX Operating System

Learning the vi Editor

MH & xmh: Email for Users & Programmers

SCO UNIX in a Nutshell

The USENET Handbook

Using UUCP and Usenet

UNIX in a Nutshell: System V Edition

ADVANCED

Exploring Expect

The Frame Handbook

Learning Perl

Making TeX Work

Programming perl

Running LINUX

sed & awk

UNIX Power Tools (with CD-ROM)

SYSTEM ADMINISTRATION

Building Internet Firewalls (Fall '95 est.)

Computer Crime: A Crimefighter's Handbook (Summer '95 est.)

Computer Security Basics

DNS and BIND

Essential System Administration

Linux Network Administrator's Guide

Managing Internet Information Services

Managing NFS and NIS

Managing UUCP and Usenet

Networking Personal Computers with TCP/IP (Summer '95 est.)

Practical UNIX Security

PGP: Pretty Good Privacy

sendmail

System Performance Tuning

TCP/IP Network Administration

termcap & terminfo

Volume 8 : X Window System Administrator's Guide

The X Companion CD for R6

PROGRAMMING

Applying RCS and SCCS (Summer '95 est.)

Checking C Programs with lint

DCE Security Programming (Summer '95 est.)

Distributing Applications Across DCE and Windows NT

Encyclopedia of Graphics File Formats

Guide to Writing DCE Applications

High Performance Computing

Learning the Bash Shell (Summer '95 est.)

lex & yacc

Managing Projects with make

Microsoft RPC Programming Guide

Migrating to Fortran 90

Multi-Platform Code Management

ORACLE Performance Tuning

ORACLE PL/SQL Programming (Fall '95 est.)

Porting UNIX Software (Fall '95 est.)

POSIX Programmer's Guide

POSIX.4: Programming for the Real World

Power Programming with RPC

Practical C Programming

Practical C++ Programming (Summer '95 est.)

Programming with curses

Programming with GNU Software (Fall '95 est.)

Software Portability with imake

Understanding and Using COFF

Understanding DCE

Understanding Japanese Information Processing

UNIX for FORTRAN Programmers

Using C on the UNIX System

Using csh and tcsh (Summer '95 est.)

BERKELEY 4.4 SOFTWARE DISTRIBUTION

4.4BSD System Manager's Manual

4.4BSD User's Reference Manual

4.4BSD User's Supp. Documents

4.4BSD Programmer's Reference Manual

4.4BSD Programmer's Supplementary Documents

4.4BSD-Lite CD Companion

4.4BSD-Lite CD Companion: International Version

X WINDOW SYSTEM

Volume 0: X Protocol Reference Manual

Volume 1: Xlib Programming Manual

Volume 2: Xlib Reference Manual:

Volume 3: X Window System User's Guide

Volume. 3M: X Window System User's Guide, Motif Ed

Volume. 4: X Toolkit Intrinsics Programming Manual

Volume 4M: X Toolkit Intrinsics Programming Manual, Motif Ed.

Volume 5: X Toolkit Intrinsics Reference Manual

Volume 6A: Motif Programming Manual

Volume 6B: Motif Reference Manual

Volume 7A: XView Programming Manual

Volume 7B: XView Reference Manual

Volume 8 : X Window System Administrator's Guide

Motif Tools

PEXlib Programming Manual

PEXlib Reference Manual

PHIGS Programming Manual

PHIGS Reference Manual

Programmer's Supplement for Release 6 (Fall '95 est.)

The X Companion CD for R6

The X Window System in a Nutshell

X User Tools (with CD-ROM)

THE X RESOURCE

A QUARTERLY WORKING JOURNAL FOR X PROGRAMMERS

The X Resource: Issues 0 through 15 (Issue 15 available 7/95)

TRAVEL

Travelers' Tales France

Travelers' Tales Hong Kong (10/95 est.)

Travelers' Tales India

Travelers' Tales Mexico

Travelers' Tales Spain (11/95 est.)

Travelers' Tales Thailand

Travelers' Tales: A Woman's World

O'Reilly & Associates—
INTERNATIONAL DISTRIBUTORS

Customers outside North America can now order O'Reilly & Associates books through the following distributors. They offer our international customers faster order processing, more bookstores, increased representation at tradeshows worldwide, and the high-quality, responsive service our customers have come to expect.

EUROPE, MIDDLE EAST, AND AFRICA
(except Germany, Switzerland, and Austria)

INQUIRIES
International Thomson Publishing Europe
Berkshire House
168-173 High Holborn
London WC1V 7AA, United Kingdom
Telephone: 44-71-497-1422
Fax: 44-71-497-1426
Email: itpint@itps.co.uk

ORDERS
International Thomson Publishing Services, Ltd.
Cheriton House, North Way
Andover, Hampshire SP10 5BE, United Kingdom
Telephone: 44-264-342-832 (UK orders)
Telephone: 44-264-342-806 (outside UK)
Fax: 44-264-364418 (UK orders)
Fax: 44-264-342761 (outside UK)

GERMANY, SWITZERLAND, AND AUSTRIA

International Thomson Publishing GmbH
O'Reilly-International Thomson Verlag
Königswinterer Straße 418
53227 Bonn, Germany
Telephone: 49-228-97024 0
Fax: 49-228-441342
Email: anfragen@ora.de

ASIA *(except Japan)*
INQUIRIES
International Thomson Publishing Asia
221 Henderson Road
#08-03 Henderson Industrial Park
Singapore 0315
Telephone: 65-272-6496
Fax: 65-272-6498

ORDERS
Telephone: 65-268-7867
Fax: 65-268-6727

JAPAN
International Thomson Publishing Japan
Hirakawa-cho Kyowa Building 3F
2-2-1 Hirakawa-cho, Chiyoda-Ku
Tokyo, 102 Japan
Telephone: 81-3-3221-1428
Fax: 81-3-3237-1459

Toppan Publishing
Froebel Kan Bldg. 3-1, Kanda Ogawamachi Chiyoda-Ku
Tokyo 101 Japan
Telex: J 27317
Cable: Toppanbook, Tokyo
Telephone: 03-3295-3461
Fax: 03-3293-5963

AUSTRALIA
WoodsLane Pty. Ltd.
7/5 Vuko Place, Warriewood NSW 2102
P.O. Box 935, Mona Vale NSW 2103
Australia
Telephone: 02-970-5111
Fax: 02-970-5002
Email: woods@tmx.mhs.oz.au

NEW ZEALAND
WoodsLane New Zealand Ltd.
21 Cooks Street (P.O. Box 575)
Wanganui, New Zealand
Telephone: 64-6-347-6543
Fax: 64-6-345-4840
Email: woods@tmx.mhs.oz.au

THE AMERICAS
O'Reilly & Associates, Inc.
103A Morris Street
Sebastopol, CA 95472 U.S.A.
Telephone: 707-829-0515
Telephone: 800-998-9938 (U.S. & Canada)
Fax: 707-829-0104
Email: order@ora.com

Here's a page we encourage readers to tear out...

O'REILLY WOULD LIKE TO HEAR FROM YOU

Please send me the following:

❏ *ora.com*

O'Reilly's magazine/catalog, containing behind-the-scenes articles and interviews on the technology we write about, and a complete listing of O'Reilly books and products.

Which book did this card come from?

_____

Where did you buy this book?
❏ Bookstore   ❏ Direct from O'Reilly
❏ Bundled with hardware/software   ❏ Class/seminar

Your job description: ❏ SysAdmin   ❏ Programmer
❏ Other_____

Describe your operating system: _____

_____

Please print legibly

Name	Company/Organization Name
Address	
City — State	Zip/Postal Code — Country
Telephone	Internet or other email address (specify network)

Nineteenth century wood engraving
of the rhesas monkey from the O'Reilly
& Associates Nutshell Handbook®
Exploring Expect.

O'Reilly & Associates, Inc., 103A Morris Street, Sebastopol, CA 95472-9902

BUSINESS REPLY MAIL
FIRST CLASS MAIL   PERMIT NO. 80   SEBASTOPOL, CA

Postage will be paid by addressee

O'Reilly & Associates, Inc.
103A Morris Street
Sebastopol, CA 95472-9902